This book's production was finished on January 30 2022, just a month before Russia's invasion of Ukraine. This act of war in Europe has proven the author's fears right, but it has also changed drastically and very quickly the situation, the debates and the atmosphere inside Europe.

In order to preserve the intellectual honesty of the book (written between in 2019 and 2021), Routledge and the author have decided to keep the text unchanged, as it stood on January 30, 2022 – this might lead to perceived anachronisms to the reader, but will inform on the harsh and painful logic of the return of war in Europe, which was and continues to be at work at the time of this book's publication.

Thibault Muzergues

"Anyone who doubts the possibility of a return to war in Europe needs to read this book. Well-written, grounded in a deep and broad understanding of Europe's past and present, Thibault Muzergues' provocative argument should prompt some serious thinking about how best to prevent a dark future."

Robert Kagan, *Senior Fellow at the Brookings Institution, USA; author of* The Jungle Grows Back *and* Of Paradise and Power

"How far away are we from war on the European continent, even inside the European Union? How long will we be able to live with the illusion that peace is permanent? Thibault Muzergues puts those questions as a shocking warning and gives an answer that future of peace is not guaranteed. This answer comes with deep analysis and that makes warning especially strong. *War in Europe?* by Thibault Muzergues is a much-needed warning for us in Europe that if peace is to be preserved, it must be constantly worked on. Thibault Muzergues once more proves that he is a great analyst of modern global processes. After his recent powerful analysis of social and political processes *in The Great Class Shift*, now he offers us a powerful and shocking warning in *War in Europe?*"

Andrius Kubilius, *former Prime Minister of Lithuania, Member of the European Parliament and Standing Rapporteur on Russia in the EP.*

"The European Union is probably the most successful peace project in history. But that should not lead Europeans to assume that because of it, war in Europe has become impossible. In a book that draws on rich historical and sociological material, Thibault Muzergues provides a powerful argument that taking peace for granted can turn out to be Europeans' most dangerous assumption."

Ivan Krastev, *Chairman of the Centre for Liberal Strategies; author of* After Europe, The Light That Failed, *and* Is It Tomorrow Yet?

"This excellent book is a powerful reminder that when it comes to peace in Europe, there is no room for complacency. The European Union might be free from War now, but Europe is already not. Europeans must read it to come to their senses and take the continent's security seriously. The survival of the European project is at stake."

Nicu Popescu, *Deputy Prime Minister of Moldova*

"In this fascinating and contrarian treatment of Europe's past, present, and future, Muzergues argues that the project of European integration is as fragile as it is revolutionary. After offering a timely and arresting warning that the continent has not yet banished war, he provides wise counsel as to the how Europe and the West can revive liberty, democracy, and enduring peace."

Charles A. Kupchan, *Professor at Georgetown University, USA, Senior Fellow, Council on Foreign Relations*

"*War in Europe?* is a creative and timely mediation on a theme as old as Europe itself, the possibility of war on the European continent. With skill and clarity, Thibault Muzergues cuts through the "grand illusions" of our times and through the political jargon that reduces European politics to technocratic platitudes. In the process, he explores the real fault lines of European security, from East to West and from North to South. Without ever descending into alarmism, Muzergues trains his readers' attention on the preconditions for peace, which begin with the careful, sober consideration of where and how war might break out. *War in Europe?* is as much a work of imagination as it is of analysis. It deserves a wide readership within and outside of Europe."

Michael C. Kimmage, *Professor of History at the Catholic University of America; author of* The Abandonment of the West

"This book is a powerful warning to us all that peace is not a given, even in Europe. Thibault Muzergues makes a compelling argument about the state of the continent's security architecture – and it hasn't been as weak as it is now for decades. Muzergues does not fall into the post-Brexit blame game so many on the continent indulge in and makes a powerful argument that today's Europe is very much the one America made – a Europe that Britain has a vested interest in seeing it thrive. Brexiteers and Remainers should read this book, for the security of the continent still matters to us – and will in the coming years."

Andrew Bowie, *Member of Parliament for West Aberdeenshire and Kincardine, United Kingdom*

WAR IN EUROPE?

In this highly provocative and documented book, Thibault Muzergues describes how war in Europe is now more likely than it has been for at least the past 30 years, how it might come back to Europe and what Europeans can do to avoid getting drawn again in fratricide conflicts.

Many consider Europe a continent of peace, with NATO guaranteeing its security and the EU providing the political glue for a Europe Whole and Free. But what if this was not the case anymore? What if, after a decade of crisis, today's Europe was much more fragile than we thought? The author challenges our assumptions about peace in Europe and forces us to face the realities of a world that has become much more dangerous. Far from being apocalyptic, this book serves as an advance warning to the dangers, both internal and external, that are now closing in on Europe – and suggests solutions to avoid them.

This book will be key reading for those interested in European politics and history, the European Union, security and strategic studies, and more broadly to current affairs and international relations.

Thibault Muzergues is Resident Europe Program Director at the International Republican Institute (IRI).

WAR IN EUROPE?

From Impossible War to
Improbable Peace

Thibault Muzergues

LONDON AND NEW YORK

Cover image: © Shutterstock

First published 2022
by Routledge
4 Park Square, Milton Park, Abingdon, Oxon OX14 4RN

and by Routledge
605 Third Avenue, New York, NY 10158

Routledge is an imprint of the Taylor & Francis Group, an informa business

© 2022 Thibault Muzergues

The right of Thibault Muzergues to be identified as author of this work has been asserted in accordance with sections 77 and 78 of the Copyright, Designs and Patents Act 1988.

The original French language copyright version remains with Le Bord de l'Eau Editions.

All rights reserved. No part of this book may be reprinted or reproduced or utilised in any form or by any electronic, mechanical, or other means, now known or hereafter invented, including photocopying and recording, or in any information storage or retrieval system, without permission in writing from the publishers.

Trademark notice: Product or corporate names may be trademarks or registered trademarks, and are used only for identification and explanation without intent to infringe.

British Library Cataloguing-in-Publication Data
A catalogue record for this book is available from the British Library

Library of Congress Cataloging-in-Publication Data
A catalog record for this book has been requested.

ISBN: 978-1-032-10537-6 (hbk)
ISBN: 978-1-032-10522-2 (pbk)
ISBN: 978-1-003-21579-0 (ebk)

DOI: 10.4324/9781003215790

Typeset in Bembo
by Deanta Global Publishing Services, Chennai, India

With the support of the ALDE Party and the European Parliament. The sole liability rests with the author; the European Parliament is not responsible for any use that may be made of the information contained therein.

The Alliance of Liberals and Democrats for Europe Party (ALDE Party) is the European political family, bringing together parties with common liberal, democrat and reform ideas from more than 30 European countries. Its role is to strengthen the liberal democrat movement throughout Europe, define a common political vision and communicate it effectively to European citizens.

https://www.aldeparty.eu/

To my Grandmother,
May she be the last in my family to have survived a war.

CONTENTS

About the author — xiv
Foreword By Daniel Twining — xv
Acknowledgments — xix

Introduction — 1
   Notes 8
   Bibliography 8

PART 1
War and Europe: It's a long story — 9

  1 Romance: War and Europe until 1914 — 11
     War and the state of nature 12
     Prisoner of Mars? 13
     Ancient culture wars 18
     The endless war 23
     Mars on steroids 28
     Notes 34
     Bibliography 36

  2 Divorce – from the European Civil War to the long peace — 38
     Causes for a suicide 39
     From the Great War to the European Civil War 44
     From civil war to total war 49
     Peace over the graveyard 52

The end of history and the triumph of peace 56
Notes 61
Bibliography 63

3 The toxic ex returns 65
   Pax Americana: extension and contestations 66
   The return of the German question 72
   Enlargement's side effects 76
   North and south 81
   Guess who's back? 87
   Dangerous paths 90
   Notes 97
   Bibliography 101

PART 2
Perilous present **103**
   Why do wars happen? 103
   Notes 108
   Bibliography 108

4 Division bells 109
   Deutschland über alles *or* Deutschland gegen alle? 110
   Notes 142
   Bibliography 147

5 Baby it's a wild world: Europe's external challenges 149
   America and Europe 150
   Russia, a low-cost power with a high nuisance potential 156
   China's rise, Europe's fall 162
   When Europe imports instability 168
   Britain and Europe: friends or foes? 175
   Notes 181
   Bibliography 184

6 War ain't what it used to be 186
   Low intensity and low-cost warfare 188
   Mars's new toys 191
   The effects of economic warfare 195
   The virtual weapon 200
   Disinfo-wars 204
   Notes 211
   Bibliography 214

PART 3
The future   215

7 Seven scenarios for the future of Europe   217
   Paralysis 219
   War in the Baltics 221
   Europe, battlefield of a Sino-American Cold War 226
   Southern disintegration 229
   The Yellow Vest wars 232
   The post-Brexit war 236
   A difficult reform 239
   Notes 242
   Bibliography 243

8 What to do?   245
   Facing the toxic ex- 247
   No salvation beyond NATO 251
   Building Europe's internal market 255
   Europe's "F" word 260
   Federalism and nationalisms 266
   Dealing with Europe's borders 270
   Notes 281
   Bibliography 284

9 What's in it for the Anglosphere?   286
   2016: a turning point 287
   Are we all Americans? 293
   Euros versus Anglos: a long story 295
   Saving the Europe America made 299
   Britain and Europe – avoiding catastrophe 303
   Reclaiming the West to uphold the peace 306
   Notes 310
   Bibliography 313

Conclusion: It ain't over till it's over   314
   Notes 323
   Bibliography 323

Index   *325*

ABOUT THE AUTHOR

Thibault Muzergues is Resident Europe and Euro-Med Program Director at the International Republican Institute (IRI), currently based in Rome, Italy. In his ten years on the job, he has traveled extensively around Europe and has experienced from the inside, with national leaders, the deterioration of geopolitical and social conditions in Europe. He is the author of *The Great Class Shift* (Routledge, 2019), which already looked at the sociopolitical strife that has been rocking our political landscape since 2008.

FOREWORD

By Daniel Twining

Could war erupt in today's Europe, currently a bastion of peace in a dangerous world? For at least five centuries until 1945, Europe was the world's cockpit of conflict. For the four long decades of the Cold War, Europe was the central front in the armed superpower confrontation between the United States and the Soviet Union. Since 1989, a Long Peace has reigned, with the European Union at the center of a regional architecture consciously designed to leave behind great-power military rivalry in favor of integration and development. Most Europeans understand war as something that happens far away, in distant lands such as Afghanistan and Syria, not in their bastion of safety and prosperity.

Yet beneath the surface, the peace of Europe is fraying. European technocrats have pursued a visionary path of post-conflict modernity, turning the page on Europe's martial history. In many ways, the modern European project has been remarkably successful – Germany and France are close allies, the Baltic nations are embedded in NATO and frontline states like Poland enjoy unprecedented prosperity. But authoritarian revanchists, nationalist politicians and external pressures may mean that Europe ultimately cannot escape its own history of militarized rivalry.

This book serves as a timely warning – not that peace and security are impossible or that the post-modern European project is doomed but that the miracle of peace in Europe is worth defending and preserving and that doing so will require positive and coordinated action. In fact, one of Thibault Muzergues' signal accomplishments is to remind us how extraordinary is the construction of a Europe whole, free and at peace, anchored in the security provided by the NATO alliance and the prosperity and freedoms provided by the European

Union. That this is not a natural condition but a product of considerable effort and sacrifice makes it all the more urgent to sustain.

This is the peace that millions of Europeans – and Americans – fought for in the twentieth century. The success and integration of a united Germany into a pillar of both NATO and the European Union is a reminder that the destiny of nations is not fixed by power or geography, but that enlightened leadership and enmeshment in institutions of cooperation can produce entirely different outcomes. The integration of former Warsaw Pact states into NATO and the European Union demonstrates how nations can chart their own course to freedom and development, rather than being cursed by geography or history as captives to sphere-of-influence politics at the hands of predatory neighbors.

What could go wrong? The answer, unfortunately, is a lot. Europe could Balkanize in various ways, as growing East–West and North–South splits compound existing structural economic tensions to break up the Union. It could become a new playground of great-power rivalry, as a global Sino-American strategic competition splits the continent into pro-Washington and pro-Beijing camps. Conflicts along Europe's periphery – such as Russia's military assault on Ukraine – could spread to Europe's core, should the Kremlin be foolish enough to attack Lithuania, Latvia or Estonia. Growing migration pressures – Africa's population will go from twice Europe's today to five times Europe's within just decades – could lead a continent whose governance is premised on open borders and free movement of peoples to erect all sorts of internal and external barriers to movement, which may nonetheless be insufficient to stem the human tide, fueling domestic extremism and fracturing European comity.

Political radicalization of the kind already evident across parts of the European core could intensify, with populist-nationalist movements that see Brussels as an enemy growing in intensity in France, Italy and parts of Eastern Europe. Territorial irredentism favoring a greater Serbia, a greater Hungary or other lost causes could reignite, as it recently has just beyond Europe's borders in the conflict between Armenia and Azerbaijan over Nagorno-Karabakh. The US withdrawal from NATO and retreat to Fortress America could expose the fact that it is the United States – not Europeans – that has solved the security problems of Europe for decades; without that reassurance, security-dilemma dynamics could lead European nations into rearmament and open hostilities.

The author lays out these and other scenarios with sobriety, prescience and conviction. They are based not on apocalyptic visions of Europe's future but on a sophisticated historical review of Europe's past. The reality is stark: war and conflict made modern Europe. Its geography produced not an internal empire of the kind evident, for instance, in China, but the fragmentation of power and politics, giving rise to a number of small states and principalities. Innovation in armament and finance was essential to sustaining competitive advantage among European nations constantly jockeying for territory and security. Intensive competition among these smaller polities led to forms of technological and military innovation that produced disproportionate capabilities for power projection.

Europe's extensive coastline encouraged maritime exploration that, combined with new military and economic capabilities, led European nations to develop far-flung overseas empires. The importation of the extraordinary wealth from those empires – whether the silver mines of South America, the sugarcane plantations of the Caribbean or the spices of the East Indies – helped produce the economic and industrial revolutions that made European nations the world's decisive great powers, until the rise of the United States and the Soviet Union in the twentieth century and the Chinese ascendancy in the twenty-first. Indeed, across the seventeenth, eighteenth and nineteenth centuries, it was European investment in and migration to North America, and the European opening of China and Japan to trade with the wider world, that ultimately helped produce a new global balance of power, with an international economy no longer anchored in Europe and the United Kingdom but along the Atlantic and Pacific peripheries.

Of course, Europe destroyed itself in multiple rounds of warfare in the twentieth century. From 1945 to 1989, a dangerous form of peace on the continent only prevailed, thanks to the presence of outside powers in the form of the United States and the Soviet Union, both poised to fight a nuclear war to secure the prize of Europe. East–West standoffs over Berlin in the 1950s and 1960s, and the Soviet use of armed force to crush the political revolt in Budapest and Prague, served as reminders of the fragility of the Cold War compact. More recently, despite the Kantian narrative of a Europe of perpetual peace that developed after the Cold War, bloody conflicts in the Balkans in the 1990s were followed by Russia's invasion of Georgia in 2008 and annexation of parts of Ukraine in 2014. Russian cyberattacks in the Baltics and against major European powers such as Britain and France underscore how interstate conflict is coming ever closer to the European core.

Europe is a domain of extraordinary pluralism. The author helpfully deploys history to help imagine how models including the Hanseatic League or the Austro-Hungarian Empire, as well as new forms of devolution, federalism and subsidiarity, could animate governance within the European Union in ways that lead to fruitful reform. But the future of Europe is not only a question for Europeans, given the positive role the United States has long played on the continent. Thibault Muzergues correctly calls for a dynamic new campaign to reunite the West to confront the global strategic challenge of predatory Chinese state capitalism, accompanied as it is by the export of authoritarian norms that pose a fundamental challenge to the interests and values of free societies on both sides of the Atlantic. This includes new forms of cooperation within a "global West" that unites the transatlantic allies with Japan, South Korea, Australia, India and other partners to preserve a free and open international order.

Ultimately, this book deploys history to help chart Europe's future. Its author, a Frenchman working for an American institute who has spent part of his career based in Central Europe and has collaborated with political and civic leaders throughout the continent and the UK, is perfectly placed to present a holistic perspective on why the European model is worth preserving – and what must be done to defend its extraordinary accomplishments in delivering security and prosperity to nearly half a billion citizens. Americans and their British cousins, as much as residents of the continent, have an enormous stake in understanding the dangers to Europe today so that we can work with allies to fortify themselves against them, so as to protect and preserve a European peace that history reminds us is priceless.

Dr. Daniel Twining
President of the International Republican Institute (IRI)

ACKNOWLEDGMENTS

Writing a book is a fantastic and fascinating journey. It is also an intellectual (and at times physical) challenge for the author, particularly when the subject is as dark as this one, and even more, if the writing is done at a time of personal upheavals and in the middle of lockdowns – a double-edged sword for authors. As I lay down my pen after three years of constant work in French and English on the subject of the complex relationship between War and Europe, I have to thank many people who helped me put on paper what I hope will be a book of interest to the readers.

One person played an indispensable role at all times, my wife Alisa Muzergues. She has been of incredible patience and understanding as I locked myself up (physically and intellectually) to write this book in French and then adapt it in English, and I am forever grateful to her, not only for this but also for the love she gives me every day. I surely could not have finished this book (let alone started it) without her total support. She is the love of my life, and I will forever be grateful for her encouragement and the discussions that helped me polish my arguments.

I am also especially thankful to French diplomat Alexandre Vulic, who played a very important part in the production of the French-language version of the book and read the first draft of the last chapter of the English-language version. Our brainstorming sessions at Café Schwarzenberg in Vienna during our central European years were always fascinating, and they played an important role in shaping the arguments of this book.

I am also thankful to the people who read and edited the draft manuscript of this book, correcting some of my mistakes and providing useful feedback to make this book readable. Bram Delen, Nicolas Tenzer, Thierry Wolton and Pierre Prévot Leygonie are to be thanked by the reader for streamlining the contents of the French version of this book, as well as my father Georges Muzergues, who reminded me on different occasions to keep things simple, so that the argument can be accessible not only to a few scribes in capital cities but potentially to a larger public. For their part, my IRI colleagues Sean Nottoli and Dan Scaduto were brave enough to take on the task of editing parts of the manuscript, taking on their free time while I was already pushing them during their work time. They greatly helped to make this book more readable for English speakers.

Sean and Dan were not the only work colleagues who helped me out in this endeavor. I am especially grateful to the International Republican Institute, for whom I have been working for ten years now, for allowing me to take upon this extracurricular activity. Obviously, what I wrote in this book reflects my views only and not that of the organization, and I am thankful for the debates I've had with my director Jan Surotchak and other members of the team, which allowed me to present stronger arguments in this book. I am also especially grateful to Dan Twining for his feedback on the manuscript and for agreeing to write the foreword, which I feel is making my case much more elegantly than I ever could.

I would also like to thank my publisher, Routledge, and, in particular, Andrew Taylor and Sophie Iddamalgoda. This is the second book I publish with Routledge, and I have been lucky enough to work with them on both my previous project and this book – they made the experience in both cases much easier than it could have been. I am also thankful to ALDE for their financial support in making this book happen – as for IRI, the reader should remember that the writings of this book are the fruit of my personal reflection only and should in no way be attributed to ALDE.

I am also thankful to the public officials and authors who read the manuscript of the English-language version of this book, provided useful feedback and gave me the honor of endorsing this book. I am especially grateful to Robert Kagan who went to the bottom of the book and helped me avoid a couple of embarrassing mistakes, as well as Andrius Kubilius (whose long-term support means a lot), Ivan Krastev, Nicu Popescu, Charles Kupchan, Michael Kimmage and Andrew Bowie. Their encouragements and enthusiasm for the book mean a lot to me, and I hope their writings will encourage the reader to read this book with a critical and interested eye.

Finally, I wanted to dedicate this book to my grandmother, who could not see this book in its final version (including in French), as she passed away while I was writing it. She transmitted to her grandson the taste for history (including the family history) and writing. This book owes a lot to her, and as the reader will discover in the introduction, she provided me with the raw material from which this reflection would emerge over the long term. A faithful Catholic, she never seemed to have seen a contradiction between her Frenchness and the idea that this could be admirably complemented by belonging to a common European civilization. She would not have liked reading this book, which would have brought too many sad memories from the past. I, therefore, hope that the warning it constitutes will allow us all to avoid another 1914 or 1918 for Europe.

INTRODUCTION

It is a box with no apparent value given to me by my grandmother a few days before my departure from the family nest. It doesn't contain anything of high monetary value: a crucifix and a figurine of the Virgin Mary well protected in a wooden cartouche, a military identity plate, a telegrapher's insignia, a few pieces of shrapnel and military decorations, including a commemorative medal of the battles of Verdun and a *Croix de Guerre*, won in the trenches of the North of France in 1916. I take these items out of their box only once a year, on November 11 – one occasional look at these vestiges of a time that seems long gone by and that many of us in Europe hope will remain so.

These artifacts belonged to my great-grandfather, Élie Morange. He was no hero, just a provincial Frenchman like many others at this time. The owner of a small hotel, he ended up becoming a municipal councilor in post-war La Bourboule, a small spa resort in the Puy-de-Dôme. Like all Frenchmen and so many Europeans of his generation, the Great War left a deep mark on him. Each of my great-grandfathers served as soldiers in the Battles of Verdun or the *Chemin des Dames*. Their experiences in the trenches changed them forever. They definitely adopted French as their mother tongue during this time, and all of them forged their character against the background noise of cannons, the smell of death and the mud of the trenches – an experience they would never want to live through again. These experiences were so traumatic that many relived them in their sleep every night (we would call this today post-traumatic syndrome), and at least one of them had to relive the hell of Verdun during his agony.

The story I have just told is by no means edifying: any French person who looks a little in his genealogy will find at least one forefather who fought in the forts and trenches of Northern France between 1914 and 1918. This generation of Frenchmen was the first – and hopefully the last – to experience total war as soldiers. Although tested, their children were not necessarily the unlucky ones:

DOI: 10.4324/9781003215790-1

despite defeat and occupation (and for some of them, destruction by air bombs or deportations), the French collective experience of the Second World War was not as direct or traumatic as that of their German, Soviet, British, American or Japanese counterparts. Of course, there is no question here of minimizing the French trauma that followed the debacle of June 1940, but this collective memory cannot be compared to the butchery of 1914–1918 trench warfare, the horrors experienced (and perpetrated) East of Berlin during the period 1938–1945 or the terror of carpet bombings in London, Coventry or Dresden. In any case, whether the starting point is placed in 1918 or 1945, the fact remains that the "Silent Generation" was the last to experience war in Western Europe. It seemed natural to my grandmother, the last familial survivor of her generation, to give these remnants of war in the family memory to her history-loving grandson before he started roaming around a unified continent. The box gradually became a kind of portable private monument – to those who died but also to those lucky enough to escape alive from the continental massacre, which historians are beginning to agree forms a kind of continuum of European history from 1914 to 1945.[1]

Despite being at the center of the Cold War, many Western Europeans seem to understand the Second World War as the last, final conflict in Europe, despite uncomfortable "exceptions," in ex-Yugoslavia in the 1990s or in Georgia and Ukraine in the late 2000s and 2010s. The building and the enlargement of the European Union, allowed by the *Pax Americana*, seemed to guarantee prosperity and peace among the nations of Europe forever. This also explains why so many post-communist countries "East of Eden" flocked to join the European Union (EU). The fall of the Berlin Wall in 1989, quickly followed by the collapse of the Soviet Union, allowed Europeans to dream of a continent finally at peace, a "Europe Whole and Free," as George H. W. Bush put it in his Mainz speech of 1989. Despite the wars that tore the Western Balkans apart during the 1990s, the disarmament of Europe after the Cold War and the EU's successive waves of enlargement between 2004 and 2013 seemed to give substance to this vision of a continent that looked finally united in peace.

"Europe brings peace" is indeed one of the most common mantras to have been used by Europhile politicians over the past 30 years when promoting the Union. The phrase not only irritates many Eurosceptics who contest its validity. It also fails in delivering the force it once carried. As the last generation that lived through the wars of twentieth-century Europe fades away, so too does the impact of the slogan. Today, more than 100 years after the 1918 armistice, and for the first time in European history, a majority of Europeans have never experienced war and, therefore, cannot really know what it looks like. Today, peace in Europe is considered a given, even though war remains close by, be it in the Eastern marches of the continent (Ukraine, Georgia) or on the other side of the Mediterranean. In 2015, the refugee columns from Syria and Libya reminded Europeans that armed conflict at their gates could have consequences for them too.

As the sounds of war drums draw closer to Europe, clouds also gather above Europeans' heads: the terrorist wave of 2015–2016 brought mini-war scenes into the heart of the European Union, while the 2018 revolt of the Yellow Vests in France showed just how angry (and sometimes violent) crowds could become, even on a rich continent. The year 2016 also saw a major member of the EU, the United Kingdom, leave the Union. It remains unclear whether this set a precedent for the future of Europe or that of the British Isles, as separatisms and nationalisms fueled by the West's identity crises have gained ground over the past ten years.

If the 2010s showed how quickly the situation in Europe could deteriorate, the 2020s started with a bang. The COVID-19 health crisis put the European Union to the test as its members "took back control" in the early days of the pandemic, closing their borders and bickering over recovery funds before reaching an agreement that could transform the union – or accelerate its demise – in the coming years. Another last-minute deal also closed the Brexit negotiations, though not before Prime Minister Boris Johnson threatened to send warships to protect British fishermen. Tensions over the North Sea fisheries, however, were nothing compared to the major military build-up between Turkey and Greece in the Eastern Mediterranean, with incidents involving the French navy during the summer of 2020, a few weeks before a short war actually changed the face of the South Caucasus in Nagorno-Karabakh. If international tensions were not enough, social tensions are probably going to define the political agenda of the first half of the 2020s, as governments will likely struggle to deliver recovery to their populations and restore pre-pandemic quality of life to all. If history has taught us anything, it is that pandemics, from the plague of Cyprian to the Black Death, have long-term consequences for social relations. And they often favor instability and unbalance rather than appeasement and reconciliation.

No longer can anyone ignore that today's Europe is more fractured than it has ever been since the end of the Cold War (including in Brexit Britain, which remains tied to the continent geographically and, in many ways, culturally). Indeed, from the Greek crisis of 2011–2015 to the Yellow Vest movement in 2018–2019, without forgetting the refugee crises of 2015–2016, Brexit or the Catalan separatist episode of 2017, the European Union seems to have become more of a crisis producer than an exporter of stability. Across the continent, the divisions are many – both between states and also within societies. The current Europeanization of the political debates and fault lines, already visible during the 2019 European election campaign, could well accentuate rather than mitigate these divisions, and it is not unimaginable that these could come to a boiling point in an uncertain post-COVID-19 environment.

After so many years of what seemed a perpetual peace, is Europe about to become a battlefield once again? Such a provocative question would probably have seemed totally inappropriate – even outright insane – just a few years ago. And yet, there are many signs that should make us wonder about the future – starting with the a priori incongruous nature of the suggestion. Talks about perpetual peace are not new; in 1909, British essayist Norman Engell published a very popular essay, *The Great Illusion*,[2] in which he demonstrated with flawless logic that war between Europeans had become impossible due to unprecedented economic development and commercial interdependence between the continent's states. We all know how that story ended; five years later, European elites sleepwalked[3] into a conflict that would bleed Europe out. After the disaster of the Great War, in 1926, French and German foreign affairs ministers Aristide Briand and Gustav Stresemann were awarded the Nobel Peace Prize for having sketched the outlines of Franco-German reconciliation – an indispensable for peace on the continent. Only two years later, the Frenchman and his American counterpart gave their name to the Briand-Kellogg Pact (then signed by Germany, Italy and Japan, among others). The pact was the first international treaty that outlawed war, while at the same time a major peace movement was developing throughout Europe. Only 11 years later, the continent would once again sink into horror and ruin, this time in proportions that would make the economic recovery that ensued look like a continental "miracle."

This story of peace in the first part of the twentieth century seems to fit a recurring – and disturbing – pattern in European history. In fact, it looks as if each great conflagration that has shaken Europe's foundations was almost inevitably preceded by periods of pacifist euphoria, with perpetual peace seemingly within reach. Before Briand and Engell, many politicians and intellectuals dreamed of a great reconciliation between peoples. In the Middle Ages, the Pope saw himself as the spearhead of a Christianity thought as the best way to impose peace in Europe. However, the periods of pious union where Christian knights exchanged peace at home for crusades in the Holy Land were ephemeral and followed by multiple and bloody conflicts back home. At the start of the Renaissance, humanist intellectuals such as Erasmus or Thomas More considered the possibility of perpetual peace on the continent, advising their sovereigns to negotiate it with their counterparts. The Wars of Religion soon reminded these idealists of Europe's much more belligerent realities, with Thomas More losing his head in the process. A few centuries later, the Enlightenment once again explored the idea of perpetual peace between nations, may it be with the Abbé de Saint-Pierre (who proposed a plan of perpetual peace following the bitter negotiations to end the War of the Spanish Succession[4]) or Immanuel Kant, whose philosophical sketch *Towards Perpetual Peace* is self-explanatory.[5] Not only did the successive wars of the eighteenth century quickly shatter the Philosophers' dreams but the revolutionary and then imperial wars of 1792–1815 showed that technical progress and the emergence of new ideologies not only made war more deadly but also more tangible for every European citizen. Following the Napoleonic Wars, the *Pax Britannica* guaranteed a relatively peaceful period from 1815 to 1914, although this first long peace prevented neither the revolutionary outbursts of 1830 and 1848 nor the unification of Italy and Germany, both forged above all in the blood and steel of the battles of Solferino, Sadowa and Sedan.

At each of these moments in European history, continental peace seemed within reach, either by the force of ideas emerging at the time or because the experience of especially violent wars had vaccinated whole generations against waging war. And yet each time, the force of new religious or political ideas (may they be the Reformation, the Jacobin ideas of the French Revolution, nationalism, communism or fascism) or new circumstances led Europeans toward new cycles of self-destruction.

Are we today witnessing a similar transition? As the last generation to have endured war on a mass scale across the continent fades away, the risk is becoming very real. This is not only due, in part, to the extinction of a living collective memory of war but also due to this memory's distorted ossification: the image of war that our generations have in mind, which stems from the experience recounted by our grandparents and great-grandparents, has been progressively deformed. For most of us, war has an ultra-moral and a Clausewitzian nature: to be "real," war must be global and involve the whole nation. The problem is that today's reality is completely different and much more nuanced, both in its moral aspects and in its intensity. And if one should not flush away the possibility of a general conflagration similar to the Great War, most wars today follow models of hybrid, low-cost or, to borrow the provocative expression used by Ian Morris, unproductive warfare,[6] as the example of the ongoing war in Eastern Ukraine shows.

As war becomes easier and less costly to wage in general, tensions continue to build up among (and within) European nations, making it possible that conflicts that were once effectively managed by policies could be considered as so entrenched, so inextricable that only war could now solve them. The economic crisis that has plagued Europe after 2008 – and of which the post-COVID crisis could be an extension, if not an accelerator – has greatly weakened Europe's renowned social fabric, dividing societies into liberal and illiberal camps and also among existential lines: rich vs. poor, millennials vs. baby boomers, urban vs. rural and suburban, etc. These new cleavages have often reinforced geographical divisions within Europe: the contempt of the Yellow Vests for their elites (and vice versa) is, in many ways, as strong as that of a Protestant, hardworking, exporting and Germanic/Baltic Europe against a Mediterranean (or Latin?) Europe that finds itself impoverished by ten years of economic and moral crisis. This North–South division is, in turn, matched by an increasingly clear confrontation between a conservative Central Europe, undermined by the traumas of the twentieth century and its demographic decline, and a Western Europe that is certainly more advanced but too often incapable of questioning its own prejudices – and ends up treating Easterners in much the same ways as Neville Chamberlain treated Czechs, Slovaks and their problems with Germany in 1938.

These growing issues are arising in a time of dramatic decline for Europe's standing worldwide. The continent which, for better or for worse, practically ruled over the world just 125 years ago is today increasingly outmatched militarily and (even more worryingly) technologically by the two behemoths of the twenty-first century, China and the United States. Worse still, Europe has also disarmed at the very moment when the rest of the world started to rearm. The result is a strategic weakness that makes Europeans vulnerable to new types of hybrid warfare and domination strategies: recent controversies over the 5G projects of the Chinese giant Huawei have often left Europeans to play the role of pawns in the confrontation between Beijing and Washington, despite having two companies at home capable of providing this technology. The COVID-19 pandemic also uncovered Europe's extreme geopolitical weakness in a world that has once again become dangerous: during the lockdowns, as each country was left on its own device to contain the spread of the virus, Beijing did not hesitate to exchange its "solidarity" for visible support from local governments toward China (which of course had to contrast with selfishness on the part of Brussels, Berlin or Washington[7]). In this sense, the outburst of Serbian President Alexander Vučić against the European Union during the coronavirus first wave[8] was not only a spectacular show of fealty toward Beijing but also confirmation that allegiances are no longer guaranteed, which implies that instability is once again rising – and with it potentially comes war.

In the early 2000s, at the height of the crisis between "old Europe" and the United States, Robert Kagan pointed out that Europeans had lost their lust for power and war and entered a post-historic paradise of perpetual peace – which explained its international impotence and reluctance in joining American wars overseas.[9] This is no longer the case today. Whether Europeans like it or not, history is now back on the continent, and its return has highlighted Europe's vulnerabilities in the 2010s, both around the EU (with wars in Ukraine, Libya and Syria) and inside. In turn, these political and social tensions undermine the fundamental institutions of European societies, leading to a long-term risk of a latent civil war that could become even more insoluble because of the increasing possibility for foreign powers to intervene in Europe's internal debates. Such intervention would actually not always be seen as inopportune for some political actors who dream more or less openly of using the new dynamics at work to settle long-forgotten conflicts at home and abroad.

This book discusses the possibility of a return of war in Europe, and it is quite certain that it would not have been treated seriously a decade ago, when the European Union won the Nobel Peace Prize. But times change, and European public opinion seems to have integrated this idea much faster than their elites: a poll conducted by YouGov for the European Council on Foreign Relations (ECFR) shows that not only do a majority of French, Italians, Poles and even Germans consider realistic the idea that the European Union will explode within ten to twenty years but also 22% to 38% believe that a war between countries of the European Union is possible in the coming decade. Even more worrying young people are almost always most likely to consider war possible within the EU.[10] In sum, to recycle Raymond Aron's observations about Europe during the Cold War (where peace was impossible and war improbable), it seems today that Europe is moving from impossible war to improbable peace.

I have been traveling, working and training political elites around and inside Europe for more than ten years now, after having worked in British and French politics. Through my work at the International Republican Institute (IRI), I have trained young leaders (some of whom are now in decision-making positions in their countries) and discussed domestic and international politics with actors and decision-makers in Brussels and throughout Europe. Since the beginning of 2010, when I started working for IRI, I have observed a continuous deterioration of the situation on the continent, not only between states but also within societies, and even within the major political families, whose choices are shaping the politics in Europe. These personal observations have led me to this book, which is an analysis based not only on my personal observations but also on serious background research and discussions with political leaders across the Transatlantic space.

The purpose of this book is not to plunge the reader into apocalyptic catastrophism. On the contrary, it was written as a warning in the hope that it can be of some use: although it is difficult to assess whether a Norman Engell book discussing the possibility of war in the 1910s would have had an impact on European governments in the summer of 1914, I can only hope that *War in Europe?* will, directly or indirectly, inform our political leaders of the current risks and threats so that they take the right decisions at the right moment. As we will see in the next chapters, these decisions may not always look pacifist a priori, but history has shown us that peace does not preserve itself, and it sometimes requires forceful action (or the threat of it) to be maintained.[11] Before getting to this point though, this book will adopt a historical approach to understand why war is actually part of Europe's DNA, why it (mostly) disappeared from the continent after 1945 and why current developments seem to threaten this long peace. Part 2 will then examine the current factors actively damaging Europe's social fabric and security architecture: among them, divisions within societies are as important as tensions between states and with the rest of the world, while new developments in warfare, which make low-cost wars easier to conduct and more difficult to recognize, make peace more difficult to maintain. Finally, Part 3 will try to look at the future and examine various scenarios that could lead to war over the next ten years, before exploring the solutions Europeans could pursue to pacify the continent. The final chapter will deal specifically with the Anglosphere and its relation to Europe: in many ways, European peace also depends on the goodwill and interest of Britain and, especially, the United States.

German Emperor Wilhelm II certainly did not leave a positive mark in history due to his role in the start of the Great War. His bravado and expansionist ambitions in the pre-war period helped fuel the subsequent image of the bloodthirsty Kaiser that became a classic in post-war year history books. But the last German Emperor was also a product of his time and was capable of incredibly astute observations which, if they could have helped him avoid his notorious *faux pas* in foreign policy, would probably have changed his destiny. Wilhelm once said that "Peace in Europe is like a patient with a heart disease. It can live for a long time – sometimes a very long time, but it can also die suddenly and at the most unexpected moment."[12] This book was written in the hope that it will help the patient to take care of itself, and the doctors to pay more attention to its condition, so that the idea of Europe as a future battlefield may be considered in ten years as the work of a slightly crazy political scientist and not as a prophecy.

Notes

1 See Ernst Nolte, *Der europäische Bürgerkrieg, 1917–1941: Nationalsozialismus und Bolschevismus*, Berlin: Propyläen, 1987.
2 Norman Engell, *The Great Illusion: A Study of the Relation of Military Power in Nations to Their Economic Advantage* (3rd edition), London: G.P. Putnam & Sons, 1911.
3 Christopher Clark, *The Sleepwalkers: How Europe Went to War in 1914*, London: Penguin, 2013.
4 Charles-Irénée Castel, *Projet pour rendre la paix perpétuelle en Europe*, Utrecht: A. Schouten, 1713.
5 Immanuel Kant, *To Perpetual Peace: A Philosophical Sketch*, Cambridge: Hackett Classics, 2003.
6 Ian Morris, *War: What is it Good for? The Role of Conflict in Civilization, from Primates to Robots*, London: Profile Books, 2014.
7 https://www.washingtonpost.com/gdpr-consent/?next_url=https%3a%2f%2fwww.washingtonpost.com%2fworld%2funder-fire-over-coronavirus-response-china-turns-to-a-familiar-fall-guy-trump%2f2020%2f03%2f13%2fbb324c84-64d2-11ea-8a8e-5c5336b32760_story.html
8 https://www.euractiv.com/section/coronavirus/news/serbia-turns-to-china-due-to-lack-of-eu-solidarity-on-coronavirus/
9 Prior to 1945, it was America that was not a believer in power, while Europe was binging on it. See Robert Kagan, *Of Paradise and Power*, New York: Alfred A. Knopf, 2003.
10 YouGov opinion poll carried out among 50,000 European voters in 14 EU countries between March and April. See Susi Dennison, Mark Leonard, and Adam Lury, *What Europeans Really Feel: The Battle for the Political System*, ECFR Policy Brief, May 2019, available online: https://www.ecfr.eu/publications/summary/what_europeans_really_feel_the_battle_for_the_political_system_eu_election
11 Donald Kagan, *On the Origins of War and the Preservation of Peace*, New York: Anchor Books, 1996.
12 Quoted in Christian Baechler, *Guillaume II d'Allemagne*, Paris: Fayard, 2003, p.258.

Bibliography

Castel, Charles-Irénée, *Projet pour rendre la paix perpétuelle en Europe*, Utrecht: A. Schouten, 1713.
Engell, Norman, *The Great Illusion: A Study of the Relation of Military Power in Nations to Their Economic Advantage* (3rd edition), London: G.P. Putnam & Sons, 1911.
Kagan, Donald, *On the Origins of War and the Preservation of Peace*, New York: Anchor Books, 1996.
Kagan, Robert, *Of Paradise and Power*, New York: Alfred A. Knopf, 2003.
Kant, Immanuel, *To Perpetual Peace: A Philosophical Sketch*, Cambridge: Hackett Classics, 2003.
Clark, Christopher, *The Sleepwalkers: How Europe Went to War in 1914*, London: Penguin, 2013.
Morris, Ian, *War: What is it Good for? The Role of Conflict in Civilization, from Primates to Robots*, London: Profile Books, 2014.
Nolte, Ernst, *Der europäische Bürgerkrieg, 1917–1941: Nationalsozialismus und Bolschevismus*, Berlin: Propyläen, 1987.

PART 1
War and Europe
It's a long story

1
ROMANCE
War and Europe until 1914

When Robert Kagan drew his famous parallel between Europeans hailing from Venus and Americans hailing from Mars in the early twenty-first century, he was of course doing this in the context of the split that was taking place between "old Europe" and the United States over Iraq. But the author himself warned his readers that this state of things was the result of a reversal of roles after 1945 – prior to that, it was the Europeans who were warriors, binging on power while the Americans were the isolationists and pacifists.[1] Indeed, for a very long time, Europe had a passionate relationship with war: not only was it part of Europe's DNA, but it was also what allowed Europeans to dominate the world in the nineteenth century. The paradox, of course, is that war also ruined the continent in the twentieth century, leading to a breakup between Europe and Mars that, for a long time, was thought to be definitive – leading Robert Kagan to his conclusions about Europeans coming from Venus and Eurocrats in Brussels to proclaim that "Europe is peace" – here again something that might look (partially) true from a perspective of the late-twentieth-century Brussels bubble but completely off the mark in the greater historical perspective.

Europe has a long common history with war, and it is precisely because the relationship is complex that it is necessary to look at it in more detail. Otherwise, we will not be able to understand why Europeans curbed their natural warring instincts in the twentieth century and why the conditions that made the "Long Peace"[2] possible since 1945 have recently started to fade away. But before talking about the divorce between Europe and Mars, it is worth looking in detail at their long honeymoon.

DOI: 10.4324/9781003215790-3

War and the state of nature

Are human beings naturally inclined toward violence and war, or are they on the contrary peaceful animals that have been corrupted by society and private property? The debate has been raging for centuries between the man-is-a-wolf-to-man discourse of Thomas Hobbes and the descriptions of the peaceful savage dear to Jean-Jacques Rousseau. Unfortunately, research in social sciences since then does not seem to have brought us any closer to solving this philosophical mystery. Among the twentieth-century anthropologists who took part in the debate using their own social science tools, two names stand out: Margaret Mead and her study among the peaceful Samoans,[3] on the one hand, and Napoleon Chagnon[4] and his works on the warring Yanomami tribe in the Amazon basin. Each came to almost opposite conclusions about the presence of violence and war in primitive societies – and each was accused of amateurish behavior, falsifying their research, or even in the case of Chagnon conspiring with the Brazilian government to divide and conquer the subject of their studies.[5]

The controversies surrounding both anthropologists may tell us a lot about the endemic sectarian and verbal violence that exists between researchers in the field of social sciences, but it does not help much to resolve the question of humanity's natural penchant for war or peace. A biological approach can be equally confusing: on the one hand, it is beyond doubt that violence is everywhere in the animal world, with teeth, tusks and horns being developed over time by animals as "weapons" to survive – following Hobbes' argument, if wolf is a wolf for itself, it seems reasonable to imagine that man in the state of nature should be a wolf to man. But violence is not warfare – war is an organized form of violence involving more or less distinct groups of individuals, and it thus requires social skills to be waged – which means that only certain types of animals, such as ants, apes and humans have acquired the ability organize collectively to attack an enemy, whether for food, territory or reproductive purposes. But not all social animals engage in organized violence: while chimpanzees are naturally inclined toward territorial violence and organize murderous raids into enemy territory,[6] bonobos, other close cousins of humans, are not at all inclined toward violence. In fact, their propensity to settle their conflicts through love rather than war has led biologists to give them the nickname of "hippie-chimps."[7]

Recent research tends to suggest that humans tend more toward the killing chimp than the hippie chimp, though. Richard Wrangham and Dale Peterson argue in their book on the origins of human violence among the great apes[8] that for geographical, genetical (but also gender) reasons, it is the violent, territorial and possessive nature of apes that is most commonly found in the behavior of gangs of hunter-gatherers – they may prefer intimidation (to minimize the risk) when they are unsure of the balance of power, but they are also capable of staggering violence when it is clearly in their favor. This leads Francis Fukuyama to conclude that there is a natural propensity for man to use violence to settle conflicts:[9] humans are tribal animals by nature, which means that they will want to protect members of their group (seen in a very strict and narrow sense) and attack those who are not part of the group. This does not, however, exclude another penchant for peace: depending on the balance of power, and often after a fierce fight that will decimate a group, it is not uncommon for survivors to become part of the winning group. Even if humans are not totally violent by nature, organized violence is clearly part of their daily life.

Archeology seems to confirm this thesis, with hard evidence of armed conflict actually going back a long way in time – 14,000 years ago, about 9,000 years before the appearance of the first states.[10] Illinois University professor Lawrence H. Keeley has also shown that the state of peace is by no means what defines the history (and prehistory) of humanity, quite the contrary. According to his research, between 90% and 95% of all known societies practice or have practiced war.[11] This does not mean, of course, that war is necessarily a natural state for mankind, since peace is sought when groups have an interest in it. No society has been able to survive in a permanent state of war, and evidence shows that humanity evolves in a spacetime where periods of peace alternate with periods of war. Moreover, war is not the only instrument of conflict resolution for mankind: when the balance of power is obvious before the fight, flight, cooperation or submission are equally instinctive choices for a group.

To the extent that humanity alternates between war and peace, can we isolate certain conditions that would make war more likely in one environment than in another? This is where geography kicks in.

Prisoner of Mars?

Although Greek mythology portrayed the young maid Europe as a captive of Zeus, a more modern perspective of the tale would more actually depict here as a prisoner of Mars, if not symbolically then at least physically – or to be more precise, geographically. As American author Robert Kaplan explains in his 2012 book, geography has done much to constrain human decision and attitudes, and strategists and politicians alike have begun to recover a certain awareness of its importance over the past two decades: if "The 1990s saw the map reduced to two dimensions because of air power […] soon after the three-dimensional map would be restored in the mountains of Afghanistan and the treacherous alleyways of Iraq."[12]

This is not to say that we should rely on geography only: as Kaplan himself concedes, it "informs, rather than determines. Geography […] is not synonymous with fatalism. But it is, like the distribution of economic and military power themselves, a major constraint – and an instigator of – the actions of states."[13] Technological advances may well transform our environment and free us from some of these physical constraints, but freedom will always be partial or at least fragile: while the Internet allows for instant communication between individuals, it does not replace a physical encounter between them. And while a bridge can allow us to cross rivers, lakes and straits, as soon as it is swept or blown away, the obstacle it was supposed to eliminate reappears instantaneously. Whether we like it or not, we can only escape the constraints of geography at our own risk, as the American military (re-) discovered in Vietnam and more recently in Iraq and Afghanistan.

In this sense, the geography of Europe tells us a lot about its nature. And when it comes to war, even a superficial look at the physical map of the continent leads to the conclusion that Europe is probably the most perfect place in the world to prepare, create and sustain warfare. From a geopolitical point of view, Europe differs from other continents by three major characteristics: first, its particularly rugged terrain with many mountain ranges clearly cuts it into many small pieces; the Alps are a good example as they mark (some would say *create*) a border between Latin Europe to the South and Germanic Europe to the North. Second, and this is partially a result of the first point, Europe also stands out with its rugged coasts, which are themselves home to thousands of coves, bays and, importantly, islands and peninsulas – which themselves are very indented and encircled by numerous seas (the Atlantic Ocean and the North Sea in the West, the Baltic Sea and the Arctic Ocean in the North, the Black Sea and the Mediterranean Sea in the South). Third, Europe opens up to its East to the vast Eurasian plain, and this unclear eastern border makes it difficult to define where Europe ends or where it begins: nineteenth-century geographers arbitrarily opted for the Ural Mountains, but this "natural" border between Europe and Asia is neither intangible (the ancient Greeks made their world end at the Don, not in the Urals) nor apolitical – including the South Caucasus as a European Mountain chains and Mount Ararat (5,137 meters) as its summit carries consequences as to where Georgia and Armenia, for example, can legitimately claim European aspirations.

These three physical characteristics have led historically to very a high degree of political fragmentation in Europe, making its pacification very difficult, if not impossible. First, mountain ranges are obstacles to communication between peoples; they, therefore, favor the constitution of distinct communities and institutions: just as the Alps crystallized a North–South divide between Latin and Germanic Europeans so the mountains surrounding the Pannonian Plain (the Alps in the West, the Carpathians in the North and East and the Balkans in the South) literally enclosed the Magyar conquerors of the ninth century in what became greater Hungary until 1919. These "natural borders" are, of course, at the origin of the extraordinary diversity that is constitutive of Europe, but this diversity is also a source of conflicts and, therefore, of potential wars. Diversity is also encouraged by the presence, on Europe's maritime peripheries, of many islands, difficult to subjugate – Britain, although close to the mainland, has not been conquered since 1066. The same could be said of Europe's numerous peninsulas: the three great southern land protrusions are also civilizational worlds in themselves, and the rugged terrain helps to further fragment them linguistically, culturally and sometimes politically. The Iberian Peninsula is a prime example of this: apart from Spain and Portugal, the Catalans, Basques and Galicians all claim a heritage and a language of their own. Diversity is also present on the Italian

Peninsula, which was only re-unified in the middle of the nineteenth century, after 1,400 years of divisions; finally, the name "Balkans" itself suggests in our vocabulary extreme fragmentation.

The combination of rugged terrain and jagged coastlines also favors a remarkable diversity in the flow of rivers, which are particularly effective vehicles for forming homogenous cultures: it is difficult to imagine the development of modern America without considering the importance of the Mississippi River and its waterways for the dissemination of goods, passengers and also newspapers, music and language in the nineteenth century – especially before the railway revolution.[14] Similarly, Chinese civilization could only develop around two river basins, the Yellow River and the Yangtze, which flowed in the same direction and were quickly connected by a canal – allowing those who controlled these two rivers, from the First Emperor of the Qin Dynasty to Mao, to dominate the Middle Kingdom. But Europe's great rivers do not follow any of these logics: the Rhine flows from South to North into the North Sea, the Danube flows into the Black Sea following a West-East course and most of the other rivers (Seine, Po, Elba, Vistula, etc.) remain small in size compared to the Mekong, Nile or Ganges, which are all civilization-markers. Here again, geography favors fragmentation: where control of the Mississippi guarantees that of a vast plain stretching from the Appalachians to the Rockies, where the submission of the Yellow and Blue Rivers in the East allows almost uncontested domination of the vast expanses that make the "Chinese world", control over one or even two rivers does not guarantee domination over Europe – or even of one of its main peninsulas: if control of the Po or the Tiber guaranteed control of Italy, it would not have waited 1,500 years to be reunited.

If geographical fragmentation favors political fragmentation, the latter in turns favors conflict, which can easily turn into war: in a single, geographically framed ensemble like China, there is no other way out of dissent than victory, submission or death: if a group fell out of favor, flight through the Himalayan mountains, the Gobi desert or the vast Siberian forests remained an option, but the high risk of the enterprise made it extremely difficult for large numbers of people to flee, while distance made it impossible for the groups to then organize into rival principalities that could fight back into enemy territory. Europe's geography, on the other hand, is full of options for would-be renegades: even if hunted down by an organized state on a given territory, rebels could always flee into the nearby mountains and settle there to regain strength, organize guerillas and counterattack (a recurring feature of Balkan and medieval Italian history); they could also leave to a nearby island and either take over its administration to organize it as a rival separate entity or serve for a sovereign with no interest in seeing the mainland unified – an enterprise made easier by the physical protection of the seas (any allusion to the history of the United Kingdom's history of relations in Europe would, of course, be fortuitous).

Finally, the lack of clear natural borders is an aggravating factor for Europe's security. True, it is bordered to its west by a great ocean that the ancients long believed to be impassable, to the north by another ocean that was until recently ice-bound and to the south by the Mediterranean Sea. The latter already constitutes a problem, insofar as the Med is relatively small and navigable: far from being a frontier, it has also been throughout history a vehicle bringing together very different peoples through trade or war[15] – the Greek and Roman civilizations' heritage may be claimed by the Europeans, but both were above all oriented toward the Mediterranean, not the mainland. Moreover, the three bottlenecks that separate Europe from Africa and the Middle East (the Straits of Gibraltar, of Sicily and the Marmara complex around the Bosporus and the Dardanelles) can be seen as borders or invasion platforms, in one direction or the other: the Turks' control of the Bosporus allowed them to dominate for nearly 400 years a large part of the Balkan peninsula and even to twice lay siege to Vienna; the Strait of Gibraltar was crossed by a number of powers initially based in Africa (Carthaginians in ancient times, Arabs in the seventh century) to invade the Iberian Peninsula and beyond, before being crossed in the other direction by the Spanish and Portuguese after the sixteenth century. As for the Strait of Sicily, the widest of the three, it is only 145 kilometers long, barely more than between Normandy and Portsmouth, and it was used not only by Charles V to lay siege to Tunis in 1535 but also by the Allies to land in Sicily from Algeria in 1943. Unlike the Americas, protected by two immense oceans, or India, sheltered from a massive invasion from the North by the Himalayas (although not from those coming from the mountains of Afghanistan in the North West) and in other directions by the Indian Ocean, Europe is vulnerable in at least three points – not counting, of course, the much larger question posed by its eastern flank.

Europe's Eastern equation is actually simple: there are no insurmountable obstacles between Vladivostok and Paris, even on horseback as none of the Siberian Mountain ranges is high enough to stop invaders. The Urals, the commonly accepted "natural" border between Europe and Asia, are far from resembling the Alps, let alone the Himalayas. With Mount Narodnaya (1,895 m) as its highest point and a Southern slope that blurs itself into the immensities of the vast Kazakh steppe land, it can easily be crossed and circumvented, as Huns and Mongols proved in the fifth and thirteenth centuries. This is of course not to mention the countless incursions of peoples actually stemming from this Eurasian region who came in, came back and sometimes settled in Europe, among them the Scythians, Sarmatians, Bulgarians and Magyars – all gave Byzantium serious headaches in the Middle Ages. The latter did take advantage of their military superiority to take possession of the Pannonian Plain in the tenth century, Christianize and settle there indefinitely, thus creating the (unmistakably European) Kingdom of Hungary.

While Europe is separated from Africa and the Middle East by porous but very real obstacles, there is none that separate Europe and Asia: the Urals is too small to form a real obstacle, and the immense rivers that water the Eurasian landmass (in a North-South or South-North direction), from be the Don to the Lena, the Volga or the Yenisei, do not form impassable obstacles but rather ideal communication – and invasion – routes. The Ryurik dynasty, which founded the powerful kingdom of Rus' in the tenth century around Kyiv, is originally Viking: its early members used the Dnieper to descend from the Baltic area to nowadays Ukraine, submitting the river basin to form a powerful empire. The vastness of the spaces in Eastern Europe made the region difficult not only to control but also to delimit. This in itself is not necessarily a bad thing: even more than the seas, the "steppe highway" was from ancient times to the end of the Middle Ages a crucial axis of communication between Asia and Europe – with not only raw materials (spices) and manufactured products (silk) but also armies and germs transiting through the silk road: the Black Death, brought to Europe via the Crimea and the Genoese merchants, originated in Central Asia.

If the border between Europe and Asia is not clear, the definition of Europe's steppe invaders (Europeans? Asians? others) is in turn difficult to determine. If Europeans readily recognize the Mongols as Asian people because of their geographical origin, the presence of a modern Mongolian state located in Asia and their physical appearance, the distinction is much more difficult for other peoples who came from the steppes and settled in Europe: could one deny today the European-ness of the Hungarians, a people settled on the continent for more than 1,000 years but who proudly keep the memory of their Uralic (and nomadic) origins in their national narrative? The question may not be of much importance for people who generally identify themselves as European and are recognized as such. It is, however, much more acute in the case of Muslim Turkey and may be even more for Russia, whose intellectual heritage is defined by a controversy as old as the Moscow's principality between Westerners and Slavophiles. Because of these contradictory influences, Russia has defined itself as a Eurasian world in itself, and this, in turn, has had consequences for Europe: Russia often wants to be part of it but on its own conditions and, more particularly, with a hinterland that can provide the strategic depth it deems crucial for its own security. Russian elites are particularly aware of their history, having been raised on the memory of the conquest of the Eurasian steppe by the Mongols, the capture of Moscow by the Polish-Lithuanian Commonwealth in the seventeenth century, by Napoleonic troops in the nineteenth century and the German invasion of the twentieth century; they are therefore eager to extend their control over the non-Russian territories west of Moscow for what they define as vital security reasons. As history has shown that the Eurasian power has no "natural" borders to provide for an objective or symbolic end to its extension, Russia's only "frontier" remains the strength of its neighbors, and if those are weak, it then sees no problem in ending the *Russkii mir* (or "Russian world," a message in itself) at Kharkiv, Warsaw or Berlin depending on circumstances and hard power balance. This feeling of insecurity, shared by the other powers of the North European plain (Germany and Poland), is one of the issues that defined some of the deadliest conflicts on the continent and, in particular, the Second

World War, which for this very reason became a conflict of colonization and extermination.[16]

The absence of a clear border in the East – and the immensity of the no-man's-land between Europe and Asia – poses a cornelian security problem for both Europe and the power (or powers) that controls the Eurasian space. Moreover, if the lack of mountains in Northern Europe opens the space to invasions from the steppe (the Huns reached the gates of Paris in 451, as did the Russians victorious of Napoleon in 1814), conquering the steppe highway remains very difficult for European powers because of the great distances. The four powers that were closest to it (seventeenth-century Poland, early nineteenth-century France, twentieth-century Germany and Russia) ultimately lost control of at least parts of the space, either because they had met their match in the West or because they could not overcome the enormous logistical constraints of deploying troops in the vast and empty spaces of the East. Furthermore, the failure of the Soviet army, despite its overwhelming military might, to impose its will on the Western Balkans, whether with Tito's Yugoslavia or Enver Hoxha's Albania, says much about the opportunities of resistance that mountainous terrain offers, even in the era of modern warfare. Seen as a whole, the geography of Europe seems to only favor fragmentation, insecurity and conflict, even though it should also be noted that other recently unified spaces, and notably India, have relatively similar characteristics: indeed, for relatively similar geographical and logistical reasons, the subcontinent was never completely unified, not even by the Mughals, until the arrival of the British in the nineteenth century.[17]

Ancient culture wars

It is of course entirely possible to reject this purely geographical and necessarily deterministic vision of Europe's destiny. World history has shown it many times, historical inevitability is often only underlined ex-post by the winners, who have the easy task of re-writing the event so as to put destiny on their side. A deterministic approach to war's relationship with Europe would therefore be both presumptuous and incomplete, especially since, as British journalist Tim Marshall reminds us, airpower and the Internet among others have also changed the rules of the geopolitical game.[18] Even if geography constrains the field of political action, it is also guided by the experience of man – for conservative authors like Niall Fergusson, these cultural elements are even crucial to understand the development of Europe and more generally of the West throughout history.[19]

How does Europe distinguish itself culturally from the rest of the world? The question is of particular interest to Europeans these days, as the globalization they initiated centuries ago has now gone way beyond their control – to the extent that the term no longer is a synonym with Westernization, let alone Europeanization. There were of course simpler times: in the Middle Ages, Christianity was the constituting factor of Europe – indeed, it was the only element that brought many different people from different origins and walks of life to start thinking of themselves as one civilization. But this distinction has lost its specificity ever since groups of Europeans took their leave to evangelize the Indies in the sixteenth century – of course, secularization, which has accelerated since the mid-twentieth century, makes this Christian character of Europe ever less convincing. In the nineteenth century, when secularism really did displace Christianity as a European religion, Europeans did see their modernity and technological advance as a marker of their specificity (a marker that took little time to turn into racialist considerations), but the industrial development of North America and then China or India today has made this distinction totally obsolete.

Europe's cultural identity must, therefore, be found not in one essential element but rather in a mixture of three major components of its history: Antiquity, Christianity and the Enlightenment. Individually, these elements are certainly not unique to Europe. The Europeans are not the only ones to have adopted Christianity – the Americas, part of sub-Saharan Africa, South Korea and many Pacific Islands are also Christian; similarly, as Ian Morris notes, the ancient West includes not only Rome and Greece but also the civilizations of the Near and Middle East;[20] finally, the Enlightenment left its mark on North America just as profoundly as on Europe so much so that it is the founding principle of the Constitution of the United States. But only Europe draws its roots directly and geographically from all three legacies at the same time – and its understanding of these constitutive elements is increasingly at odds with those developed on the other side of the Atlantic.[21]

It is impossible to deny the influence of classic Roman and Greek Antiquity to Europe: a large part of its architecture, its cultural heritage (from the theater to sports), but also its political structures derive from the specific ancient Greek and Roman experiences - all modern forms of government, kingdom, democracy, empire or republic. It would also be foolish to deny the heavy mark that Christianity has left not only on Western thought, as Tom Holland recently argued,[22] but specifically on Europe, shaping its whole societal structure during the millennium and a half in which it enjoyed a monopoly on European souls. As French political scientist Olivier Roy puts it,

> things as specific as the police investigation (the gathering of clues, the search for confession, still central in the police forces of Catholic Europe, or the neighborhood investigation) and the criminal courts (where truth derives from the subject's confessions) were built by the Church's jurists, and by the Inquisition in particular. The Council of Trent played a great role in the definition of a Christian anthropology that still defines Europe's cultural base (the family centered on the couple and not on the group, the symmetry between the spouses, which is indeed a break with the vision of Roman law).[23]

Finally, the third component of Europe's identity, the Enlightenment, paved the way to our technical modernity but also shaped our thinking in a way that was particularly fitted for the economic expansion of its time: our explanation of things and events by reasoning and causality and not by the will of one (or more) god(s), our (re-)discovery of the separation of powers to avoid tyranny but also the great experiments of representative and direct democracy are all markers that have made and still make Europe since the eighteenth century.

The three legacies that have made Europe as a cultural whole are not separate items, they are intertwined. One cannot understand the idea of the separation of powers, or the separation of Church and State, without first understanding the differentiation between the spiritual power of the Pope and the temporal power of princes – a legacy of the fall of the Roman world and the lack of authority in Rome at the time of the barbarian invasions. Likewise, and despite the temptation for many eighteenth *Philosophes* to break (at least in part) with Christian tradition to return to the sources of antiquity, the reality is that the legacy of Rome and the ancient Greeks that they re-discovered (through their Christian lenses) could only be transmitted through the monasteries that preserved the knowledge and ancient manuscripts during the long period of turmoil we call the Middle Ages. It should also be remembered that when the philosophers were not themselves practicing Christians (and they were in any case shaped by their Christian upbringing[24]), their intellectual reasoning was guided by predecessors such as Erasmus, Bossuet or Thomas More, who were all fervent Christians educated with respect, even reverence, for the heritage of antiquity, having studied most of the classical texts in their original language, since they mastered Greek and Latin – the language of the court in the Holy Roman Empire until the early nineteenth century. Finally, even if Christianity rejected the polytheism of the Greeks and the first Romans, the construction of its institutions and its creed owe as much to the Greek and Roman tradition as to the elements of Jewish history reported in the Old Testament. If Jesus was indeed himself a Jew and his doctrine derived from the Old Testament, the Gospels were all written by subjects of the Roman Empire, and the ecclesiastical institutions (from *ecclesia*, the Latin word for assembly, before it became synonymous with the church) were built within the cultural system of the Roman Empire – they could only have been deeply imbued with it, despite the revolutionary character of Christian thought.[25]

Europe's identity is defined by these three legacies – Antiquity, Christianity and the Enlightenment – three factors of unity that very often fuel the discourse of those who support the deepening of European integration. But just as these three elements can be seen as factors of unity between Europeans, they also carry within them the seeds of discord. The conflict between them is first and foremost a struggle for the primacy of one over the other two, due in large part to the Christian religion, which is monotheistic and therefore finds it difficult to cohabit with other systems of thought – after all, there can be only one God and, therefore, only one truth. The French are well aware of the tensions that can exist between the Christian and Enlightenment heritage – after all, French modern history is littered with varying degrees of conflict between Church and State over spiritual leadership on society, from the separation of Church and State in 1905 to the debates over same-sex marriage in 2013. This tension is equally visible in other states of the European continent, as current tensions in Poland over abortion and the links between the state and the catholic church testify, and the fragmentation of polities has meant very different outcomes from one country to the next. Today, the division between "an enlightened, revolutionary and republican Europe on the one hand, and a conservative, traditional Europe, [...] more instinctive and identity-based," on the other hand, to use Belgian MEP Guy Verhofstadt's wording,[26] may well be over-simplistic, but it remains a reality and, in many ways, it overlaps with the separation between Western Europe and Central Europe – where the East–West divide of the twentieth century over communism overlaps with that between liberal Europe and the Holy Alliance in the early nineteenth century. As unifying as Europe's three legacies can be, the ambiguities of the combination can also be a source of inextricable conflicts – in many ways, this is actually a European specificity, as America has so far been able to combine the Christian and the Enlightenment heritage much more peacefully, due to the fact that, unlike in Europe where the State had to force a separation with religious authorities against the will of the Church, in the United States this separation was actually operated to protect (rather than tame) the autonomy of the churches.[27]

If tensions between Europe's defining cultural components were not enough, each of them carries within itself the seeds of discord that have repeatedly led the continent to division, conflict and war. The heritage of antiquity is not necessarily the least divisive: the Roman Empire, despite its high degree of industrial and administrative standardization, was from the outset divided into two parts, later sanctioned by the tetrarchy: one, in the Western Mediterranean, spoke Latin, and the other, to the East, Greek. It should come as no surprise that the dividing line between the two worlds, continued under Christianity between Catholicism and Orthodoxy, is to be found around the eastern coast of the Adriatic, in the very region that saw a bloody conflict break out in the early 1990s between Catholic Croats and Orthodox Serbs. As if this was not enough, the heritage of antiquity also cuts Europe in two following a North–South axis: Rome may have been vast, but it was the center of a Mediterranean Empire, not a European one, and most of the continent north of the Danube and east of the Rhine was beyond its control – both politically and culturally. This division between "civilization" and "barbarians" was blurred with the great invasions of the fifth to eleventh centuries, which greatly complicated the social and ethnic composition of what was to become France or Italy, but traces of it have remained, for example in the dividing lines that have separated the Catholic and Protestant kingdoms that waged war on each other for several centuries after the Reformation in Western Europe. Today, the division is not expressed in a religious way, but it is still remarkably visible with a clear cultural fault line between a Latin, Catholic, demonstrative and prodigious Southern Europe and a Nordic Northern Europe, which is more closed, more discreet, Protestant and takes much greater attention of controlling public spending. We will see in the next chapters that this cultural division is quite contemporary and that it has shattered the unity of Europe during the Euro crisis in the early 2010s.

The Christian heritage is also in itself a source of discord among Europeans: the division between Catholics and Protestants is actually a constitutive element of our modern states, following the Treaty of Westphalia and its principle *cujus regio, ejus religio* (to each realm its religion) which has practically defined the early formation of modern states prior to the nineteenth century, thereby guaranteeing a high degree of atomization. But Christianity also magnified pre-existing divisions, such as that between the Latin-speaking Rome and the Greek-speaking Constantinople, leading to a rivalry between Catholic and Orthodox Christians that found an expression in the Sack of Constantinople by Venice and the Latins in 1204 – an episode of history that Greeks, for one, still have not forgotten. The tensions between the Latin, catholic West and the Greek, orthodox East found many other fields of expression in Europe, whether in Ukraine between Polish Catholics and an Orthodox Church installed since the conversion of the State of Rus' by Volodymyr the Great in 988. More recently, the great schism found an expression in the conflict between Croats and Serbs during the wars of Croatia and Bosnia-Herzegovina during the 1990s. One can of course answer that in each case, the religious aspect of the conflict was only one element among many others in the outbreak of the war and usually not the most important: control of trade in the eastern Mediterranean in the case of Constantinople, land ownership for the Polish nobility in the case of Ukraine, or nationalism for the Serbs in the wars of the 1990s played a much more important role in leading to war than religion. But once the religious element stuck in, they became more entrenched and made war almost intractable. As French scholar Olivier Roy points out, "there is nothing to negotiate in religion [...]. Religions are incapable of making peace among themselves precisely because one cannot negotiate on dogma, only on the place of religion in the public space."[28] Historically, conflicts with a religious dimension have been the most difficult to manage, and the experience of the long wars in Yugoslavia shows us that once sectarian violence is ignited with a cultural or religious dimension, it is very difficult to put the lid back on it.

Finally, the Enlightenment, which originally developed as a response to these conflicts over religious dogma, came to show over time its potential as an equally divisive and, sometimes, destructive force. Edmund Burke's *Reflections on the Revolution in France*, even though they were themselves a product of the Enlightenment, provide a prescient canvas to show how the ideas of the *Philosophes*, once unleashed, could lead to an orgy of sectarianism and violence, whether internal (via the French revolution) or external (the French revolutionary wars). This of course is not to say that the Enlightenment made Europe more prone to war: on the contrary, by freeing the continent from religious sectarianism, it did contribute to pacifying the relations not only between states but also between the individuals who were now put, for the first time ever, at the center of European thought. But the Enlightenment also did produce the ideologies that progressively replaced religion starting from the nineteenth century in

Europe: nationalism, of course, but also communism and the right-wing nihilism which, coupled with the Nietzschean vision of a post-Christian moral order, was to lead many intellectuals of the early twentieth century to embrace fascism and its steroidal version, Nazism. The rise of these two side-products of the Enlightenment (which themselves were critiques of liberalism and Christianity) led after the First World War to the most vicious ideological conflict in European history, in what German historian Ernst Nolte has called the "European Civil War."[29] Whether taken individually or as a whole, the three constitutive elements of Europe's cultural identity are as much a source of concord and unity as a source of discord, and they have regularly turned the continent into a battlefield.

The endless war

Whether looked at from a geographical or cultural perspective, Europe seems almost conditioned to be defined by its relationship with Mars. But if war is part of the continent's DNA, this does not necessarily mean that Europe has to find itself in a permanent state of war, as the history of the past 75 years has shown. We will get back to this period in a moment, but it is worth examining the long history of the continent to understand the complexity of the relationship between Mars and Europe. Viewed over a long period of time, that relationship does look straightforward, and it is passionate. While it is true that there have been periods of peace in Europe for varying lengths of time, an overview of the continent's long history shows that the peaceful times Europeans have been living constitute a remarkable exception in an otherwise very bellicose record.

That European history may be principally punctuated by battles and armed conflicts should come as no surprise, for war has in fact defined the rise and fall of nations as much as the wellbeing and ruin of European communities and individuals. War has actually followed a pendulum movement between two opposite dynamics: one went toward unification (expansion of Rome, constitution of the Carolingian or Napoleonic Empire, etc.), the second toward atomization, which again presupposed more or less long and bloody conflicts.[30] This double movement was almost perpetual in European history, in the sense that there were very few periods when the international or imperial system stabilized sufficiently to make war unnecessary. Moreover, an examination of these periods of *Pax Europaea* shows that when they did occur, they were geographically limited and fragile enough to guarantee the existence of armed conflict in one part of the continent even when the other was prosperous and peaceful – the 1990s come to mind here, as Europe found itself at peace and (at least in the West) prosperous while the Balkans disintegrated.

If we are to take a look at the history of the relationship between war and Europe, our paths must first lead us to Greece before Rome. Greece is the true cradle of European civilization. The continent's first cities developed there (although they were then more oriented toward the Mediterranean than toward the hinterland, unlike Egypt, for example[31]), and it is also in Greece, more precisely during the battles of Thermopylae and Salamis, that the first break between a Greek civilization based in Europe and the Near and Middle Eastern civilizations occurred. For the needs of the fight against Xerxes's Persia, the Greeks had coalesced into an alliance to defend their homeland – but as soon as the threat disappeared, they took up their weapons again to fight among themselves and thus make sure that no power could take over the others. Athens's attempt to build hegemony was checked by the declining power of Sparta. They locked themselves into 30 years of destructive warfare.[32] Much like Europe, the Greek world of the time, its rugged coastlines, its uneven mountain ranges and its fiercely independent (and war-prone) city-states favored war rather than hegemony.

Paradoxically, and pretty much like Europeans in the twentieth century, the Greeks' unity would be achieved not by Greeks themselves but by outsiders. Alexander the Great may have been educated in the Greek culture, but the Kingdom of Macedonia was not part of the Greek world – in his Philippics, Athenian orator Demosthenes denounced Alexander's father Philip as a barbarian.[33] The construction of the Hellenistic Empire, the first to emerge from European soil, thus began with the conquest of one European country by another, but its subsequent expansion was aimed not at Europe but toward the much richer South and East. This makes Alexander's conquests not only a very ephemeral construction but also and above all a Near and Middle Eastern empire, insofar as most of the conquered territories (and by far the richest ones) were located in Asia Minor, the Middle East and Africa.

If Alexander's Empire was geographically Middle Eastern, that later built by the Romans was more European in the sense that the center of power was and always remained on the European continent, whether in Rome itself or in the last years of the Empire in Constantinople (located on the European bank of the Bosporus). Although the Roman world was essentially Mediterranean, its expansion (most often by war, more rarely by diplomacy) also took place inlands north the Mediterranean to encompass not only the three southern peninsulas of the continent (the Balkans, Italy and Hispania) but also all lands west of the Rhine and south of the Danube. In this sense, Rome was the first empire that had a true European dimension since it united a large part of the continent or at least its Western and, especially, Southern parts, by far the most developed at the time.

Rome may have been made by war, but as British scholar Dominic Lieven rightly points out, once it is established, empire brings peace.[34] This is, of course, the case of Roman rule, which once entrenched – be it in Gaul, Hispania or Brittany – imposed a 400-year peace on the conquered European territories, allowing the flourish of a common civilization over large parts of the continent. But the *Pax Romana* was often more nominal than factual, even in the glory days of the empire. What Rome lacked was a clear rule of succession for its sovereign, and this often prevented a smooth transfer of power from one ruler to another, encouraging violence during periods of transition. This was especially the case when the emperor died a violent death, a common occurrence at the time: since the beginning of the Empire had been built around the murder of Julius Caesar (many others would follow), succession by regicide had much legitimacy in Roman culture and almost immediately became as commonplace as the civil wars that almost invariably followed them. From assassination to open rebellions in the marches of the Empire, Rome soon found itself in a situation of almost permanent civil war, which eventually accelerated its fall.[35]

Internal strife was not the only problem the Romans had to deal with: despite having tamed the Celtic and Gallic tribes that had previously sacked the Italian Peninsula at various times, the arrival of Roman soldiers on the banks of the Rhine and the Danube confronted them with the specific strategic issues of Northern Europe's great plain. Once settled on the banks of these two rivers, and in spite of enormous fortification works, Roman generals found themselves confronted with a vast open flat space, from which more or less civilized hordes could organize deep incursions into the territory of the Empire. Confronted with the constant flow of Germanic peoples on these borders, the Romans often acquiesced to invite these barbarians to settle on their territory – in exchange for the protection of the Empire and the development of the land, the newcomers were asked to integrate and become true Romans, with their rights but also their duties, a process of acculturation which originally worked.

The bargain between the barbarians-turned-citizens and the Roman state lasted as long as the latter could hold some authority. But as Roman institutions deteriorated and migratory (and military) pressure from other peoples from the Urals and Central Asia increased, this authority progressively withered away. The only way out for an increasingly debile state structure was to delegate more power to barbaric warlords and from compromise to compromise, Gothic, Frankish and Vandal rulers were recognized as Rex under an increasingly nominal suzerainty of the emperor – in the Eastern part of the Empire, the Slavs and Bulgarians preferred the even more equivocal title of Basileus, with the Bulgarians breaking a taboo by crowning their sovereigns as Tsar, a Slavic version of Caesar. All the Huns had to do is to finish the job – after their short-lived conquests, no one in the West had the strength to take back the title of Caesar, and the Western Empire finally died out, leaving in its place a multitude of kingdoms, while in the East Byzantium did recover to hold out against the migrations and invasions of the Slavic, Bulgarian and Arab peoples (but also the Franks and the Venetians) before falling to the Turks in 1453.

The 1000 years between the fall of the Roman Empire and the discovery of the Americas has long been considered, not without reason, as a time of turmoil, or Dark Ages for Europe. Outsiders' invasions extended almost to the fifteenth century. They came along with not only large-scale population movements but also armed conflicts that undermined the continent from the beginning to the end of this long period, from Attila's invasions to the Hundred Years' War, the Reconquista in Spain or the Mongol invasions. The Middle Ages were, not are also marked by the rapid rise and fall of many kingdoms (Moravia, Sicily, Lombardy, etc.), many of which resulted from military campaigns. But to define the medieval era only by war would be an over-simplification: the millennium also saw periods of cultural expansion (the Gothic cathedrals were only surpassed in splendor – and height – in the eighteenth century). It was also the moment when the idea of a united Europe really started to emerge, courtesy of the Christianization of the continent. In fact, the ancient Greeks and Romans would certainly not have defined themselves as European but as Mediterranean, oriented as they were toward the *Mare Nostrum*, "our" sea "between two lands" (so the translation of the modern term from Latin says). But from the seventh century onward, when the southern coast of the Mediterranean came effectively under the control of the Muslim Arabs, the Mediterranean was no longer a Roman sea – it rather became as much of a frontier as a trade route. This new status made the fortunes of the republics of Genoa, Venice and many other maritime republics, but it made the consolidation of a common Mediterranean culture absolutely impossible: from then on, each shore would have its own god, and in a monotheistic world where there could be only one deity, Christianity would become the marker of the civilization North of the Mediterranean, Islam to that of the South.[36]

North Africa's fall to Islam was as much the end of a Mediterranean world as the start of a new civilization that blossomed on the European continent. The main agents for shaping this new world were the Roman and Greek churches which, now faced with a spiritual wall south of the Mediterranean, turned to the North to evangelize the peoples beyond the old Roman world. The church already had a long experience of evangelizing the barbarians that had already settled in the historical territories of the Empire (the king of Franks Clovis is one example among many), but the loss of the rich parts of the Mediterranean pushed Rome and Constantinople to look North for a compensatory expansion, thereby leading the way to the civilization we now call European. In the ninth century, the brothers Cyril and Methodius were sent on a mission to the pagan Khazars, then to the Slavs, whom they converted. As rulers came to understand the power that this particular monotheism could give them, mass baptism occurred and Christianity spread beyond the Roman realm: the empire of Great Moravia, which Cyril and Methodius Christianized, lied north of the Danube, Rome's traditional borderland, and the faith then progressively spread North and East during the Dark Ages. Hungarians adopted Christianity in 950, followed by the Kievans in 987 and then Scandinavia (at least nominally). The Balts resisted much longer and were, as a result, the target of extremely violent campaigns, the Teutonic Crusades, but in the end, the Lithuanians, the last European people that had remained Pagan for much of the medieval era, finally converted in 1387 with their king Vytautas, who converted to cement the dynastic union of his family with the powerful Jagiellonian dynasty of the Kingdom of Poland. By the end of the Middle Ages, the whole of Europe was Christian, and indeed it was, at the time, the only region in the world where Christianity was practiced as a state religion, thereby providing a strong identity against the outside world. As Dominic Lieven points out, "as Chinese civilization defined itself against the barbarians of the northeastern steppe, so in time the 'other' against which Christian [and therefore, in the medieval sense, European] civilization above all defined itself came to be Islam,"[37] as Europe's pagan gods joined their Latin and Greek counterparts in the dustbins of history.

Within this framework, the constitution of the Carolingian Empire marks the first attempt at proper European unification. Charlemagne's construction was intended to be both a reconstitution of the Roman Empire under the banner of Christianity,[38] the union of a large part of the Germanic peoples under Frankish rule, and a new alliance between the Throne and the Altar, which explains why the coronation took place in Rome, the seat of the Papacy, and not in Aachen, the seat of Carolingian power. This Holy Roman Empire, which was to last a thousand years, intended to unite the whole of Christianity and expand its realm, bringing Europe under one rule. The dimensions of Charlemagne's empire would remain in memories, and it became the first empire centered and entirely constituted in Europe. The enterprise, however, remained incomplete, for even at the height of its power the Empire comprised only parts of Western Europe – remaining beyond Charlemagne's grasp were many territories such as Britain, Southern Italy, modern Spain, Central Europe and the Balkans. Indeed, the kingdom of Rus', founded by a Viking prince (Valdemar/Volodymyr) and centered around its capital Kyiv, formed a larger ensemble than Charlemagne's empire, as it extended from Karelia to the Black Sea, and from Galicia to the Don.

The Carolingian ensemble also proved ephemeral: after Charlemagne's death, territorial divisions among his descendants led to the formation of three different kingdoms, including what were to become France and Germany. The former struggled for its survival throughout the Middle Ages, warring against invaders from the North (the Norsemen who gave its name to Normandy), powerful neighborly barons in the North and East, as well as the English, the Burgundians and unruly subjects. For its part, what remained of the Holy Roman Empire was to evolve into a fairly decentralized, Germanic structure with an elected, rather than hereditary emperor. This ensured the prosperity of certain cities like Nuremberg or the Hanseatic ports, but it could not avoid conflicts inside the Empire. Tensions between powerful barons often degenerated into open warfare in which the emperor was more of an arbiter than a judge (meaning that his judgments could, therefore, be ignored when he was weak). Further, the tensions between the Emperor and the Pope resulted in regular warfare between them and their supporters (who often jumped on the bandwagon to solve their own differences), leading to many factional wars, notably between Guelfs and Ghibelins, with roads leading more often to the altar of Mars than to Canossa. In any case, the Papacy's aspirations to unite Christian Europeans against an external threat brought only limited results in space and time, with Crusades only temporarily (and imperfectly) uniting Christendom against a common foe that was not always considered as such. During the thousand years that make up our Middle Ages, Europe started to take its modern form, but it was as much by division and war as by the construction of Gothic cathedrals.

Mars on steroids

The end of the Middle Ages did not change the nature of the relationship between Europe and Mars. On the contrary, it seems to have given it a steroid boost. The Renaissance that began with the discovery of the Americas and the printing press led to the first mass diffusion of new ideas – and with it the Reformation. Protestants' conflicts with Rome (and vice versa) brought at least one hundred years of religious bloodshed in Western Europe. The civil strife that defined the time rendered the Holy Roman Empire obsolete long before its dissolution and brought Europeans to kill each other in protracted conflicts all over the continent. The only way out of this cycle of destruction ended up being the institutionalization of Europe's atomization under the principle *cuius regio eius religio* (to each kingdom its religion), and even this didn't stop sovereigns from fighting each other: after the Treaty of Westphalia, new generations of much more cynical sovereigns went to war against each other not to defend their faith but simply to check each other's rise. As armies benefited from technical progress and better organization, these wars wreaked havoc and destruction wherever they were fought, in particular in the many smaller German principalities (there were around 300 of them at the time). Even those countries that lived through long periods of internal peace at the time ended up trading peace inside their borders with a war outside of them, as they jockeyed with rival powers for predominance in different regions of Europe. Their enemies were not always European: the rise of Russia in the seventeenth and eighteenth centuries did preoccupy Sweden and Poland the most, while the latter was in alliance with the Habsburgs to try and check the growing power of the Ottomans in Europe's South East and the Mediterranean: The Turks were stopped in Malta and at Lepanto and reached the gates of Vienna twice (in 1529 and 1683), while the Polish-Lithuanians fought them almost everywhere in the territory of present-day Ukraine – it was the troops of the Rzeczpospolita, led by Jan Sobieski, who freed the Viennese from the second siege imposed by the Turks.

With the discovery of America, Europeans were now exporting war to other continents. In 1492, when Christopher Columbus crossed the Atlantic for the first time, Europe was truly on the periphery of the known world: the continent was then economically and technologically behind the Middle East, India and China,[39] and its western end was itself on the periphery of the periphery – the center of the Western world was then located in the Mediterranean, where the spice and silk routes ended – even if new centers of civilization had begun to appear around the English Channel and the North Sea in the late Middle Ages. The discovery of America radically changed the geopolitical position of Europe and, in particular, its western end. Instead of being small peripheral states struggling for survival, Spain, Portugal, France, the Netherlands or England found themselves with privileged access to the open seas that were no longer the end of the world but the departure point to the riches of the "Indies."

In America, the Europeans originally envisaged to create trading posts similar to the ones they had begun to build in Africa and on the coasts of the Indian

Ocean (recently explored by the Portuguese) in order to bypass Muslim intermediaries. But three factors radically changed the Europeans' outlook, as they realized that their Western voyage had brought them not to the East of Asia but to a new continent. *Guns, Germs and Steel*, to use Jared Diamond's wording,[40] suddenly allowed a small group of warriors from a peripheral continent to carve for themselves and Christendom empires larger than Alexander's in the space of a few decades.

The conquest of refined and organized civilizations[41] that had developed over large parts of the American continent occurred because of an unexpected combination: first, the relative geographical proximity between Europe and America and the currents and dominant winds of the Atlantic gave Europeans the discovery of the new continent before China. Second, with the more sophisticated weapons developed by Europeans – swords' steel as well as rifles and cannons, Spain's conquistadores recorded minimal losses when they fought the Aztecs or the Incas. The battle of Cajamarca of 1532 between Atahualpa's 8,000 Inca warriors and Pizarro's 200 soldiers equipped with swords, arquebuses and a few cannons, ended up in a spectacular victory for the Spaniards: at the end of the day, Pizarro only deplored one wounded and no death, while the Incas had lost 2,000 men killed in combat, and their emperor, now a captive.[42] Ceaseless wars served the Spaniards well: facing big armies equipped with clubs and slings, they benefited from a technological advantage that centuries of war and exchanges had brought. Thus, Europe was able to effectively claim for itself an entire continent, make the Atlantic a major trade axis (for better or for worse) and take advantage of the global competition that transformed a small peninsula of the Eurasian continent into a global leader for the next 400 years.

To be fair, Europeans did no achieve such a feat on their own. Prior to the battles, much of the carnage had actually been done by the viruses that European settlers transported with them, in particular smallpox. The aboriginal populations, which had developed in complete isolation from the deadly germs that had been exchanged for centuries between the East and West of the Eurasian landmass, were decimated more surely and definitively than any guns or swords, with estimations of populations killed by smallpox currently running as high as 90–95%.[43]

That viruses played a major role in Europeans' victories in America is confirmed by the fact that their triumph was limited to that continent. In fact, the other regions of the globe did not fall into the hands of the Europeans, and the latter remained in positions of weakness (sometimes extreme weakness) whenever they set foot on land in Africa (where the viruses worked against them) or Asia. In his History of Modern India, French scholar Claude Markovits recalls that at the beginning of the eighteenth century,

> European activity [in the subcontinent] was still a marginal element, confined to coastal regions, vulnerable because it remained far from its bases. There is no doubt that their survival in Asia owed much to the discovery

of America and its silver mines. The appearance of the Spanish *real* on the markets of Goa had played a decisive role in ensuring European merchants' prosperity. More prized than gold, silver came from all sides: from Acapulco by the Manila galleon, from America through Spain to buy silk, indigo and spices, from Japan through Batavia.[44]

The conquest of the Americas allowed Europeans to set foot all over the world and to progressively take over markets that were previously inaccessible to them but not to dominate militarily Africa or Asia. As late as 1793, when Lord Macartney established the first permanent British Embassy in China and presented Emperor Qianlong with a trade treaty, the latter brushed away the proposition, informing the bemused Westerner that China already produced everything it needed.[45] The Americas may have been subjected thanks to smallpox, but it would take much more to subjugate Africa, the Middle East or Asia.

War came to provide that extra advantage to the Europeans, as they fought each other in ever larger numbers throughout the sixteenth, seventeenth and eighteenth centuries. As European states exhausted themselves in conflicts of continental dimensions, they developed new weapons and strategies of warfare that gave them an absolute advantage over their rivals. They were able to put these in practice first at the service of indigenous princes on the Indonesian and Indian subcontinent, before turning the weapons against them to extend the territory of their original trading posts. The French, British and Dutch were thus to gradually gain military ascendancy over the indigenous kingdoms in these regions, progressively achieving results similar to that of the Spanish conquistadores but without viruses. In 1746, a small French army won a decisive battle on the Adyar River in India – about 500 men defeated a local army of 10,000 soldiers. "It was a decisive victory that showed for the first time that disciplined, trained and well-equipped European troops could defeat Indian armies that were ten times larger but fought without order or method."[46] The advantage of the French, and, more generally, of the Europeans, was actually more strategic than technical, proof that superiority had indeed been acquired through a long practice of war, as Claude Markovits points out:

> European military technology was certainly ahead, especially in the field of artillery, but the Indian states, thanks to French and other specialists, had an easy access to this technology. In sum, it is not so much technological superiority that allowed the army of the various East India Companies to defeat those of the Indian states as their more effective organization.[47]

As they started to feel this overwhelming superiority acquired on home battlefields, Europeans set out to conquer the world. They may have lost the Americas in the late eighteenth century and throughout the nineteenth century, but Europeans would find other riches to exploit in the South and East: India was conquered by the British from the end of the eighteenth century, roughly at the same time as Australia and New Zealand became colonies of settlement for His Majesty's demographic surplus. In the nineteenth century, the rest of the world followed, so much so that in 1913, with the exception of the Americas (where states had already acquired independence from European colonization), only a dozen or so countries remained effectively independent of any European power. Even counting Turkey and Russia as non-European actors (which they were not in the nineteenth century), Europe's domination over the world was beyond contestation, even for a rising power like the United States. As British historian Ian Morris puts it, "in 1914, Europeans and their colonists ruled 84% of the land and 100% of the sea."[48]

The nineteenth century, thus, ended up being a triumphal march for Europe, whose nations took benefit of the military superiority they had acquired during 13 centuries of almost uninterrupted fighting to conquer the world. For sure, Europeans' successes in the African hinterland and parts of Southeast Asia were also due to the progress of science, notably the treatments that allowed them to survive tropical diseases. But the successes of the English, French, Belgians, Dutch, Germans and Italians were primarily military and were directly linked to better organization and armament, as the industrial revolution further extended their technological advance, especially with the production of fast-loading guns and new battleships that could cause considerable damage in coastal and river areas while staying out of range from other canons, as the experienced military in China and on the Indochinese peninsula were to discover at their own expense. The revolutionary and Napoleonic wars, however bloody and destructive, further expanded Europeans' advance, as 25 years of almost uninterrupted warfare allowed generals to experiment with new weaponry and, importantly, new tactics.

The Congress of Vienna and the battle of Waterloo, which effectively ended the cycle of the Napoleonic Wars, represented a first break in the history of the continent. Indeed, despite geographically limited warfare, particularly around the mid-century, there would be no conflict with continental dimensions in Europe between 1815 and the assassination of Archduke Francis Ferdinand in 1914. There are several reasons for this – and they also shed light on the causes of the peace Western Europe has known since 1945. The first one is certain exhaustion, as continental Europe did come out morally, financially and demographically worn out from the revolutionary cycle that began in 1789 in Paris. Only two peripheral powers came out of the carnage stronger: Russia, which had increased its prestige and had acquired new territories in Europe, and the United Kingdom, which had not experienced war and destruction on its territory – an advantage acquired thanks to its island status. Thanks to the superiority of its fleet, Britain had conquered or consolidated all the maritime hotspots between Europe and China and had served as a banker for all the powers that had fought against Napoleon – and as there is no such thing as a free meal, these continental powers were all indebted to Albion, whose prestige and mastery of the seas guaranteed for the first time that status of a global superpower. For the first time since the Roman Empire, a European power was thus in a position of quasi-hegemony over its rivals. But Britons, already busy with their very lucrative overseas colonies, did not push their advantage on the continent to consolidate a territorial empire. Rather, they thrived to ensure a balance of power that would keep their hands untied overseas. Unlike *Pax Romana*, *Pax Britannica* was not based on direct territorial domination, at least in Europe, but on the commercial and maritime power of the United Kingdom, coupled with the balance of power on the continent – once that was lost after 1870, the deconstruction of peace took time but it became a strong undercurrent that led to Britain's intervention in the Great War.

A similar combination of general exhaustion (along with fear of new revolutionary outbreaks) and a clear balance of power led to similar results in 1945. But for the moment, it is worth getting back to the period between 1815 and 1914, which despite the many localized conflicts that marked it (notably in the period 1848–1870), was actually the least violent until then in the history of Europe. Built on the ruins of the Napoleonic wars and fueled by the industrial revolution, it came to be a century of unprecedented technological progress and prosperity, although the latter was certainly badly distributed, with wealth partly created at the expense of a new local lumpenproletariat and the newly conquered colonies. But from a strictly European perspective, colonization actually helped pacify the continent, as colonial endeavors allowed the (many) young and restless adventurers of the nineteenth century to satisfy their thirst for action and glory outside of Europe.

The European Century was not only marked by conquests outside Europe. There were indeed many internal armed conflicts, may these be revolutions that in some countries turned into short civil wars (in 1820, 1830 and 1848), but also violent wars between states that, although localized and brief, were particularly violent. The wars of unification of Italy and Germany, in particular, were the first in which soldiers experienced industrial warfare. Following the battle of Solferino, by all accounts a bloodbath, Henri Dunant a shocked Swiss businessman who visited the battlefield, founded the Red Cross to allow humane treatment of the prisoners and wounded.[49]

The industrialization of war and its deadly consequences led Europeans to start thinking of ways to limit it, or even abandon it altogether. The cycle of peace conferences initiated in The Hague and Geneva between 1899 and 1907 proved perpetual peace was not just wishful thinking but an ideal that had become much more widespread than anticipated, among the general public and parts of the continent's elites. The realities, however, were not as romantic: much of the texts adopted at the time concerned the rules of conduct in warfare (*jus in bello*). Much as chivalry in the Middle Ages, the idea was to make war more "humane," but certainly not to eliminate it – the right to war (*jus ad bellum*) remained indisputably a means to solve international differences.[50] Indeed, while the desire for peace expressed by the Hague conference participants was to be taken with a pinch of salt (as he gave the impetus for the discussions, Tsar Nicholas II had begun a major effort to rearm the Russian Empire[51]); other powerful actors advocated for European nations to consider leading preventive wars, in particular in the German high command.[52] The objective of this new type of warfare was to prevent long-term negative developments that were considered to favor rivals, and appetite for war was further fueled by an excitable public opinion. Recent experience, from Austerlitz and Waterloo to Sedan and Sadowa,[53] had told everyone that war was short and its outcome defined by a single battle, very limited in time and space. While war certainly was a dreadful thing, its ephemeral nature made it a conceivable solution to solve a crisis just as decisively as an international conference, if not more.

Europe's Great Powers thus came close to conflict on several occasions between 1890 and 1914, as the continent's old "balance of powers" had been irredeemably shattered by German and Italian unification, with debates about how to best accommodate the new powers. But while crises had mostly developed in the core of the European continent between 1815 and 1870, they now appeared most threatening either outside of it (the Fashoda incident in 1898 brought Britain and France on the brink of war, while the Agadir crisis between Germany and France in 1911 was over Morocco) or on its periphery, namely in the Balkans. The peninsula was already in a state of quasi-permanent war since the end of the nineteenth century as the new states that had formed following the retreat of the Ottoman Empire throughout the period were pitted against each other for influence and border delineations. Bulgaria, Greece, Albania, Serbia, Montenegro and to a lesser extent Romania had already been at war with each other a number of times before the start of the twentieth century, but rivalries turned into generalized regional warfare in 1912–1913. The two Balkan wars, which practically expulsed the Turks from the region while pitting Russian and Austrian interests against each other (along with those of their client states), also gave a leading role to an expansionist Serbia, allowing an organization ran in parallel to the Serbian state, the Black Hand, to successfully plan the attack on Austrian Archduke Franz Ferdinand in Sarajevo on June 28, 1914, thereby precipitating the Great War.

★ ★ ★ ★ ★

In view of this brief history of the continent from its origins to 1914, one can only conclude that up to then Europe's historic relationship with war was very close. It was favored from the start by geographic and cultural fault lines that made war remarkably easy on European soil, whether between states or inside communities. The political atomization that resulted meant that the few attempts to unify and pacify the continent (Roman, Carolingian, Habsburg or Napoleon empires) were both to remain geographically incomplete and of limited duration. In the case of the Roman Empire, as in that of the *Pax Britannica* of the nineteenth century (which consecrated the effective but indirect and non-nominal domination of the United Kingdom over Europe), the peace brought by Empire was also very limited: Rome was torn by internal struggles that regularly turned into civil wars almost, while British disinterest in continental affairs in the nineteenth century meant that its peace remained imperfectly applied on the continent. That being said, the *Pax Britannica* did also mark a period of remarkable stability and peace on the continent, even though the war was never far away – whether at home or in the colonies that European powers carved for themselves. In fact, it was precisely because they had been fighting each other for so long that Europeans had a competitive advantage over their rivals throughout the nineteenth century – paradoxically then, it was Europe's marriage with Mars that gave it the edge it needed to dominate the rest of the world. How the relation turned sour to the point of destroying Europe almost entirely, thereby putting an end to the idyll, is the subject of the next chapter.

Notes

1 Robert Kagan, *Of Paradise and Power*, New York: Alfred A. Knopf, 2003.
2 John Lewis Gaddis, *The Long Peace: Inquiries into the History of the Cold War*, Oxford: Oxford University Press, 1987.
3 Margaret Mead, *Coming of Age in Samoa: A Psychological Study of Primitive Youth for Western Civilization*, New York: William Morrow, 1928.
4 Napoleon Chagnon, *Noble Savages: My Life among Two Dangerous Tribes – The Yanomamö and the Anthropologists*, New York: Simon & Schuster, 2013.
5 If local police reports are to be trusted, the reality of violence in the Samoas at the time tends to prove a more natural penchant for violence in pre-industrial societies. See Ian Morris, *War: What is it Good for? The Role of Conflict in Civilization, from Primates to Robots*, London: Profile Books, 2014, p.58.
6 Ian Morris, *War: What is it Good for? The Role of Conflict in Civilization, from Primates to Robots*, London: Profile Books, 2014, pp.288–294.
7 Ibid., pp.288–294.
8 Richard Wrangham, and Dale Peterson, *Demonic Males: Apes and the Origins of Human Violence*, Boston: Houghton Mifflin, 1996.
9 Francis Fukuyama, *The Origins of Political Order: From Prehuman Times to the French Revolution*, London: Profile Books, 2012.
10 Lawrence H. Keeley, *War before Civilization: The Myth of the Peaceful Savage*, Oxford: Oxford University Press, 1997, p.37.
11 Ibid., p.28.
12 Robert D. Kaplan, *The Revenge of Geography: What the Map Tells Us about Coming Conflicts and the Battle against Fate*, New York: Random House, 2012, p.17.
13 Ibid., p.29.
14 Tim Marshall, *Prisoners of Geography*, London: Elliott & Thompson, 2015.
15 See David Abulafia, *The Great Sea: A Human History of the Mediterranean*, London: Allen Lane, 2011.
16 Thimothy Snyder, *Bloodlands: Europe between Hitler and Stalin*, London: Vintage, 2010.
17 Claude Markovits et al., *Histoire de l'Inde Moderne: 1480–1950*, Paris: Fayard, 1994.
18 Tim Marshall, *Prisoners of Geography*, London: Elliott & Thompson, p.xvi.
19 Ferguson considers that Europe – and more generally the West, has built its supremacy not due to geography but through the development of six distinct cultural traits – the six "killer apps" that have made its fortune, namely competition between nations, science, the rule of law, medicine, consumerism and work ethics. See Niall Ferguson, *Civilizations: The West and the Rest*, London: Penguin Press, 2011.
20 Ian Morris, *Why the West Rules – For Now: The Patterns of History and What They Reveal about the Future*, London: Profile Books, 2010.
21 See Bruno Macães, *History has Begun: The Birth of a New America*, London: Hurst, 2020.

22 Tom Holland, *Dominion: The Making of the Western Mind*, London: Little Brown, 2019.
23 Olivier Roy, *L'Europe est-elle Chrétienne?* Paris: Seuil, 2018, p.17.
24 Tom Holland, *Dominion: The Making of the Western Mind*, London: Little Brown, 2019.
25 Rémi Brague, *Europe, la voie romaine*, Paris: Folio, 1999.
26 Guy Verhofstadt, *Le Mal Européen*, Bruxelles: Marque Belge, 2016, p.93.
27 George Weigel, *The Cube and the Cathedral: Europe, America and Politics without God*, New York: Basic Books, 2005.
28 Olivier Roy, *L'Europe est-elle Chrétienne*, Paris: Seuil, 2018, p.22.
29 Ernst Nolte, *Der europäische Bürgerkrieg, 1917–1941: Nationalsozialismus und Bolschewismus*, Berlin: Propyläen, 1987.
30 This back-and-forth movement in many ways corresponds to Ian Morris' dichotomy between productive and unproductive warfare. The former tends to gather estates and territories together and ultimately systematizes their management, while the second promotes dismemberment and productivity losses. See Ian Morris, *War: What is it Good for? The Role of Conflict in Civilization, from Primates to Robots*, London: Profile Books, 2014.
31 See David Abulafia, *The Great Sea: A Human History of the Mediterranean*, London: Allen Lane, 2011.
32 Thucydides, *History of the Peloponnesian War* (revised edition), London: Penguin Classics, 1972.
33 Demosthenes describes Philip as "not only not a Greek nor related to the Greeks, but not even a barbarian from a land worth mentioning; no, he's a pestilence from Macedonia, a region where you can't even buy a slave worth his salt." Quoted in Thomas R. Martin, *Ancient Greece: From Prehistoric to Hellenistic Times*, Yale: Yale University Press, 2013, p.240.
34 Dominic Lieven, *Empire: The Russian Empire and its Rivals from the Sixteenth Century to the Present*, London: Pimlico, 2003.
35 Adrian Goldsworthy, *How Rome Fell*, Yale: Yale University Press, 2009, p.84.
36 See Henri Pirenne, *Mahomet et Charlemagne*, Paris: Presses Universitaires de France, 1937.
37 Dominic Lieven, *Empire: The Russian Empire and its Rivals from the Sixteenth Century to the Present*, London: Pimlico, 2003, p.34.
38 Charlemagne's campaigns of Christianization, particularly to the East in Pagan Saxony, was particularly violent. See Tom Holland, *Dominion: The Making of the Western Mind*, London: Little Brown, 2019, pp.191–205.
39 Ian Morris, *Why the West Rules for Now: The Patterns of History and What They Reveal about the Future*, London: Profile Books, 2010, pp.331–383.
40 Jared Diamond, *Guns, Germs, and Steel: The Fates of Human Societies*, New York: Norton & Company, 2005.
41 The Mesoamerican civilizations and the Inca Empire are by now well known to Europeans because of the immediate conquest of the Aztec and Inca empires and the romanticism associated with the searches for Maya ruins, but these were not the only groups that occupied the vast American space, building cities and, therefore, civilizations. We are not only starting to discover these lost civilizations' refinement, which remain very difficult to track because of the vastness of the American spaces, but also the fact that many buildings had been built with biodegradable materials such as lime, earth and wood. Among them, the civilizations of the Mississippi – from which the first Conquistadors suffered terrible losses – and those of the Amazon are probably among the most underestimated. See Charles C. Mann, *1491: New Revelations of the Americas before Columbus* (2nd edition), New York: Vintage Books, 2011.
42 Jared Diamond, *Guns, Germs, and Steel: The Fates of Human Societies*, New York: Norton & Company, 2005, pp.67–81.

43 Even discounting these estimates as exaggerations or internalizing the fact that this high figure results not of one but several pandemics which spread across the Americas through three centuries, the figure remains impressive and does not capture the social chaos that the epidemics also caused for survivors in societies that faced rapid extinction and became even more vulnerable as a result – in fact, the weakening of the Inca and Aztec Empire prior to their conquest by the Spaniards had much to do with the spread of smallpox. See Charles C. Mann, *1491: New Revelations of the Americas before Columbus* (2nd edition), New York: Vintage Books, 2011, p.106.
44 Claude Markovits et al., *Histoire de l'Inde moderne: 1480–1950*, Paris: Fayard, p.168.
45 Ian Morris, *Why the West Rules for Now: The Patterns of History and What They Reveal about the Future*, London: Profile Books, 2010, p.484.
46 Claude Markovits et al., *Histoire de l'Inde moderne: 1480–1950*, Paris: Fayard, p.261.
47 Ibid., p.296.
48 Ian Morris, *War: What is it Good for? The Role of Conflict in Civilization, from Primates to Robots*, London: Profile Books, 2014, p.168.
49 Henri Dunant, *Un souvenir de Solférino*, Paris: Hachette, 2001.
50 As War historian Lawrence Freedman rightly points out, "the logic of the Hague conferences [...] was not to outlaw war but to make it more palatable by smoothing down its rougher edges." Lawrence Freedman, *The Future of War: A History*, New York: PublicAffairs, 2017, p.27.
51 Ibid., p.25.
52 Graham Allison, *Destined for War: Can America and China Escape Thucydides's Trap*, Boston: Mariner Books, 2018, p.275.
53 Lawrence Freedman, *The Future of War: A History*, New York: PublicAffairs, 2017, p.9.

Bibliography

Abulafia, David, *The Great Sea: A Human History of the Mediterranean*, London: Allen Lane, 2011.
Acemoglu, Daron, and Robinson, James A., *Why Nations Fail: The Origins of Power, Prosperity and Poverty*, London: Profile Books, 2013.
Allison, Graham, *Destined for War: Can America and China Escape Thucydides's Trap*, Boston: Mariner Books, 2018.
Brague, Rémi, *Europe, la voie romaine*, Paris: Folio, 1999.
Chagnon, Napoleon, *Noble Savages: My Life among Two Dangerous Tribes – The Yanomamö and the Anthropologists*, New York: Simon & Schuster, 2013.
Diamond, Jared, *Guns, Germs, and Steel: The Fates of Human Societies*, New York: Norton & Company, 2005.
Esdaile, Charles, *Napoleon's Wars: An International History 1803–1815*, New York: Penguin, 2008.
Ferguson, Niall, *The Ascent of Money: A Financial History of the World*, London: Penguin Book, 2009.
Ferguson, Niall, *Civilizations: The West and the Rest*, London: Penguin Press, 2011
Freedman, Lawrence, *The Future of War: A History*, New York: PublicAffairs, 2017.
Fukuyama, Francis, *The Origins of Political Order: From Prehuman Times to the French Revolution*, London: Profile Books, 2012.
Gaddis, John Lewis, *The Long Peace: Inquiries into the History of the Cold War*, Oxford: Oxford University Press, 1987.
Goldsworthy, Adrian, *How Rome Fell*, Yale: Yale University Press, 2009.
Holland, Tom, *Dominion: The Making of the Western Mind*, London: Little Brown, 2019.

Kaplan, Robert D., *The Revenge of Geography: What the Map Tells Us about Coming Conflicts and the Battle against Fate*, New York: Random House, 2012.
Keeley, Lawrence H., *War Before Civilization: The Myth of the Peaceful Savage*, Oxford: Oxford University Press, 1997, p.37.
Lieven, Dominic, *Empire: The Russian Empire and its Rivals from the Sixteenth Century to the Present*, London: Pimlico, 2003.
Kagan, Robert, *Of Paradise and Power*, New York: Alfred A. Knopf, 2003.
Macães, Bruno, *History has Begun: The Birth of a New America*, London: Hurst, 2020.
Mann, Charles C., *1491: New Revelations of the Americas Before Columbus* (2nd edition), New York: Vintage Books, 2011.
Markovits, Claude et al., *Histoire de l'Inde moderne: 1480–1950*, Paris: Fayard, 1994.
Marshall, Tim, *Prisoners of Geography*, London: Elliott & Thompson, 2016.
Mead, Margaret, *Coming of Age in Samoa: A Psychological Study of Primitive Youth for Western Civilization*, New York: William Morrow, 1928.
Morris, Ian, *Why the West Rules for Now: The Patterns of History and What They Reveal about the Future*, London: Profile Books, 2010.
Morris, Ian, *War: What is it Good for? The Role of Conflict in Civilization, from Primates to Robots*, London: Profile Books, 2014.
Nolte, Ernst, *Der europäische Bürgerkrieg, 1917–1941: Nationalsozialismus und Bolschewismus*, Berlin: Propyläen, 1987.
Pirenne, Henri, *Mahomet et Charlemagne*, Paris: Presses Universitaires de France, 1937.
Thucydides, *History of the Peloponnesian War* (revised edition), London: Penguin Classics, 1972.
Roy, Olivier, *L'Europe est-elle Chrétienne*, Paris: Seuil, 2018.
Snyder, Thimothy, *Bloodlands: Europe between Hitler and Stalin*, London: Vintage, 2010.
Verhofstadt, Guy, *Le Mal Européen*, Bruxelles: Marque Belge, 2016.
Weigel, George, *The Cube and the Cathedral: Europe, America and Politics Without God*, New York: Basic Books, 2005.
Wrangham, Richard, and Peterson, Dale, *Demonic Males: Apes and the Origins of Human Violence*, Boston: Houghton Mifflin, 1996.

2
DIVORCE – FROM THE EUROPEAN CIVIL WAR TO THE LONG PEACE

Europeans celebrating the dawn of the New Year on December 31, 1913, had reasons to look at the future with optimism. Europe was at the height of its power and dominated the Eurasian mass, as well as Oceania and Africa. In the Eastern hemisphere, apart from the exceptional case of Japan, which had managed a successful modernization program and was on its way to become a great power, the states that had managed to retain formal independence had only done so, thanks to the will of the United States (Liberia) or of Europeans, who preferred to leave Siam, Iran, or Afghanistan as buffer states between their zones of influence. Even the once-mighty China was dominated by European powers who had carved zones of influence to exploit its riches. Of course, astute observers of 1913 knew that America's rapid growth threatened European hegemony in the long run, but its isolationist tendencies seemed to commit it to dominate the Western hemisphere exclusively,[1] while leaving Europeans free of their movements in Eurasia and Africa. In any case, in 1914, Europe remained beyond doubt the world's financial, scientific, artistic and intellectual magnet, pretty much in the way that the United States has been after 1945. Of course, this domination was not without its downturns, and for those areas of the world that had come under European rule, this meant exploitation and underdevelopment, but Europe's dominion over the "old world" was at the time uncontested.

Timothy Snyder has admirably summarized Europe's enviable situation as it stood on the verge of the precipice: "no adult European alive 1914 would ever see the restoration of comparable free trade; most European adults would not enjoy comparable levels of prosperity during the rest of their lives."[2] The remarkable freedom of movement enjoyed by Europeans is summed up by this telling incident, which happened just a few days before the great powers declared war on each other: on July 6, 1914, French diplomat Louis de Robien crossed the border between Germany and Russia at Wirballen (now Kyrbatai in Lithuania). The

Russian authorities' request for his passport at the border astonished him: "in that era of liberty, one travelled everywhere in Europe except for Russia without carrying a passport."³

Fast forward to 1918, and the picture had drastically changed: as the great powers (or what remained of them) signed the armistice in November, they were only the shadow of their former selves – dominance had left place to financial and moral ruin. The conflict had turned into a long war of attrition, ruining the lives and futures of a whole generation. Thirty years later, the entire continent would complete its ruin with the Second World War: in 1945, it was destroyed, defeated by its own ideologies and divided between two zones of influence, each dominated by a non-European power (although both shared a very strong cultural link with Europe). Europe would reunite after 1989 and the collapse of the Soviet Empire, but this time unification was achieved not by war but through soft-power and reform.

The period between 1914 and 1989 was a long and painful divorce between Europe and Mars – but what is not clear is how and why this unlikely separation happened. It would of course be easy to take this process through a moralist lens and see Europe's domination by outsiders as a punishment for its previous sins, a sort of purging process to alleviate its failings, but such an analysis would be as dangerous as incomplete, for the imposition of peace in Europe is the result of very specific circumstances and factors that were not as self-evident as they might seem today. This chapter will try to explain why Europeans changed their relationship with war, by looking first at the process of self-destruction they embarked on between 1914 and 1945. We will try to explain the titanic suicide committed by Europeans, for it informs us on why they were forced to find other ways to resolve their differences after 1945. Once we will have understood the specific circumstances that led Europe to its longest peace, we will then be able, in the next chapter, to understand why all the factors that safeguarded it have progressively unraveled in the past decade.

Causes for a suicide

The causes of the outbreak of the First World War have been the subject of numerous brilliant analyses. Among them, Christopher Clark's *Sleepwalkers* stands out as it reminds us at times how modern the dilemmas faced by the then decision-makers could look to us.

> What must strike any twenty-first century reader who follows the course of the summer crisis of 1914 is its raw modernity. It began with a squad of suicide bombers and a cavalcade of automobiles. Behind the outrage at Sarajevo was an avowedly terrorist organization with a cult of sacrifice, death and revenge; but this organization was extra-territorial, without a clear geographical or political location; it was scattered in cells across political borders, it was unaccountable, its links to any sovereign government

were oblique, hidden and certainly difficult to discern from outside the organization.[4]

Of course, the first parallel that comes to mind is the 9/11 attack on the Twin Towers, but as we will discover in Chapter VI, Clark's account can allow for many others: in fact, not only do the circumstances of 1914 seem somehow familiar but the dynamics of asymmetric warfare, internal tensions and the elites reasoning do as well.

Understanding the exact reasons why Europe threw itself in the abyss is way too ambitious an endeavor to be contemplated in this chapter, but it is worth getting back to some of the specifics that led European elites to take the decision to go to war – not so much to focus on the deeply personal motives that led individuals to embrace war but rather to look at the larger picture of why Europeans came to think that war was their best option. As a result, we will see that the Great War was not only the outcome of an unfortunate set of bad decisions taken with an unfortunate sequencing but the result of a logic that progressively became inescapable as the decision-making moment arrived – leading to what seems to us *ex-post* as an irrational decision.

The first important lesson from the outbreak of the First World War is that its detonator was not an extraordinary occurrence. The decision to go to war was not made over a direct great-power crisis over a colony or a contested European territory such as Alsace-Lorraine but over an incident that took place in Europe's periphery. Furthermore, the assassination of Archduke Franz Ferdinand, heir to the Habsburg crown, however tragic and criminal it might have been, was nothing exceptional for the time: in the previous 35 years, political leaders as diverse as Tsar Alexander II of Russia (1881), French President Sadi Carnot (1894), Empress Elizabeth of Austria (aka Sissi, 1898), King Umberto I of Italy (1900) and Russian Prime Minister Piotr Stolypin (1911) had all been assassinated, without their death ushering in a major crisis. Even taking into account the fact that the terrorist organization behind the assassination of Archduke Franz Ferdinand was linked to the Serbian state – although there was never any smoking gun[5] – the probability that this tragic event could lead to a continent-wide slaughter by itself was almost nil, and even in the aftermath of the attack, it was still very low – what should have happened at worst was a brief conflict between Austria-Hungary and Serbia.

The unfortunate sequence of events that led a purely bilateral crisis to become a series of mobilizations and declarations of war on a continental scale is a textbook case of game theory applied to war, in which each of the protagonists believes that the other will have to respond to their bluff by de-escalation – except that the opposite happens. But it would be wrong to talk of war as "accidental" in 1914: at any moment, the actors could have chosen to back down, not to mobilize, not to declare war, or even in the last minute to recall their troops. The road to war was, in the end, a series of conscious decisions, taken in a very specific context (which is what is of interest to us), and its irrationality can only be proved *ex-post*.

What is also remarkable is that the crisis of 1914 was probably less likely to turn into a general war than the Fashoda incident of 1898 between France and Britain or the Agadir crisis of 1911. Sarajevo was peripheral to the major powers' interest, and the obvious asymmetry of forces between Austria-Hungary and Serbia in 1914 should have convinced local actors to back down and other actors to stay out of the crisis. And yet, it took barely more than a month for the Austro-Serbian conflict to turn into a war of continental dimensions. This, no doubt, proves to us that the war trigger, a unique event, is not so important to analyze as the set of substantive elements that make possible the transition from crisis to war. In fact, the Sarajevo terrorist attack could only turn into a war because of a specific set of circumstances or causes, which shaped the decision-making of the leaders of the time.

The first one is directly related to the location of the attack and to the situation in the Balkans, which caught the attention of the great powers at the beginning of the twentieth century – particularly during the Balkan Wars of 1912–1913. The slow agony of the Ottoman Empire had forced the Turks to gradually withdraw from both North Africa and Southeastern Europe, leaving behind territories with ethnic, religious, and national borders that were difficult to delineate – the 400 years of Ottoman domination over the Balkan region had naturally mixed-up populations, identities and religions. The expulsion of the Ottoman Empire from Europe had felt a vacuum that was quickly filled by new kingdoms with contested legitimacy, ill-defined borders (due to the absence of clear "ethnic," religious or linguistic boundaries) and contradictory territorial ambitions. The young kingdoms saw their appetites develop as Ottoman retreat accelerated: Italy's successful efforts to expulse the Ottoman in North Africa as they took Tripolitania and Cyrenaica in 1911 had not gone unnoticed. It convinced the kinglets of the Balkans that they too could expand their kingdoms at the expense of the Turks and of their neighbors. In fact, each sovereign had developed a hypertrophied vision of the future of his kingdom, whether a Greater Bulgaria, a Greater Serbia or a Greater Greece including Constantinople as its capital and the Western Anatolian coast. The confrontation of these "grand ideas" between states armed to the teeth had everything to bring trouble to the region.

The Balkan powder keg had already exploded several times in the past 75 years, as the Ottomans accelerated their retreat from Europe. Apart from a few romantics, other Europeans hadn't taken much notice, as the violence remained mostly contained within a relatively small geographical area. At that time, the Balkans remained a relatively isolated ecosystem where only the surrounding powers (Austro-Hungarian, Russian and Ottoman empires) had the capacity – and will – to invest. But the globalization of continental rivalries (encouraged in part by the question of control of the Dardanelles and Bosporus Straits[6]), combined with the matrimonial policies of kingdoms seeking dynastic prestige to fuel their ideals of grandeur, quickly contributed to the internationalization of local conflicts. By 1914, the region was fully connected to the system of alliances on the continent. The Bulgarians had become clients of the central powers, thanks to Tsar Ferdinand of Saxe-Coburg – son of a Germanic princely family, while Serbia could count on the military and political support of France and Russia. The ambitions of Balkan leaders, combined with the complex interweaving of their alliances with other European powers, transformed what was initially a purely bilateral crisis between Austria and Serbia into a conflict of continental proportions. Today, the risks of seeing the Balkans becoming once again a grand chessboard where regional and global powers could jockey for influence is one of the most worrying developments for Europe.

The present situation in the Balkans will be looked at in more detail in Chapter 5 of this book. But for the moment, it is worth returning to 1914, for the transformation of a local crisis into a global war cannot only be explained by subregional factors. Beyond the local situation in the Balkans, the real issue that fueled the drive for war in most military headquarters (including, paradoxically, in Berlin) was the "German question." Since the discovery of America, which had shifted the European center of gravity toward the Atlantic, and the Reformation, which had effectively castrated the Holy Roman Empire and divided German-speaking lands into a confetti of sovereignty, Germany had turned into a battlefield where bigger powers fought out their rivalries. But the rise of a liberating nationalist movement focused on a common German language and a *Volk* fantasized by the Romantic movement had allowed a rising Prussia to progressively gather the patchwork of German-speaking principalities into a second Reich, successor to the first (Holy) Roman Empire. The united Germany thus represented a new challenge for Europe, in the sense that it was too big for the European balance of power inherited from 1815, but at the same time, it was not powerful enough to become THE hegemonic power in Europe.[7]

The German question poisoned Europe's geopolitical situation until 1945 – and its resolution by partition opened up the possibility of a long, albeit very tense, peace until 1989. Germany's quick rise had taken all European leaders by surprise. Unification took place in the space of a decade and three short, victorious wars led by Bismarck's Prussia: against Denmark in 1864, against Austria in 1866 and against France in 1870.[8] British Prime Minister Benjamin Disraeli took the measure of the momentous changes, as he declared in the British Parliament the day after the proclamation of the Empire at Versailles (following the crushing of France in 1870), that "the balance of power has been entirely destroyed, and the country which suffers most, and feels the effects of this great change most, is England" – for, with the balance of powers, the prospects of *Pax Britannica* were also gone.[9]

Until its unification, Germany had been a factor of instability because it was in effect characterized by a power vacuum. After 1870, it became a factor of instability precisely for the opposite reasons: its unity and power. The economic boom experienced by Germany after 1870 was spectacular: between 1895 and 1913, the industrial production of the Empire increased by 150%, with a 150% increase in metal production and 300% in coal, the main source of energy at the time. The German economic miracle sure gave its neighbors reasons to worry, and in particular the British, whose leadership was directly challenged: in 1880, the United Kingdom controlled almost a quarter (22.4%) of world trade, far ahead of Germany's 10%. In 1913, that number had collapsed to 14.2%, compared to 12.3% for Germany.[10] To make matters worse, the new Kaiser in Berlin, Wilhelm II, had decided to build a fleet that threatened British naval supremacy,[11] the very basis of its power. As the prospects of naval competition became real, London had to abandon its policy of splendid isolation to get involved in European politics and protect its naval supremacy. Even though Britain eventually won the naval arms race with Germany, the vivid memories of the rivalry combined with fears of German ascent had much to do with Britain's decision to go to war in 1914, in a crisis that did not concern Britain directly (at least until Germany's failure to respect Belgian neutrality).

Britons were not the only ones afraid: Germany's spectacular rise was also frightening to France, who shared a border with Germany and sought to take back the Alsace-Lorraine territories it had lost to the Kaiser in 1870, and also to Russia, who found in Prussia not only a model to emulate but also a competitor for the mastery of Europe's Northeastern plain.[12] The problem here was actually not Germany's power itself – if it had been undisputable, it would not have been a problem, but rather the fact that despite this ascent, Germany still fell short of imposing its superiority to other actors. Chatham House researcher Hans Kundnani has marvelously described this *Paradox of German Power* in a way that finds echoes in today's Europe (although the problem is now posed in geo-economic rather than geopolitical terms): "the unified Germany was too big for a balance of power in Europe and too small for hegemony."[13]

The paradox of Germany's rise and the fear generated by the arrival of new actors conditioned political leaders' calculations in the summer of 1914: many of them were by then convinced that considering the dynamics of the time, it was better to risk a war today than to let negative long-term dynamics continue to take hold. In other words, better make war now in a position of force rather than be forced to make one in five years, when the enemy's situation will have improved. Indeed, one of the remarkable features of leaders' thinking at the time is that all these Europeans had a panic fear of decline: that of British power had made the headlines ever since the Boer War and led governments to reaffirm their power in the face of Germany's ascendency in the sea and Russia's in the Middle East and North of India. The French, for their part, were all too aware of their relative decline after the disaster of the 1870 war, and although the republican regime had managed to bring back some luster to France's reputation, Paris was seeking to avenge the loss of Alsace-Lorraine before Germany would become too strong to fight. For his part, the Emperor of Austria-Hungary was also well aware of the relative decline of his estates and the difficulties to hold together a multinational empire sandwiched between Germany and Russia – going to war was seen as an existential question, and history proved that it was indeed. Even the ascendent powers had reasons to worry: Russian Tsar Nicholas II had been made aware of its empire's weakness after a military defeat in the hands of the Japanese had led to revolution at home – political instability had made his politics at home and abroad more nervous.

Kaiser Wilhelm had other reasons to worry. Even if Germany's dynamic was much more favorable than that of England or France, Berlin looked very nervously at Russia, which despite its political instability was experiencing rapid economic and military growth. On all sides, the idea of an absolute or relative decline, present or imminent, was in all the minds of European leaders, and it conditioned, more than any other, the decision to go to war. What Europeans feared most was that the future was about to bring bad news to their countries – a sentiment that is unfortunately all too common today in Europe.

European leaders also took the fateful decision to go to war because they imagined that, beyond victory or defeat, it would be short. Everything in recent European history pointed to wars that were increasingly deadly but had been decided over a short period of time, often by one single battle. War could be costly but not to the point of compromising the continent's long-term prosperity. As historian Lawrence Freedman remarks, the image of what war looked like had been shaped by the strategic experience of the past century, in which "a climacteric encounter between two armies or navies, expending resources accumulated over decades, might, in a matter of hours, change history's course."[14] Von Moltke's victories in the wars of German unification, at Dybbøl in 1864, Sadowa in 1866 and Sedan in 1870, followed this narrative, and the feeling of the military staffs in Paris, Berlin or St. Petersburg was that any future war would follow the same logic. What they had failed to appreciate was that technology had now given an advantage to the defender, not the assailant,[15] and that once offensive plans had failed, forces on each side would have to either make peace over a stalemate (which had by then become unacceptable) or bury themselves in trenches, transforming the war of movement that had defined European conflicts in the nineteenth century into a war of attrition. This was to decisively change Europe's position in the world – and ultimately its relationship to war.

From the Great War to the European Civil War

Whatever the causes of the Great War, its consequences were far-reaching. The conflict was long and exhausting, as trench warfare stretched along the Western front all the way from 1914 to 1918. It was also truly continental in its dimensions: in 1917, only Spain, Switzerland, Norway, Sweden and Denmark were not involved, and Europeans fought all around the continent: in the North of France, in the Turkish Straits, in Northern Italy's Dolomites, in the Balkans, in the Baltics, etc. Despite all these battlefields and the attempts to break the deadlock by opening new fronts or bringing in new belligerents, the war had become unfinishable and exhausted the continent's resources.

In 1914, Europe dominated the World, international finance, global trade and the oceans – the two came together. In 1918, the situation had completely changed, and the two European sides that signed the armistice in Rethondes on

November 11 were doing so over the ruins of their past glories. Having wasted all their human and financial capital in the trenches, European victors and vanquished shared a similarly precarious situation. For sure, the French and the British were in a stronger position as they expanded their colonial possessions and influence over the remains of the Russian, Ottoman, German and Austrian empires, but they were as financially and humanly exsanguinated as Germany: Europe's nations had literally bled themselves dry to achieve an elusive (and illusive) victory. France tried to make up for it by claiming to "make the Boche pay," as French Premier Clemenceau claimed, but the terms of the French government were acceptable neither to the Germans nor to the British, who would have liked to reclaim their central economic position by allowing Germany to quickly recover.

All these ideas, however, proved illusory, as money and power had already changed hands – the new center of the world was now in New York, not London. The United States, which had experienced a spectacular growth in the past decades, had reluctantly come to the rescue of the Allies in 1917, sending their boys just in time to thwart a decisive offensive decided by the German Military Headquarters. The extra men provided by Uncle Sam were decisive for the Anglo-French to absorb the shock and then lead a successful counter-offensive – but so were the loans granted to the allies and the foodstuffs sold to them. In victory, however, the Americans proved as demanding to the victors as they were of the vanquished: all were ruined, but they had been equally responsible for their actions, and all had to pay their debts. French historian Pierre Miquel gave a comprehensive picture of the situation in 1918:

> The United States of America held Europe's survival in their hands. Feeding the ravaged Balkans, the hungry Austria, Italy, France and Belgium, supplying Europeans with coal and wheat, safeguarding currencies, everything depended on the Americans. The French and the English had spent all their assets, accumulated prodigious amounts of debts. In France, there was nothing left but diminished rentiers with ruined savings. As they supported the war effort and lent money to Europeans for the continent's reconstruction, the United States had become by far the world's largest producer of coal, and had doubled their steel production and wheat exports. They were the world's creditor and they held in their coffers half the gold stock of all nations. America's once feeble merchant navy was already equal to half of the huge English fleet, and it had allowed them to take over many markets in Asia and Latin America. Through war debts, they kept the European states in a position of constant inferiority. The enormous profits made by the banks, industries and agricultural circles made the United States the real winners of the bloody confrontation from which Europe emerged defeated.[16]

This description may be interpreted by some Americans as a whining exercise by sore losers who only got what they had deserved. It may be so, but it nonetheless accurately shows how the balance of power had irredeemably and decisively shifted. America had, for the first time, given up on its tradition of isolationism and non-entanglement out of the Western Hemisphere,[17] but the decision was not taken unconditionally: President Wilson's 14 points, which French premier Clemenceau violently criticized by reminding that God himself had only had Ten Commandments, advocated a new European order based on liberalism and self-determination. But liberalism did not survive the 1929 crisis, and self-determination presupposed the dismantling of Empires, which by nature were bringing together and mixing very different nationalities, making the delimitation of borders according to the national principle a very difficult job indeed – in particular if no higher authority was there to enforce the rules. To give one example among others, the village of Kittsee, located on the border between the new Austrian and Czechoslovak republics and not far from the border with the new Hungary, was not populated by any of these nationalities but by Croats, Southern Slavs who had migrated a couple of centuries before to find work and arable lands. These Croats could not easily be attached to their "homeland" via the principle of nationalities – even if their village had been situated further South, a problem would have remained as Croats had been incorporated in a union of Southern Slavs (literally, Yugoslavia), whose legitimacy was contested by many Croats.

In this complex and volatile environment, the newly liberated nationalist passions and tensions generated many stories of post-imperial instability varying between the tragic and the burlesque, from the creation of the "Heinzenland Republic" over the estates of the Eszterházy family, which lasted two days before a plebiscite separated the territory into Austrian Burgenland and the Hungarian Sopron District, to Italian poet and adventurer Gabriele d'Annunzio's expedition to "liberate" ethnic Italians from Yugoslav domination in the port of Fiume. The Free State of Fiume ended its course a few years later in a tragicomedy that led to the territory's annexation a few years later by fascist Italy.

The new liberal self-determined order advocated by President Wilson was not off to a great start. But things got even worse when America, the power that had imposed its conditions on Europe, refused to guarantee the order it had created: as soon as the Peace of Versailles was signed, America turned back to isolationism and decided not to take part in the security architecture of the continent. It declined to be part of the very League of Nations it had inspired and would not guarantee the security and independence of the newly formed states in Central Europe – the task was devoted to the French and Brits, who were clearly no longer as strong as before and were already finding the governments of the new, small countries too provincial and too exotic. In the aftermath of the Allied surrender to Hitler in Munich in 1938, the British Prime Minister Chamberlain declared in the House of Commons: "how horrible, fantastic, incredible it is that we should be digging trenches and trying on gas-masks here because of a quarrel in a faraway country [Czechoslovakia] between people of whom we know nothing."[18] As a new great power, America had set its terms to end an endless war, but it now refused to take responsibility for protecting the security architecture it had created. France and Great Britain, the pyrrhic victors of the Great War, were too weak to hold it in the long run.

Even more so as the war never really ended. For sure, peace treaties were signed in Versailles, Trianon and Sèvres, but the orgy of violence of 1914–1918 did not end completely. Rather, it morphed in nature and intensity: in Germany, the military, who had not had to fight on German soil and had withdrawn from France and Belgium in order, was already preparing for the next war. General Erich Ludendorff, who had wanted to bleed the French army dry and had had to lead his army to the armistice, could not admit the "betrayal" of the Reich's civilian population, even though their demoralization had been caused by four years of increasing deprivation. The German Army's myth of the "stab in the back" by its own civilian population quickly became the creed for all those who refused to accept defeat, whose implications for the future Ludendorff understood before others: if the still-powerful army in Weimar Germany wanted its revenge, it would, in Ludendorff's own words, have to wage total war, which would "involve a whole territory and a whole population, not just its armed forces."[19]

This perspective pointed toward an intensification of the war, while European societies had already been particularly brutalized by four years of combat. Young Europeans before 1914 had grown up with the idea that the world was becoming more civilized, thanks to technical progress, and the war was, for many of them, a memory from their time in military service. The Europeans of 1918 who returned from the front did so with a defining experience of battle, far removed from the pre-1914 romantic idealization of the soldier-knight defending civilization. All these young conscripts had spent their formative years killing, destroying and living in the mud. Most of them came out of this experience scarred for life and would do anything to avoid having to bury themselves (or their children) again in trenches in another war. But other individuals came back fascinated by their experience at the front, seeing it as a new model for society as the armies *esprit de corps* and trench fighting greatly reduced class differences. For a smaller group, it was also the excitement of combat and the raw power given by war that was attractive. Benito Mussolini, Hermann Göring, Adolf Hitler and many other future far-right leaders were veterans of the Great War, and their ideology was shaped by a vision of war experienced as a positive value, theorized as a shaper of a more perfect society. Once violence had been unleashed, it proved very hard for states to fully take back control.

In reality, for many people, and particularly in Central and Eastern Europe, 1918 did not mark the end of the war, but its transformation. Just a year earlier, another cycle of violence, directly linked to the Great War, had started in the East. In February 1917, exhausted (and brutalized) by three years of war in which undecisive successes against the Austrians were eclipsed by bitter defeats against the Germans, Russia went into revolution, which quickly turned into chaos.

Originally a marginal branch of the Russian socialist movement, the Bolsheviks used their iron discipline to take advantage of the vacuum of power left by the government's contradictions, broaden their base by promising peace, power and land redistribution and seized power in November 1917. In the minds of these communists, this was only the first step in the march toward a World Revolution, whose center had to be the much more industrialized Germany. They, therefore, encouraged other Europeans to rise against the political leaders whose folly had buried their youths in trenches for years and imposed ever-increasing food restrictions on ordinary folks. But as the revolution seemed to spread to Europe, the Bolsheviks knew they were also themselves very weak internally: they quickly faced rural discontent and revanchism. The original Russian Army had pretty much disbanded itself and weapons were therefore readily available to all in a society already brutalized by three years of war. The anarchy of 1917 thus quickly turned into a civil war. It would consume the Eurasian space until 1921 – and eject Russia completely from the European cultural and socioeconomic space.

The October 1917 revolution was paradoxical in more than one respect: the Bolsheviks effectively kept their promise of immediate peace by pretty much surrendering most of Imperial Russia's Western territories to Germany at the Peace of Brest-Litovsk. At the same time, their authoritarian methods, coupled with the ambient anarchy, transformed Russia itself into an immense battlefield. Also paradoxically, as Russia plunged into the chaos and atrocities of the civil war, the very victors that had extracted so many concessions from Soviet Russia were themselves on the verge of revolution, as the German and Austro-Hungarian empires collapsed: deprived of even basic foodstuff by four years of war and economic blockade, the central powers' populations turned against their masters. In the power vacuum left by the fall of the Habsburg and Hohenzollern monarchies, new Soviets were now being formed in Berlin, Budapest, Riga and Munich. Europe was on the verge of a Marxist revolution: at the signing of the Armistice, German center-right politician Matthias Erzeberg warned his French counterpart Marshal Foch that if Germany falls to the Bolsheviks, "you will be next."[20]

Peace may have been signed, but it could no longer be decreed by governments. In this revolutionary atmosphere, the order could only be re-established by force, and it came at the price of a ferocious repression by paramilitary groups, the national army or foreign intervention. In Germany, a militia of Great War veterans, the *Freikorps*, terrorized German cities before their own attempts to seize power were stopped by regular troops of the Weimar Republic, who finally restored order. As political order crumbled, violence was easy to unleash after four years of war that had starved citizens and brutalized conscripts – back from the front, they were now experts in the use of weapons and many were all too ready to continue the fight – this time not necessarily for their nation but for a higher ideal.

War, therefore, continued after 1919, even though it became for a while an underground phenomenon, as Europe enjoyed a short respite of prosperity during the Roaring Twenties. Of course, violence was more diffuse as states were no longer mobilizing armies to fight, but it remained nonetheless as a social and political struggle (with its load of violence), with three ideologies in competition. The first, democratic liberalism, had triumphed in Europe in the aftermath of the First World War, and it, therefore, had become the ideology of the establishment. The consequences of the financial crisis of 1929, however, greatly weakened its legitimacy, as its main appeal of delivering justice and prosperity for all lost much of its luster: in the words of historian Timothy Snyder, "the market had brought disaster, no parliament had an answer, and nation-states seemingly lacked the instruments to protect their citizens from immiseration."[21] The parallels with the current crisis of liberal democracy is as scary as it is accurate, and we will get back in Chapter 4 on the current weakness of the liberal democratic consensus. But getting back to the interwar period, this ideological weakness allowed for the rise of two competitors who had been there ever since the Great War and wanted only one thing: to take on the liberals before fighting each other for ideological supremacy.

By definition, the two totalitarian ideologies had an all-encompassing ambition: to entirely rebuild society and submit individuals to a whole. The communism that emerged from the Russian Revolution had been further shaped by the experience of the civil war; its aim was to build a society free from the exploitation of the rich and powerful – which very quickly ended up being the physical elimination of the rich, the powerful, and more generally anyone who stood in the way of utopia. The other ideology, fascism, rejected both liberalism and communism *en bloc*, and its ideal of a harmonious society was based on the values of soldier comradeship, considered as the healthiest and best way to erase social inequalities – coupled in many cases by a search for ethnic purity. War was a central part of fascism's political platform, even more central than for the communists, as war was not only a means to an end but an end in itself. In both cases, however, war was the main instrument to create a new society – may it be a class or racial struggle. As they grew, these two ideologies transformed the Great War into a "European civil war," to use the expression popularized by German historian Ernst Nolte.[22]

From civil war to total war

The Great War had transformed European warfare into a war of attrition, and despite armistices and peace treaties, violence never truly ended after the official hostilities. The European Civil War that followed could only be more savage, as barbarity invited itself in every aspect of life. In the trenches, the fighting was total, the violence and filth were absolute, but the battlefield was physically limited: armies remained separated from the civilian populations, and their departure signaled a return to peace.

As the conflict turned into a civil war, this distinction between the battlefield and normality, between civil and military life, totally vanished. By definition, civil wars blur the line between civilians and soldiers, since each inhabitant is summoned to choose his or her side. The transition from high-intensity to civil war strengthened the case for total warfare – now possible as technological innovation had allowed the military to project their power beyond the front line, whether through long-range cannons or through the use of airpower against urban areas. Airplanes had mostly bombed strategic targets during the Great War. Starting in the 1930s and the carpet bombings of the Spanish Civil War, cities as a whole (and therefore their population) became targets, thereby legitimizing the annihilation of entire cities from the air.

War also became total because the confrontation between communism, fascism and liberalism could only result in an absolute winner: victory ended up being a question of survival, as two of the ideologies were totalitarian and could not accommodate dissent. But ideology was not the only culprit. Military doctrine and the lessons from 1918 also moved toward total warfare. General Ludendorff, who also took part in Hitler's failed putsch in Munich in 1923, had learned the lessons of the war of attrition: to win in the next all-out conflict, Germany would have to wage all-out war. Of course, that meant mobilizing an entire population for the front. But it also meant mobilizing the civilian population as an actor of the war, which also meant destroying or subjugating enemy civilian populations. For this, the Germans (but also, more generally, all Europeans, including the French and British) used their experience in colonial warfare, where they got to know that the best way of breaking down a population's resistance to a foreign presence was the use of brute force – as the carrots used to coax local elites ready to collaborate often proved insufficient. As war historian Lawrence Freedman puts it:

> Colonialism established the idea of whole populations as legitimate targets. Such practices as massacring local people, destroying villages, eradicating crops, and slaughtering domesticated animals arose for largely strategic reasons – as the available means Western armies had to "defeat elusive, highly mobile people who were adept practitioners of guerilla war".[23]

The English, Belgians and French had also experimented with these techniques in part of India, and in the Congo, Algeria and Morocco. Germans and Russians, for their part, had used them in Namibia, the North Caucasus and Central Asia. In all cases, the war theater was far enough from the metropolitan center and national public opinions. In the absence of an independent war press, military headquarters had all leisure to employ *any* means to "pacify" the Herreros or the Daghestanis – including practices that would today be considered as acts of genocide.

The British, French, Belgians and (to a lesser extent) Italians had been able to keep these actions overseas, limiting awareness of their practices. What the new masters in Berlin and Moscow did was to import the atrocities of colonial warfare back to Europe. The logic was implacable: since war was now total, populations had become stakeholders in the conflict, and could, therefore, in no way be treated separately from combatants. At the very end of this logic, it became legitimate to deport or even massacre entire populations guilty of belonging to a nation at war with the government to a class or to a "race" considered as a threat to the survival of the whole. As war had become more "democratic" in the trenches of the Great War, it became a matter of survival and, therefore, of extermination. The logic was pushed furthest in Central and Eastern Europe, Timothy Snyder's "Bloodlands": more than half of the soldiers who died in the deadliest war in history were killed in this region,[24] but they were not the only casualties of the war. The horrors of the Shoah and the systematic extermination of Jews, Roma, Sinti, homosexuals and other undesirables in the gas chambers of Auschwitz, Majdanek, Treblinka and other camps obviously come to mind, and it is worth noting that almost all of the death camps were located between Germany and Russia. But the population at large, not only groups of "undesirables", suffered directly from the war, with a terrible weapon being used against them: hunger. As Snyder reminds us, "of the fourteen million civilians and prisoners of war killed in the bloodlands between 1933 and 1945, more than half died because they were denied food" – mainly Ukrainians, Poles, Belarusians, etc.[25]

The war of extermination had its logic: for Stalin, this was a fight to the death between socialism, which had found a homeland in the Soviet Union, and fascism, the ultimate form of capitalism. For Hitler, beyond the existential question for the German *Volk*, the conquest of the East was inspired, in part, by Germany's colonial experience and accounts of America's Western expansion, which Hitler adapted to his own ideology to produce his own Germanic version of manifest destiny, the messianic mission of the German race to find a Lebensraum, or vital space, for its sustained growth. Here too, the concept was derived from the experience of the First World War: as Snyder recalls, "Hitler wanted Ukraine 'so that no one is able to starve us again, like in the last war'."[26] The colonization of space in the East would allow Germany to be self-sufficient and "to become a global power on model of the United States."[27]

Total on the Western front, colonial in the East, the war that developed in Europe between 1939 and 1945 was an orgy of destruction. The enumeration of a few places that marked the conflict gives a measure of the extent of the violence: Katyn and its 22,000 officers killed in an effort to exterminate the Polish elite, Babi Yar and his 33,000 Jews shot in the space of only two days, Auschwitz and all the Holocaust, etc. During the war, historic European cities became collective graveyards: Warsaw, Minsk and many others were completely destroyed with their civilian populations inside (more often than not by design); smaller towns and villages were literally burnt to the ground as a reprisal for acts of resistance; others were destroyed by air raids – among them Coventry, Hamburg or Dresden, where 3,900 tons of explosives and incendiary bombs were dropped in a couple of days, killing 22,000 to 25,000 people between 13 and 15 February 1945.[28]

British military strategist Basil Liddell Hart regretted the transformation of war from "a fight to a process of destruction."[29] But it was already too late for Europe: before 1914, the war had given the continent an almost undisputable dominion over the world. In 1945, it now laid literally in ruins, with peace imposed by two non-European powers, the United States and the Soviet Union. In this situation, it was only a matter of time before the collapse of European colonial empires in Africa, Oceania and Asia – in little over fifteen years, these were almost all gone. The thirty years cycle of destruction that ruined her financially could only transform Europe's relationship with war.

Peace over the graveyard

Europe came out of the Second World War totally destroyed, and the collective memory of the disaster left deep scars. The trauma of the massive collective suicide that represented the cycle of the two world wars contributed greatly to appease the situation: there is usually less to gain from fighting over a field of ruins than over a land of plenty. But the conflict in Afghanistan shows us that ruin, horror and destruction are not in themselves sufficient to impose peace. If it had, the inter-war period, with its mass pacifist sentiment, the Briand-Kellog Pact to outlaw war and the more elitist idea of creating a pan-European political union (originally championed by Count Richard Coudenhove-Kalergi[30]), could have been an early candidate for the pacification of Europe – in many ways, the continent was already ruined after 1918. Indeed, the experience of the outbreak of the Second World War shows that even a strong pacifist movement, in vogue even in Hitler's Germany in 1938–1939, tells us how much war depends on elites: as long as an absolute consensus reigns among them that war is not a legitimate option to settle differences, war is unlikely. But suffice it that parts of it deviate from the consensus and decide that war is not only acceptable but a necessity and the situation can deteriorate very quickly.

In 1947, Europeans had reasons to worry: as the Cold War engulfed Europe, it was by then in no ways clear whether it would remain cold for long. As early as 1946, Winston Churchill had understood that the victorious powers of the war in Europe were no longer united; as he put it in his famed Fulton speech, "from Stettin in the Baltic to Trieste in the Adriatic, an iron curtain has descended across the continent."[31] Europe would be divided into 2 for 45 years, with each half evolving in a different system, divided by a heavily militarized border. But despite this division and the massive presence of troops on both sides of the iron curtain, there would be no return to war, and while crises would be numerous and sometimes deadly, mostly on the Eastern side, the period between 1945 and 1991 can be described for Europe as much of a Cold War as a "Long Peace"[32] – even though the conditions of existence on each side of the Iron Curtain were much different.

To understand why this uneasy peace was made possible, it is necessary to focus on what changed after 1945. And the most important development, as depressing as it may sound for Europeans, was that they were no longer truly masters of their own destiny. In the East, the Soviets made it clear that the countries they had just conquered would henceforth be part of an exclusive sphere of influence: in a few years, all the zones "liberated" by the Soviet Union were either annexed or placed under the control of a local communist party totally subservient to Moscow, and what remained of the local elites was purged to establish the domination of the USSR.[33] From show trials to deportations and massive population transfers, the new masters of Central and Eastern Europe made it clear to their new vassals that there would be clear limits to their deviations, and when the Hungarians and Czechoslovaks would test them too hard in 1956 and 1968, the consequence would be invasions which, in other times, would probably have amounted to an act of war but in a bipolar world was treated as an act of policing in one's own sphere of influence.

The situation in the West was different, even though the Europeans who fell on the right side of the Iron Curtain found some of their options constrained under American military protection, as the British and the French discovered during the Suez crisis of 1956. As they faced a threat dangerously close to them, both physically and politically (many countries like France and Italy had a very strong communist party), the weakened elites of Western Europe were clearly dependent on the United States if they wanted to avoid domination by the Soviets.[34] On their side, the Americans had understood after the disasters of 1930s isolationism that it would ultimately be cheaper to protect what remained of free Europe than to have to intervene once again after the entire continent had been placed under the control of an enemy power, as they had to do in 1941.

Pushed by the Europeans who did not want to be left on their own to face the Soviet bloc, the United States decided to not only to stay in Western Europe, but also invest in it: the Marshall Plan of 1948 successfully rebuilt the economies of Western Europe so that its governments could strengthen themselves against the communist threat, gain legitimacy and also buy products made in the United States; on the military side, the Washington Treaty established the North Atlantic Treaty Alliance (NATO) in 1949, guaranteeing a continued US military presence – there would be no pullback as there had been in 1919. To this day, Article 5 of the treaty still guarantees mutual protection in the event of aggression, which at the time was perceived principally as a threat from the East. This mutualization of armed forces for defense purposes spoke volumes about the new American approach, combining Wilsonian idealism and a more realist internationalism;[35] for behind the symbolism of multilateralism, everyone understood that only the United States had the political, economic and military power to stand up to the Soviet Union, whose gigantic army had just rolled over half of the continent. The United States would try to encourage Europeans to pool their armed forces together and better share the burden with America to protect themselves, but although national defense budgets ran considerably higher than where they are now, the formation of a European Defense Community (EDC), which would probably have changed the history of European integration thereafter, did not become reality. The plan had been encouraged by the United States and carried out in France by Jean Monnet – a strong proponent of Europe and the Atlantic Alliance, and Prime Minister René Pleven. Signed in 1952, the treaty was never ratified by the French National Assembly, due to strong Gaullist and Communist opposition. This was to be the first post-war occasion where France managed to masterfully shoot itself in the foot, as the EDC (although modest in its ambition, the proposed 100,000 men were far from the 500,000 requested by Uncle Sam) had been imagined as a way to avoid German rearmament out of French control. In the end, the death of the EDC gave the signal for the Americans to encourage the German Federal Republic to rearm, which the French originally wanted to avoid at all costs.[36]

In any case, the formation of a strict (and, with the exception of Yugoslavia, relatively impervious) bipolar system with determined boundaries, guaranteed an uneasy armed peace in Europe, but it was peace nonetheless. What is called the Cold War could just as well go down in European memories as a "long peace,"[37] in the sense that despite sometimes acute crises and violent deaths (in the Eastern bloc in the late 1940s, 1956 and 1968, and in the West with secessionist and left-wing terrorism), there was no new armed conflict on the continent until 1991, with the notable exception of the brief Cyprus War of 1974, which partitioned the island. The bipolar system largely contributed to this stability: it became much more difficult for Europeans to wage war among themselves without having to consult at least one of the two superpowers.

Americans and Soviets were themselves constrained in their choices to wage war by the destructive capacity of the weapons that emerged at the end of the Second World War: the fire of the atomic bomb, also mastered by the Soviets by 1949, guaranteed instantaneous mass destruction. At the same time, the development of rockets made it possible to produce medium- and then long-range missiles, guaranteeing Mutually Assured Destruction, a concept better known thanks to its (well-deserved) acronym MAD. Superpower competition had reached a new stage in warfare, as Lawrence Freedman remarked:

> the simplest if depressing assumption was that war had become progressively more murderous, with ever more sophisticated means being found to slaughter people on a large scale, and that future wars would be even more intense and existential. This prospect encouraged great caution, even when it came to quite minor crises.[38]

In this context, and as Europe clearly became the grand prize of the competition between the United States and the Soviet Union, any crisis was treated with extreme care: the crises of Berlin (1949), Budapest (1956) or Prague (1968), in the last two cases direct invasions of a sovereign country by another, did not lead to all-out war, as each party knew the risks of intervening directly in each other's sphere of influence.

Despite temptations to interfere on one side or the other of the Iron Curtain, intrusions remained covert or discreet, may these be through the broadcasting of Western Radio to the East (Radio Free Europe, the BBC) or the assistance to left-wing terrorist groups such as Italy's Red Brigades or Germany's Red Army Faction[39] in the West. The idea was that Europe was clearly and durably divided between two impervious spheres of influence and that if it was considered by both parties "fair game" to try to weaken the adversary by devious means, it was far too dangerous in view of the economic and strategic importance of Europe to try to intervene militarily in the opposing camp. While parts of Africa, Asia and Latin America became the theater of proxy wars, Europe was almost entirely deprived of this tool to resolve its political disputes. The Cypriot conflict and the invasions of Hungary and Czechoslovakia are exceptions that confirm the rule, but Europe's long peace of 1945–1991 was initially and paradoxically conditioned by the Cold War and the domination of the United States and the Soviet Union on the continent.

Muzzling European leaders' warring tendencies was one thing, but this could not be the only reason why the continent remained at peace after 1945. For, this time, Europeans had learned their lessons, and they also contributed to the pacification of their continent, at least in the West, where they could actively play their part. The task was made easier by the fact that the Second World War had acted as a great simplifier of the continent's map, greatly lowering the number of *casi bellorum* on the continent – indeed, it did seem for a while that the only confrontation in Europe was between communism and capitalism, which was being taken care of at higher levels. In the early stages of the war, inspired by their theories about the *lebensraum* for the German Volk, the Nazis had carried out policies of expulsions and mass murder for the "inferior races" to make way to the Aryans, but as the Germans retreated, they too, along with others, became targets for deportations and murder. In 1945, as the Allies decided on the peace terms, borders were moved by several hundred kilometers (in Poland, for example), while the advance of Soviet troops toward Berlin meant an extremely harsh treatment on remaining German civilian population, in part, as a retribution for the treatment inflicted by Nazi troops on civilians inside Soviet territory.[40]

As the Soviet advance moved borders hundreds of kilometers to the West to make way for the USSR's expansion, the countries of Central Europe found themselves in a situation where their ethnic composition got greatly simplified, precisely through war and the horrors imposed on civilian populations. In the interwar period, Prague and Bratislava were two linguistically (and therefore ethnically) heterogeneous Czechoslovak cities, where one could hear Yiddish, German, Hungarian, Czech or Slovak spoken – this had been an issue of the young Czechoslovak state, and in many ways a source of weakness as the presence of minorities had given pretexts for irredentists in Germany, but also Hungary and Poland, to destabilize and eventually carve out the Czechoslovak state. But in 1945, Czechoslovakia was much more uniform: both cities had seen their Jewish ghettos emptied, and the Beneš decrees had condemned Germans and

Hungarians to choose between total assimilation or expulsion to their original "homeland," which some had never set foot in.[41] This is a truth difficult to tell, but the reality is that the genocide, ethnic cleansings and mass forced population movements that happened during the period 1939–1945 greatly simplified the linguistic (and in some cases ethnic) composition of each state, allowing for the consolidation of nation-state building in Europe, particularly in Central Europe. In a continent where uniformity had often been an obsession for governing elites, this, in turn, provided for the pacification of relations inside and between states.

In many ways, parts of this simplification had been motivated by a willingness to solve or at least simplify the "German question," which had been the main factor of instability in Europe between 1870 and 1945. With minorities abroad reduced to a minimum, an industrial and urban landscape reduced to a pile of rubble, and a division in zones of occupation which would soon become two separate states, the strategic challenge that Germany represented had become one for the two superpowers, not Europeans to solve. The relatively small size of the German Democratic Republic (GDR) and deliberate Soviet policies would ensure that it would always remain loyal to Soviet power – on which it absolutely depended for its existence. In West Germany, support from the United States allowed German leaders to look for and seek redemption while quickly rising back to an industrial size corresponding to its reduced ambitions – as other Europeans had much less reasons to fear a Germany ready to accept and pay for its sins, the Federal Republic joined the Western European club. By partially copying some of the recipes of its American victor (for example, by adopting US style federalism), the Germany of Adenauer and Willy Brandt realized that it could only regain its place in Europe by accepting deep repentance for the crimes committed during the Second World War (without publicly dwelling on the suffering of German civilians during the bombings or mass expulsions of 1945). Divided, reduced to a size bearable for its neighbors, framed by NATO (whose main function was to "keep the Russians out, the Americans in and the Germans down," according to Lord Ismay's famed expression), Germany had constrained itself within a European collective system that included not only the Atlantic Alliance but also the European Communities, which were to become a Union after the Cold War.

The end of history and the triumph of peace

If the Atlantic Alliance and bipolarity played a major role in imposing and consolidating the Long Peace that is better known as the Cold War, it is worth noting that peace could not have been sustainable had the Europeans not decided to actively give it a chance, through the European integration project. On the Eastern side of the Iron Curtain, the question of European unity did not pose itself insofar as everything revolved around Moscow: the local communist parties were in a logic of subjugation to the USSR, although the relationship was often reminiscent of Hegel's famed master and slave dialectic, with servants at times forcing Moscow's hand: in 1968, European members of the Warsaw Pact literally begged the Russians to send in tanks to put an end to developments that were directly threatening their power in Budapest, Sofia and Warsaw – a similar situation would arise in 1988–1989, and it was, in fact, Gorbachev's decision to let the Eastern Bloc go, as the USSR was ruined, which allowed the peaceful fall of the Berlin Wall.

In the West, the logic was different: the Americans of course had their own interests in mind when dealing with Europe – indeed, the Marshall Plan was as much an aid mechanism as an investment to create new customers for US manufactured products, while NATO opened new markets for the American military-industrial complex. But their main desire was to let Europeans take their destiny into their own hands. By inclination, as much as by necessity, Washington acted more as a benevolent and distant overlord, not as a bully. This of course did not go without friction: Washington did show great concern when De Gaulle's France left NATO's integrated military command, when Willy Brandt developed links with Eastern Europe through his *Ostpolitik* or when the French Communist Party was associated to the government in François Mitterrand's first left-wing government in 1981. Diplomatic tensions happened in the West, but there were never even talks of American tanks rolling in the streets of Paris, Rome or Bonn, unlike in the East. In this flexible and free environment, Europeans were encouraged by the US administrations to find ways to come together and find institutional solutions that would consolidate peace and cooperation between them. In many ways, the return of a constrained West Germany to the European mainstream, as it rebuilt its industrial capacities, provided encouragement for this integration – if you can't beat them, join them. This very specific situation, along with the memory of a ruinous cycle of war, gave the impetus to a new generation of leaders to build common security, economic and (if possible) political framework to bring European nations together, with the United States taken as a model. Thus, the ideal of the United States of Europe, which had already started to take shape in the interwar period, now turned into a strong dynamic to unify the Western half of the continent.

Much like America's Founding Fathers, the inspirers of Europe had diverse social origins, and although predominantly Christian democrats, they represented different political philosophies, very often defined by their national background and experience. If most hailed from the Christian Democratic movement, like Konrad Adenauer, Alcide de Gasperi or Robert Schuman, others such as Paul-Henri Spaak were Socialists. In many ways, what brought them together was defeat: all six countries that came together in the European communities had been military losers of the Second World War. The French, Belgians, Dutch and Luxembourgers had been defeated by Germany, and Italy and Germany had then been defeated by the Allies. For Europe's political leaders, the logic was simple enough: Europe had been ruined by war, and it was important to break with the past – not by outlawing war but by making it practically impossible. The best way to do that at the time was economics – and federalism. For sure, the idea of a European federation was not new – its traces could be brought as far back as 1464 and Bohemian King George Poděbrady's *Tractatus*. It re-appeared many times in European intellectuals' writings in the following centuries, most of the time associated with the idea of perpetual peace.[42] But federalism was now no longer understood as a utopia, it was a model whose effectiveness was beyond contestation, with the United States a clear model to emulate.

The six that signed the Treaty of Rome and founded the future European Union (EU) formed a club of countries defeated in and by the Second World War. This status strongly defined their psychology: as they integrated the reasons for their defeat, they tried, via federalization, to adopt and adapt the winning recipe of their American victor. The logic followed what German academic Wolfgang Schivelbusch has called *Culture of Defeat*:[43] once the shock of defeat has been absorbed, the vanquished seek to reinvent themselves by copying part of the recipes that they believe made the victorious power successful. This, of course, explains why Britain, who was a military victor of the Second World War, did not join the project originally, but to get back to the logic of the defeated continentals, if Europe wanted to become prosperous again, it had to take inspiration from the American institutional model and create the United States of Europe. EU founding father Jean Monnet, who had made many transatlantic trips since the beginning of the century (for his Cognac selling business or for more official reasons) and spent the beginning of the War in the United States, was one of the most ardent supporters of the American model, which he had seen function. It guided his political vision, while the political networks he had built during his sojourns in Washington helped lobby for US support.[44] The American administration was ready to listen: from the outset, the United States wanted as much as possible to share the burden of defending the continent with the Europeans and the project of bringing them together in a common project that also corresponded to the US objective of checking Communist advance in Europe was, therefore, most welcome.

Despite strong impetus, European integration was not self-evident, and almost from the very beginning, it also caused much resistance from parts of the national elites. In Germany, Social-Democrats were originally the most skeptic, while in France, it was the Gaullists and the Communists who found themselves in an unlikely alliance to throw the European Defense Community project under the bus. The economic dimension, however, proved much less controversial, partly because it was more technical: Frenchman Robert Schuman's plan to bring together European economics and, in particular, the steel and coal industries into a single market was welcomed not only by his own government but also by Italy, the Netherlands, Belgium, Luxembourg and especially West Germany – Chancellor Konrad Adenauer is said to have exclaimed that *Das ist unser Durchbruch*, "this is our breakthrough," for redemption and re-integration among the European civilized powers.[45] The six founding members signed the Treaty of Rome establishing the three European Communities on March 25,

1957: they included the Economic Community, Euratom for atomic energy and the European Coal and Steel Community or CSCE, which had been created in 1952. The idea was not only to pool sovereignty over economic affairs – it was also to share it over the particularly sensitive and strategic sector of energy policy, at a time when coal was still a major source of energy on the continent and atomic energy was on the rise. Bringing these under one roof, under one single community would make any new war between members "materially impossible," to use Robert Schuman's own words. Europe had to be made to give peace a chance. It would "not be made all at once, nor will it be built as a whole, but through concrete achievements, to establish de facto solidarities."[46]

But if the Treaty of Rome was a political and economic success in the context of Europe's post-war boom, any attempt to go beyond economic integration was vetoed by the French. In 1958, a nationalist Charles de Gaulle had come back to power, and while he was ready to accept the Treaty of Rome (which greatly benefited France, as it technically got German industry to pay for the country's agricultural modernization), he would remain adamant about any further pullback on national sovereignty. Interestingly, in his efforts to resist federalization, De Gaulle set up another pillar of European integration, the famous "Franco-German couple," which he put in place with Konrad Adenauer, as both countries settled for reconciliation in the 1963 Élysée Treaty. As remarkable as this reconciliation proved to be, it was also specifically formed in De Gaulle's mind to counter the federalism defended by Schumann, Monnet and the other founding fathers. In his 11 years tenure, President De Gaulle had many occasions to reassert his sovereigntist approach: the "empty chair crisis" of 1965–1969 clearly showed to EU partners the limits that France intended to give to the European project. The Treaty of Rome had been accepted by Paris because it had set up a Common Agricultural Policy through which the modernization of French Agriculture would be subsidized by Germany's booming re-industrialization, in exchange for France's opening of its markets. But when the new European Commission proposed to endow Europe with its own resources (and down the road to raise taxes itself), de Gaulle gave a clear *non*, and to make sure his point was taken, he recalled France's permanent representative in Brussels and refused to sit on the European Economic Communities' Council of Ministers, technically blocking any decision – unanimity was still the norm then. The "empty chair crisis" ended with the Luxembourg compromise, which greatly weakened supranational institutions. Another opportunity to push toward a political Europe has just been wasted.[47]

The European integration movement was all but blocked by the 1970s, as Europe entered a phase of sluggish growth after 30 years of fast-paced reconstruction. Valéry Giscard d'Estaing did convince his peers to peg all the European currencies together following the US exit from the Bretton Woods system – a way for France to have a say in the monetary policy of Germany, whose economy was by now clearly more productive than France. However, the first attempt to create a European Monetary System did not achieve the results its proponents hoped for: European growth continued to slow down, as French and other deficits began to widen.[48] In the early 1980s, the election of Socialist François Mitterrand as President of France also brought great suspicion in Western Europe and particularly in Germany, as French economic policy went into a spending spree while communists were brought to the government in the midst of renewed tensions in the Cold War. But the new French president reassured his partners, as he quickly turned back to a more orthodox monetary and budgetary policy, while providing guarantees of France's continued alignment with the West – Mitterrand defended the US Euromissiles in the German Bundestag and, thanks to double-agent Vladimir Vertov (aka "Farewell"), provided US intelligence with invaluable information about the extent of Soviet infiltration in the West.

France was conscious of its economic weakness vis-à-vis Germany and wanted to at least have a say in a monetary policy – it was by now clear that it would be set in Frankfurt and not in Paris. Pegging currencies together had not worked, so Paris decided to push directly for the next step: full monetary integration. The idea did not please the Germans, as they considered that their economic miracle of the past decades had actually been based on the stability and strength of the Deutsche Mark. Sharing sovereignty over currency, the symbol of Germany's economic success, was out of the question. But Europe had managed to set itself in motion once again under the Commission leadership of Jacques Delors as member states progressively understood that they needed to move forward together to get out of the multiple economic crises Western Europe was stuck in at the time. European economies were brought more strongly together by the Single European Act in 1986, and although the monetary union was still far away, there was motion once again in the European project.

Paradoxically, it was a national event, German reunification, that precipitated subsequent developments. Chancellor Helmut Kohl may not have been a supporter of monetary union, but he was ready to pay a high price for achieving German reunification. In 1989, after years of stagnation and crisis in the East – and a last ditch by Mikhail Gorbachev to reform via Glasnost and Perestroika, which ended up in epic economic and diplomatic failure[49] – the Soviet bloc collapsed. On August 19, 1989, Hungarians and Austrians met in the border town of Sopron for a pan-European picnic where Europeans were finally allowed to cut the barbed wire separating East and West. A few weeks earlier, Solidarność won Poland's first free elections after years of repression and negotiations. Just a few more months and the Berlin Wall, a symbol of the separation between the two Germanies, had fallen.

Things were changing in Europe – but outside Germany, celebrations were mixed with a sense of panic: a reunification of Europe meant above all a reunification of Germany and, therefore, a return of the German question: would a stronger, unified Germany become once again too big for Europe and yet too small for hegemony[50]? Margaret Thatcher had the harshest words at the time, as she promised to prevent the Germans from achieving "in peace what they could not achieve in war." Although not as publicly profligate, French President Mitterrand shared British preoccupations, along with his Foreign Minister Roland Dumas (who had had to bury his own father himself after he was shot by the Nazis). German chancellor Helmut Kohl was very much aware of these fears, and he succeeded in convincing his European, American and Soviet partners that a reunified Germany would not be a threat to the balance of power in Europe by agreeing to imprison it willfully in the institutions of NATO and the European Union.[51] The price for reunification consisted in a double constraint: Germany would remain an important member of NATO under American leadership – this gave security guarantees to France and, down the way, to Poland as well. And it would abandon the Deutsche Mark for a new, common currency that would avoid total German economic hegemony on the continent. Mitterrand's direct answer to Thatcher was clear – and, from a French perspective, realistic: "without a single currency we are all of us – you and we – already subordinate to the Germans' will."[52] Building Europe was the only way of constraining Germany, and in many ways, it meant answering the wish of German novelist Thomas Mann, who had pleaded in 1953 for a European Germany in order to prevent a German Europe.

Germans – and more largely Europeans – faced the prospect of unification, and the atmosphere was understandably one of jubilation and euphoria. The mood may have been different in Moscow, but Europeans had truly the feeling that they were living the "end of history" and had got rid of war for good. Indeed, Robert Kagan's "Americans are from Mars, Europeans from Venus" analogy in his famed *Of Paradise and Power* was generally accepted as common and eternal truth in the early 2000s, even though the author himself warned that before 1945, it was Americans who hailed from Venus and Europeans from Mars. The spectacular enlargement of the European Union in the 1990s, combined with that of NATO, seemed to suggest that Europeans had found their way to perpetual peace, with two guarantees just to make sure: to the military *Pax Americana* provided by the Transatlantic security pact was added an economic *Pax Europea*, which seemed to guarantee commerce and prosperity around the continent, as a quickly reforming Central and Eastern Europe started to catch up with the West. With solid economic growth and memory of European collective suicide by war still relatively fresh, Europe really seemed to have turned its back on war.

A few decades later, Europe's toxic ex came knocking back on the door, and unexpectedly, circumstances and other factors made it that at least some Europeans seemed to be ready to listen.

Notes

1 See Charles Kupchan, *Isolationism: A History of America's Efforts to Shield Itself from the World*, New York: Oxford University Press, 2020.
2 Timothy Snyder, *Bloodlands: Europe between Hitler and Stalin*, London: Random House, 2015, p.1.

3 Christopher Clark, *The Sleepwalkers: How Europe Went to War in 1914*, London: Penguin, 2013, p.433.
4 Christopher Clark, *The Sleepwalkers: How Europe Went to War in 1914*, London: Penguin, p.xxv.
5 Ibid.
6 Ibid., p.251.
7 Hans Kundani, *The Paradox of German Power*, Oxford: Oxford University Press, 2015, p.6.
8 Lawrence Freedman, *The Future of War: A History*, New York: PublicAffairs, 2017, p.7.
9 Hansard Parliamentary Debates, Ser. III, vol. cciv, February–March 1871, pp.81–82.
10 Christopher Clark, *The Sleepwalkers: How Europe Went to War in 1914*, London: Penguin, 2013, p.164.
11 Historian Margaret MacMillan reminds us that the building of the German fleet was actually not thought by German authorities as an act of war or even a direct challenge to Britain but stemmed from the Kaiser's desire to emulate the British leadership and gain the respect of his cousins in the royal family on the other side of the North Sea. The perception in London was quite different and led to a naval race that strongly conditioned British reactions in June–July 1914. See Margaret MacMillan, *The War that Ended Peace: The Road to 1914*, New York: Random House, 2013, p.xxvi.
12 See Sean McMeekin, *The Russian Origins of the First World War*, Cambridge: Belknap Press, 2013.
13 Hans Kundani, *The Paradox of German Power*, Oxford: Oxford University Press, p.8.
14 Lawrence Freedman, *The Future of War: A History*, New York: Public Affairs, p.9.
15 One telling example is the range and rate of fire of rifles and guns, which developed exponentially throughout the nineteenth century and the beginning of the twentieth century. The consequence, as Lawrence Freedman recalls, was that "it was becoming increasingly difficult to obtain a rapid result against an enemy of similar size and capability." See Ibid., p.14.
16 Pierre Miquel, *La Grande Guerre*, Paris: Fayard, 1983, p.610.
17 See Charles Kupchan, *Isolationism: A History of America's Efforts to Shield Itself from the World*, New York: Oxford University Press, 2020.
18 Quoted in Lawrence Freedman, *The Future of War: A History*, New York: Public Affairs, p.53.
19 See Ibid., p.57.
20 Quoted in Pierre Miquel, *La Grande Guerre*, Paris: Fayard, 1983, p.594.
21 Timothy Snyder, *Bloodlands: Europe between Hitler and Stalin*, London: Random House, 2015, p.17.
22 Ernst Nolte, *Der europäische Bürgerkrieg, 1917–1941: Nationalsozialismus und Bolschevismus*, Berlin: Propyläen, 1987.
23 Lawrence Freedman, *The Future of War: A History*, New York: Public Affairs, p.36.
24 Timothy Snyder, *Bloodlands: Europe between Hitler and Stalin*, London: Random House, 2015, p.vii.
25 Ibid., p.xiv.
26 Quoted in Ibid., p.161.
27 Quoted in Ibid.
28 Rolf-Dieter Müller, Nicole Schönherr, Thomas Widera et al., *Die Zerstörung Dresdens: 13 bis 15 Februar 1945. Gutachten und Ergebniße der Dresdner Historikerkommission zur Ermittlung der Opferzahlen*, Göttingen: V&R Unipress, 2010, p.46.
29 Quoted in Lawrence Freedman, *The Future of War: A History*, New York: Public Affairs, p.186.
30 Richard Coudenhove-Kalergi, *Pan-Europa*, Independent Publishing, 2019 (the original, in German, Vienna. dates from 1923).
31 https://winstonchurchill.org/resources/speeches/1946-1963-elder-statesman/the-sinews-of-peace/

32 John Lewis Gaddis, *The Long Peace: Inquiries into the History of the Cold War*, Oxford: Oxford University Press, 1987.
33 Stéphane Courtois et al., *Le livre noir du communisme: Crimes, terreur, répression*, Paris: Robert Laffont, 1997, pp.423–529.
34 Robert Kagan, *The Jungle Grows Back : America and Our Imperiled World*, New York : Alfred A. Knopf, 2018, pp.54–55.
35 See Charles Kupchan, *Isolationism: A HIstory of America's Efforts to Shield Itself from the World*, New York: Oxford University Press, 2020.
36 Matthieu Calame, *La France contre l'Europe: Histoire d'un malentendu*, Paris: Les petits matins, 2019, p.98.
37 John Lewis Gaddis, *The Long Peace: Inquiries into the History of the Cold War*, Oxford: Oxford University Press, 1987.
38 Lawrence Freedman, *The Future of War: A History*, New York: PublicAffairs, p.280.
39 The findings in Germany of the Federal Commission on Archives of the Stasi police (*Bundesbeauftrage für die Unterlagen des Staatssicherheitsdienstes der ehemaligen Deutschen Demokratischen Republik*, or BStU), has documented the links between the terrorist organization and the Stasi. See BStU (ed.), *Anarcho-terroristische Kräfte: Die Rote-Armee-Fraktion und die Stasi*, Berlin: BStU, 2017.
40 Timothy Snyder, *Bloodlands: Europe between Hitler and Stalin*, New York : Basic Books, 2012, p.315.
41 Alfred Maurice de Zayas, *A Terrible Revenge: The Ethnic Cleansing of East European Germans* (2nd edition), New York: Saint Martin's Press, 2006.
42 Patrick Pasture, *Imagining European Unity since 1000 AD*, Houndmills: Palgrave MacMillan, 2015.
43 Wolfgang Schivelbusch, *The Culture of Defeat: On National Trauma, Mourning and Recovery*, New York: Picador, 2001.
44 Éric Roussel, *Jean Monnet*, Paris: Fayard, 1996.
45 Ashoka Mody, *Eurotragedy: A Drama in Nine Acts*, Oxford: Oxford University Press, 2018, p.24.
46 The full text of the May 9, 1950, Schuman declaration is available on the EU's website: https://europa.eu/european-union/about-eu/symbols/europe-day/schuman-declaration_en
47 Matthieu Calame, *La France contre l'Europe: Histoire d'un malentendu*, Paris: Les Petits Matins, 2019, pp.100–101.
48 Ashoka Mody, *Eurotragedy: A Drama in Nine Acts*, Oxford: Oxford University Press, 2018, pp.57–64.
49 Peter Kenez, *A History of the Soviet Union from the Beginning to the End*, Cambridge: Cambridge University Press, 1999, pp.243–277.
50 See Hans Kundani, *The Paradox of German Power*, Oxford: Oxford University Press, 2015, pp.40–41.
51 If the Russians today speak of an American "promise" not to enlarge NATO to the East at the time of the fall of the Iron Curtain, this idea is more of a Soviet pious wish than anything else, as there is no proof of any reality of this agreement (the Budapest Memorandum, which guaranteed the territorial integrity of Ukraine in exchange for its disarmament is, for its part, perfectly documented). See Robert Kagan, *The Jungle Grows Back: America and Our Imperiled World*, New York: Alfred A. Kopf, p.73.
52 In Mitterrand's words: "Without a single currency we are all of us – you and we – already subordinate to the Germans' will." Quoted in David Marsh, *The Euro: The Politics of the New Global Currency*, New Haven: Yale University Press, 2009, p.135.

Bibliography

Calame, Matthieu, *La France contre l'Europe: Histoire d'un malentendu*, Paris: Les Petits Matins, 2019.

Clark, Christopher, *The Sleepwalkers: How Europe Went to War in 1914*, London: Penguin, 2013.
Coudenhove Kalergi, Richard, *Pan-Europa*, Independent Publishing, 2019.
Courtois, Stéphane et al., *Le livre noir du communisme: Crimes, terreur, répression*, Paris: Robert Laffont, 1997.
Freedman, Lawrence, *The Future of War: A History*, New York: PublicAffairs, 2017.
Gaddis, John Lewis, *The Long Peace: Inquiries into the History of the Cold War*, Oxford: Oxford University Press, 1987.
Kagan, Robert, *The Jungle Grows Back: America and Our Imperiled World*, New York: Alfred A. Kopf, 2018
Kundani, Hans, *The Paradox of German Power*, Oxford: Oxford University Press, 2015.
Kupchan, Charles, *Isolationism: A History of America's Efforts to Shield Itself from the World*, New York: Oxford University Press, 2020.
MacMillan, Margaret, *The War that Ended Peace: The Road to 1914*, New York: Random House, 2013.
Marsh, David, *The Euro: The Politics of the New Global Currency*, New Haven: Yale University Press, 2009.
McMeekin, Sean, *The Russian Origins of the First World War*, Cambridge: Belknap Press, 2013.
Miquel, Pierre, *La Grande Guerre*, Paris: Fayard, 1983.
Mody, Ashoka, *Eurotragedy: A Drama in Nine Acts*, Oxford: Oxford University Press, 2018.
Nolte, Ernst, *Der europäische Bürgerkrieg, 1917–1941: Nationalsozialismus und Bolschevismus*, Berlin: Propyläen, 1987.
Pasture, Patrick, *Imagining European Unity since 1000 AD*, Houndmills: Palgrave MacMillan, 2015.
Roussel, Éric, *Jean Monnet*, Paris: Fayard, 1996.
Schivelbusch, Wolfgang, *The Culture of Defeat: On National Trauma, Mourning and Recovery*, New York: Picador, 2001.
Snyder, Timothy, *Bloodlands: Europe between Hitler and Stalin*, New York: Basic Books, 2012.

3
THE TOXIC EX RETURNS

Between 1989 and 2001, the West went through a period of collective euphoria rarely experienced in history: victors of the Cold War, Western Europe and North America were more than ever models for the rest of the world to follow; with the Soviet threat gone, Europeans were once again able to decide for their future and embarked in a process of unification materialized by the enlargements of the European Union in 2004, 2007 and 2013; finally, with the eastern extension of the *Pax Americana* to almost the whole continent, Europeans could glimpse at the possibility of perpetual peace. It is worth noting that even in that time, the narrative was not followed perfectly, as the wars in Yugoslavia showed the limits of that peace. It took two American interventions, first in Bosnia and then in Kosovo to put an end to a decade-long cycle of violence in the Western Balkans.[1] The wars in Yugoslavia may have been seen at the time as the exception confirming the rule, but they also showed how much the reality of *Pax Europaea* was in fact dependent on the continuation of the *Pax Americana*.

As violence receded in the Western Balkans, however, reservations withered away: whatever problems remained in the region would soon disappear, thanks to future Euro-Atlantic integration, and conflicts in Europe were relegated to the continent's eastern marches in the post-Soviet space – often in places too remote at least for Western Europeans to be worried about.[2] The time was for celebrations, and the enthusiasm of the epoch was famously encapsulated by Francis Fukuyama's claim that this was the end of history.[3] On December 31, 2001, as the Euro became the new currency of the European Union, the EU was getting ready for its largest enlargement in history, and its borders moved East to englobe most of Central Europe in 2004, along with Cyprus and Malta. The European Union had become an economic behemoth, the largest market in the world. At that moment, the continent was united as it had never been before, while peace returned to the Balkans. The color revolutions in Serbia (2000),

Georgia (2003) and Ukraine (2004) suggested that this new perpetual European peace, guaranteed by the United States, would not only consolidate but also continue to expand.

It is precisely in this period of intense euphoria that the first signs of degradation started to appear, becoming more and more apparent as time went by: one by one, the elements that had prolonged and extended the imperium of peace in Europe started to weaken, at first in a barely perceptible way, before a spectacular degradation after 2008. In this sense, the period we have just lived has shown a spectacular decay of the economic, political and security environment in Europe, with the return of war at the very borders of the European Union. As the war has got nearer, more factors have contributed to destabilizing Europe from the inside, with socioeconomic difficulties, a migrant crisis that left deep scars in the European psyche, the rise of populism, Brexit and the coronavirus crisis, whose long-term consequences are not yet known. In this chapter, we will try to understand why and how the safeguards that had until now guaranteed the security of the continent have weakened in the last decade to the point of making war possible again. Indeed, some Europeans could reasonably be content that war has already come back to Europe: since 2014, the war in the Donbass has claimed more than 15,000 lives, and to this day, parts of Ukraine are still occupied by a foreign power, who still denies any implication.

Pax Americana: extension and contestations

One of the main reasons to be fearful about the future of Europe is the current perceived weakness of the *Pax Americana*, which until now has guaranteed Europe's security and unity: after all, the idea of a "Europe whole and free," largely realized with the enlargement of the EU in 2004, 2007 and 2013, was first expressed by George H. W. Bush in his Mainz speech of May 1989, although it was later enthusiastically adopted by a large number of European leaders.[4] Following its successes in Western Europe, where Europeans had laid down their arms to take advantage of collective security and the US military umbrella, America was in a position to extend *Pax Americana* in the 1990s and 2000s: for 20 years, the United States worked tirelessly to anchor Central Europe to the West, promoting a cultural change among the region's economic and political elites and guaranteeing in return their security: the exceptions of former Yugoslavia – which did not originally fall into the US plans[5] – show how complicated the situation could have become if America had shown no interest in Central Europe: the region would probably have ended up as it had been in the 1930s: atomized and vulnerable.

For a while, it also seemed that this extension would go even further than Central Europe: Ukraine abandoned its nuclear arsenal through the Budapest Memorandum in 1994 in exchange for a guarantee of its borders by Russia, France, Great Britain and of course the United States (a decision that the Ukrainian elites would bitterly regret upon Crimea's illegal annexation in 2014).

A few years later, with the Orange Revolution in full swing and great hopes for reform, it seemed that Ukraine too would transition from East to West, along with Georgia and Moldova.

In Washington, enthusiasm for the extension of democracy's *imperium* was also at an all-time high: despite early calls from retrenchment, the late 1990s and early 2000s represented a high tide for American liberal internationalism, and the idea of the formation of an enlarged and free Europe was met with enthusiasm in foreign policy circles. The few voices that raised the alarm mostly did so to warn of the systemic danger that a united Europe could pose to American hegemony, which now as then looked like a fantasy: Europeans remained powerless faced with bloodbaths taking place just a couple of hours away from their national capitals, and they were way too happy to invite the United States to play the policeman for them.[6] In the Western Balkans, it was indeed the US intervention that proved decisive: not only through diplomatic intervention (with the Dayton Accords for Bosnia) but also though military intervention with the bombings of Belgrade putting an end to the bloodbaths in Kosovo. America's reluctant but ultimately successful interventions were a reminder to Europeans that despite their good words and ambitions, they remained extremely dependent on their partner across the Atlantic to guarantee peace within their own continent.

There were reasons for these Europeans to actually be comfortable with the situation: with existential threats now far away (Russia had retreated to its borders of the time of Peter the Great) and the threat of Islamist terrorism seemingly still manageable, Europe had everything to gain by remaining under the American umbrella. The United States had an annual defense budget of more than $600 billion, more than China, Russia, Saudi Arabia, India, France, the United Kingdom and Japan combined,[7] and the countries of Central Europe that had been subjected to the Soviet Union could thus hope for effective protection against a possible – and then still distant – Russian resurgence. But in Warsaw as much as in Prague or even Paris, US presence was also a guarantee that a certain balance of power would remain in Europe. As Robert Kagan puts it,

> "when Germany reunified in 1991, only the promise that Germany would remain in NATO and that US troops would remain on German soil calmed Germany's neighbors. Even France, which had sometimes regarded NATO as a tool of American hegemony, sought closer integration in the alliance.[8]"

At the time, unified Germany itself didn't look like a likely hegemon as it struggled to digest reunification: after the euphoria of 1989–1991, the 1990s were a time for crisis, and reinvention would only come in the early 2000s.

This ideal moment could have endured for decades, as all actors seemed comfortable with it. But Europeans had to face the unfortunate "opposition of events," to use Churchillian terminology, as subsequent developments proved less favorable to the tranquility of Europeans. September 11, 2001, represented a first turning point: attacked on their soil for the first time since Pearl Harbor, the United States responded to the challenge with a plan whose ambition was equaled only by the ultra-dominant position of American hyperpower at the time.[9] Extending the *Pax Americana* (and with it liberal democracy) to the Arab world would not only ensure the security of Americans would it also fulfill the messianic mission of idealist America while extending American power inside Eurasia's heartland, thereby ensuring uncontested global dominance. The project proved overambitious, but one of its side effects was that Europe almost immediately ceased to be a real issue for Washington as the war on terror drew security circles' attention. After 2008, the decision was taken to pull back from Central Europe and the Western Balkans as much as possible. As democratization and Euro-Atlantic integration were declared a success throughout the continent, the State Department waved the "mission accomplished" flag and reduced efforts in Europe, very often to re-deploy them in the Middle East. The Obama administration's reset with Russia and its abandonment of the missile defense shield project, which was supposed to protect Europe from any ballistic attack, is symptomatic of Washington's strategic retrenchment.

If the financial and human abyss represented by America's endless wars in the Middle East was already visible in 2006, it became even more so after the 2008 financial crisis, which exposed the weaknesses of the American colossus – and Europeans initially failed to see that it exposed their weaknesses too. As US diplomats started to realize that China's rise had become a problem, they understood that the great Middle Eastern strategy of the Bush era had to be abandoned, although they could not pull out from the region altogether. Robert Kagan wrote in 2014 that Americans were tired of the world, in particular the new generations, whose lesson from Iraq and Afghanistan was that "America has neither the power nor the understanding nor the skill to fix problems in the world."[10] This does not necessarily mean that Americans are necessarily and inevitably reverting to a cycle of isolationism (although the risk is real[11]), but just like in the 1970s after the Vietnam War, they have entered a phase of retrenchment and introspection. This has meant not only a lot of anger expressed in the public space, which has, in turn, translated into internal polarization, but also a call for America's soldiers to come home. Back home, these vets have, in turn, influenced the way America votes: they may be much better treated than the Vietnam returnees, but they are numerous, and come back with a world vision very much defined by their experience in service. Furthermore, they often come back overwhelmingly to those states of the Rust Belt and the Midwest that have become battleground states in US presidential elections. As Benjamin Haddad of the Atlantic Council reminds us,

> fewer Americans have been killed in Iraq than in other wars such as Vietnam, but this number should not blind us to the conflict's direct – and profound consequences on American society. And especially in those communities with high concentrations of veterans, who have come back

wounded, physically and mentally. Thanks to major advances of field medicine, they are especially numerous: In Vietnam, the ratio of dead to wounded is one soldier for every three, compared to one for every seven in Iraq.[12]

America is facing a period of introspection, but it is not only doubting its Iraq or Middle Eastern strategy: the entire global outreach of America is potentially at play. In the words of Robert Kagan, this retrenchment

> cannot be attributed only to the failure of Iraq and Afghanistan, even compounded by the effects of the 2008 financial crisis and the recession that followed. Rather, it is due to the widespread conviction that the role the United States has been playing in the world for the past seven decades is no longer necessary, perhaps was never necessary, and in any case no longer serves American interests.[13]

In this sense, Haddad is correct when he claims that, at least from a foreign policy perspective, "Donald Trump is not an accident of history [...] but rather the accelerator of a deeper transformation of the United States, its relationship to the world, and the international system."[14] While isolationism used to be a taboo in Washington in the post-Second World War area, today think-tanks like the Quincy Institute for Responsible Statecraft, which promotes retrenchment in US foreign policy approaches, manage to fundraise from both left-wing liberals like George Soros and conservative philanthropists like Charles Koch – a sign that the pendulum is moving toward a less militant role of the United States in the World.[15] On this issue as on many others, the US public remains divided: according to a 2019 survey carried by Gallup, the Council on Foreign Relations and National Geographic, 45% of respondents wanted the United States to increase or keep its role in the world, while 46% want it to shrink or end altogether.[16]

These numbers also show how wrong it would be to believe that America is about to return to a pre-Pearl Harbor type of American isolationism. Americans are split on the subject, and at this stage, full retrenchment is not likely – but what is almost inevitable is that the United States will recalibrate its presence in the wider world, pretty much like in the 1970s after the Vietnam War. And much of the calculations around this strategic change will have one denominator: China. The Pacific/Asia zone is now the priority for Washington, not Europe. The move had already started during the Obama administration, and it is likely to continue; as contrary to what many in Brussels and elsewhere believe, Europeans are no longer the center of the world. Today's global economic growth is driven by North America and the Asia-Pacific region. This is of immense importance for the United States, as it is itself a center of growth and has easy access to Asia via its long Pacific Coast. It is indeed where most of the major "new" American industries are concentrated, from Boeing (Seattle) to Hollywood (Los Angeles) and, of course, Silicon Valley in the San Francisco Bay Area – the corollary of this economic power is also that the United States holds strategic key points all around the Pacific Ocean, from San Diego to Okinawa via Hawaii, Midway or Samoa. With the confrontation between China and the United States now a given in world affairs, the geopolitical hotspots are no longer in Berlin, Szczecin and Trieste but in the China Sea and the Strait of Malacca. With slow growth now becoming almost endemic, Europe has once again become a periphery of the world – a periphery that is still rich, of course, but not necessarily the place where the strategic efforts of the United States should be concentrated. This may be analyzed as good news by Europeans, as this means that they are no longer systematically on the radar of great power competition, but it also means that Europe is more vulnerable: indeed, it was precisely because Europe was the grand prize of the Cold War that the United States and USSR made efforts to avoid war on the continent, preferring to fight by proxy in more peripheral areas of the globe.

Europe's new position also has consequences for America, as it tries to pull more resources out of peripheries to re-deploy elsewhere, may this be on the home front or in the Asia-Pacific region. This means on the US side a renewed (and often frustrated) demand from European allies to share the burden of their defense with them. In 2006, Europeans had informally committed to increasing their military spending to 2% of GDP.[17] But with the 2008 crisis and in the absence of an immediate threat, military spending was among the first budget lines to get cut in Europe, which quickly led to exasperation in Washington – as Haddad recalls, before Donald Trump, it was Barack Obama who denounced

> the European free riders who dragged him (with Hillary Clinton) into the Libyan conflict, which he considered to be his main foreign policy mistake [...]. Drawn into a confrontation with Russia at the end of his second term, he left it to the Europeans to assume the economic cost of the sanctions and entrusted diplomatic leadership to Angela Merkel and François Hollande during the cease-fire negotiations in Minsk II.[18]

Indeed, America decided to pay attention in Europe only when Russia annexed part of a European territory (Crimea). But while the Obama administration had to pay more attention to Europe, they also had Europeans renew their commitment to increase defense spending – solemnly this time, at the 2014 Cardiff NATO summit. The fact that some countries, and most notably Germany, have continuously slowed down this process has exasperated Washington even more, on both sides of the aisle. Berlin may have good reasons to avoid building up an army for internal purposes, but this is not the problem of the United States, after all.

In the early 2020s, America is definitely in trouble, but that does not mean that it is on its knees or even contemplating the idea of leaving world leadership to China – quite the contrary. Today, as at the end of the Cold War, the United States accounts for almost a quarter of world GDP, and pre-pandemic dynamics actually showed that growth rates between the United States and China tended to converge, as American growth potential increased and China's "factory of the world" model of the 2000s was clearly showing signs of fatigue. With European growth rates often stuck below the 2% bar, at least in Western Europe, Washington elites have started to ask questions about what they see as the European free riding, with the United States protecting Europe but getting too little in return. The estrangement between Europeans and North Americans is reinforced by demographic changes on the other side of the Atlantic as the United States has become more diverse and distinctively less "European": with fewer Americans of European descent, general affinities to Europe are becoming less obvious, and cultural changes in America and Europe contribute to adding distance in the relationship, with America becoming a cultural world in itself, less capable of influencing European culture precisely because it is culturally more alien.[19]

That Americans and Europeans do not understand each other in the way they used to is illustrated by a recent incident in Berlin: during the celebrations of the fall of the Berlin Wall in November 2019, the US Embassy inaugurated a monument to Ronald Reagan within its walls. The municipality of Berlin had repeatedly refused to erect the statue in a public place, using a public order pretext that seems rather difficult to explain, particularly considering that statues of Karl Marx and Friedrich Engels are still standing in the German capital.[20] Of course, the Americans' insistence of viewing Ronald Reagan as the prime, if not, sole actor in the fall of the Wall is certainly an overstatement (as his successor George H. W. Bush, but also Mikhail Gorbachev and Helmut Kohl played a crucial part), but the unwillingness of the authorities in Berlin to authorize the erection of a statue on shaky grounds was yet another proof of the estrangement between Europeans and Americans, including on commemorations that should actually bring them together.

Between 2016 and 2020, it was easy to put these tensions on the personality of Donald Trump, but as on many other subjects, he was the symptom rather than the cause of the problem. Looking at facts on the ground, the then-Republican administration actually did not act against American interests in Europe: Trump got his arm twisted by Congress and the military establishments on key issues, he eventually reversed its campaign statements in which he had declared NATO "obsolete," but most importantly under his administration America contributed much more to the alliance than under his predecessor ($6.5 billion devoted in 2019 to the European Deterrence Initiative, almost double Obama's balance[21]). But in politics, perception is everything, and even if the weariness of the United States toward Europe has not turned into disengagement (courtesy of Russia's invasion of Ukrainian territory), the suspicion in many capitals of the Old Continent is that, in the long run, an American re-entrenchment, may be even withdrawal, is inevitable. When President Macron clumsily declared in November 2019 to *The Economist* that NATO was "brain dead," he was not only indulging in an old Franco-Gaullist fantasy but also pointing at real contradictions of the Atlantic Alliance in the Mediterranean and anticipating that these could not be resolved in any other way than reform or US disengagement – the latter options seeming all too real after Donald Trump's announcement that American troops' presence in Germany would be reduced. We are not there yet, but the future is now uncertain enough to envisage this eventuality. The end of US presence in Europe would then mean de facto the end of *Pax Americana*, without which a *Pax Europea* seems difficult to uphold – even more so as Germany represents a seemingly intractable problem both to itself as well as European geopolitical and geo-economic balance.

The return of the German question

The German question represents a double paradox for Europe: if Germany is fragmented, its central position in Europe makes it a source of instability for the continent – this is what the German lands experienced between the sixteenth and eighteenth centuries. If, on the contrary, it is united, as is the case today, it becomes too strong for the balance of European powers and thus tends toward hegemony. But, a paradox within the paradox, if a united Germany is too strong for its neighbors, it is not strong enough to become hegemonic. The result is a position of "semi-hegemony," to use Hans Kundnani's term,[22] and it becomes itself a source of instability for Europe, as this position generally convinces neighboring powers to dissociate themselves or to join forces against Germany to weaken it – as happened in 1914–1918 and again in 1939–1945.

Whether Germans like it or not, Germany is once again in a similar position of semi-hegemony, although it is expressed in geo-economic rather than military terms: once it had digested reunification, the Federal Republic could only find itself in a dominant position in Europe, if only for demographic reasons: as long as it was divided by the Iron Curtain, Germany had a population still comparable with France and the United Kingdom. By adding 17 million citizens at the time of reunification, it became by far the largest demographic power in the EU,[23] which logically translated into a greater weight in the European Council and a greater number of Members of the European Parliament (MEPs) than other EU countries. This has not been without consequences for the functioning of the European institutions, insofar as they are now dominated by Germans – due to their demographic weight and the bad political (and organizational) choices made by the French, British and Italians.

The reality of this domination is evident when one is willing to pay attention to who holds the important positions in Brussels: today, the Commission is chaired by a German, Ursula von der Leyen – it was an openly expressed campaign goal for Angela Merkel and the her party, the Christian Democratic Union (CDU) ahead of the 2019 European elections. The Commission itself has also long changed its culture – from quite French in the 1980s and 1990s, it has turned more Germanic, as former British ambassador to Berlin Paul Lever pointed out in his book *Berlin Rules*.[24] But Germany's dominance is perhaps even clearer in the European Parliament, which for different reasons the French and British have traditionally looked with much contempt – leaving a vacuum that German leaders naturally filled: according to Paul Lever, the Germans

> occupy more senior positions in the European Parliament than any other nationality. Of the presidents of the Parliament in the last 20 years, five have been Germans. [...]. Germans hold more committee chairs than any other nationality. Germans are also disproportionately represented in the key roles of committee rapporteur.[25]

German over-representation is also obvious in the European political families, a consequence of political interest in the process and of the strength and stability of the German party system: The Christian Democratic European People's Party is clearly dominated by the CDU and the CSU – it is no coincidence that the parliamentary group is chaired by Manfred Weber from Bavaria, and the party was until recently led by Frenchman Joseph Daul, an Alsatian who spoke much better German than English; on the left, the Party of European Socialists is also dominated by Germans, even though this dominance is less visible today after the departure of Martin Schultz, an emblematic figure of social democracy in Brussels, and bad results for the SPD prior to the 2021 German elections. Among the Greens, the German delegation is also the largest and clearly the most powerful. Even inside the Alliance of Liberals and Democrats for Europe (ALDE), where the FDP has never enjoyed a truly dominant position, Germans have also used their assets to covet important positions, although here again, this should be put not only on the smart thinking and better structuring the German party system but also on the inability of parties in the other "big" countries to work over the long term to gain influence in these groupings. An excellent example of this was given by Emmanuel Macron's *La République en Marche*, who instead of joining a European political family to build its power there (the liberal ALDE was an obvious choice), chose to try and break up the whole party system and after failing to do so ended up in relative isolation after making up a common group with ALDE (Renew Europe) without becoming a member. The decision of David Cameron's Conservative Party to leave the European People's Party (EPP) and build its own group outside the decision-making circles of Brussels was even more consequential for his party and for Britain, as it marginalized British positions in the European Parliament (not that this matters anymore in a post-Brexit environment of course).

It would indeed be too cheap a shot to explain German dominance in European institutions by demographics alone – or by some sort of evil plan. The reality is that German elites did not really "seek" this dominant position, but they acquired it by default, thanks to a mix of luck, good organization and above all else an effort to cultivate relationships that the British, the French, the Italian and the Poles (among others) have always treated as a waste of time. The Germans' ability to listen to smaller actors, even if the end result is a polite "no," contrasts with the arrogance or detachment (sometimes both) of others. In the meantime, the powerful party foundations, very generously funded by the German state (they are actually larger than their American counterparts[26]), have allowed Germany to develop an impressively dense network of friendships – and when push comes to shove, these friends inevitably come to the rescue – voluntarily or with a bit of friendly pressure. At the EPP Congress in Helsinki in November 2018, where the party chose its *Spitzenkandidat* for the European Election – the candidate who, in case of an EPP victory, was supposed to be the first nominee to head the EU Commission, representatives of the Konrad Adenauer Foundation worked very hard to make sure that national delegations would support Manfred Weber's candidacy, and their work produced a triumphant election for Weber, despite a remarkably well-designed challenge by former Finnish Prime Minister Alexander Stubb. The result was even more remarkable because many of the national delegates I talked to on that day off-the-record were telling me that they thought that Weber had fewer chances than Stubb to be accepted by the European Council as President of the Commission.[27]

Germany's success in Europe did not come by chance – it is the product of a long, laborious work that has come to fruition as the country's economy expanded. This economic success took time to mature: in the 1990s and early 2000s, Germany was still digesting the incorporation of the former German Democratic Republic (GDR), and it was then, at least for *The Economist*, the "sick man of Europe"[28] – a brand more readily appropriate for France or Italy these days. Germany managed to turn the tables rapidly, in part thanks to the series of reforms dubbed "Agenda 2010" passed by the Gerhard Schröder government to revitalize the German economy and make its job market more flexible. The Hartz plan relied on a severe restriction of benefits and wages and had the modernization costs of Germany's economy carried mostly by German workers. But one of the unsung reasons why the reform was so successful is that its implementation coincided with the introduction of the Euro, which was a de facto devaluation of the German currency that made Germany's high-quality products more competitive overnight. Thanks to this double pressure, Germany not only managed to preserve its impressive industrial model relying on the consideration of manual labor and an extremely dense network of small and medium-sized enterprises but also completely reversed its trade balance, which went from a deficit of 1.7% of GDP in 2000 to a surplus of 7.4% in 2007.[29] Just in time for the worst financial crisis since the stock market crash of 1929, Germany had managed to operate a spectacular reversal of its economic fortunes – and was ready to act once again as a model.

Indeed, in the aftermath of the 2008 crisis, Germany's standing in Europe was all but confirmed: with a GDP of almost $4,000 billion in 2018 (compared to $2,600 billion for France, the second economic power of the EU-27), Germany is clearly the largest economic power in the Union, and the relative dominance of the German economy has been all but reinforced after Brexit and the departure of the UK's $2,600 billion in GDP.[30] And while proponents of a "Carolingian Europe" often quote that together, Paris and Berlin weigh no less than 42.5% of the EU's current GDP, there is also no doubt that Paris is the junior economic partner in the Franco-German "couple," with a GDP one third lower than that of Germany.[31]

When money talks, everyone listens. And so, it was only natural – and inevitable – that the country that had so clearly taken the economic advantage in Europe should translate this economic ascent into political power – and even though Germans are reluctant to assume it (for perfectly sensible reasons), the reality is that they are now de facto mostly in charge. This was already clear during the late 2000s and early 2010s: despite the talks about the "Merkozy" leadership over Europe, with Germany's Angela Merkel and France's Nicolas Sarkozy leading the EU's response to the financial and then the Euro-crisis, insiders were left in no doubt that despite President Sarkozy's communication, it was the German chancellor who decided, with an eye first and foremost on Germany's interests – which was quite logical: after all, she had not been elected by Italians or Greeks but by Germans. As a *Times* publisher recalled at the time of the Greek crisis, "The First Iron Law of Europe is simple enough to be learned by rote. Europe proposes. Angela Merkel disposes."[32]

Berlin's dazzling economic success of course made its European partners envious. As very often, their first reaction was mimicry: all governments (almost all of them from the EPP between 2008 and 2012) thrived to follow the German example by introducing their version of the Schröder reforms, with varying degrees of success. But while a government could adopt measures to "flexibilize" the job markets and flatten the salary curve, they could reproduce neither the quality of Germany's Mittelstand production nor the access to the Chinese consumer market nor for that matter the boosting effect that the Euro's lower value had for German products compared to the Deutsche Mark. When economic results failed to materialize in Southern Europe, admiration gradually turned into resentment and sometimes even hatred in countries like Greece, where anti-austerity demonstrators were seen holding signs with fellow European Angela Merkel restyled with a Hitler-like mustache. The attack was cheap but in line with the desperation of the Greeks, who were asked to accept impoverishment without any guarantee for their future (or that of their children).

Former chancellor Helmut Schmidt had warned Germans at the SPD Conference in 2011:

> If we Germans were to be tempted by our economic strength into claiming a leading political role in Europe […], an increasing majority of our neighbors would mount effective resistance. The concern among the states on the periphery about the center of Europe becoming too strong would return very quickly. The likely consequences of such a development would cripple the EU and Germany would lapse into isolation.[33]

Schmidt died four years later, and developments following his passing have tended to prove him right. Whether in Italy, Poland, France or Hungary, the populist contestation of the present "ordo-liberal" order very often described Germany as the main culprit for the country's woes. The German elites, for the first time entirely relieved of direct experience from the period 1933–1945, did not understand that their dominance, once it found political expression (even if natural and unconscious), could generate the same type of resentment as during the period 1871–1914. Even more so since the two other major post-Cold War developments in Europe – the introduction of the Euro and enlargement – have also strengthened Europe's imbalances, in both cases in favor of Germany and to the detriment of the EU's peripheries.

Enlargement's side effects

In the early 1990s, when the countries of Central Europe commenced their journey from socialist democracy to market capitalism, few would have predicted that their ambition to join Euro-Atlantic structures would become reality in little less than a decade. Considering the economic ruin that Soviet communism had left, the idea of a Europe Whole and Free from Lisbon to Vilnius seemed, indeed, a very distant goal. And yet, in less than two decades, the European Union and NATO had absorbed almost the whole of Central Europe: the three Baltic States (Estonia, Latvia and Lithuania), the Visegrád four (Poland, Czech Republic, Slovakia and Hungary) and Slovenia joined the EU a few years after NATO (as far as the EU was concerned, they were joined by Malta and Cyprus in the Mediterranean), followed by Romania and Bulgaria in 2007 (they were NATO members since 2004) and Croatia in 2013. Croatia had also joined NATO in 2009, along with Albania, and they were followed by Montenegro in 2017 and North Macedonia in 2020. At the end of this road and with more countries knocking on the door, it could be argued that despite differences, the whole of the European continent was on its way to join a common security framework, courtesy of a new enlarged *Pax Americana et Europea*.

That the enlargement was carried out in record time is certainly a fact. That it might have been carried out too fast is an argument one too often hears among the power corridors of net losers of enlargement. But if processes were accelerated, there were perfectly good reasons. This unprecedented expansion of Europe as a political unit had to take place quickly, first of all for geopolitical reasons understood as well in Paris and Berlin as in Warsaw or Bucharest: with the Russian/Soviet threat removed for an unknown time, the European continent found itself facing a real political vacuum at its center, and that vacuum had to be filled in quickly, one way or another. Yugoslavia, left to its own devices due to American disinterest in the early hours of the crisis and the inability of Europeans to agree on a common strategy, is a perfect example of what could have happened in Central Europe if the West had not committed itself early to a quick, conditional integration. If this had been the case, this book would not deal with a possible European war by 2030, but the one that would have occurred between 1991 and 2005, when a resurgent Russia would have once again changed the security equation on the continent, leaving Warsaw, but also Berlin and Paris dangerously exposed.

It was necessary to move quickly, and this is precisely what Europeans on both sides did: many Western companies (German and Austrian in particular) did not hesitate to take risks and invested in the region, while Europeans and Americans invested massively in the democratic and state structures of the candidate countries. For their part, leaders in Central and Eastern Europe had taken upon themselves the difficult transition from a bankrupt socialist economy to a market economy and did not hesitate to make their population pay a high price for a quick transition: in the years 2006–2012, when a new painful economic transition was to become a question again, memories of the 1990s convinced many in Central Europe that support for populist leaders would allow them to avoid the poverty and humiliations they had suffered back then. But back to the 1990s, it is remarkable to take a look at the philosophy of the great, transformative figures of the time: Václav Havel in the Czech Republic, Lech Wałęsa or Aleksander Kaśniewski in Poland, Mart Laar in Estonia, Mikuláš Dzurinda in Slovakia or the young and then-liberal Viktor Orbán in Hungary, etc. Looking at these leaders' credentials at the time, it is remarkable to see how much Western they were, or were aspiring to be. Latvians went probably the furthest, as they elected as President an émigré compatriot who had had to spend most of her life in exile in Canada before returning to Riga, Vaira Vīķe-Freiberga – she presided over Latvia's accession to both NATO and the EU.[34]

The double movement of westernization and willingness from the part of the West to enlarge was strong long enough for fast and successful integration of Central Europe in Euro-Atlantic structures. But while much thought and energy had been given to the transition process itself, very little thinking had been done about the aftermath of the transition: once the countries had made their way back to Europe, they often were considered as graduated (although many harmful stereotypes remained in place, on both sides) and pretty much left to cope on their own devices. The contradictions that followed brewed enough in the late 2000s to explode in the face of European leaders in the 2010s.

The 2000s were a time in which politics were pretty much overlooked compared with economics. It was a real mistake, as the political consequences of enlargement were massive: combined with German reunification, the inclusion of 10 who subsequently became 12 and 13 new members inside the Union could only change the geopolitical balance of the European Union: if it was consensual and even logical to give Strasbourg or Brussels the status of capital to a European Union with of 12 or 15 members, that choice made much less sense in an EU-25, then 28 and 27 after Brexit. Indeed, the UK's departure has accentuated the eastern movement of the Union's center of gravity – which in turn has strengthened Germany's central position. This is true, of course, not only from a geographical point of view but also from an arithmetic point of view, for the reallocation of the number of seats in the European Parliament gave less weight to Western Europeans, to give space for the new entrants. But consequences were also economic, as British, French and Italian companies – not necessarily helped by their government – proved much more reluctant to try their luck in Mitteleuropa, leaving the field wide open for Swiss, Austrian and especially German companies to move in. The result, in the words of Chatham House analyst Hans Kundnani, has been that much of the region has "become an integral part of Germany's industrial supply chain," giving it a competitive advantage over its neighbors and "aligning to a large extent the economic interests of these countries with those of Germany and thus [increasing] German power within the EU."[35]

European governments' reactions to this new situation were mixed: in the United Kingdom, Tony Blair opened the doors wide open for Central European immigration – setting the stage for the main argument for Brexit a decade later. Italy didn't react; it was left with a structural disadvantage as its natural Eastern market, Yugoslavia, virtually disappeared in the 1990s with war and instability. France probably had the worst reaction, taking a condescending attitude toward the new entrants, as President Jacques Chirac allowed himself to lecture the Central European leaders who had missed "a good opportunity to keep quiet" during the Iraqi crisis of 2003, a year before their integration into the EU. The French President was then compared to Leonid Brezhnev by the Polish press,[36] and Central European leaders did not forget or forgive the French once they got in. Relations further deteriorated the following year, as the "Polish plumber" became the villain of the European Constitution referendum of 2005. Eleven years later, Polish and Eastern European immigrants were to become an easy target during the Brexit vote of 2016 – after all, racism is much more socially acceptable in Western societies when it is targeted at white and Christian (or post-Christian) populations.

Around the same time, Central and Eastern Europe started to feel the first effects of a "Westernization" fatigue. The transition to the West had been done in effectively less than a generation and had produced not only huge winners but also losers, and those who paid the costs were often peripheral populations, living in rural areas and small towns, and those that precisely today tend to vote for populist parties. There was much talk in the West of unfair advantages in Central Europe, of "social dumping" and at the home of the downward pressure that eastern workers exerted on a number of low-skilled occupations. But to be fair, Western critiques paid little attention in return to the huge human drain that occurred when Central Europe moved into the EU, as factories were not the only ones to move: in fact, economic migrants also came to Western Europe to look for a better life. With Poles and Balts proving particularly eager to move West, the choice destinations were often Germany, Sweden and also Ireland and Britain as Tony Blair had made the conscious choice to open his country for free movement of people before the others. The United Kingdom gained a competitive advantage in its headhunt for Central and Eastern European talents, but a backlash soon followed. With nearly a million nationals leaving for London and other British cities, Poles became the UK's largest foreign minority. And while the side effects of these (voluntary) population transfers soon became visible in Western Europe, those in the countries of origin were even more visible, as Central Europe lost huge chunks of its population to emigration. In the first ten years of its membership of the European Union, between 2007 and 2017, Romania lost no less than 3.4 million inhabitants, or 17% of its population, a statistic unheard of in Europe in peacetime.[37] Even worse, it was often not the least educated (or the very rich, who had gorged themselves on corruption and had all incentives to stay home) who left but the middle class: during the pandemic of COVID-19, Romania regretted having let go of many of its doctors, trained by the Romanian state – they were missed at a crucial moment, having left their country to settle down for much better wages and working conditions in France, Italy and the United Kingdom.

This demographic disaster could only have major consequences on the national political scene: the young and the middle class, those most likely to carry projects of liberalization and westernization in their countries, left them at a crucial time in their development – very often allowing Western economies to use their skills at a low cost and compensate for bad public policies in education and health sectors recruitment. As Bulgarian political scientist Ivan Krastev explains, when the émigrés had a chance to lead what they considered a normal life at little cost, they took it without hesitation:

> The mass anti-government protests that took place in Bulgaria in 2013 captured well the paradox of open borders. Protesters on the streets were shouting "we don't want to emigrate," but in reality, some of them did because it is easier to go to Germany than to make Bulgaria function like Germany.

On the other hand, those who stayed behind were probably the least prepared for the challenges of globalization and the most reliant on crumbling social services (or corrupt politicians' paternalistic promises) to stay afloat. For Krastev, "the biggest beneficiaries of the opening of the borders turned out to be brilliant individual émigrés, the bad eastern European politicians, and the xenophobic Western European parties."[38]

As an unprecedented peacetime demographic disaster unfolded in Central and Eastern Europe, local populations' views were also heavily impacted, especially in the small towns and rural areas most affected by emigration. Once perceived as an El Dorado for inhabitants of the region, the West started to be seen as a problem: it was no longer a provider of wealth and freedom but often reverted to its pre-1989 image as decadent, corrupt and even corrupting. Immigration, which after the wave of emigration had become an especially sensitive issue, and same-sex marriage became symbols of this struggle to regain a Central European virtue corrupted by Western influence. As Ivan Krastev recalls:

> Post-communist societies, most of which are very secular as a rule, are quite tolerant when it comes to sexual life. But for many conservatives, gay marriages signify fewer kids and further demographic decline. For an eastern European nation haunted by low birth rates and migration, the endorsement of gay culture is like endorsing your own disappearance.[39]

Migration, reproduction, conservative values, etc. The decor was planted for unscrupulous local politicians to exploit fears and – let's face it – a gigantic lack of understanding and compassion from Western European leaders, who themselves had to deal with a quite similar backlash in their own countries, as depopulation and the closing of social services in many poor peripheral areas in Western Europe solidified a strong electorate for populist politicians.[40] People in Central Europe have been raised with a sense that the existence of their nation was by no means a certainty,[41] and the history of the region has tended to prove them right. With mounting pressure for cultural changes coming from the major cities and the West, depopulation a real problem and disinformation riding high on all sorts of conspiracies about a "great replacement," all ingredients were set for a cultural backlash against Westerners who were themselves often to blame for their lack of sensitivity to Central Europeans' objections or ideas.

It did not take long for what Krastev called the "bad politicians" to understand the electoral potential of this frustration, especially as the 2008 crisis had reinforced the idea among Central Europeans that they remained second-class citizens inside the European Union. The financial crisis hit Central Europe immediately and violently – economic historian Adam Tooze called it a "monetary Stalingrad"[42] – and while Western European countries like France and Germany were mobilizing their resources to withstand the financial shock, countries like Hungary (where the authorities had encouraged people to take mortgages in Swiss francs) or Latvia were pretty much left to deal with the crisis on their own. The local populations, who still remembered how hard they had been hit 20 years before at the time of capitalist restructuring, were of course in the front lines as they paid the price of the resulting austerity policies, which in turn created a very large popular resentment, exploited by politicians like Viktor Orbán, who masterfully drove the wave of public anger to obtain a super-majority in the 2011 parliamentary elections, allowing him to completely redefine Hungary's political trajectory.[43] Three years later, when Southern Europe went broke and Western European governments asked EU citizens to show some solidarity with the Greeks (whose turn it was to face massive austerity programs), Central Europeans logically answered "no." And in 2015, when the same Western European countries asked again for Central Europe's solidarity, on the equally delicate issue for migrations, the "no" answer was equally predictable.

The populist leaders that got elected in the aftermath of the 2008 crisis (notably Viktor Orbán) and the 2015 migrant crisis (with the victory of the nationalist-conservative Law and Justice, or PiS, in Poland) did not come out of nowhere. Indeed, the ground was especially fertile for them, and the bar had been set pretty low to earn the trust of their fellow citizens: with levels of cynicism in the region one of the highest in the world,[44] any leader with enough charisma to articulate popular (sometimes legitimate) fears and frustration and credible enough in their promise to defend them, if not to protect them, was enough to turn the tables in some – though not all – countries in the region. As a result, a new cleavage developed not only between Europeans of urban centers and peripheral areas but also between governments of East and West, as the former was accused of leading nationalist peoples out of liberal democracies, while others were depicted as decadents disrespectful of Central Europe. A continent that had united itself a few years earlier now found itself, in many ways, cut in two again. This time, however, the division was no longer physical but psychological and economic, with the countries of Eastern Europe remaining trapped, despite their spectacular catch-up, in a position of economic inferiority vis-à-vis the West, with a model now in exhaustion due to the revaluation of wages and the increasingly glaring lack of manpower. For their part, the citizens of the West could also present legitimate frustrations against an economic convergence that very often took place at their personal expense.[45]

North and south

Of course, migrations and the East–West divide were not the only issue that dangerously fragilized the European construct. For quickly after the 2008 financial crisis, the Euro-crisis was to cut the European Union in two, this time between its North and South.

Interestingly enough, the Euro had been until then (and still is) one the biggest, most concrete achievements of the European project. The fact that one can pay for a coffee in Paris, Madrid, Bratislava or Tallinn with the same currency is certainly something that helps bring down trade barriers and also bring people together. The idea of it, though, was very much ingrained in a simple appreciation of geo-economics at work: Paris had understood early on that the money of reference in Europe had become the Deutsche Mark, and considering German ascent over the European economy, if the French (or the Italians, for that matter) were to keep at least a little bit of control over monetary policy, they had to push for a common currency that would not be the Deutsche Mark. The path to the Euro was tortuous, but it somehow delivered, with two French heads of the Central Bank (Jean-Claude Trichet in 2003–2011 and Christine Lagarde since 2019) and one Italian, Mario Draghi, who technically saved the Euro by putting an end to monetary orthodoxy in the mid-2010s.

The pill, however, had been hard to swallow for the Germans, for whom a stable and strong Deutsche Mark had become the symbol of the post-war economic miracle. The idea of coupling their currency with the much more volatile Franc or the Lira had given headaches to German chancellors and prompted them to answer "nein" to French suggestions until German reunification. The Germans, however, could not ignore French demands and agreed to a "snake in the tunnel" and then a full-fledged European Monetary System (EMS) to peg together national currencies. But while the system delivered for some economies, it could not cope with major bifurcations, and the crisis of 1990–1992 brought the system down, as speculative attacks against the Peseta, the Lira, the Franc and the Pound Sterling took a heavy toll on the national economies – in many ways, the real start of the long road that led to Brexit can be traced back to Britain's 1992 Black Wednesday, which convinced even the more Europhile British elites to act with extreme caution when it came to European integration, especially monetary integration.[46]

The EMS crisis did much to convince Helmut Kohl to give way to the Euro, as the common currency came to be identified as the price to pay for German reunification. The Germans would still keep a currency controlled from Frankfurt, but the teams would not be entirely German, with French and Italian policymakers ensuring that the continent's monetary policy could not be systematically and exclusively serving German interests. With a central bank set with European objectives rather than national ones, one of the biggest flaws of the previous monetary systems was thus erased, but the price to be paid for the less competitive countries was very heavy: as British diplomat Paul Lever recalls,

> once locked in a single currency, the other Eurozone members no longer had the ability to enhance their competitiveness through the devaluation of their national currency. They could only survive and prosper by increasing the efficiency of their enterprises and/or by reducing their wage costs. Unsurprisingly this has been monumentally difficult for some of them.[47]

In fact, and not unsurprisingly considering their monetary history, the Germans had posed conditions to the other countries for a single currency. Public deficits were to be limited to 3% and public debt to 60%. In many ways, Germany was inviting other countries to follow its virtuous path to economic well-being. But by doing so, Southern European countries were losing not only their monetary sovereignty but also their budgetary sovereignty – indeed, heavy constraints were placed on budgets and structural adjustments proved very difficult in Italy, Spain, Greece and, indeed, France. The 1990s austerity measures had a social cost difficult to swallow for many, and public unrest often made the reforms themselves difficult – France all but abandoned its pensions reform after two months of a well-followed general strike in the public sector in 1995. But even when reform was made, it could never be enough: debts had to be repaid, and those were included in the cap on public debt; meanwhile, the Southern Europeans had to catch up with a locomotive that was already at full speed and would not wait for them. Germany remained much more competitive than the other countries, special thanks to the relative weakness of the Euro compared to the Deutsche Mark. In the words of Hans Kundani,

Germany said it wanted to see deficit countries in Europe to become more competitive, but it did not accept that, as a corollary of this, Germany must itself become less competitive. At the same time, Germany could not abandon the Euro altogether because a stronger German or even northern European currency would instantly make German exports less competitive everywhere."[48]

The efforts made by the French, Italian or Spanish were, therefore, never enough, and few solutions remained at their disposal to stay within the limits of the fiscal compact: one of them was to cook the books (with the tacit approval of the European partners) and another was to temporarily ignore them, which the Germans and French agreed to do in 2003 as their numbers came off the marks; yet another was to impose austerity for long periods of time, hoping that the sacrifices of the day would finally put the country's finances afloat – they rarely did, for even when the accounts got better, the crisis of 2008 totally changed prognoses and budget previsions. Without budgetary or monetary solutions, states in difficulty just had to hope for the best, and that did not prove enough for a number of them, since the European Central Bank (ECB) could neither lend as a last resort nor play on interest rates to promote growth or fight unemployment. Former World Bank economist Ashoka Mody has described the situation remarkably well, and the fact that his Eurosceptic view is relayed here by a self-confessed federalist says a lot about the nature of the problem:

> The Maastricht contract [of 3% deficits and 60% public debts] essentially said that if a member country had a heart attack, it would receive no emergency care; it would rely for recovery on the equivalent of a regimen of diet and exercise. The supposed stability of the entire structure rested on this one threat that a country would receive no or only token assistance if it got itself into trouble. This threat was expected to induce good behavior and thus prevent the heart attack from occurring in the first place. But even with the best of intentions, human beings do have heart attacks, and countries do fall on bad times.[49]

The rules were in fact so untenable that as soon as the new official currency was officially introduced, they were ignored. Back in the early 2000s, everyone knew that in the current circumstances, Greece's deficits did not allow it to join the Euro. But Brussels, Berlin and Paris decided to turn a blind eye and banks continued to lend the money so that Greece would join the single currency. There were political reasons for this, and they could have been forgiven had the 2010 crisis not focused on Greece. But perhaps even more importantly, in 2003, France and Germany broke the very rules that they had imposed and decided to ignore the 3% deficit rule as they tried to restructure their economies. As Guy Verhofstadt, Prime Minister of Belgium at the time, recalls, "for purely political reasons, all governments chose to turn a blind eye." Of course, this gave an incentive to other economies in difficulty to politely ignore the rules: "since France and Germany had been trampling on the Stability Pact in 2003, why should anyone make such a fuss in the case of Greece or Italy?"⁵⁰ Europeans were going to pay dearly for these contradictions after 2008. When the crisis hit, it would be easy for everyone to accuse the other of not having played fair: the Greeks, for "cooking the books" and also the French and Germans, who had set the bad example and encouraged their banks to invest heavily in Southern Europe, ignoring, on purpose, the risks of insolvency.

The Great Recession didn't hit the Europeans as immediately as it did the Americans, which gave German and French leaders an occasion to criticize "Anglo-Saxon greed" and brag about the superiority of the Rhenian capitalist model. But it was, in fact, a Transatlantic crisis, and when Europeans ended up in the eye of the storm, it was already too late: to quote economic historian Adam Tooze the crisis was

> not merely American but global and, above all North Atlantic in its genesis. And in a contentious and problematic way, it had the effect of recentering the world financial economy on the United States [and not on Europe,] as the only state capable of meeting the challenge it posed.⁵¹

This is now obviously easier to understand with hindsight, but it was far from evident in the period 2008–2010. Hans Kundani has summarized the mood in Berlin thus:

> above all, Germans saw the crisis as one that had been caused by others [i.e. greedy Americans and lazy Greeks]. Even though Germany had been the first to break the terms of the [Stability and Growth Pact] in 2003, they saw the crisis as one caused by the fiscal irresponsibility of other countries. They did not recognize the role that German banks had played in irresponsible lending to countries such as Greece during the boom – at the end of June 2009 Greece owed German banks €38.6 billion.⁵²

The Greek crisis of 2010–2015 had actually two faces: the one that we all heard about is the financial bankruptcy of the Greek state, which had borrowed too much, notably to keep its own banks afloat and needed to reform its public finances. But even if Greece (and many other countries in the South) had borrowed too much, it was not the only culprit, as the providers of easy money in the years prior to 2008 were first and foremost Northern European banks.⁵³ In the early stages of the crisis, as Lehman-like revelations exploded to the faces of governments, political leaders did pretty much like everyone who could and bailed out their banks, using the occasion to restructure a banking sector that had failed everywhere in the Transatlantic World. But the side effect of this was to make governments' debts explode all around Europe – and those governments most exposed were (mostly) in Southern Europe. As the crisis hit the real economy, pressure built on all governments to start austerity measures that would depress the economy in the short term but hopefully provide healthy bases for a long-term restart. And while pressure was building everywhere, countries in the North and East opted for national solutions: it was hard enough to sell austerity to national populations but way too risky to ask compatriots to tighten their belts and help other Eurozone countries. The French and German governments thus decided that Southern Europeans would have to pay a dear price of "their" exuberance – so that they or their banks would not have to pay that price in full. In other words, instead of thinking about the crisis at the European level and resolving it accordingly, as the United States had done in 2008, Europeans actually turned in on national solutions, thereby refusing to follow the budgetary logic implied by a single currency: either Member-States were individually responsible for their debts and could therefore file for bankruptcy (which would have consequences for the valuation of the currency and therefore for all the Member-States) or a federal State was to guarantee the solvency of all Member-States (as has been the case in the United States since the 1930s), which, in turn, meant that there would be a price to pay collectively to avoid the bankruptcy of one country.

Faced with a similar situation in 2008, the United States bailed out the banks that had to be saved, and even if states like Florida and California were in for a rough ride, they knew that they could count on federal support. The federal government of course had to pay the price, including politically, since both Occupy Wall Street (against the banks) and Tea Party (against the federal government) started with the bailout programs. But the results were indisputable: in the years following the crisis, the American economy recovered much more quickly, while the Eurozone fell into a trap of stagnation from which it still had not escaped by the time the coronavirus hit, despite a late monetary stimulus in 2015–2016.[54] Without budgetary or monetary instruments, European governments had no choice but to find resources by exerting sometimes extreme downward pressure on wages and employment, which in turn depressed output and European productivity in the long term, particularly in Southern Europe.[55]

Hard austerity measures not only had effects on growth in Europe as a whole but also threatened the cohesion of the European Union: in fact, some countries had been able to tighten their belts (or rather were forced to, as they did not get any assistance from anyone, their economies being less financially linked with Western Europe). This was notably the case in the Baltic States, where austerity was brief but particularly severe. In these countries, life had been hard enough, and it was out of the question to make the slightest sacrifice for countries that were actually richer: Iveta Radičová's coalition government in Slovakia fell in October 2011 over the Greek bailout, and the parties that had been part of the coalition suffered a historic defeat in the following early elections of March 2012.

The message was clear: European solidarity was a myth, and Member-States were pretty much on their own. As a member of the European Commission recalled at the time: "no German or Estonian is going to accept Brussels spending *his* money to rescue a failed Greek bank."[56] Popular hostility did not need much encouragement, but it did receive much from Northern European tabloids, especially German and British, who railed against the lazy, lying Southerners.[57] Germany's *Bild* went as far as to suggest to the Greeks that they sell their islands (and their Acropolis) to bail out their coffers[58] – which may have been funny to some modern Germans but was much less so to their elders when, 90 years earlier, the French had suggested Weimar Germany to cede the Rhineland, occupying it in the process, so that it could pay its war reparations – European nations' memories can be both selective and short-sighted.

In the South though, humiliation was the lesser of the problems, as populations had to deal with massive financial loss and impoverishment. True, a phase of "restructuring" had become unavoidable after the excesses of the 2000s, but the effects could somehow have been softened with an adequate fiscal policy and financial help from Northern Europe. But in the end, there was no other choice than harsh austerity measures. Official unemployment figures in Spain ran as high as 25% in 2014, with half of under-35's out of jobs. For their parts, Greeks households lost a third of their income between 2007 and 2013, with extreme poverty rates skyrocketing.[59] Italy also lost out: as Ashoka Mody points out, "in 2007, the average German had a 10 percent higher income than the average Italian; in 2014, the gap had increased to more than 30 percent [while] the Italian economy fell into a near-perpetual recession."[60] Countries that had been some of the most pro-European members of the EU since their accession started to entertain second thoughts: Greece saw an early rise in the left-Eurosceptic SYRIZA and the neo-Nazi Golden Dawn, Italy saw support for the Union plummet as the anti-system parties Lega and the Five Star Movement rose in the polls,[61] and even Spain saw parties critical of the EU emerge during the 2010s with Vox and Podemos. While left- and right-populist movements rose in Southern Europe, in Northern Europe it was right-wing populist parties that used popular hostility to support for Greece, combined with anti-migrant rhetoric to make gains in the political debate.

To be fair to Europeans, it is true that a backlash of resentment was probably unavoidable after the debacle of 2008. In the much more homogenous environment of the United States, the rather generous response of the US government also led to protest movements on both left and right which in turn led to the polarization of the American electorate. But while the United States faced particularly strong challenges and divisions, the foundations of its union were much stronger than Europe's, and talks of sawing off New England, California or Texas usually never go much further away than drunks' discussion in bars. Yet this is precisely what almost happened during the Euro-crisis, when resentment on both sides reached such a peak after the election of Alexis Tsipras that Greece was almost excluded from the Eurozone, which would undoubtedly have had a domino effect on the single currency, perhaps the entire European Union. The catastrophe was averted at the last minute, but resentment over financial situations still remains very strong between Northern and Southern Europe; indeed, tensions ran high again very quickly in the spring of 2020 when the EU in general (but particularly the South) faced another economic meltdown – with very emotional clashes between Italian and Dutch officials in Council Meetings.[62] Even though the right decisions were made this time, the resentment is here to stay, and it might turn again into full detestation if the result of the European rescue package fails to deliver the expected recovery: in this case, it would not take long to see Northern Europeans asking for their money back and Southern Europeans bringing back their demonstration posters depicting a German chancellor with a Hitler-style mustache. The economic crisis has definitely been a test for European unity, and the fact is that we do not know at this stage whether the European Union has passed it: if much depends on the success of the EU Recovery Fund, the outpour of nationalism in North and South has produced gaps that will be very difficult to bridge in the next few years.

Guess who's back?

As they entered a new economic cycle in 2008, Europeans were still living in the myth of the *End of History*, and war seemed like a distant concern to them, something that would happen literally overseas, not in their neighborhood. But at the very moment, their economic fortunes started to change, war also got closer – first as an imperceptible, background noise, before moving dangerously to Europe's borders and, in many ways, beyond them.

After the wars in ex-Yugoslavia, European elites had come to see that time had really come for perpetual peace on the whole European continent. With the extension of the EU and NATO to the East and prospects for membership in the Western Balkans and further afield in Ukraine, Moldova and Georgia. Europeans may have been forgiven at the time for indulging in over-optimism. But if any illusions had remained in 2008, they should already have been swept away by Russia's invasion of Georgia. With the United States turning back to "nation-building at home," as Barack Obama put it at the time, and Russia's state budget over-inflated, thanks to very high commodity prices, the periphery of NATO and the European Union found itself once again vulnerable. To use Robert Kagan's metaphor, the jungle of international relations was now growing back, and it hit first the marches of Europe,[63] getting closer and closer as the 2010s developed.

Georgia was first on the list: in the summer of 2008, Russia intervened militarily to make sure that the separatist territories of Abkhazia and South Ossetia would stay away from Tbilisi's control. The attack had been carefully planned and had the effect of convincing most Western European countries that they should refuse any further initiative to open NATO's doors to Georgia, Ukraine or Moldova – all territories with separatist movements directly linked to Moscow.[64] Russia, whose military budgets had benefited from the oil bonanza of the 2010s, had modernized its army and military doctrine, and Vladimir Putin had clearly embarked on a project to restore at least parts of the old Russian/Soviet empire, this time under the umbrella of a "Eurasian Community," whose geographical contours furiously resembled those of the former empire. What many Europeans failed to understand was that part of this "near abroad" also comprised territories of now members of NATO and the EU, Lithuania, Latvia, and Estonia, the latter two hosting sizeable Russian-speaking.

Not that the Russians had hidden their intentions: in 2005, Vladimir Putin had publicly described the fall of the Soviet Union as "the greatest geopolitical catastrophe of the 20th century,"[65] and it was now clear that an extended European Union was considered as a geopolitical rival in Moscow – something that elites in Berlin, Brussels and Paris somehow found difficult to comprehend. Russia's war in Georgia led to a barely concealed annexation of both Abkhazia and South Ossetia and gave the Russian army an opportunity to test and draw lessons from its new playbook, which already included the innovative use of hybrid warfare – Westerners would be particularly exposed in the following years.

For Moscow, Georgia was not an end itself. The real prize was Ukraine, and the Kremlin put much of its attention on getting Kyiv to fall back in line, after dangerously drifting away from Moscow's orbit after the Orange Revolution. Kyiv was at the heart of the Eurasian project, which was itself thought of as a way to prevent liaison between the EU and China to take place without Moscow's intermediary.[66] Vladimir Putin did not spare any efforts to achieve his objectives, from the infiltration of the Ukrainian State by agents of various Russian secret services to the use of geo-economic tools,[67] and of course direct assistance to local politicians more interested in filling their pockets than in Ukraine's national interest. The Kremlin got terribly close to achieving its objectives, but despite all these efforts, Kyiv did not enter the Kremlin's sphere of influence. Summoned by both sides to choose a camp by opting either for association with the European Union or for integration with Russia in the Eurasian Union, the Ukrainians got rid of a cumbersome and corrupt leader and clearly opted for Western strategic alignment. The blow was huge for the Kremlin, as Vladimir Putin actually agreed with Zbigniew Brzezinski that "without Ukraine, Russia ceases to be an empire, but with Ukraine suborned and then subordinated, Russia automatically becomes an empire."[68] A battle had been lost, but the war was not over. It actually just started.

The annexation of Crimea had been prepared for a long time and the speed of Russian troops deployment on the peninsula, using hybrid warfare and undercover special forces, took all the other players – Ukrainians, Americans and Europeans – by surprise. The success was so one-sided that the Kremlin decided to go further and embarked on a much more ambitious, project: to annex the entire South and East of Ukraine, which Russian propaganda quickly renamed *Novorossiya*, the New Russia that Catherine the Great had conquered from the Turks in the eighteenth century. If successful, the project would have allowed Russia to control the entire northern shore of the Black Sea, consolidate its gain in Crimea and create a land link with Transnistria, another Russian separatist enclave in Moldova. However, the military operation had been much less prepared Crimea and the area much larger: in the end, despite local tragedies,[69] the Russians did not manage to turn Southern Ukraine into a battlefield, but they managed to gain a foothold in the Donbass, thanks to two proxies, the self-proclaimed republics of Luhansk and Donetsk.

Contrary to Moscow's expectations, the Ukrainian army had not melted down and it had re-organized very quickly, very often from the bottom-up, to counter Russian aggression. As the dreams of a *Novorossiya* evaporated, Moscow consolidated its gains in the Donbass and worked with its proxies to fight the Ukrainians for the control of the Donbass. The war started in 2014 is still ongoing. It has already cost the lives of at least 15,000 people (military and civilians), not counting the one and a half million internally displaced persons in Ukraine and the one million people who have left the country, notably to settle in Poland.[70] The war may have taken place in Europe's geographical borderlands, but it was soon to have consequences in the European Union: when Western Europeans demanded that Warsaw accept a quota of migrants in 2015, the then-liberal Polish government was itself facing a surge in immigration from Ukraine. The fact that this was totally ignored by Brussels, Paris and Berlin played a role in shifting public opinion from the civic platform to the populist-conservative Law and Justice party, which won the subsequent elections and durably changed power balances within the EU.

War was also getting closer to Europe from the South and Southeast. The economic crisis of 2008 had also hit the Maghreb and the Near East very hard, pushing populations to despair – and ultimately revolt. The Arab spring took the entire region (and the West) by surprise: In Tunis, Cairo, Damascus, Manama or Sana'a, the mobilization of urban, young and educated populations were threatening regimes that were thought to be stable, and the modernity of these connected young liberals in Tahrir Square or Bourguiba Avenue fueled the romanticism of Western reporters. What pundits did not see or predict was that, first, the regimes in place would fight back and (importantly) that rural populations, far from sharing the liberal ideals of the urban demonstrators, had actually joined forces with them to topple hated authoritarian regimes before voting conservative Muslim leaders in. It would soon transpire that the dreams of a modernized, democratic Mediterranean envisaged by some would turn out to be a mirage, as an Arab winter followed the Arab spring, with Libya and Syria descending into civil war – and creating opportunities which the so-called Islamic State in Iraq and Syria (ISIS) quickly exploited.

War's return in Europe's periphery was anything that anecdotal: it signaled that the "soft power" that Europeans thought sufficient to guarantee their security was weakening or at least losing in efficiency. The world was moving on from the liberal order and the inevitability of the end of history,[71] and Europe was completely unprepared for it. As war got closer from home the EU, Member-States soon discovered that war at one's borders could have consequences at home, providing opportunities for new crises and instabilities, this time inside the EU.

Dangerous paths

The migrant crisis of 2015 will probably be remembered as one of the most consequential moments of the decade in Europe. Its genesis lays in two distinct factors, one very long term and the other very immediate – both linked to the reappearance of war in Europe's neighborhood. The long-term factor is the demographic surplus currently developing in large parts of the Sahel and the Middle East, which has pushed many inhabitants of regions with finite resources to aspire to leave. Here, the question is not only demographic but also environmental: in 1961, Mali had about 4.5 million inhabitants and 19 million in 2012 – in other words, the population quadrupled in just 50 years. This exponential demographic growth has taken place in the backdrop of global warming, with an increase in droughts over the region and potentially disastrous consequences in the long term. In Pakistan, whose civilizational heartland is even more centered than the Sahel on one river basin, the Indus Valley is experiencing similar problems. As the fragile ecosystem of these regions continues to deteriorate, wars, dictatorships and violence become more likely, and people get an incentive to leave for good.[72] The destinations actually vary: major urban centers in the region are usually prime destinations but so are the Middle East's petro-monarchies, Southern Africa, Turkey and, for what is of immediate concern here, Europe. The European Union, with rich markets and a shortage of manpower in certain sectors, is an obvious destination. The 2015 migration crisis is therefore part of a very long-term problem that will probably see a very large number of nationals from the Sahel, Afghanistan or Pakistan to seek new opportunities in other parts of the world, as the environment in their immediate neighborhood has become too crowded.

The long-term nature of the migration crisis is a mystery for nobody, not least for the inhabitants of the islands (Lampedusa, Lesbos, etc.) that are in the frontlines of the European migration routes. But to become acute, the crisis needed a more immediate cause: the trigger was the war in Syria, which displaced about half of the country's population (about 12 million people). Many of these Syrians settled down in other areas of the country, but others decided to leave, mostly for neighboring countries (3.5 million found refuge in Turkey, and most of them are still there), sometimes for Europe – with the idea of not getting back. Further south, the civil war in Libya created a huge vacuum in the heart of North Africa and thus became a platform for many young Sahelian migrants to try and reach either the Balkan peninsula or the Italian boot. The result in 2015 was the arrival of more than a million migrants on European soil,[73] and the inflow, although less massive than in Turkey for example, had profound consequences on the psyche of Europeans, particularly in those areas that were threatened with de-population.

Nobody had anticipated the massive influx of people, and institutions found themselves in a position where they communicated to their public that they were in control, while it was clear they were not. The images of refugees on the road were certainly moving (or worrying) for Europeans, but they left the sentiment that nobody knew what to do. The countries of Northern Europe, which were usually the final destinations of the migrants, were soon overwhelmed. They were very quick to ask countries in the South and East – the ones who had been told to tighten their belts or die on their own just a few years earlier – to show solidarity. Needless to say, these calls were usually not well received. But Northern and Western Europeans had problems of their own at home, as parts of their own populations turned equally recalcitrant to taking more refugees in. The elites proved particularly insensitive to their own people's pleas, dismissing them as rants of xenophobia that didn't have their place in the public debates. In the words of Ivan Krastev, "the resistance of liberals to conceding any negative effects of migration has triggered the [...] reaction that is convulsing political life in democracies in so many places today."[74] As elites rejected any public debate on migration, discontent was channeled in other ways: populist parties had already started to rise, thanks to the social consequences of the economic crisis; the migration crisis provided them with more political oxygen, allowing them to take a completely different dimension. After all, immigration and borders had been their historic argument for years, sometimes decades before the crisis.

If national solidarity with migrants had its limits, then surely the solution was to Europeanize the problem, diffuse it by settling new arrivals under a quota system to different parts of the European Union and thus be able to better absorb the inevitable social shock. The solution may have looked good on paper, but coming from Brussels, Stockholm and Berlin, it looked like once again the Northern Europeans were trying to impose their will on the peripheries of Europe, asking them to show the very solidarity toward foreigners that they had refused to give to other Europeans.

British diplomat Paul Lever gave a detailed description of the events that led to the European quota crisis, and it is worth quoting him at length here:

> Most of the refugees came to Germany through Bavaria. The minister president there, Horst Seehofer, took the lead in demanding limits on the number of refugees. He argued that Germany should accept no more than 200,000 asylum seekers in any one year, and he overtly criticized the policy of the federal government. Angela Merkel's response was to demand that Germany's EU partners should shoulder more of the burden. The Commission duly came up with a proposal for a mandatory distribution of 120,000 refugees among the members of the Schengen zone. Under the decision-making procedures which apply to that part of EU Treaty the proposal could be adopted by a qualified majority vote.

Seeing little enthusiasm in Warsaw, Athens or Bucharest for this solution, Berlin then applied pressure on countries that resisted the quota policy – the stakes were high, since German public opinion had to be relieved from what was becoming a real problem. To get back to Lever's account,

The Commission, under German pressure, maintained its proposal and it was brought to a vote. The Polish government caved in and voted for it - with the lame explanation that it was going to happen anyway. But Hungary, the Czech Republic, Slovakia and Romania voted against. The German interior minister, Thomas de Maizière, expressed his satisfaction at the outcome. He went on to suggest that countries which failed to take their quotas on refugees should be denied access to EU structural funding on the grounds that the obligations of solidarity cut both ways.[75]

Not only was a German minister weaponizing structural funds on a purely political issue, but he was also crossing a "red line," basically challenging dissenting governments to not follow the rules – which politicians like Viktor Orbán were all too happy to indulge in. Defiance allowed them to win on all fronts: they could defy the EU's orders and in this way consolidate support at home; they had a perfect occasion to criticize the selfishness and double standards of North-Western Europeans, and of course they made much more difficult the implementation of sanctions against illiberal governments that would really infringe on fundamental values of the European Union like democracy and the rule of law, as it became easy for them to dismiss these threats as politically motivated. The victim in the process was Europe's cohesion, as the gap between the East and West of Europe but also more generally between the heart of Europe and its periphery grew wider.

Had the Europeans been lucky and no trouble ensued, tensions would have probably eased gradually, even more so as Germans, Swedes and especially Austrians took drastic steps in 2016 to cut the migration routes. But, instead, they flared up again as Western Europe experienced a wave of terrorist attacks in the period 2016–2017, all of them ordered by the Islamic State (ISIS) from their base in Syria and Iraq. Of course, the migrants who had arrived from war-torn regions in the Middle East and North Africa had nothing to do with ISIS, but geographic provenance trumped other considerations in the eyes of many, even more so as the integration of the new populations was not without issues, with cases of sexual assault, sometimes covered-up by authorities, multiplying in places like Germany or Sweden.[76]

There was indeed a link between the migration and the terrorist waves: the Islamic State had experienced a meteoric rise in 2014–2015, thanks to the complicity of former Iraqi Ba'ath Party officials and the Assad regime, which had opened the prisons at the beginning of the civil war to create chaos, releasing hundreds of jihadists. ISIS had used its conquered territory in the desert zone between Syria and Iraq to attract and recruit a significant number of young Europeans from very diverse backgrounds,[77] using innovative recruitment methods and making full use of social networks.[78] Although Europe was not the prime target of ISIS, the jihadists had understood that striking the West in its heart with spectacular attacks could allow them to meet two objectives: to demobilize public opinion in the West and ensure retreat from the main theater of war in the Middle East and to bring in new international recruits, as attacks in Europe allowed for global publicity on all major news channels.

ISIS strategists quickly understood that they could use the refugee flux to their own advantage if they could infiltrate a small number of their own into the caravans of migrants – those who could not be monitored adequately due to their numbers and the authorities' unpreparedness. Once inside the Schengen zone, they could join local networks, plan and execute terrorist attacks. The number of infiltrated combatants was extremely tiny but, in the mass of refugees at the time, they logically went unnoticed, especially since the internal intelligence services in Western Europe were already busy monitoring terrorists who had never left and were planning attacks on their own – for example, the Paris attacks on French newspaper *Charlie Hebdo* in January 2015.

The wave of terrorist attacks of 2015–2016 that hit Europe, and France in particular,[79] was a trauma for many Europeans: it briefly, but visibly, brought back scenes of war in the heart of the continent. Even more importantly, it strengthened the internal divisions within European societies, which were already experiencing polarizing discussions on Islam and its place in Western civilization. European countries turned out to be almost as divided on the subject from within as they were between themselves: populist activists in Central European countries did not miss a chance to express *schadenfreude* on social media at the sight of Paris, Nice, Berlin or Brussels being hit by terrorist attacks while citizens of Budapest or Warsaw could carry on their day-to-day work, and populist leaders around the continent could get back to their constituents with a moral victory over Brussels, Paris, Stockholm or Berlin elites who had gotten it "all wrong" after indulging in moralistic sermons for years. For Beppe Grillo or Viktor Orbán, it was now easy to answer to the Northern European elites that the Italians might be lazy and the Hungarians might be selfish racists, but at least they knew who they were, they knew where their roots were and they knew danger when they saw it and they could protect themselves against it, unlike the acculturated and cosmopolitan northerners who were sowing chaos across Europe. The divisions between Europeans were now obvious for everyone, and the Union was now approaching the danger zone where these divisions could have real long-term consequences.

One of these consequences was Brexit. This is not to say that the Brexit vote of 2016 was only caused by the immigration debate, but the migration crisis clearly played a major role. The Brexit referendum had been called by then-Prime Minister David Cameron for purely national reasons, to silence the Eurosceptic wing of his party at a time when the conservatives were facing a spectacular rise of Nigel Farage's United Kingdom Independence Party (UKIP). Its unexpected result, though, was as much the logical outcome of the dynamics we have just mentioned as a potentially consequential event for the security of the European continent.

This is not to say that there was no rationale for Brexit. Even though the electoral campaign more often than not verged on the irrational (as almost always in the case of referendums), there were many good reasons for perfectly decent people to vote for Brexit. Having said that, and even though Brexit did have its own long-term dynamic, the reality is that had it happened ten years earlier, the referendum would have most likely ushered in a decision to stay in the EU, as the Union's power of attraction trumped the appeal of the open sea and the cultural proximity with the Anglosphere.[80] But 2016 was probably the worst possible year to hold a referendum on the subject: the United Kingdom had gone through difficult times with harsh austerity policies accelerating the marginalization of a number of social groups (including the old British working class in the North of England); it faced difficult foreign policy choices as its courting of China had not brought as many benefits to the City as it had to the German Mittelstand. Finally, Britain had not digested the arrivals of large numbers of immigrants from Central and Eastern Europe, encouraged by the government during the 2000s.[81] In these circumstances, the crisis in the Eurozone and the sluggish growth of continental Europe (especially compared to North America, India and more generally to the Commonwealth countries) didn't give the Remainers much economic argument for staying in the Union. Nor did the migrant crisis of 2015, as the United Kingdom was one of the most sought destinations for many migrants, and Britons showed little eagerness to take more in. As the situation seemed to get out of hand in continental Europe, it was easy for Brexiteers to focus their campaign on the idea to "take back control," as continental Europeans seemed at this very moment to have lost it completely.

It would, of course, be unfair to blame the entirety of the Brexit debacle on the elites in Brussels and Berlin, and it is true that the long-term negligence of the British elites to "sell" the European Union, including during the Blair years, and poor campaigning on the part of the Remain camp played a major role. But the reality is that, at the time of the referendum, the European Union was not exactly covering itself with glory as it faced the Eurozone crisis and the migrant crisis. The decision to leave a ship that, viewed from Britain, looked like it was sinking, was all the more rational as the insularity of the United Kingdom and its cultural and (at least in the minds of Brexiteers) commercial links with countries like Australia, Canada, or even the United States and India gave power to the idea of leaving – following this rationale, Brexit was indeed Britain's Plan B.

The marriage between London and Brussels had always been one of convenience: Britain joined at a time in which it was weak on the world stage, with socioeconomic problems aplenty and influence in free-fall after losing its empire. After 30 years of mainly robust growth, Britons looked at the situation with a completely different outlook. What did the European Union have to offer Britain at the time of the referendum, particularly against the promise (which many Britons understood to be untrue from the beginning) of a return to imperial glory? With migrants coming in from all corners of the continent over the past decades, Europe had been assimilated with problems, a region where red tape and inflexible mentalities were harnessing growth, where migration was out of control and where Germany was reigning supreme – a prospect much more difficult to swallow for a country that had actually won the Second World War, although here again, British elites hesitations toward the European project and their inability to build stronger coalitions inside Europe did help lower the prospects of British influence in Europe. Seen in this light and with the benefit of hindsight, the British decision to leave the European Union seems not only much more logical – and should be read as a failure of British elites who believed in Europe but never seriously tried to sell it to their citizens (Tony Blair comes to mind), but also as a failure for the European Union.

Whatever the responsibilities, Brexit is not an inconsequential event. Indeed, the departure of Europe's second-largest economy[82] is depriving the European Union of significant long-term funding – despite its famed rebate, the United Kingdom contributed more than 10 billion Euros to the EU budget. Perhaps as importantly, it has lost a leading global financial center that will be impossible to recreate on the continent, even if some international banks have left London to set up operations in Frankfurt, Paris, Warsaw or Amsterdam. Perhaps even worse, Britain's departure completely changes the balance of powers on the continent, and it is not certain that either Germany or countries like France, Italy or Poland will have enough time to adapt and find a new equilibrium. Even though some might see in Brexit an opportunity to finally move forward toward a federal Europe, for which London was always hostile, it was perhaps preferable to have them "inside the tent pissing out, rather than outside to pissing in," as Lyndon Johnson said in 1971 to justify John Edgar Hoover's continued presence in the FBI. The reality is, and we already have seen hints of that over the past few years, now that Britain has left the Union, it has automatically become an "economic competitor" for the EU and particularly for Germany, as Angela Merkel recognized herself in November 2019.[83]

Brexit has the potential to become a geopolitical catastrophe for Europe (and Britain itself) over the long term, as it cuts Europe's economic heart, centered on the North Sea, in two. Now that London is no longer part of the European project, the potential for rivalry with the continent makes Britain a potential suspect for continentals if no way is found to cultivate a good relationship between the two – this will be especially difficult if European (and British) economies do not find a stable path back to growth and stability in the post-COVID-19 world. The result of a rivalry between Britain and the European Union would probably mean closed markets for Britain and costly isolation, but it would also prove hard to digest for continental Europeans: in addition to Russia, which considers itself as a rival to the European Union, Europeans would also feel a threat on their Western flank, and it will be even more worrisome if it is perceived to be coming not only from the United Kingdom but from the whole Anglosphere. This would not be a position dissimilar to that which Germany experienced after 1870, which carried tragic consequences both for Britain and for the rest of Europe.

Of course, we have not reached that stage yet, but the mere fact that it has become logically conceivable says a lot about Europe's recent downward trajectory. The continent is now threatened by the specter of an American withdrawal, a poorly controlled (and barely assumed) German semi-hegemony that has brought a number of imbalances inside the European Union, Russian revanchism and increasingly salient internal divisions, among others. Of course, none of these factors automatically and immediately leads to war, but they now make it conceivable. as Robert Kagan recalls, the Americans and Europeans of the 1930s "learned, and we have now forgotten, that when things start to go wrong, they can go wrong very quickly, that once a world order breaks down, the worst qualities of humanity emerge from under the rocks and run wild."[84]

★ ★ ★

Human beings can adapt to all sorts of the situation – including the worst ones. Paradoxically, they also tend to take comfort for granted. As luxury becomes a habit and then a God-given right, the effort made to obtain is quickly forgotten, and it is then taken for granted. In many ways, Europeans are treating peace this way. The (false) idea that the continent was living the end of history reinforced Europeans in the conviction that war had become unnatural on their continent. This is itself surprising, for war has never been very far from Europe, even after the end of the Cold War: In the 1990s, it tore Yugoslavia and Moldova apart; in 2008, a young European state, Georgia, was invaded by Russia – to which Europeans mostly turned a blind eye: Tbilisi was too far away. Six years later, in 2014, it was Ukraine's turn to be invaded, and this time Europeans took notice. Finally, the wave of terrorist attacks of 2015–2016 finally showed that the streets of Paris, Brussels or Berlin could become again a battlefield, although for a very brief period. In the aftermath of the attacks – as during the coronavirus pandemic – European elites were quick to declare that they were "at war," but were they themselves convinced that they were? The use of rhetorical artifice has long plagued European political discourse, and it is not clear whether European governments have really understood the reality of the situation – and its implications.

For in reality war never left the Europeans. Everything in Europe, its geography, its culture or its history, favors man's warlike instincts in a way that is unique in the world – indeed, it was through warfare that Europeans acquired the knowledge and strategies that enabled them to dominate the world between the eighteenth and nineteenth centuries. But it was precisely the unbridled competition between the European powers, the source of so many wars, that led them to commit the long suicide that began in 1914 and, in many respects, did not truly end until 1945. Europe then emerged destroyed and ruined – both morally and financially – from this cycle of wars, and if peace could be given a chance, it was because of very special circumstances, including the vivid memory of Europe's destruction through war, the settlement of the German question and the *Pax Americana*, which initially covered Western Europe and gradually extended to almost the entire continent between 1989 and 2008. These elements, in turn, allowed visionaries such as Jean Monnet, Robert Schuman, Konrad Adenauer,

Paul-Henri Spaak and others to begin a process of an economic union that was to become a political union in the early 1990s.

History could have ended there. But Europeans discovered at their own expense during the 2010s that it did not have an end. Even if we cannot explain all the events that marked the decade with the 2008 financial crisis, it did mark a turning point in the history of Europe, as it coincided with a spectacular and rapid deterioration of the economic, social and security situation around the continent, to the extent that war became almost a common occurrence on its marches. Adding to that the fading memory of the Second World War with the passing of the last living veterans, the internal soul-searching currently going on in the United States, which raises doubts inside and outside Europe about the persistence of the *Pax Americana*, the return of the German question due to its geo-economic semi-hegemony and the prospects for peace and prosperity in Europe no longer look that good. Even more so as the continent's divisions have seemed to widen dangerously within the past decade: not only between North and South, East and West but also with bitter social- and identity-based divisions, which will be the subject of our next chapter.

Notes

1 See Viktor Meyer, *Yugoslavia – A History of its Demise*, London: Routledge, 1999.
2 These 1990s post-Soviet wars usually confronted successor states with separatist groups. That was the case for Transnistria in Moldova (1992), for Abkhazia and South Ossetia in Georgia (1992), for Nagorno-Karabakh between Armenia and Azerbaijan (1988–1994, the conflict was reactivated in 2020) and for Chechnya in Russia (1994 and 1999). Other conflicts led to tensions without getting to war. See James Hughes, Gwedonlyn Sasse et al., *Ethnicity and Territory in the Former Soviet Union: Regions in Conflict*, London: Frank Cass, 2002.
3 Francis Fukuyama, *The End of History and the Last Man*, New York: Free Press, 1992.
4 President George H. W. Bush's Mainz speech of May 31, 1989, became a classic of presidential foreign policy speeches. It is available at website of the US Embassy in Germany, among others: https://usa.usembassy.de/etexts/ga6-890531.htm
5 The American disinterest in Yugoslavia was almost total until the first reports of Iranian jihadists participation in the Bosnian conflict. Then Secretary of State James Baker famously declared "we don't have a dog in this fight," although the quote originates from US Ambassador to Yugoslavia Warren Zimmermann. See Niall Mulchinok, *NATO and the Western Balkans: From Neutral Spectator to Proactive Peace Maker*, London: Palgrave MacMillan, 2017, p.15.
6 Belgian Prime Minister during the 2000s, Guy Verhofstadt, summed up not only the impotence of the Europeans but also their vanity. Recalling the aftermath of the Kosovo crisis, he remembers that "once the dirty work was done by the Americans, we hastened to give Pristina a ton of good advice and an army of 4 X 4 vehicles. They called it soft power in Brussels and elsewhere. Cowardice' seems a more appropriate term to me." Guy Verhofstadt, *Le mal européen*, Brussels: Marque belge, 2016, p.57.
7 Benjamin Haddad, *Le paradis perdu: L'Amérique de Trump et la fin des illusions européennes*, Paris: Grasset, 2018, p.28.
8 Robert Kagan, *The Jungle Grows Back: America and Our Imperiled World,* New York: Alfred A. Kopf, 2018, p.84.
9 Lawrence Freedman summarized this position of ultra-dominance during the period 1991–2007: "The West now enjoyed a remarkable military preponderance, with the

United States alone spending as much on its armed forces as the rest of the world combined. It was in a position to act if it chose to do so." Lawrence Freedman, *The Future of War: A History*, New York: Public Affairs, 2017, p.166.
10 https://newrepublic.com/article/117859/superpowers-dont-get-retire
11 Charles Kupchan, *Isolationism: A History of America's Efforts to Shield Itself from the World*, New York: Oxford University Press, 2020.
12 Benjamin Haddad, *Le paradis perdu: L'Amérique de Trump et la fin des illusions européennes*, Paris: Grasset, 2019, p.46.
13 Robert Kagan, *The Jungle Grows Back: America and Our Imperiled World,* New York: Alfred A. Kopf, 2018, p.100.
14 Benjamin Haddad, *Le paradis perdu: L'Amérique de Trump et la fin des illusions européennes*, Paris: Grasset, 2019, p.26.
15 Charles Kupchan, *Isolationism: A History of America's Efforts to Shield Itself from the World*, New York: Oxford University Press, 2020, p.364.
16 Ibid., p.348.
17 See Jan Techau, *The Politics of 2 Percent: NATO and the Security Vacuum in Europe*, Carnegie Center, September 2, 2015, available online: https://carnegieeurope.eu/2015/09/02/politics-of-2-percent-nato-and-security-vacuum-in-europe-pub-61139
18 Benjamin Haddad, *Le paradis perdu: L'Amérique de Trump et la fin des illusions européennes*, Paris: Grasset, 2019, p.187.
19 See Bruno Maçães, *History has Begun: The Birth of a New America*, London: Hurst, 2020.
20 https://www.dw.com/en/berlin-gets-unwanted-ronald-reagan-statue/a-51147688
21 Benjamin Haddad, *Le paradis perdu: L'Amérique de Trump et la fin des illusions européennes*, Paris: Grasset, 2019, p.184.
22 Hans Kundnani, *The Paradox of German Power*, Oxford: Oxford University Press, 2015, p.6.
23 Ibid., p.39.
24 Paul Lever, *Berlin Rules: Europe and the German Way*, Londres: Tauris, 2017, p.11.
25 Ibid., p.183.
26 Each party represented in the Bundestag is allowed to set up not only a foundation (Stiftung in German) with a think tank mission but also an international wing, with a budget indexed to its results in the federal elections. In the end, all parties choose to do (on the far-right, the *Alternativ für Deutschland* has a Desiderius Erasmus Foundation since 2017, while on the far-left *Die Linke* also has a Rosa Luxemburg Stiftung). The largest, the Konrad Adenauer Stiftung (or KAS), had a budget of 120 million Euros in 2009. In comparison, the annual budget of the American International Republican Institute at the same time was "only" $78 million.
27 Personal experience of the author.
28 https://www.economist.com/special/1999/06/03/the-sick-man-of-the-euro
29 Hans Kundnani, *The Paradox of German Power*, Oxford: Oxford University Press, 2015, p.76.
30 Source: World Bank: http://datatopics.worldbank.org/world-development-indicators/
31 The numbers date from 2008. Source: World Bank: http://datatopics.worldbank.org/world-development-indicators/
32 Cited in dans Paul Lever, *Berlin Rules: Europe and the German Way*, Londres: IB Tauris, 2017, p.21.
33 Schmidt's speech to the SPD Congress in Berlin on December 4, 2011, is available online on SPD's website: https://www.spd.de/fileadmin/Dokumente/Beschluesse/Bundesparteitag/2011_bpt_berlin_protokoll.pdf; an English translation is also available on the website of the Friedrich Ebert Stiftung: https://library.fes.de/pdf-files/id/ipa/08888.pdf

34 Ivan Krastev and Stephen Holmes made these "politics of imitation" the center of their book on the current crisis of international Western liberal democracy. See Ivan Krastev and Stephen Holmes, *The Light that Failed: A Reckoning*, London: Allen Lane, 2019.
35 Hans Kundnani, *The Paradox of German Power*, Oxford: Oxford University Press, 2015, p.75.
36 https://www.economist.com/europe/2003/02/27/frosty-for-the-french
37 https://emerging-europe.com/news/new-statistics-confirm-romanias-demographic-catastrophe/
38 Ivan Krastev, *After Europe*, Philadelphia: University of Pennsylvania Press, 2017, p.53.
39 Ibid., p.51
40 See for example, in the case of France, Christophe Guiluy, *La France périphérique: Comment on a sacrifié les classes populaires*, Paris: Flammarion, 2014.
41 National history books, even in the English language, often give a good guidance of the main idea that transpires between interpretation of national history. Among them, the words "struggle," "existence" and "survival" most often trump more glorious ones. See for example Stanislav J. Kirschbaum, *Slovakia: The Struggle for Survival* (2nd edition), New York: St. Martin's Press, 2016; Andrew Wilson, *The Ukrainians: Unexpected Nation* (2nd edition), New Haven: Yale University Press, 2002, etc.
42 Adam Tooze, *Crashed: How a Decade of Financial Crises Changed the World*, Londres: Penguin Random House, p.233.
43 Ibid., pp.227–238.
44 See for example the polling conducted by IRI and Fondapol on 65 democracies in the world – Dominique Reynié et al., *Democracies under Pressure: A Global Survey*, Paris: Fondapol, 2019, pp.144–147. Also available online: http://www.fondapol.org/wp-content/uploads/2019/06/DOSSIER_FICHES-THEMES_GB_2019_06_18_w-derni%C3%A8reversion.pdf
45 Ivan Krastev & Stephem Holmes, *The Light that Failed: A Reckoning*, London: Allen Lane, 2019.
46 Ashoka Mody, *Eurotragedy: A Drama in Nine Acts*, Oxford: Oxford University Press, 2018.
47 Paul Lever, *Berlin Rules: Europe and the German Way*, Londres: IB Tauris, 2017, p.60.
48 Hans Kundani, *The Paradox of German Power*, Oxford: Oxford University Press, p.95.
49 Ashoka Mody, *Eurotragedy: A Drama in Nine Acts*, Oxford: Oxford University Press, 2018, pp.92–93.
50 Guy Verhofstadt, *Le Mal Européen*, Brussels: Marque belge, 2016, p.284.
51 Adam Tooze, *Crashed: How a Decade of Financial Crises Changed the World*, Londres: Penguin Random House, pp.5–6.
52 Hans Kundani, *The Paradox of German Power*, Oxford: Oxford University Press, 2015, p.90.
53 Ashoka Mody, *Eurotragedy: A Drama in Nine Acts*, Oxford: Oxford University Press, 2018, p.173.
54 Over the period 2008–2016, hardly a memorable time for American prosperity, US GDP average annual growth was at 2.1%, with significant improvements toward the end of the period. The EU's numbers were almost half, with 1.2% average annual growth. See Graham Allison, *Destined for War: Can America and China Escape Thucydides's Trap*, New York: Mariner, 2018, p.12.
55 See Ashoka Mody, *Eurotragedy: A Drama in Nine Acts*, Oxford: Oxford University Press, 2018, p.127 et p.176.
56 Quoted in Ibid., p.217. Emphasis added.
57 See Ibid., p.247.
58 *Bild*, October 27, 2010, p.1.
59 See Donatella Della Porta, Joseba Fernández, Hara Kouki, and Lorenzo Mosca, *Movement Parties against Austerity*, Cambridge: Polity, 2017, pp.36, 45.

60 Ashoka Mody, *Eurotragedy: A Drama in Nine Acts*, Oxford: Oxford University Press, 2018, p.339.
61 https://www.politico.eu/article/italy-euroskeptic-surge-migration-crisis-eu/
62 https://www.politico.eu/article/virtual-summit-real-acrimony-eu-leaders-clash-over-corona-bonds/
63 See Robert Kagan, *The Jungle Grows Back: America and Our Imperiled World*, New York: Alfred A. Kopf, 2018.
64 A few months earlier, at the Bucharest Summit, NATO had submitted a very prudent declaration congratulating Georgia and Ukraine for their "aspirations for membership" in the alliance. Despite US insistence, France and Germany made sure there would be no mention of any path for membership. Even this careful wording was dropped after 2008. https://www.nato.int/cps/fr/natohq/official_texts_8443.htm?selectedLocale=en
65 https://www.independent.co.uk/news/world/europe/putin-collapse-of-the-soviet-union-was-catastrophe-of-the-century-521064.html
66 Adam Tooze, *Crashed: How a Decade of Financial Crises Changed the World*, London: Penguin Random House, 2018, pp.485–509.
67 Robert D. Blackwill and Jennifer M. Harris, *War by Other Means: Geoeconomics and Statecraft*, Cambridge, MA: Harvard University Press, 2016, p.21.
68 Zbigniew Brzezinski deserves to be quoted (once again), as he reminded us that "without Ukraine, Russia ceases to be an empire, but with Ukraine suborned and then subordinated, Russia automatically becomes an empire" Zbigniew Brzezinski, "The Premature Partnership," *Foreign Affairs*, Vol. 72, No. 2, March-April 1994, p.80.
69 https://www.bbc.com/news/av/world-europe-27261010
70 Source: UNHCR – https://www.unrefugees.org/emergencies/ukraine/#:~:text=More%20than%20three%20years%20of,anything%20in%20search%20of%20safety
71 Timothy Snyder opposes this inevitability conundrum with the concept of eternity that autocrats like Vladimir Putin have used to legitimize their power. Timothy Snyder, *The Road to Unfreedom: Russia, Europe, America*, London: Penguin, 2018.
72 Stephen Smith, *The Scramble for Europe: Young Africa on its Way to the Old Continent*, Cambridge: Polity Press, 2019 (subsequent quotes will point to the original, French-language edition).
73 The numbers come from UNHCR. See https://www.reuters.com/article/us-europe-migrants-idUSKBN0U50WI20151222
74 Ivan Krastev, *After Europe*, Philadelphia: University of Pennsylvania Press, p.50.
75 Paul Lever, *Berlin Rules: Europe and the German Way*, Londres: IB Tauris, 2017, pp.198–199.
76 The case of the 2015 New Year's Eve sexual assault wave is probably the most famous, but it was not the only one. See https://www.independent.co.uk/news/world/europe/german-police-search-1-000-men-after-mass-sexual-assault-cologne-a6797126.html for a more detailed account on the most spectacular wave in Cologne or https://www.france24.com/en/20160112-swedish-police-covered-music-festival-sex-assault-allegations for Sweden.
77 See David Thomson, *Les Revenants: Ils étaient partis faire le jihad, ils sont de retour en France*, Paris: Points, 2018.
78 David Patrikarakos, *War in 140 Characters: How Social Media is Reshaping Conflict in the Twenty-First Century*, New York: Basic Books, 2017, pp.202–229.
79 See Dominique Reynié et al., *Islamist Terrorist Attacks in the World*, Fondapol, November 2019, http://www.fondapol.org/wp-content/uploads/2019/11/ENQUETE-TERRORISME_GB_2019-11-18versionfinale.pdf
80 See Michael Kenny and Nick Pearce, *Shadows of Empire: The Anglosphere in British Politics*, Cambridge: Polity, 2018.
81 See Andrew Adonis et al., *Half In Half Out: Prime Ministers on Europe*, London: Biteback Publishing, 2018, pp.234–235.

82 http://datatopics.worldbank.org/world-development-indicators/
83 https://www.politico.eu/article/angela-merkel-sees-post-brexit-uk-as-potential-competitor-to-eu-emmanuel-macron/
84 Robert Kagan, *The Jungle Grows Back: America and Our Imperiled World*, New York: Alfred A. Kopf, 2018, p.24.

Bibliography

Adonis, Andrew et al., *Half In Half Out: Prime Ministers on Europe*, London: Biteback Publishing, 2018.
Allison, Graham, *Destined for War: Can America and China Escape Thucydides's Trap*, New York: Mariner, 2018.
Blackwill, Robert D., and Harris, Jennifer M., *War by Other Means: Geoeconomics and Statecraft*, Cambridge, MA: Harvard University Press, 2016.
Brzezinski, Zbigniew, "The Premature Partnership," *Foreign Affairs*, Vol. 72, No. 2, March–April 1994.
Della Porta, Donatella, Fernández, Joseba, Kouki, Hara, and Mosca, Lorenzo, *Movement Parties against Austerity*, Cambridge: Polity, 2017.
Freedman, Lawrence, *The Future of War: A History*, New York: Public Affairs, 2017.
Fukuyama, Francis, *The End of History and the Last Man*, New York: Free Press, 1992.
Guiluy, Christophe, *La France périphérique: Comment on a sacrifié les classes populaires*, Paris: Flammarion, 2014.
Haddad, Benjamin, *Le paradis perdu: L'Amérique de Trump et la fin des illusions européennes*, Paris: Grasset, 2019.
Kagan, Robert, *The Jungle Grows Back: America and Our Imperiled World*, New York:Alfred A. Kopf, 2018.
Kenny, Michael, and Pearce, Nick, *Shadows of Empire: The Anglosphere in British Politics*, Cambridge: Polity, 2018.
Krastev, Ivan, *After Europe*, Philadelphia: University of Pennsylvania Press, 2017.
Krastev, Ivan, and Holmes, Stephem, *The Light that Failed: A Reckoning*, London: Allen Lane, 2019.
Kundani, Hans, *The Paradox of German Power*, Oxford: Oxford University Press, 2015.
Kupchan, Charles, *Isolationism: A History of America's Efforts to Shield Itself from the World*, New York: Oxford University Press, 2020.
Hughes, James, Sasse, Gwedonlyn et al., *Ethnicity and Territory in the Former Soviet Union: Regions in Conflict*, London: Frank Cass, 2002.
Lever, Paul, *Berlin Rules: Europe and the German Way*, Londres: IB Tauris, 2017.
Maçães, Bruno, *History has Begun: The Birth of a New America*, London: Hurst, 2020.
Meyer, Viktor, *Yugoslavia – A History of its Demise*, London: Routledge, 1999.
Mody, Ashoka, *Eurotragedy: A Drama in Nine Acts*, Oxford: Oxford University Press, 2018.
Mulchinok, Niall, *NATO and the Western Balkans: From Neutral Spectator to Proactive Peace Maker*, London: Palgrave MacMillan, 2017.
Patrikarakos, David, *War in 140 Characters: How Social Media is Reshaping Conflict in the Twenty-First Century*, New York: Basic Books, 2017.
Reynié, Dominique et al., *Islamist Terrorist Attacks in the World*, Paris: Fondapol, 2019a.
Reynié, Dominique et al., *Democracies under Pressure: A Global Survey*, Paris: Fondapol, 2019b
Smith, Stephen, *The Scramble for Europe: Young Africa on its Way to the Old Continent*, Cambridge: Polity Press, 2019.

Snyder, Timothy, *The Road to Unfreedom: Russia, Europe, America*, London: Penguin, 2018.

Thomson, David, *Les Revenants: Ils étaient partis faire le jihad, ils sont de retour en France*, Paris: Points, 2018.

Tooze, Adam, *Crashed : How a Decade of Financial Crises Changed the World*, London: Penguin Random House, 2018.

Verhofstadt, Guy, *Le Mal Européen*, Brussels: Marque belge, 2016.

PART 2
Perilous present

Why do wars happen?

Why do wars happen? This general question needs to be asked if we are to understand not only why peace has become less probable but also why war is becoming more possible in Europe. The question itself needs to be asked the right way: Europeans' disbelief about the chances of war in their region is linked to a badly formulated question – for it should not be "*how* could a war happen in Europe?," but rather "*why* could a war happen in Europe." As will be shown in the next chapters, once that question is answered, it, unfortunately, becomes much easier to envisage scenarios for the return of war in Europe.

Focusing on answering the question "how can war happen" leads us to another problem, which is an immediate (and therefore excessive) focus on the events that can trigger hostilities. History tells us these are almost diverse as the number of wars that have taken place across the world. Even getting to a typology of triggers is not necessarily useful: these can be as meaningful and spectacular as Japan's attack on Pearl Harbor, but they can also look much more banal. A 1969 war between El Salvador and Honduras was actually directly triggered by a football game[1] – not for the last time, as it turned out. Getting back to Europe, most Croats consider that their country's war of independence, which itself conditioned the beginning of hostilities in neighboring Bosnia and Herzegovina, started with a riot in a soccer stadium on May 13, 1990, during a derby between Dinamo Zagreb and Red Star Belgrade.[2] At this stage of the discussion, focusing on the trigger, on the "how," is therefore of little value, as it tends to make each conflict unique[3] and does not allow the study of the deeper causes that lead to war. To get back the example of the Pacific War of 1941–1945, Pearl Harbor happened in a very specific context of geopolitical rivalry and economic warfare, which, in turn, explains the Japanese surprise attack. Explaining the war solely through Pearl Harbor, while occulting the rising geopolitical and geo-economic tensions between the United States and Japan over the Asia-Pacific region in the previous months and years, misses the point.

Asking the right question gives a few keys to understanding the causes of war in general, which can then be used to explain why current developments could lead to war in Europe. The first of those keys is that the root causes of war can be usefully summarized to three general sentiments, which Greek historian Thucydides had already isolated some 25 centuries ago: fear, honor and interest. These three general principles are often on their own enough to explain why wars happen and the succession of events that transition countries from a state of peace to a state of war. The second key is that, despite the reality of more democratic, low-cost warfare, wars are actually inevitably decided by elites, may they be at the national or at the local level. Elites are the ones who declare war (when they choose to do so, as most wars actually do not start with an official declaration of war), and most importantly they are the only ones who can mobilize supporters and collective resources for armed struggle.

But beyond elites' decisions, are there rules that actually push them to war? Some schools of thought suggest that war obeys a natural law in history, thereby imprisoning the choice of human leaders. The venerable British historian Arnold Toynbee considered that war and peace followed a cycle of approximately a hundred years, starting with the peaceful generation that comes after a great, destructive general war. The next generation, brought up in peacetime, is more war-prone, but its bellicose instincts are checked by the influence of the previous generation, whose still vivid memory of the previous great conflict constrains the choice of their successors. In this phase, conflicts can return, they can be bloody, but they are usually much shorter. The third generation is once again more inclined toward peace after having gone through the battlefield in their youth, but as the last survivors of the great cataclysm die, the tendency toward a return to general war becomes irresistible for the unfortunate representatives of the fourth generation.[4] Toynbee's cyclical theory, of course, applied a bit too perfectly to his time, and Europe's current Long Peace run disavows it, at least partly. However, it cannot be entirely dismissed: today, the disappearance of the last survivors of the Second World War is making us much less conscious of the realities of war – what a battlefield can look like, the privations that one has to endure in wartime and the difficult moral choices individuals have to make during these troubled times. As the vivid memory of war disappears, it can be replaced by ideas of glory on the battlefield and visions of it as a necessary moral crusade (which can be on paper but rarely is on the battlefield itself). In this way, the justifications for war can become more potent in the minds of stakeholders, to the point that idealistic views lead elites to consider that war is a reasonable option to sort out differences. Without consisting in an indisputable "cause" of war, Toynbee's iron law tells us about how the passage of time can make wars easier.

Another theory of inevitability is provided by the Marxist school of thought, based itself on the inevitability of human development, and for which war is part of the deterministic path toward socialism. Lenin saw armed conflict not only as the inevitable consequence of the concentration of capitalism but also as following the logic of the capitalist market: not only do arms dealers need war to maximize their profits and expand their activities but the elites also need war to prevent the working class from uniting against their real oppressors.[5] This Marxist interpretation may look simplistic, insofar as it reduces all conflicts to economics and wild conspiracy theories; it also explains neither the causes of the many wars of the pre-capitalist era nor those that can happen between communist countries (the Russian-Chinese conflict of 1969 for example) nor the violent explosion of Yugoslavia, which took place in a socialist federation. Nevertheless, like Toynbee's theory, the Marxist theory is informative about the mechanisms that lead to war, how economic interests can influence (and support) decisions to go to war and why it can be in some elites' interests to choose war over peace. The fact that this theory has regained popularity in some American academic circles following the wars in Afghanistan and Iraq speaks volumes about the post-liberal disillusionment generated by these two endless conflicts.[6]

Beyond these general considerations, identifying more specifically the causes of war to give them an application for our times is no easy task: the number of conflicts to be studied is such that one will often find an exception to the rule, or another ideological interpretation. To better identify the causes of war, we must dig deeper and return to its simplest definition, namely a state of armed conflict between several constituted political groups, which may or may not be nation-states. From this simple definition, it becomes clear that a state of war cannot exist without "an intense dispute and available forms of violence," to use Lawrence Freedman's phraseology.[7] For war to occur, therefore, there must be weapons – and as we will see in Chapter 6, they are much more numerous, much cheaper and even more dangerous today (although not all of them are lethal). But above all, for there to be war, there must be a dispute, a conflict that divides states and populations into irreconcilable camps. Those disputes are aplenty in Europe today, as we have started to discover in the previous chapter. Indeed, Ivan Krastev strikes a chord when he states that

> "all the crises Europe faces today divide the Union one way or another. The Eurozone crisis divides the Union over a north-south axis. Brexit highlights the division between the core and the periphery. The Ukraine crisis divides Europe into hawks and doves with respect to dealing with Russia. But it is the east-west divide that reemerged after the refugee crisis that threatens the survival of the Union itself.[8]"

It is probable that the coronavirus crisis will usher in either creating new divisions or enlarging old ones, and if those are not well managed, they could spell the end of the experiment of peace in Europe.

Of course, the divisions Krastev mentions have already been touched upon in the previous chapter, but it is worth looking at them from a different angle, using less history and more sociology, international affairs and other social sciences. For, the description of issues and imbalances is not enough. To have the potential of turning into an armed conflict, a dispute must be both intense and perceived as dynamic by the different stakeholders. A static disagreement or imbalance, without dynamics, can be managed peacefully, as stakeholders know that the problem exists, that it is not going away and that the balance of power between the sides remains stable: in this instance, the conflict is predictable, and all sides prefer to manage it rather than take the risk of an uncertain outcome through war. For war to be considered by the elites, there must be a dynamic in the dispute. And when the long-term outlook in peacetime looks negative, the idea of going to war makes sense. For Harvard professor Graham Allison, "behavioral scientists have explained this at the basic psychological level, noting that people's fear of loss (or intimations of 'decline') trumps our hopes of gain – driving us to take often unreasonable risks to protect what is ours."[9] In other words, and for our purposes here, the sense of absolute or relative decline, so present in Europe's public debate today, encourages us to see violence as a solution to our dispute or problem: if we feel trapped in a vicious circle and have the feeling that we have lost control in peacetime, then any solution that gives us the chance to take back control becomes reasonable – at least we will have "tried to do something." This was the logic followed by the passengers of United Airlines Flight 93, which crashed in Pennsylvania on September 11, 2001, as they rebelled against the terrorists who had taken control of their plane and were about to launch it on Capitol Hill. It also provided the intellectual framework for Michael Anton (aka Publius Decius Mus) to provide a rationale for the Trump vote in 2016.[10] Even more consequential, as unlike the election of Donald Trump, it did lead to war, it was similar reasoning that led to the collective decision taken by European nations to go to war in 1914.

The term "decision" is important here since the transition from peace to war can only be made on the basis of the decision of at least one actor. That actor may start the conflict with a "surprise" attack or with a formal declaration of war, but war always begins with a decision by political leaders. This decision is thus a rational choice, even if the individual or collective passions can contribute to it and even if the subsequent consequences of war end up being completely out of proportion to the aspirations of the time. The choice to go to war is therefore a rational decision guided by a risk/opportunity and win/loss evaluation by political leaders. The latter choose to go to war after examination of the information available to them at a given time, history deciding ex-post if it was the right decision.

As Geoffrey Blainey reminds us in his study of the causes of war between the eighteenth and the twentieth century around the world,

> "any nation's decision to fight, or to cease fighting, is based on a picture of what that war or what peace will be like; and one of the many influences

on that picture is the fluctuating and intensely-colored memory of past wars or past periods of peace.[11]"

Thus, to echo Toynbee's theory, the vivid memory of a particularly long, bloody and costly conflict has an influence on the decision to go to war. But it is not the only factor: the perception of the enemy's power and his capacity to react at a given moment, the anticipation of the budgetary and human cost of the war and the possible gains in the event of victory have an impact on the fateful decision.[12] When Europeans went to war in 1914, they each considered that they had at that moment a military advantage over their adversary that they might not have in a few years' time – going to war at this moment allowed them to maximize their advantage,[13] and they anticipated a costly but short war – for these leaders at that given time, war made complete sense, even though their decisions would look completely irrational ex-post. Fast-forward 25 years: when Adolf Hitler made the decision to declare war on Poland, he knew the risks of a long and widespread European conflict, but he believed that the potential gains (and the probability of victory) were far greater than the costs that Germany might have to pay – through war or negotiation, even though the British and French had given him Czechoslovakia on a silver plate one year earlier. Hitler's idea was that he could more surely impose his will on his opponents through armed confrontation than through negotiations, since German military superiority (and cohesion) was for him beyond doubt. Hitler's build-up and decision to go to war, which had matured for many years, is also a reminder of the folly of unilateral disarmament.

In our times, Europe needs no Hitler, no Attila and no evil scarecrow to go back to war. As soon as an actor considers that the state of peace is more costly in the long run than the gamble of war, war becomes more likely. Europe has not (yet) reached that point, but the current dynamics, if they are not stopped in time, could bring the heart of the continent much closer to breaking point in the coming years. After all, Europe has no shortage of leaders who actually enjoy risk-taking, and the 2010s have stirred up intense divisions within the continent and within the Union, with internal and external dynamics that could push future actors to take decisions that may seem irrational to us today. Adding to this, our idea of war is no longer necessarily in line with the very diverse range of instruments available to leaders to fight their battles, and the ensuing mix can indeed prove explosive within the next ten years.

In Part 2, we will try to explain the reasons why imbalances and negative dynamics could bring Europe back on the warpath. To do so, we will first focus on the internal fault lines within Europe, before studying the continent's external challenges. We will then examine how recent changes in the art of war make it potentially less costly, more democratic and therefore necessarily more likely. Having done that, we should be able to understand why war is possible again in Europe, before imagining in Part 3 how this return could happen and what can be done to avoid it.

Notes

1 Ryszard Kapuscinski, *The Soccer War*, London: Granta Books, 1990.
2 https://www.euronews.com/2020/05/13/red-star-belgrade-vs-dinamo-zagreb-the-football-match-that-started-a-war
3 Of course, at various points in history, the war trigger was similar – that was notably the case in the eighteenth century where most wars broke out in Europe over dynastical succession, in Spain, Austria and Bavaria among others. In a world where legitimacy no longer rests on familial ties, the triggers have much diversified. See Geoffrey Blainey, *The Causes of War*, Third Edition, New York: The Free Press, 1988, pp.88–90
4 Arnold J. Toynbee, *War and Civilization*, Oxford: Oxford University Press, 1951.
5 Vladimir Ilich Lenin, Imperialism, *The Highest Stage of Capitalism: A Popular Outline*, New York: International Press, 1969.
6 Mark P. Worrell, *Why Nations Go to War: A Sociology of Military Conflict*, New York: Routledge, 2010.
7 Lawrence Freedman, *The Future of War: a History*, New York: Public Affairs, 2017, p.285.
8 Ivan Krastev, *After Europe*, Philadelphia: University of Pennsylvania Press, p.44.
9 Graham Allison, *Destined for War: Can America and China Escape Thucydides's Trap*, New York : Mariner, 2018, p.50.
10 https://claremontreviewofbooks.com/digital/the-flight-93-election/
11 Geoffrey Blainey, *The Causes of War*, Third Edition, New York: The Free Press, 1988, p.9.
12 Ibid., p.122.
13 It is certainly the case for the Russians vis-à-vis the Germans but also vice versa. See Sean McMeekin, *The Russian Origins of the First World War*, Cambridge: Harvard University Press, 2011, and Christopher Clark, *The Sleepwalkers: How Europe Went to War in 1914*, London: Penguin, 2013.

Bibliography

Allison, Graham, *Destined for War: Can America and China Escape Thucydides's Trap*, New York: Mariner, 2018.
Blainey, Geoffrey, *The Causes of War*, Third Edition, New York: The Free Press, 1988.
Clark, Christopher, *The Sleepwalkers: How Europe Went to War in 1914*, London: Penguin, 2013.
Kapuscinski, Ryszard, *The Soccer War*, London: Granta Books, 1990.
Krastev, Ivan, *After Europe*, Philadelphia: University of Pennsylvania Press, 2017.
Lenin, Vladimir Ilich Ulyanov (aka), *Imperialism, The Highest Stage of Capitalism: A Popular Outline*, New York: International Press, 1969.
McMeekin, Sean, *The Russian Origins of the First World War*, Cambridge: Harvard University Press, 2011
Toynbee, Arnold J., *War and Civilization*, Oxford: Oxford University Press, 1951.
Worrell, Mark P., *Why Nations Go to War: A Sociology of Military Conflict*, New York: Routledge, 2010.

4
DIVISION BELLS

The contemporary European Union is an exceptional construct: not only has its security architecture provided the longest run of peace in the continent's history but the geographical scope of this emporium of peace is exceptional; even with Britain out, the EU is the largest political entity ever constituted entirely on European soil: Alexander's Empire was immense, but geographically centered on the Near and Middle East; the Roman empire was above all a Mediterranean Empire; those of Charlemagne and Charles V were European but did not include a large part of the continent's territories; the British Empire was certainly based on a metropolis in Europe, but its ambition was global and its power based on the mastery of the sea, not the European battlefield that Britain wanted to avoid when it could. Finally (and more controversially), Napoleon's and Hitler's empires, vast as they were, remained very temporary in construct and, in any case, never translated in direct incorporation in their ensembles, as protectorates were often used to ensure some control over peripheral territories. The European Union is, thus, an unprecedented construct in the history of the continent, in terms of size, of its foundation by and on the rule of law, and of its aspiration for democratic governance and equal representation. And although the two organizations do not recoup the same membership, the EU's security is greatly enhanced – even guaranteed – by NATO, which covers most of Europe. In many ways, the current construct looks too big to fail. But things change, and at the start of the 2020s, Europe looks more fragile than it ever has in living memories. Divisions are aplenty, whether geographic, technological, sociological, identity-based or ideological, and if Europeans do not manage to master them in the years to come, they hold the potential to become the background causes of new European wars.

DOI: 10.4324/9781003215790-7

Deutschland über alles *or* Deutschland gegen alle?

Whether we like it or not – and more specifically, whether Germans like it or not – the first challenge for the future of the continent is the "German question." Of course, thanks to the changing nature of European (and German) politics, it does not pose itself in the same terms as it did in 1914, 1938 or 1945. But if it is not addressed, it could indeed become a real political problem and, ultimately, a potential cause for war, for the challenge for Europe (and for Germany itself) is to accommodate itself with a semi-hegemonic Germany.

Today, the German question is first and foremost posed in economic terms: Germany has a GDP worth almost $4 trillion, which gives it undisputed leadership in the Eurozone and the European Union, even more so after Britain's departure from the Union:[1] in a 27-member EU, the German economy is by far the largest country in the Union and alone, it accounts for about a quarter of its total wealth – the equivalent to what the US economy weighs on a global scale. Add to this the unparalleled organizational capacity of the political parties and the political ties that the German foundations have built over the years, and the picture of Germany's ascendancy in the period 2005–2015 is complete. The French, Italians, Poles and (when they were members) British may at times have been uncomfortable with this situation, but the truth is that they have hardly been in a position to truly rebel against the almighty Angela Merkel. Rather, all strategies seem to have reinforced the pattern: the British Conservatives' decision to leave the European People's Party (EPP) in 2009 accentuated the dominance of the German Christian Democratic Union (CDU) within Europe's main umbrella party, which further isolated the United Kingdom and played a role in Brexit a few years later;[2] Nicolas Sarkozy's opposite strategy to go along and use the Franco-German "couple" to magnify France's European policy, via the famed "Merkozy" entente of 2010 and 2012, may have looked better on paper, but in the end, despite the French president's efforts to sell to his public that the relationship was one between equals,[3] the harsh reality eventually kicked in: "Europe proposes, Angela Merkel disposes." Back then, nobody could really mount an effective resistance to Germany, who ended up getting away with some unilateral *faux-pas* that are kicking back today. Germany's dominance, and the perverse effects it could have on the EU's cohesion, was seen during the debates on the migrant crisis where the initial "no" of the Visegrád Four (Poland, Czech Republic, Slovakia and Hungary) could not prevent the decision on quotas – much worse, the countries that didn't want the migrants got their arms twisted to accept quotas from Brussels, then went back home to condemn it, didn't comply and got away with it (which is a perfect metaphor of the problems of semi-hegemony). The Nord Stream 2 pipeline project is another example of the problems posed by this half-hearted German dominance: the project to build a second pipeline under the Baltic Sea to allow Russia to directly provide gas to Germany has been met with equal hostility throughout the Baltic region, with Poland, the Baltic States and also Sweden and Denmark originally opposing the project. Reasons for opposition varied, but all were admissible: environmental impact, dangerous isolation of the Eastern European countries, empowering a corrupt regime in Moscow, building up a one-sided dependence for Germany's energy supplies on an unreliable partner, etc. But each country attacked the project individually, and even when they got together, they remained too weak to counter Germany's will to finish the project, which was a priority in Berlin. Italy was not interested, as the project does not concern her directly, and France – who would have had some interest in opposing it and use this to make friends in Central Europe – only voiced formal opposition when it needed to get something else in return from Germany. In this configuration, Germany has been able to get its way in a project that was practically opposed by everybody to various degrees, because it was a priority that itself stemmed from an ill-advised unilateral decision, that of ending the production of nuclear energy in Germany. In the end, only US economic sanctions against participating companies slowed down construction and made Berlin realize that there would be a price to pay for a project that is benefiting no other country than Germany.[4] This is yet another proof of the current incapacity of Europeans to sort out their problems on their own and that of countries like France or Poland to organize effective coalitions within the EU to act as counterweights to Berlin, where their interests are threatened – responsibilities for this lie not in Berlin but rather in Paris, Warsaw, Rome and other capitals.

Today, Germany's dominant position in Europe is beyond contestation, and some could argue that part of the problem is not so much this dominance but the fact that Germans are actually still in denial that it exists. This is certainly a powerful argument, but it is also true, as Hans Kundani argues, that

> "although Germany's increased power and France's relative weakness has allowed Germany to impose its preferences on the others in the Eurozone, it is too small to be a European hegemon. This is strikingly similar to the position of Germany within Europe between 1871 and 1945."[5]

Needless to say, this is not a discourse that is much appreciated in Berlin, but that is so precisely because it rings true. German dominance in European affairs can and will be accepted by its neighbors up to a certain extent, but it will never be strong enough to convince the said neighbors to blindly follow the "German Way." We have seen first signs of rebellion during the 2010s, with the rise of populism and an anti-German discourse in capitals across Europe, and even though the wave has recently receded, thanks to the European Recovery Fund (there is now "free" money to redistribute in Europe's periphery), it will not be long before more political issues start to kick in again. And even more so as Germany is now facing not only the end of a glorious and extremely stable political cycle with the end of Angela Merkel's chancellorship but also importantly the end of an economic cycle, with China becoming less dependent on products *Made in Germany* and tough economic choices waiting to be made in the next few years.⁶ For Germany, the news of a long-term economic slowdown, potentially blamable on the European Recovery Fund in the long term, is all the more worrisome since contestations of German leadership have sprouted up over the past years. Those started, timidly, with Alexis Tsipras in Greece in 2014–2015 (he was quickly convinced to fall into line),⁷ but they also took shape in Central Europe, where Poland's refusal to work with Germany on a number of issues after 2015 has greatly complicated Germany's reliance on its Eastern periphery. Probably even more serious is the carefully calibrated challenge that Viktor Orbán poses to the Germans, as he uses interdependence to get what he wants from Berlin without having to pay the price for it (a situation that is clearly ushering in the worst of both worlds for the Germans, who see their authority challenged while not being able to sanction the troublemaker).

In this regard, the change of government in Poland through the victory of Jarosław Kaczyński's Law and Justice Party (PiS) in the aftermath of the migrant crisis was a strategic turning point in the European balance of power. Until the end of 2015, only Hungary and Greece had really dared to enter into a more or less direct confrontation with Berlin (with Brussels acting as a proxy target on both sides). Nevertheless, the relatively low economic weight of these two countries ($155 billion in GDP for Hungary, $218 billion for Greece⁸) made their rebellion certainly unpleasant but nevertheless manageable from Berlin's perspective. But when Poland, the largest economy in Central Europe, with 38 million inhabitants (compared to 10 million in Greece and Hungary), $585 billion in GDP and an annual growth rate of 5.1% in 2018, decided to turn its back on the alliance with Berlin, this had consequences for the whole European power system. PiS considers that the policy of Poland's previous liberal governments, which consisted in relying on Germany to strengthen Poland's position in Europe was tantamount to subordinating the country to German interests, which are indeed very present in Poland. Considering Poland's history of the past 200 years, PiS's thinking is that Warsaw cannot be too dependent on either Germany or Russia and certainly not when the two cozy up together (which takes us back to Nord Stream 2, among others). The current Polish government, therefore, considers that the only strategy is to rely on the United States for its security, oppose Berlin as much as possible and reduce dependence on Germany. This is exactly the agenda that Warsaw has been pursuing since 2015, including in its illiberal political agenda (parts of the strategy of "media nationalization" is to stop any news outlet from being owned by foreign groups, which in Poland are mostly German). Warsaw has found allies in this crusade, notably Viktor Orbán in Hungary, and the two countries (now joined by Janez Janša's Slovenia) are making sure to protect each other from possible sanctions from Brussels. This is, of course, not to say that Poland and Hungary are in an all-out alliance against the European Union: although they do share some interests in opposing Brussels on such issues as migration, they also take great benefit from membership, which their populations recognize. Besides, the Hungarian-Polish couple also has its limits, as important divergences remain on crucial issues, such as foreign policy and the relationship with Russia and China. In any case, the irruption of an illiberal problem in Central Europe has become a thorn in Berlin's foot, and it is encouraging other countries to follow suit.

In fact, discordant voices with Germany's "ordo-liberal" discourse of the early 2010s have also been mounting outside of central Europe. Italy has been a particularly tricky case here because its size makes it much less vulnerable to restructuration imposed from Brussels in the Greek fashion, while its precarious economic situation makes it a prime candidate for popular dissatisfaction and economic trouble: if the Greek crisis had been tricky enough to endanger the eurozone in the mid-2010s, one could only imagine the consequences of an Italian default, Italy being the third-largest economy of the EU. Italians have their reasons to be frustrated, as the belt-tightening policies of the past 25 years have neither taken the country out of a slow but painful economic decline nor given hope to young Italians, who are left to pay for the cost of readjustment of the Italian economy while their elders have continued to enjoy relatively high standards of living.[9] Many Italians also hold a grudge against Northern Europe for leaving them and other Southern European countries on their own in dealing with the refugee crises in the last decade. The combination of economic and migration grievances against Northern Europe have ushered in a new rise of Euroscepticism in a country that traditionally has been among the most pro-European[10] in the Union, which in turn has led to the rise of political parties promoting a Eurosceptic agenda: Matteo Salvini's League, although it has recently softened its language on Europe as a result of the European Recovery Fund,[11] remains a pole of attraction for critics of the EU, while Beppe Grillo's Five Star Movement and Giorgia Meloni's Fratelli d'Italia have built their political DNA around a discourse that is critical of Brussels – and Berlin.

Since the COVID-19 crisis and, importantly, the decision to mutualize a European Recovery Fund for which Italy is set to be the single biggest beneficiary, political passions about the European Union have thankfully receded, but this could only prove temporary: as in many cases around Europe, the measures taken by national governments against the socioeconomic consequences of the pandemic and its lockdowns have resulted in putting a lid over European societies. Once that lid is removed and consequences are plain to see (including long-term job losses), it might take years for many to get back to their pre-pandemic income. A bad exit of the first phase of the crisis, leading to more social misery, would surely strengthen the voices of Eurosceptic and populist voices in Italian politics, further endangering the country's fragile compact. If such a crisis were to occur, Europe would be at pains to find a suitable solution: Italy is not Greece, and it weighs more than 2 trillion dollars, making it the third economy and the second-biggest manufacturer of the EU. Its size and economic situation (with public debt at 130% of the nation's GDP, held in large part by the Italians themselves[12]) would make a crisis much more problematic than the 2010–2015 Eurozone crisis, and one can imagine the anxiety of Italians at the prospect of being treated like their Greek colleagues if their banks were to be the target of speculative funds. The threat of a specifically Italian crisis (which would affect 10% of the Union's economy), made possible once again by the coming economic consequences of the coronavirus crisis, could have particularly harsh consequences for the whole of Europe and continue to push Rome further away from Berlin.

Italy is not the only country that Germany could worry about. For similar reasons, France, the second economy on the continent, is also showing signs of dissatisfaction. After a short idyll in 2017 between Emmanuel Macron and Angela Merkel, the famed Franco-German couple has turned into a somehow sour relationship, even though it has been able to move forward on some important issues in the past few years. In fact, the COVID-19 rapprochement should not hide the reality of the long-term dynamics of Franco-German relations, which is much more uncertain than many would like to show in Paris or Berlin. Even though France and Germany have been able to create an impressive network between their public officials at all levels, mutual frustration has mounted on both sides of the Rhine in the past few years. German leaders are understandably disappointed by France's chronic inability to "reform" its economy – a story that has been going on for nearly twenty years already; on the other side, the French are becoming increasingly frustrated with Germany's inertia when it comes to reforming the European Union, a process that Berlin understands is necessary, but that it does not want to rush as the current institutional and economic framework has served Germany's interests well over the past 15 years. Emmanuel Macron, himself under pressure from an impatient French electorate, has become increasingly frustrated with German inertia, while a populist, Eurosceptic electorate has consolidated at around 20–25% on the right, possibly 10–15% on the left. On the other side of the Rhine, Macron's taste for personal diplomacy has also unsettled Berlin, for whom Paris's disruptive and unpredictable policy is a worry, not least since Franco-German initiatives are now viewed with increasing suspicion by other EU partners.

France's position is, therefore, not necessarily viewed in Berlin as that of a reliable partner, and Paris can both block German initiatives and build coalitions to force German officials to rethink Europeans' policies. In effect, Germany's acquiescing to an ambitious European Recovery Fund – which represents a de facto economic North–South transfer of funds – represents a triumph not so much for the Franco-German couple, although it was Emmanuel Macron and Angela Merkel who ultimately drove the project in the EU council of ministers, but for an alliance of Southern countries, including France, which were in a desperate situation and put enough pressure on Germany to end budgetary orthodoxy. This time, the result was to force Germany into making the right decision, but it is by no means certain that any future large coalitions to force Berlin into taking a decision it does not want will be as successful, or that it will not result in rising tensions between EU members – particularly if the EU recovery plan fails to produce enough tangible results to reverse the tide of populism in Europe.

As Germany has to face a new environment with more headwinds in Europe, it will also have to adapt to a changing Transatlantic relationship. Even before the Trump era, the United States started to show signs of frustration with Germany, as the Obama administration already despaired at Berlin's failure to appreciate the nature and scope of geopolitical dangers rising in Europe's neighborhood. During the Trump years, frustration turned into outright hostility: Germany was often openly portrayed by the President as a free rider taking advantage of US generosity and plundering its protector's industry while not paying its dues. Of course, the problem was that if Germany really started "paying its dues," its neighbors – especially France and Poland – would then become alarmed by the sight of an already economically dominant Germany now building an army. Basic mathematics comes handy here: when the continent's largest economy spends 2% of its GDP on its army, its military spending becomes far more important than that of the Union's second-largest economy. This is of course of little importance in the framework of a collective defense with the American ally, but if the United States were to lose interest in Europe, the consequences could be far-reaching. Germany thus finds itself in a catch-22 situation, where it runs the risk of being blamed by its partners either for its strategic weakness or for its preponderance – in any case, it cannot afford to be blamed for both at the same time.

Of course, it is possible to argue that much of the Trumpist discourse on Germany has disappeared with the new administration coming in. But despite a much more diplomatic tone, Joe Biden's team has already found reasons to worry about the relationship with Berlin: even before taking the oath, it had to deal with a particularly assertive German push for the EU to finalize a foreign investment deal with China that was clearly favored in Beijing to weaken the Transatlantic relationship.[13] A few weeks later, when faced with the imprisonment of Aleksey Navalny in Russia, the German government (under pressure from German business) continued to push for completion of the Nord Stream 2 pipeline, despite mounting pressure not only from the United States but also in Europe to abandon the project.[14] Of course, the new US administration is not as vociferous in its opposition to Germany, but it is taking note of German behavior, which is now clearly considered a problem as Berlin wants to continue to do business as usual with Russia and China – two countries that are now engaged in a systematic competition with Washington. The picture that is emerging is one of slow but steady estrangement of German and American interests, as Germany adopts a more isolationist and "continentalist" approach to its foreign policy. This tendency to a new "Ostpolitik" is probably most clearly affirmed in the social-democratic circles that have shaped German foreign policy in recent years (including during the Obama era), but they have also become more common on the right – first and foremost within the far-right, with the Alternativ für Deutschland (AfD) taking clearly orientalist positions but also in some circles in the CDU, insofar as the business interests they represent are attracted to business in the East.

This, of course, does not mean that Washington and Berlin are on the verge of breaking point, but a prolonged deterioration of relations between Berlin and Washington could end up feeding German nationalism and continentalism, and this would certainly have harmful consequences for the balance of power within the European continent – and encourage European countries, East and West, to further distance themselves from Berlin.

Considered almost omnipotent at the beginning of the last decade, Germany finds itself today in a situation where its leadership is more and more contested in Europe. To take an analogy that may appear shocking to some Germans, it seems that Germany is transitioning from a situation where it was superior to all other actors, and its particular interests reigned supreme (*Deutschland über Alles*[15]) to one where it has to face increasing opposition from its traditional partners (*Deutschland gegen Alle*). This comes at a particularly delicate time for Berlin, as the transition from the very stable years of Angela Merkel's chancellorship may not turn out not to be a smooth ride: with a post-COVID-19 crisis to manage and an uneasy coalition to uphold at home, Chancellor Olaf Scholz has to maneuver in a difficult international environment and a closing Chinese market that will need fewer German products, as its own production is now starting to equal (or even better) the quality of German industries – in the automobile sector, for example.

Germany's environment is changing at the worst possible time, and Berlin might end up regretting some of the unilateral decisions it took in the 2010s (as did all semi-hegemonic powers in Europe in the past). As the world becomes more dangerous and soft power less important, Germany's military impotence and its over-reliance on trade for its prosperity in a time of increased protectionism may well give the impression to different actors, both inside the European Union and outside of it, that internal dynamics are changing and this could lead to a new period of uncertainty. If Germany's strength in the 2010s guaranteed continuity – and most importantly resilience – for the European Union, the perspective of a weakened, or less effective Germany could give different actors new ideas that would not necessarily play for Europe's stability. As Geoffrey Blainey reminds us, "wars usually end when the fighting nations *agree* on their relative strength, and wars usually begin when fighting nations *disagree* on their relative strengths."[16] If Germany's fortunes were to fluctuate too fast and too strongly, the whole European edifice would suffer, and the European balance of power could be destabilized for the worse, in particular in the continent's peripheries, where grievances are strongest and trajectories unpredictable.

Center vs. peripheries

One should not indulge too much in German-bashing. If war were to start again in Europe, it would probably not do so because of Germany: the still vivid memory of the first half of the twentieth century and the culture of the German elites clearly push Berlin toward conciliation rather than conflict in international relations. As war is considered both against morality and also against the interests of Germany, it is unlikely that German elites will revert to martial discourses any time soon. What is much less unlikely is to see Germany losing control over its own geo-economic zone of influence, getting tired of being systematically criticized by its neighbors and partners, and adopting a sort of home-grown isolationism or passive-aggressive attitude. Frustrated by the attitude of ungrateful partners who would have received substantial transfers of wealth from North to South in the immediate aftermath of the COVID-19 crisis, Germany would then start to disengage from the rest of Europe, especially its Southern and Eastern peripheries. The risk here is to see rich Northern Europe secede and recreate its own internal system centered on a northern sea (which could be the North Sea or the Baltic Sea). This would leave the rest of the continent on its own, with the danger of war and instability crippling back in as a result.

As described in the previous chapter, the North–South and the East–West cleavages have been particularly salient throughout the 2010s, and they were fueled by the impact of the economic crisis and the regional disparities in its effects. But while these divides have been magnified by the socioeconomic difficulties of the past decade, they are hardly new. In many ways, they follow an ancestral logic: the North–South divide very much follows the dividing line between Latin and Germanic nations, somehow (though not entirely) between Catholic and Protestant Europe, or between a poor Europe naturally oriented toward the Mediterranean and a rich Europe turned toward the North and the Baltic Sea. In the same way, the East–West divide can be interpreted through a purely socioeconomic lens, using the Cold War years as a defining moment (although, 30 years after its end, this interpretation is less and less pertinent); but it can equally be seen – as indeed it was in the late nineteenth century – as a cleavage between Germanic and Slavic peoples or through the ideological lens inherited from the Enlightenment, with a liberal Western Europe and much more conservative and absolutist Central Europe[17] or even through a historical division between the political and administrative heritage of the Holy Roman Empire and that of the Byzantine Empire, between Orthodox and Catholic/Protestant traditions. Of course, these divides are not thought through by ordinary people; rather, they are the product of elites reflections, but those elites are the ones who decide on war and peace, not peoples, and the fact that these divides are reappearing in common discourse is a sign that what Benedict Anderson described as imagined national communities[18] are taking a regional, parochial character rather than a global one.

In fact, the North–South and the East–West divides are much more complex than they appear at first sight. The famed "Eastern" bloc is very far from united: true, Central and Eastern European countries can come together on some areas of common interest (e.g., the refusal to take in refugees in 2015), but they are at odds with each other on many issues: old tensions remain between the countries in Central Europe, whether ethnic (between Slavs and Albanians, Slavs and Magyars or Magyars and Romanians, for example), religious (between Catholic countries like Poland and Lithuania, Protestant countries such as the two northern Baltic States, and orthodox countries like Romania, Serbia or Bulgaria) or historical; a remarkable feature of electoral maps in both Poland and Romania is that their geographic electoral fault lines often correspond to the old borders between provinces that belonged to extinct empires – those between Prussia and Russia in the case of Poland, and between Austro-Hungarian territories and principalities under Ottoman suzerainty in Romania.[19]

In the same way, the "Visegrád Four" (V4), which became a media sticker during and after the migrant crisis, may be an occasional instrument for Poland, the Czech Republic, Slovakia and Hungary to work together on some common issues, but in reality, co-operation remains limited, and members of the group are divided on crucial issues such as the strategy to adopt vis-à-vis Brussels, Moscow, Washington or Beijing.[20] Recently, sensing that their belonging to the V4 had toxic implications for their image in Brussels, the Czech Republic and Slovakia have moved away from V4 co-operation and opted to work under the Slavkov or Austerlitz format, which allows them to move away from the orbit of the "illiberal democracies" currently built by PiS in Poland and Viktor Orbán in Hungary and work together with Austria.[21] Central Europe is of course not the only area that is traversed by multiple fault lines: in the summer of 2020, when the temperature rose in the Eastern Mediterranean, Euro-Med countries were divided as to what to do with Turkey's assertive behavior at sea, with France following Greece and Cyprus in a hard line against Ankara, while Italy and Spain proved initially much more reluctant to endanger their relationship with Turkey.

The divides in Europe, far from following the logic of an iron curtain are many, with the size of each Euro-confetti varying from the national to the regional or socioeconomic sizes. For, if the East–West and the North–South fault lines are currently the most salient, they are not the only ones. In many ways, if one is looking for a strong, overwhelming divide, it would be between, on the one hand, North-Western Europe, the socioeconomic heart of the continent, relatively prosperous, integrated into globalization and satisfied with its democratic institutions and, on the other hand, impoverished peripheries in the East and South, which are much less integrated into the global economy and dissatisfied with their institutions. This divide is both economic and psychological; it emerged clearly from the public opinion study conducted jointly by the French *Fondation pour l'Innovation Politique* (Fondapol) and the International Republican Institute in 2018–2019 on public attitudes toward democracy in 42 countries.[22] The maps used for this study clearly show a divide between a Nordic and Anglo-Saxon Europe, where public opinion seems satisfied with institutions and remains generally optimistic about the future, and Southern and Eastern Europe, where levels of satisfaction and trust are much lower, and the outlook about the future much more pessimistic. Between the two, France, Poland and Germany (whose results in the former German Democratic Republic (GDR) have significantly lowered the overall figures) form a sort of intermediate zone.

Here again, what emerges is that Germany plays a central role – not only geographically but also culturally – in keeping the different parts of the continent together. Just as France is in many ways a link between Southern and Northern Europe, Germany straddles the East–West divide, and its economic interests bind together the center and the periphery. And so, if Berlin decides to go its own way, or makes a conscious decision to close in on itself, many of the bridges within Europe will be cut off. Relations between European countries would then become tenser, and it would not be impossible to see old rivalries reemerge in a periphery isolated from the economic growth magnets in North-Western Europe.

A foretaste of what could await Europe, in this case, may currently be at play in Hungary, where the government of Viktor Orbán has often played the chords of Hungarian ethnic nationalism to consolidate its electoral dominance. Of course, Hungarian nationalism is not new, and it has been exploited by both the left and the right since (but also before) the fall of communism. Although in its original form a predominantly civic affair, Hungarian nationalism has become an ethnic, revisionist ideology after the 1920 Treaty of Trianon relegated the country to the status of a "small" nation, as it lost 30% of its ethnic population (who became citizens of the new neighboring states) and 60% of its territory. Of course, Hungary is not the only one to have suffered a land and population loss – Austria and Turkey in 1919 and also Germany in 1945 are other recent examples, but while the four latter digested (or rather, were forced to digest) their fate, leaving their imperial past behind, successive Hungarian elites kept the memory of the lost territories almost intact, like an open wound that they repeatedly refused to heal. Today, Trianon continues to be represented as a historical injustice, a "Passion" calling for a resurrection that is still awaited. The presence of Hungarian ethnic minorities outside the national territory in countries such as Romania, Serbia, Ukraine or Slovakia is a source of tensions with these neighboring countries, and everyone is aware that the question of minorities can be used to raise the stakes in an international crisis.

The spark of nationalist fever orchestrated by circles close to the government during the centenary of the Treaty of Trianon in 2020 shows the extent to which the myth of Greater Hungary remained a powerful lever for communication and mobilization, especially as it allows Viktor Orbán to combine his two favorite themes: nationalism and a Christian identity that is both absolute and exclusive. During the commemorations, the famous "Magyar creed" of the 1920s and 1930s was shared widely on social networks, with a phraseology that says a lot about the revisionist potential that Hungarian nationalism could unleash if it is not controlled, externally or internally: "I believe in one God, I believe in one fatherland / I believe one divine, eternal truth / I believe in the resurrection of Hungary. Amen."[23]

Today, the resurgence of the Magyar creed, and with it, the trivialization of the map of "Greater Hungary" in the communication of the Prime Minister[24] and organizations close to the government, remains a mostly electoralist folk rite, but it carries long-term perspectives that, combined with other trends, may well become an intention if nobody is there to call an end to the game: one of the consequences of Fidesz's 2011 constitutional revision was to change the very definition of Hungary, now described not only as a territory delimited by international treaties but as an idea that englobes the Hungarian people, including those living abroad.[25] This definition recalls that of the *Russki Mir*, the "Russian world" defended by Vladimir Putin, which served as a narrative to justify the invasion of Crimea. The parallel is not insignificant: Viktor Orbán did not hesitate to use similar arguments on the protection of Hungarian minorities in Transcarpathia at the height of the Ukrainian crisis, when Kyiv had to face Russia's invasion. While Moscow threatened to advance militarily much further than Crimea, Donetsk or Luhansk under the pretext of protecting the Russian-speaking populations on Ukrainian territory, the Hungarian Prime Minister used the same theme of defending "his" people to demand "guarantees" for the Magyar-speaking populations in Transcarpathia, a territory in the West of Ukraine that belonged to the Austro-Hungarian Empire until the Great War.[26] Of course, Viktor Orbán, an exceptionally gifted politician, is conscious of the balance of power (and American support for Ukraine's territorial integrity), and under the present circumstances, Budapest would not follow a policy of military confrontation – Hungary's military resources are limited, and US support for the stability of borders guaranteed. But Hungarian elites planted a seed in Ukrainian-Hungarian relations, and the diplomatic guerilla that Hungary has been waging against Ukraine with different levels of intensity, notably over Ukraine's recent law on education,[27] is a sign that it has identified a vulnerable country outside of the European Union, upon which he can act regularly to mobilize nationalism at home and create long-term opportunities, with the starting point being the dilution of Western support for Ukraine.[28]

It would be unfair to qualify Viktor Orbán's Hungary as a revisionist power like Russia. Whatever one thinks of the Hungarian Prime Minister, he is an extremely intelligent man, and he knows that the current balance of power in Europe – and the interest of both Germany and the United States – would not allow him to transform the current upsurge of nationalism in Hungary into an actual campaign to change borders within Europe. His words and deeds are above all a means of mobilizing Hungarian nationalism to consolidate his power, not a preparation for war in Central Europe. But, should interest from Germany and the United States wane in the region, should the jungle grow back in Central Europe as well, a Hungary fed for years on the idea of the unfairness of a treaty signed a century ago could gradually be seen by its neighbors as a potential threat. The fact that Hungary chose Transcarpathia as a rallying point for his discourse on "minority protection" and the defense of the Hungarian nation abroad says a lot about its strategy: Ukraine is not a member of the European Union or NATO and is, therefore, more vulnerable than Romania or Slovakia to pressure from outside.

Outside of the EU or NATO, also subject to Russian aggression in the East, the Ukrainian state is still vulnerable, and part of a super-peripheral Europe where the EU's rule of law emporium remains subject to conditions set by outside forces. Viktor Orbán knows this, and his policies of rapprochement with Russia and China, although they should also be seen from an ideological angle that we will explore toward the end of this chapter, also do allow him to envisage a much more ambitious foreign policy, should Western attention in the region wane. This may not happen during Viktor Orbán's lifetime – but the reality is that a new generation of Hungarian nationalists has been raised since 2010, and under a different international setup, they could easily contemplate the possibility of repairing what is still considered in the elites in Budapest as the injustice of Trianon. If this were to happen, the strength and reaction of Hungary's neighbors would define the future of the region, and were the balance of power to look uncertain, this would probably mean war over disputed territories or populations.[29]

It would be both wrong and unfair to stigmatize solely Hungarian nationalism: first, because a combination of factors (a nationalist rhetoric tamed by internal or external dynamics, a continued Western presence in the region, or government compliance with the rule of law reaffirmed in Hungary or by and through the European Union) can still prevent a worrying trend from developing into a nightmare in the long run. And also because Hungary is not the only European actor with revisionist potential. Alexandar Vučić's brand of Serbian nationalism finds many common points with Hungary – the frustration of a loss of territory experienced as an injustice (in the 1990s), rapprochement with China and Russia, a peripheral position in Europe with most (though not all) neighbors not part of the European Union, etc. These signs could suggest a parallel scenario in the event of a loss of Western influence, in which Serbia could reasonably be tempted to force a change in a situation that Serbian nationalists consider to be a tragic and temporary accident in their country's bumpy history. In regions where wars and border changes are still in vivid memory, the absence of an external force to impose the maintenance of the status quo would eventually push actors to define their relations by raw power rather than law. This is true not only for Eastern Europe and the Balkans, where the fortunes of states have varied over the centuries but also in Southern Europe, where autonomist and sometimes secessionist tendencies have developed recently, as was seen in Catalonia during the late 2010s; this raises the risk that the Hispanic or even Italian peninsulas (as well as the Balkans) could become subjects of a partial state collapse and/or localized violence not dissimilar to those of the Western Balkans during the 1990s.[30] Left to their own device, the weaker and more isolated peripheries of the continent would be prone to fluctuations in the balance of power between states, and the fault lines that may exist between them today could eventually transform them into new battlegrounds. At the heart of this rotting process is the concept of identity politics, which because of the continent's history carry specifically sinister implications for Europe.

Identities and secessionisms

In his remarkable work on the causes of war, Australian historian Geoffrey Blainey reminded us that war was not necessarily an international phenomenon: "the frequency of civil wars shatters the simple idea that people who have much in common will remain at peace."[31] Europe is no exception, as Europeans are just as divided within their nation-states as they are between nation-states. Indeed, as we saw in Chapter 1, they always have been, and religious, political or cultural divisions, combined with Europeans' obsession with uniformity,[32] have been the source of some of the bloodiest conflicts in Europe. Some have remained internal to each state, but many have subsequently developed to take a continental character when victory within one's borders gave ideas to a government that it should impose its "model" on its neighbors. In the context of a collapse or loss of meaning in the European political system, such a scenario cannot be ruled out, especially as the continent's history offers many precedents. During the Renaissance, wars of religion, initially confined within each state, quickly spilled over and gave way to a quasi-permanent state of war in Europe at least until the Peace of Westphalia. Fast-forward a couple of centuries, and the French Revolution also extended beyond the borders of France, embarking Europe in another long cycle of Revolutionary wars. After 1917, the Russian Revolution and its civil war, themselves the product of the First World War, provoked chain reactions across Europe, leading to what Ernst Nolte has called the European Civil War:[33] the confrontation between liberalism, communism and fascism indeed provoked many civil wars in several European countries such as Hungary, Germany, Austria or Spain from 1918 to 1939, followed by a world war waged on the same ideological bases from 1939 to 1945. And although enlightened minds post-1991 were quick to state the ultimate inevitability of liberalism's victory a half-century later, the end result of the European Civil War was by no means predestined – indeed, is also fair to say that without the intervention of the United States, the three-party fight would have turned into a binary confrontation between the two totalitarianisms, Nazism and communism. In short, to use Blainey's words,

> many international wars in Europe after 1800 were not preceded by civil strife, and civil strife did not always lead to war. Nonetheless, it is astonishing to discover how many wars had been heralded by serious unrest in one of the warring nations.[34]

We will come back in the next few pages to the social or ideological fault lines that could once again lead Europeans to civil war, but it is worth taking the time to first reflect on how identity politics are altering Europe's prospects for peace. These should not be underestimated: after all, and although economic stagnation provided the background for ultimate collapse, the resurgence of particularistic identities triggered the last regional conflict in Europe, the Yugoslav wars of the 1990s. As these questions have reemerged, sometimes crossing the Atlantic through university campuses, sometimes through a purely indigenous process, they have taken over many aspects of our current debates, to the extent that Peter Pomerantsev recently argued that "all politics is now about creating identity."[35] It is, therefore, not impossible to see identity reemerge as a factor of instability, civil strife and, ultimately, war.

Like their American counterparts, Europe's identity politics are the result of a variety of factors, both socioeconomic and cultural, but they ultimately come down to a group's demand for recognition of its uniqueness and honor – in other words, its dignity. Francis Fukuyama has described how this struggle for recognition is not conditioned only by economic considerations:

> Human beings do not just want things that are external to themselves, such as food, drinks, Lamborghini or that next hit. They also crave positive judgments about their worth or dignity. […] If they receive that positive judgement, they feel pride, and if they do not receive it, they feel either anger […] or shame.[36]

This, of course, does not mean that material goods cannot satisfy demands for dignity – they do, but only partly, as they allow individuals (or groups of individuals) to acquire social status. But they are often not sufficient to allow the individuals or the group to fully satisfy their demands for recognition. The endless quest for dignity is of course not new: back in the day, European nobles who felt humiliated by a peer took drastic steps to "restore their dignity" – a practice that kings appreciated little, as they preferred these nobles to remain obedient and serve their king at war rather than killing each other in duels. In the nineteenth and twentieth centuries, it was the demands of the working class, which included material well-being and their request for recognition and dignity that defined the left–right divide in Europe's political debate. And although dignity was not necessarily linked to working conditions or salary, acting on the latter often played a role in easing tensions. Conversely, economic crises and social distress do a great deal in making identity issues more pressing: when individuals lose some (or all) of their material goods, their dignity is all they have left, and they are then ready to do anything to save it, including by voting for extremist candidates. The way is then open for violence to become a legitimate means for a group to defend or assert its identity, which down the way leads to civil war.

In periods of severe economic hardship and rapid social change where individuals' status and habits are profoundly challenged, it is logical to see groups question their identity and cling to their dignity. In this sense, an incredibly consequential scientific discovery like the Internet, originally thought to liberate the individual, can in the long term revive the need to find dignity in belonging to a transcending collective. Fukuyama reminds us that

> human beings are intensely social creatures whose emotional inclinations drive them to want to conform to the norms that surround them. When

a stable, shared moral horizon disappears and is replaced by a cacophony of competing value systems, the vast majority of people do not rejoice at their newfound freedom of choice. Rather, they feel intense insecurity and alienation because they do not know who their true self is. This crisis of identity leads in the opposite direction from expressive individualism to the search for a common identity that will rebind the individual to a social group and reestablish a clear moral horizon.[37]

Of course, Fukuyama's description is first and foremost aimed at the American public, and the European context is somehow different, as most (though not all) identity groups claim indigenous status. But his conclusions also apply to Europe, where groups facing spiritual or numeral decline have answered to it, like in North America, by reaffirming traditional or national values. In many ways, this identarian revival is a reaction to the ideas *en vogue* in the early 2010s that promoted the advent of a globalized standardization of individuals, where local particularism would be replaced by cultural and ethnic mixing[38] and where physical or mental borders would become obsolete. The backlash since then has been far-reaching. In the words of Ivan Krastev, "the demand for more democracy in Europe has been transformed into a call to defend one's own political community and thus a demand for exclusion rather than inclusion."[39] These demands have taken many forms: exclusion of immigrants from the national community, insults and aggression against women who would not wear the veil in Muslim-majority neighborhoods (and vice versa in non-Muslim neighborhoods), refusal to teach in the Castilian language in Catalonia, etc. Although theorized by Anglo-Saxon researchers in recent years, identity politics is actually a deeply rooted European phenomenon, and it carries a powerful potential for violence when combined with the search for uniformity of the social body, itself a European obsession.[40]

This tension between uniformity and identity is certainly not new in Europe. Similar causes produced the same effects in the heydays of European history, as Ernest Gellner has shown with remarkable accuracy in his book on the sociological roots of nationalism:[41] like in the early twenty-first century, the late nineteenth century and early twentieth century were marked by accelerated modernization and rapid acculturation around Europe: technical progress had triggered a rural exodus that had brought peasant masses in unseen numbers to urban centers, in search for a better life. But, rather than a promised land, cities ended up being pockets of precarity where the world as it had stood until then – community, uniformity, hierarchy – was pretty much turned upside down. In this tough environment where everything was missing, from spiritual comfort to decent lodging, the feeling of abandonment and alienation experienced by the masses pushed them (and the intellectuals who wanted to lead them) to look for forms of identity that would allow them to defend themselves and find meaning in their existence in an environment that seemed to have lost any logic. Some turned to socialism as an emancipatory force, others opted for a return to religion, others still to a fantasized and standardized village in a national construction – thereby laying the bases for the mass nationalisms that replaced the Empires in Central and Eastern Europe after the Great War. In this respect, the differential in the development of Czech and Slovak nationalisms perfectly validates Gellner's thesis: the former was born in a context of very rapid urbanization and industrialization and found itself at the forefront of the national awakening movement; the latter, which evolved in a much more deeply agrarian society, with few industries and few urban centers, developed much more slowly.[42]

Of course, today's mental alienation has not been triggered by factory work (which has almost disappeared in Europe) or rapid urbanization. The factors today are more diverse, among others an intense drive of globalization, social deprivation and insecurity following the 2008 financial crisis, a process of ghettoization in local neighborhoods (for which local elites themselves are often the first to blame[43]) and a re-rigidification of society as meritocratic systems are ushering into social class reproduction while social discourse has actually focused on the idea of social fluidity.[44] All these social phenomena have led to feelings of alienation, which in turn have led individuals to gradually turn to a collective that can transcend them and respond to their fears for the present and future. Following this logical development, many young people from immigrant backgrounds in France, Great Britain or Germany have found different solutions to respond to alienation, sometimes turning inwards to their neighborhood against foreigners (that includes the police), sometimes outwards to the nation they belong to (which has led to full integration in the host country or serving in the armed forces – French sociologist Jérôme Fourquet reminds us that many soldiers stemming from minorities have served the French army in a combat zone[45]). More controversially, some have also turned to a turn to radical interpretations of the Koran.

But identity politics is neither a factor in Europe's inner cities nor confined to "immigrant" communities: similar processes have led populations in the Catalan hinterland, sometimes more affluent but anxious about their future, to adhere to the idea of Catalan separatism, while recruiting their children in the movement. In other instances, communities of pious and practicing Catholics have become aware of their new status as a minority and radicalized their discourse to defend what they considered non-negotiable values, such as marriage and the family – here lies the genesis of the French (and subsequently Europe-wide) movement against same-sex marriage, the *Manif pour Tous*, which managed in places to mobilize far beyond the catholic community.[46] In a completely different setting, indigenous working-class people and their families that were left behind the drive of deindustrialization in the rust belt of the North of France, in Northern Britain or in former East Germany (among others), have tried to cultivate a sense of collective identity to reappropriate the public debate after a period of individual alienation and economic hardships. This, in turn, has led to the rise of not only right-wing populism but also violent episodes such as the Yellow Vest movement in France in 2018–2019. The result has been what French sociologist Jérôme Fourquet has called an "archipelization," extreme atomization of European societies, where communities turn inward and react to any higher collective's action as an intrusion. Signs of this atomization can be seen in the increased adoption of specifically "ethnic"[47] first names, whether Muslim, Jewish, Corsican,[48] Hungarian, Catalan or Ukrainian and by the wearing of distinctive signs in public, such as the Jewish kippah, the Christian cross or the Muslim scarf (24% of French Muslim women claimed to wear it in 2003; they were 35% in 2015[49]). In a European context, these have become rallying identity objects as much as religious physical obligations. And while they may be tolerated in the United States and to a lesser extent the United Kingdom, in Europe these marks of "specificity" have quickly raised tensions between communities, and between communities and the states.

The multiplication and diversification of identities have, in turn, re-complexified our societies, and when combined with material decline, it has led to a radicalization of part of these populations. George Mason University professor Justin Gest has shown that a remarkably similar process of social and identity alienation is at work in communities as diverse as the British working class of Barking and Dagenham, in the outskirts of London,[50] or young Muslims in the working-class district of Lavapiés in Madrid.[51] When unanswered, alienation can lead to radicalization: at best, this means a polarization of political debates, as societies throughout the West have experienced in the past decade, but it can also in certain circumstances turn into violent action.

The portraits of jihadists returned from Syria sketched by French journalist David Thomson show a diversity of trajectories, including socioeconomic, of the "French jihad's footsoldiers."[52] But while their backgrounds are different, they all share one common feature: the feeling of being lost in an individualized society that no longer makes sense to them and a quest for a sense that has brought them to an ultra-minoritarian (and ultraviolent) reading of Islam. Becoming part of this sort of adventure allows them to put their person at the service of a cause greater than themselves, give meaning to their lives and affirm their collective identity in the face of a community that they consider inaccessible and, in any case, corrupt.

When the jihadists returning from Syria in 2015 planned, encouraged and committed terrorist attacks in Paris, Brussels, Nice, Berlin or Barcelona,[53] they were not only seeking to export Middle Eastern conflicts into Europe. Their goal was also to provoke reactions among the local populations: one was demoralization so that Western powers would not intervene to help Middle Eastern regimes they consider as their enemy. But they also sought a negative reaction toward the local non-Muslim population, so as to further alienate European Muslims, who would then be more tempted to join organizations like ISIS. For terrorist groups, the stronger the sentiment of alienation is among Muslims, the more fertile is the ground for a radical, uncompromising version of Islam. But radicalization goes both ways, and it could lead to a clash of identities sufficiently salient to lead to civil war, as Michel Houellebecq imagined in his fiction book *Submission* which, notwithstanding the conversion of its main character to Islam, portrays France on the brink of civil war in the run-up to a French presidential election.[54] When Houellebecq's book came out in France in 2015, just before the start of a wave of terrorist attacks, it was extremely controversial and indeed rejected by much of the left as Islamophobic. This would not necessarily be the case today, as the reality has in some ways kicked in the way of fiction – French Muslims, like French practicing Catholics and many others, are more aware of their particular identities than they have been for a long time – indeed, the last time such atomization was present at these levels was the 1930s, where the crystallization of old divisions into leagues, clubs and a fear of foreign, religious or class enemies led the country into stagnation, defeat and ultimately a short civil war.[55]

Identity has so far not totally crystallized, in France as elsewhere. Thankfully, the French (and European) identity archipelagoes are today far too fragmented to set in motion a logic of direct confrontation between well-established camps. Furthermore, French and European Muslims, like French and European Christians, do not form a compact group and their communities are also crossed by multiple internal cleavages.[56] But debates could ossify very quickly due to an unforeseen event or the willingness of elites to instrumentalize identity for their own purposes: for example, the way Catalan elites used identity to deflect their own responsibilities in the region's budgetary difficulties following the 2008 crisis led to a protracted conflict between Madrid and Barcelona in which everyone has lost out, including ordinary Catalans. This could be the canvas for future confrontation between groups in Europe – with potentially unknown consequences.

So far, identity politics and their destructive effect on Europe's social fabric have mostly been contained by local and national elites – at least to a level where war and systemic inter-community violence have remained improbable. But if economic difficulties were to accumulate after the COVID-19 crisis, it is not impossible that the same elites find in identity and nationalism an easy fix to deflect blame for social and economic problems and instrumentalize it to keep power. This would, in turn, pave the way to the confrontation between communities that would have turned inward for long enough. In many ways, the run-up to Yugoslav wars in the 1990s followed this type of scenario (especially in Kosovo[57]), and identity clashes could reemerge in the next few years, with possible domino effects across the continent: A return to political violence in Bosnia and Herzegovina may have a spillover effect on the whole Western Balkans, widespread violence between Muslims and non-Muslims in France could thus have consequences beyond France's borders, while the spillover effect of a Catalan war of secession on the Hispanic peninsula could inspire (or follow the inspiration of) other separatist movements in the Balkans and around the Mediterranean. Religious, national or regional identity could thus spread like wildfire in a cultural era, Europe, where ideas travel faster than people. The continent-wide Wars of Religion of the sixteenth century or, in a more limited context, those of the Western Balkans between 1991 and 1999 remind us how Europe's very diverse identities coupled with Europeans' obsession with uniformity can lead to the worst protracted conflicts. Once awakened, they tend to spill over borders and become tenacious, as elites often lose control over these very decentralized types of war. Of course, the situation in Europe has not (yet) deteriorated to this point, but the reappearance in public opinion and public discourse of identity politics on so many levels should encourage the greatest caution.

New class struggles

Identity politics are not the only internal challenge facing Europe as social tensions could just as well destabilize the continent in the next decade. In many ways, these social issues are linked to identity: to take the example of the white working-class electorate's radicalization in recent years, it has much to do with a social, rather than racial feeling of estrangement: as Justin Gest points out, the workers he interviewed in his anthropological studies are always embarrassed when they have to talk about immigration or ethnic minorities, but much more articulate when it comes to describe their social problems, which they feel much more directly.[58] Does this mean that class struggle is returning today, with the potential to degenerate into civil war? The French Yellow Vests certainly represented a very polarizing and sometimes very violent moment. This jacquerie introduced mini-scenes of urban guerilla in the heart of Europe, and in different circumstances, it could lead to either civil war in one country (a riot overthrows a government, a power vacuum settles in and leads to a war between legitimists and revolutionaries, as was the case in Russia in 1918) or an interstate war (a riot overthrows a government, revolutionaries succeed in gaining some legitimacy at home but frighten their neighbors, who decide to intervene militarily to restore order, as was the case in France in 1792 or in Soviet Hungary in 1919).

These scenarios would require a very strong polarization of the European social body, even though it is reputed to be much more compact than American, Asian or African societies – as Angela Merkel liked to remind her fellow Germans regularly during her career as Chancellor, Europe represents 7% of the world's population, 25% of its economy but also 50% of its social spending.[59] However, when mapping social unrest, the trajectory of a society (or social groups) is sometimes as important as its position, and the fear of decline can be as destabilizing as the feeling of continued alienation. In reality, both alienation and social decline have monopolized public debate on social issues in Europe since the 2008 crisis, as inequalities between social groups, already growing before the crisis, have become much more visible today. This is a specific issue for Europe, where high levels of inequality are much less tolerated than elsewhere, as the idea of uniformity is much more persistent in European than in American societies. Importantly, these inequalities are not only inequalities of status but inequalities in the perception of individuals' trajectories. The social gaps have continued to grow between "winners" of globalization, optimistic about their future, and those who feel that they have been left behind in an ultracompetitive environment where their skills are no longer valued.[60]

Inequality often leads to alienation. And this feeling is reinforced by self-reproduction. Today's elites have not only created their own ghettos where they now live in almost total isolation from the rest of society but also tended to reproduce themselves at an ever-increasing rate, leaving outside of their circles those smart provincial (or simply socially poorer) graduates who were knocking on their door. This "secession of the elites" has been described by several authors including David Goodhart who gave a controversial but no less interesting critique of European meritocratic systems[61] but also by French sociologist Jérôme Fourquet who has thus described the phenomenon in his *French archipelago*:

> Having developed in a vast territory their own housing, shops, cultural spaces, leisure and workplaces, the upper socio-professional categories have learnt to effectively live in ever-increasing autarky. Living their life in an environment literally shaped to suit their specific needs, the members of the privileged classes have developed social gregariousness and an increasingly homogeneous value system. [...] A motorist can travel more than 30 kilometers westward from the Place de la Concorde in the center of Paris without leaving areas where the proportion of executives, intellectual professions and independent professions is less than 40% and often even 50% of the working population.[62]

As elites have seceded from the rest of society, the middle classes (relegated to the suburbs further afield) and the working classes have also coalesced in their own, homogenized social ghetto, thereby creating an exclusive common social identity, which has turned into a uniform political identity.[63]

Of course, this phenomenon of social ghettoization is not exceptional– it certainly is a feature of French as much as US society. But it is also becoming an issue in historically much more homogenous societies such as Germany or Sweden, and increasingly uniform electoral results in specific zones (urban/rural, young/old, global/local, etc.) suggest that many communities are now breaking away from each other, as I tried to demonstrate in 2019 in *The Great Class Shift*.[64] My previous book's main idea is that four social "classes" have monopolized the public debate and imposed their values and fault-lines on the rest of society. The liberal and globalized Creative Class,[65] which has lived a brief but intense period of dominance in the early 2010s, is socially, economically as well as culturally liberal. These winners of globalization have seen their efforts to change society opposed, sometimes vehemently, by the provincial (or suburban) middle class, who may share their economic liberalism, but certainly not their cosmopolitanism and their cultural choices (flexibility, diversity, porosity between work and leisure time, etc.). But if the Creative Class and the provincial/suburban middle class are increasingly at odds over social and cultural issues, they are often on the same side of the barricade on economic issues, as both are defined by a liberal economic outlook. This is not the case of the "rebel" classes, who have been lobbying for state intervention, although for completely different reasons and with different ends in sight – their emergence as a political force has aggravated polarization in the political debate. The "New Minority,"[66] composed of the white working class and the less educated, peripheral middle class that has gone through a period of pauperization in recent years,[67] is one of them. Much like in the United States, they have been the core vote of a new right-wing populism and have been asking for the return of the state in their communities, an end to the drive for more diversity and flexibility, and above all a stop to immigration and globalization. On the other hand, the millennials (to which now the woke zillenials must be added), young graduates whose university and life experience have pushed them toward the left or even the far-left, do support far-reaching social transformation and multiculturalism on steroids, leading to new left-wing populist pushes in places like Spain, Italy and France (*Podemos*, the Five Star Movement and La France insoumise come to mind but so also do extra-democratic groups like the Antifa and Black Bloc anarchist groups). Although millennial discourses and values have departed from the mainstream over the past ten years, it is also worth noting that softer versions of millennial left-wing politics have emerged, with Green parties often making a breakthrough in Western and Northern Europe between 2018 and 2019.[68]

The emergence of these new "classes" across the continent has redefined European political systems and the fault lines in the public debate, very often leading to a more fragmented, atomized (and polarized) political landscape. This in itself is not necessarily a bad thing and not a factor of war. After all, the concepts of right and left have evolved many times over the two hundred years of their existence. It is also true that social divisions have always been a driving factor in the democratic political debate – during the times of the Roman Republic, the divide between the Plebs and the Patricians defined much of the political struggles.[69] Nearer to us, in the 1970s, British historian Peter Pulzer reminded his students that "class is the basis of British party politics …. Everything else is embellishment and detail."[70]

If the social dimension of political debates is not new, the problem lies in the increasing polarization of social situations since 2008, which then translates into a more polarized political debate. This is a sign of our democracies' perceived inability to amalgamate the contradictory interests of old and new social classes in a satisfying way. Western societies' polarization hardly needs to be demonstrated in detail – as far as Europe is concerned, the mention of the debates on Brexit, the impact of the refugee crisis in Germany and Central Europe or the French Yellow Vest movement is usually enough to give a grasp of the problem. But while polarization is not a new phenomenon, what is different today is that the actors are no longer willing to talk to each other, including at elite level, and thus prefer to operate isolated from each other: as a result of the increased ghettoization of social groups described above, each class now develops its own logic on pretty much everything – including the selection of facts to create one's own reality, with logics that do not suffer any contradiction in the environment of socially (and geographically) segregated communities. Social groups can now create their own echo chambers, where individuals' experiences will be taken as a universal and undeniable fact, because it corresponds to a uniform, closed experience. Once the echo chamber has grown and become hermetic enough to exclude other social groups, any dissenting element that contradicts the well-oiled narrative is disregarded or dismissed as "fake news." The result is a self-radicalization of actors who end up seeing the debate as a mere exercise of throwing slogans at each other to mobilize client electorates rather than a negotiation in which they have to try and convince their adversary or incite them to meet halfway. Comforted in their cognitive bias, the members of each class will thus self-censor and radicalize their discourse. Meanwhile, each slogan put forward by the adversary will be experienced as an increasingly unacceptable aggression.

The problem is that this process of radicalization not only incites a more heated political debate but can also lead to outbreaks of violence – the events of the US Capitol on January 6, 2021, come to mind, but similar events occurred in Europe, for example in France with the Yellow Vest demonstrations of November–December 2018. In many ways, they represented a jacquerie that the country regularly had to face before the advent of trade unions in the early twentieth century,[71] but the Parisian version of the movement often took the form of seditious crowds organized to have a go at the police and, in some cases, to storm French ministries and *lieux de pouvoir*. Luckily for the French elites, the police forces remained loyal and the very horizontal movement did not usher in the emergence of new political leaders capable of mobilizing and redirecting energies toward a political goal. But, considering the state of social relations in France and elsewhere, it is not unthinkable to imagine similar movements pop up again in the future, with more social despair fueling more violence and political entrepreneurs using the raw potential of a Yellow-Vest like movement to build up their way to power.

For the moment, this perspective remains unlikely. Liberal democracy has this advantage that through voting and representation, it gives everyone, including those who form an electoral collective, the ability to make their voice heard by voting for their candidate or party in an election – according to German sociologist Max Weber, it is actually the very function of a political party to be the vehicle of a social body in the public debate.[72] By opening up the possibility of political alternance between parties and the classes they represent, the democratic game can ease tensions between social classes, insofar as it leaves the exercise of power open to an alternation between political parties and the classes they represent. It could be argued that democracy works even better in fluid environments, where pre-electoral and post-electoral alliances allow for multiple combinations, and smart politicians can take previously marginalized groups under their wing to bring them back into the system – something the UK Conservative Party has managed to do under Theresa May and Boris Johnson as they moved their party from a Thatcherite consensus to embracing the values of the traditional working class, previously solid Labour voters.[73] In completely different settings, in Austria, the ruling Austrian People's Party (ÖVP) did not hesitate to switch his priorities to ditch an uneasy alliance with the Austrian far-right (which had become a champion of the Austrian working class) to build an equally uneasy alliance for his middle-class ÖVP with the Greens, whose support base is principally with young, left-wing voters.

But while this fluidity may be seen as a remarkable sign of resilience from democracies, whose qualities are too often unsung these days, nothing guarantees that this state of affairs will continue in the long term. Democracies, like all institutions, do decay, and they can tilt too much toward plutocracy or the tyranny of the majority, thereby creating imbalances that can in turn lead to violence. Democracies' success is also driven by economics, as Edward Luce points out:

> We are taught to think our democracies are held together by values. Our faith in history fuels that myth. But liberal democracy's strongest glue is economic growth. When groups fight over the fruits of growth, the rules of the political game are relatively easy to uphold. When those fruits disappear, or are monopolized by a fortunate few, things turn nasty [...]. The politics of interest group management turn into zero-sum battle over declining resources.[74]

The economic difficulties that many countries in Europe have been experiencing over the past decades (Italy, France but also Greece come to mind) have put them in a delicate situation: in these countries where growth has often stagnated or even declined in real terms, the zero-sum game has already become a reality, and too often it is the young (historically more susceptible to radical options) that have been paying the price of "adjustments" made to maintain the insiders' cash flows. The game could become dangerous if, over the longer term, one or more classes came to be collectively convinced that the democratic game is rigged in favor of a specific group. Violence, or a confiscatory and definitive seizure of power, could then become an option for these rebel groups and, especially, their leaders, who would feel deprived of their share of government by the system. Here again, the obvious example that comes to mind is the assault on the US Capitol on January 6, 2021, but similar logics are at play in Europe, notably to justify the construction of illiberal states, and it is not impossible to see riotous power grabs being attempted in the future in some Europe countries, ending up in confiscation of powers by a group of people representing a specific social group. Such a scenario could usher in another type of a revolutionary war that, in the European context, has rarely confined itself to the borders of one state – the risk is therefore to see the emergence of a new European Civil War fueled by a social, class war.

Social media: a new Gutenberg Bible?

The social divisions we have just discussed are certainly not a new phenomenon. Europe's history is full of societal (and identity) fault lines such as these, some of them superficial and some of them particularly deep, and if some have deepened enough to cause war in the continent's history, they have also brought major advances for European civilization without necessarily causing war: without class conflict between aristocracy and bourgeoisie, and then between the ruling and the working class, the right to vote would have remained limited to the privileged strata of European societies, for example. Seen in its historical depth, the return to more fragmented and divided societies actually marks a return to normalcy after an exceptional period of cohesion that had been the direct (but ephemeral) result of the Second World War, with its ethnic cleansing and the construction of a far-reaching welfare state in its aftermath.

Yet this should not hide the fact that traditionally, social divisions are also the cause of some of Europe's most vicious wars. The three longest and most severe conflicts on the continent since the Renaissance, the Wars of Religion, the Revolutionary Wars and the European Civil War, which encompasses the two world conflicts, also have in common with each other and with our times that they were all preceded and/or accompanied by periods of very rapid intellectual and technological innovation. The Wars of Religion followed the discovery of the Americas and the invention of the printing press by Gutenberg; the Revolutionary and then Napoleonic Wars were a direct product of the Enlightenment, its salons and importantly its first newspapers; finally, the European Civil War followed a period of not only intense technological change with the acceleration of the industrial revolution but also the invention of the radio and cinema. In fact, it seems that the three most vicious conflicts in the history of modern Europe have all followed major advances in communication technologies. The Gutenberg Bible at the end of the fifteenth century paved the way for the Reformation by allowing the printing of different versions of the Bible on a very large scale in more literate societies. Where Bogomils, Hussites and Cathars had been contained in Bosnia, Bohemia and southwestern France prior to Gutenberg because of the confidential circulation of writings, Luther and Calvin were able to take advantage of the printing press to disseminate their theological theses to a much wider audience. If the intransigent protestant leaders shared responsibility for the Wars of Religion with a Catholic church that stuck to its privileges and questionable behavior, printing allowed the extension of passions to new publics and larger regions. Later on, Europeans discovered in the eighteenth century that the appearance of modern newspapers and the multiplication of new ideas in the salons and clubs could lead to a much richer intellectual debate but that this also meant more violent intellectual confrontations and, down the road, terror and war. Finally, as American sociologist Larry Diamond reminds us, we discovered at the beginning of the twentieth century that "just as radio and TV could be vehicles of information pluralism and rational debate, they could also be commandeered by totalitarian regimes for fanatical mobilization and total state control."[75]

Having mentioned these three examples, one can only wonder whether the Internet and social networks could be playing exactly the same role as the

Gutenberg Bible, the first newspapers of the eighteenth century or radio and cinema in making our political debate more violent, thereby dividing our societies into irreconcilable warring camps. In fact, social media have thus far proved just as disruptive to our societies and states over the past decade and consequences could be far-reaching. First, social media puts in touch people who would not originally have had the possibility to talk to each other, let alone exchange and organize. These people could be tens, even hundreds or thousands of miles away from each other (or sometimes just a few streets away). The first demonstrations of Facebook and other social media's potential of mobilization and people's power captivated liberals during the 2010s, during the Arab Spring in 2011[76] or the Revolution of Dignity in Ukraine in 2014,[77] when urban demonstrators were able to multiply their mobilizing power and organize large demonstrations to intimidate dictators and overthrow dishonest and corrupt regimes. This, however, proved to be only one side of the social media revolution; those liberals who had enthusiastically endorsed it soon discovered that reactionary forces could also organize and that they could even manipulate social media to influence outcomes.

We will return in the next chapters to the issues of foreign interference and the use by unfriendly powers of social networks as weapons of war, but it is worth discussing here the direct effects that social media have had on Western politics over the last decade. The first unintended consequence of their irruption into the public debate is the logic of tribalization that they have encouraged. Social networks, whose addictive effect is now documented,[78] tend to bring us closer to people with whom we share common interests. In doing so, they can cut us off from reality and the diversity of opinions around us – and encourage us to associate only with people who share our views. What was supposed to be a soundboard for a broader public debate thus quickly became a series of closed echo chambers that have increasingly isolated groups from the rest of the world, in particular those individuals who did not share our views. We have all experienced this on our social media, where we engage in what is originally a political "discussion" with a "friend" or contact with whom we do not share political views. Disagreements emerge, the discussion escalates and turns into a mud fight, the conflict becomes personal as comments and responses become more acrimonious and, in the best cases, one of the parties just leaves the conversation with a "whatever," waiting for the next mud fight to take revenge on the opponent – that is, when there is an opponent remaining, as very often the latter is simply blocked or "unfriended." The effect of these incidents can be devastating for the moral and intellectual balance of individuals: in the words of cyber security expert Clint Watts,

> preference bubbles create a world of audiences where social media users, in many cases, identify with people they don't know over people they live with or see every day. We've seen the crowd not complement or compete with the core but seek to destroy it. Whoever gets the most likes is in charge; whoever gets the most shares is an expert.[79]

These preferences bubbles thus gradually lead us to what journalist David Patrikarakos defines as a state of homophilia "meaning literally 'love of the same', in which individuals bond with like-minded others, who reinforce their worldviews."[80] This process has another name, which is predominantly used to describe an individual's road toward terrorism: self-radicalization.

Of course, we are not suggesting that the use of social media makes us all potential terrorists. But it is undeniable that social networks have not only played a role in the self-radicalization of a number of individuals (it was clearly the case for the assassin of Samuel Paty in France in 2019[81] or the Christchurch white supremacist terrorist the same year[82]) but also driven societies apart, collectively. The fact that we increasingly function in isolated bubbles that reinforce our prejudices (whether liberal, socialist or conservative) is allowing us to develop a much narrower view of what is to be considered normal and acceptable. And as the fault lines between our bubbles correspond, as a result of individual experience and social ghettoization, to the dangerous social and identity cleavages described earlier in this chapter, the end result is that the gap between individuals and groups of individuals in our societies is becoming ever wider, to the extent that we sometimes wonder whether we actually do have *anything* in common with our fellow citizens.

This, of course, is the first step toward civil war, and we are only starting to explore ways in which we can regulate social media to avoid this fate.[83] One way to deal with the problem of growing tribalism is to impose one's view on all, which means instituting a new form of censorship over social networks, thereby adopting the model of population control advocated by the Chinese Communist Party. But such a drastic measure, even assuming that it would be desirable (or even effective, as Chinese and Russian censors are discovering every day), would be extremely difficult to implement in our Western cultural system where liberty and freedom of expression remain a centerpiece of political culture. The actual ineffectiveness of states, even when they want to, in imposing full censorship (including in China), brings us to another side effect of social networks, namely their capacity to weaken central states, which for two hundred years had "a virtual monopoly on the use of force and dominant control over information flows," as David Patrikarakos puts it.[84] Social networks have indeed removed most of the barriers to entering the world of media: today, an individual only needs a smartphone, internet access and a smart communication strategy to send a message to the world, where 20 years ago such a feat was possible only through the purchase and use of considerable means that only states and large corporations could afford (journalists, a TV or radio studio, equipment – cameras, microphones, mixers, etc.). Of course, it would be foolish not to applaud this irresistible democratization of communication that potentially makes us all individual broadcasters, but it would be equally foolish not to recognize the perverse effects of having millions of these broadcasters competing on the web at the same time for attention: today, anyone can go on a crusade against anything and mobilize a large number of people on an issue (including by inciting violence) without the state having the capacity to anticipate the scale of the movement, or (more problematically) the intentions of the protesters. The end result can be a peaceful demonstration that humbles the government, but the Yellow Vests riots in Paris in 2019 or the storming of the US Capitol in January 2021 show how well organized and violent groups can make use of social media to organize themselves and overwhelm security forces to turn a demonstration into a riot and, possibly, in the future a riot into a coup – which could end up into civil war. As radical groups use social networks to challenge the state's claimed monopoly on the use of violence, the diffusion of multiple narratives to a large and diverse public opens the way to new types of confrontations, some of which we will discuss in Chapter 6.

This is of course not to say that social networks are (willingly or not) fomenting a civil war in Europe or elsewhere. As in many other cases, the instrument here is not so much to blame as its users, who are learning every day, through a succession of trial and error to tame a new tool and make the difference between real and fake news as they did decades ago with the printing press or radio. The learning curve is also long for states and political actors who have often underestimated the negative implications concomitant to the positive effects brought by social networks in our lives. The elites are not entirely blameless either in the rise of public skepticism around fake news – they have not exactly covered themselves with glory since the beginning of the century, as the rise of social networks coincided with (and sometimes amplified) state or corporate scandals where authorities manipulated or concealed realities to get their way: the war in Iraq, of course, comes to mind but so do the Volkswagen emissions scandal,[85] Edward Snowden's revelations on the surveillance practices of the National Security Agency (NSA) and many other events that, once publicized, have reduced citizens' trust in institutions – and their neighbors. All these developments have deepened the rift between the people and their elites and between people and their institutions.[86] Uncontrolled and unregulated, social media have thus amplified the atomization and polarization of Western – and for what is of interest to us European – societies. This has happened in a context where public authority and nation-states were already being weakened by more than ten years of crisis and austerity, and before that, a neoliberal economic consensus that may have released an incredible amount of private energy but has also threatened the state's capacity to perform some of its essential functions. As state structures may further weaken in a post-COVID-19 environment, social media could contribute to further weaken our societal structures, to the point where online calls to violence would become common enough to be followed by actions. Even more problematically, the capacity of ill-intentioned elites or foreign governments to use the power of social media to foment social strife in a given country has become a serious issue for European governments to consider, as we will see in Chapter 6.

Twilight of liberalism

The post-Cold War period has often been defined as post-ideological, insofar as the great competition between the ideologies of the twentieth century

– communism, fascism and liberalism – ended in what seemed a decisive victory for the liberal democratic model. But we are learning today that an ideology may only retain its dominant status for a while, before being inevitably challenged one way or another. Indeed, the crisis of 2008 and the economic and social disasters that followed have greatly weakened the thus-far uncontested advantage of liberal democracy. After the rise of communist China as a systemic competitor to the United States, it was only a matter of time before new philosophies on the best way to organize society would challenge the quasi-monopoly liberalism had enjoyed on European governance for almost thirty years.

The task of the challenger was made easier by liberals' capacity to divide themselves into rival groups and to isolate themselves from other political families. The splits inside the liberal family between classic and social liberals are well known to Europeans, but they are only one of the many divisions that run through the liberal movement, and when they became too strong, these divisions have weakened not only political liberalism but also the larger consensus on the relevance and strength of liberal democracy. This has happened even more easily as liberalism has too often willingly cut itself – in the name of orthodoxy – with other forces with whom it had teamed up to defeat fascism and communism. On the left, social democracy and democratic socialism have increasingly become estranged from liberalism after a period of rapprochement after the 1960s; on the right, it is conservatism (which in its Burkean version is certainly compatible with liberalism) and civic nationalism that has drifted away from liberalism,[87] leaving the "dominant" ideology isolated and exposed on both flanks. In particular, the divorce between nationalism and liberalism is extremely problematic for the latter, as the former possesses a potential for mass mobilization that is far more powerful than an ideology whose very principle is the absolute neutrality of the state toward its citizens and vice versa.[88] Of course, the movement of these ideologies away from liberalism is not new – it started well before the 2008 crisis, but the acceleration of liberalism's isolation in the 2010s, coupled with the dominance of a certain type of social liberalism fueled by the creative class during this decade has made the problem much worse. In the absence of a common enemy to appease their differences, liberals, social democrats, conservatives and nationalists have thus moved away from each other, to the extent where they consider themselves enemies, leaving the way for anti-liberal (and often also anti-democratic) ideologies to recruit them for their cause, just like communism and fascism did in the 1930s.

So far, the most powerful challenger to the liberal order has been on the far-right. Right-wing populism is both a nationalist and an illiberal vision of the world; it considers that liberalism as it exists today only defends minorities (sexual, ethnic or immigrant) and that the promotion of these minority interests is done directly at the expense of the majority, fantasized in its size and in its embodiment by the charismatic leader. Even though it is being challenged by the necessities of COVID-19, right-wing populism remains a considerable force in the public debate, as its rise corresponds to a fundamental shift within the electorate. According to political scientist Yascha Mounk, "the preferences of the people are increasingly illiberal: voters are growing impatient with independent institutions and less and less willing to tolerate the rights of ethnic and religious minorities."[89] The active minority/silent majority conundrum is historically a very potent one in societies in crisis, as it allows to put all problems a country faces on the back of a malfeasant minority supposedly in bed with the elites in power. In turn, it allows right-wing populism to propose an ultra-majoritarian vision of power in which "the people" regain power against corrupt, liberal and cosmopolitan (read foreign) elites. One of the leading figures of this movement in Europe is Viktor Orbán, who proposes not only to build a state that he calls "illiberal democracy" in Hungary[90] but also to export his model to Europe through an "alliance of European rights,"[91] the idea being to include in it as many nationalists and conservatives as possible in his political coalition to create an illiberal majority, with the primary theme being the defense of Christian Europe.[92]

However spectacular, the rise of the right should not hide the development of another populist challenge on the left, equally embedded in the idea that it represents a fantasized "people" against a corrupt elite.[93] These anti-systemic forces take several forms, some more or less respectful of elections, others such as the Black blocs clearly rejecting parliamentary democracy as fake. Left-wing populism should not be confused with a loyal, left-wing critique of liberalism that seeks to reform society within the institutions of liberal democracy. Unlike this "liberal" left, left-wing populism seeks to replace representative liberal democracy with a model that is at once more state-centered, more dirigiste and more direct, in which referendums or consultations (most often controlled and manipulated) are presented as a way to overcome "fake democracy," today's equivalent of what German communist Rosa Luxemburg once called "parliamentary cretinism." The distinction between this "liberal left" and the "populist left" is sometimes difficult to make, insofar as the new left-wing parties that stem from the social youth movements of the early 2010s are often open to both movements for the sake of electoral appeal. Nevertheless, as Giuliano da Empoli had demonstrated in the case of Italy's Five Star movement, the reality is often that the liberals end up being instrumentalized by the populist left in controlled forums on social media that give an impression of democracy but are in fact controlled by a small group of people (the case of the Rousseau platform in Italy comes to mind).[94] The anti-liberal movement has also taken much more insidious action in recent years to impose itself in the public debate, may it be through the organization of small violent groups inside demonstrations (France's Black Bloc groups are one example among many[95]) or through direct action to establish new censorship in universities and impose minority views on race, gender and social justice to the public: after all, as Eugen Weber once wrote, "Revolution – like reformation – begins in utopia and ends in orthodoxy."[96]

The illiberal challenge from the left may be easily dismissed by those who view the far-right as currently a more immediate threat. This may be true in a pre-COVID-19 environment, but the future may hold a few surprises for us: in fact, while the support for national-populism may have reached a high tide, the numerical potential for socialist-populism is growing by the day: indeed, left-wing illiberalism feeds itself from millennials' (born between 1982 and 1996) and now zillennials' (born after 1996) frustration with a system that puts their aspirations behind those of the more numerous baby boomers. And while the boomers' numerical advantage is still guaranteed by their higher propension to vote, the reality is that their numbers have already plateaued, while those of the millennials and zillennials are growing each year. While young non-graduates increasingly join national-populist movements, young graduates often leave their universities committed to left-wing ideas and skeptical of democracy. Of course, integration in the socioeconomic system usually softens the critiques to make them "progressive" rather than revolutionary in countries like Germany and Austria (where young graduates vote Green) or the Czech Republic and Slovakia (where they vote for the Pirates and Progressive Slovakia). But this process of socioeconomic integration is slowed down or even broken in countries with high unemployment like France or Spain, where young people are two times more likely than others to be jobless. These frustrated, socioeconomically estranged youths often join movements with leaders taking their inspiration from the Cuban, Venezuelan or even the Chinese models. Young people who can harbor legitimate frustration with a system that too often ignores them are thus drawn into much more radical structures, where their moral appreciation of right and wrong becomes more important than facts and where violence can be seen as a legitimate instrument for solving or managing conflicts.

As more people move away from liberal democracy and are drawn into illiberal populist narratives, the risk is that a divided and weakened liberal model finds itself surrounded by two rival illiberal models, much like in the 1920s and 1930s. And while one can count on the more radical fringes of each camp to fight each other as much as they would fight the liberals, history also tells us that in the long run, it is the liberal model that is most at risk of weakening and disappearance, as times of polarization give very little room for nuance and institutional neutrality. That this polarization could usher into a new "European civil war," although yet not probable, is now a distinct possibility.

Indeed, one of the risks carried by this *ménage à trois* is that far-left and far-right could join forces to get rid of liberal democracy before sorting out their differences. This is in many ways what the Marxist concept of the "convergence of struggles" envisages, with the idea, of course, that the far-left will ultimately triumph, thanks to its superior ideological offer. This slogan was often heard among left-wing intellectuals in France during the Yellow Vests crisis. Such a convergence could well happen, but right now, it looks much more like it would be to the benefit of right-wing illiberalism, not left-wing populism. Countries like France today look much more like the Germany of 1932 than Russia in 1917, and the deeper roots of the populist right in political landscapes across the continent suggests that if a junction were indeed to take place, it would inevitably be to the latter's benefit. If such a scenario were to unfold, the discussion would not be about a weakened liberal consensus attacked on its left and its right but weakened and isolated liberalism facing a broad illiberal coalition that would have gathered all discontents around one banner. The confrontation could then take violent turns, leaving the way open for a civil war between supporters of "illiberal democracy" and defenders of a liberal model that would have decoupled itself from the democratic ideal for fear of ochlocracy. In fact, while Yascha Mounk acknowledges the growing appeal of illiberal policies among voters, he concedes that there are equally strong anti-democratic tendencies among liberals:

> Elites are taking hold of the political system and making it increasingly unresponsive: the powerful are less and less willing to cede to the views of the people. As a result, liberalism and democracy, the two core elements of our political system, are starting to come into conflict.[97]

Of course, we cannot anticipate the final outcome of such a confrontation between "liberal-antidemocrats" and "illiberal-democrats," but if history can provide us with elements of an answer, they plead for atomization of Europe between states that would have succumbed to illiberalism and others that would have remained faithful to the liberal model. Such a situation would not be unlike that of the Reformation, where the conversion of some German princes to Protestantism while others remained Catholics led to a cycle of fratricidal wars; it would also echo the Napoleonic Wars and the great revolutionary waves of 1830 and 1848 – which were also punctuated by short but bloody military interventions in Belgium (1830, success of the insurgents and independence of the Belgians) or Hungary (failure of the insurgents and direct rule by Vienna). In all cases, the ideological confrontation between elites, fueled by social and identity-based opposition among the population, led to war.

Oceanism and continentalism

The ideological confrontation between liberalism and illiberalism is not the only dimension that could one day lead Europeans to more physical confrontations. In fact, the ideological competition between the two systems is taking place in the background of more profound geopolitical realignments resulting from the rise of authoritarian powers like China. In fact, behind the confrontation between liberals and illiberals, we often (though not always) see another geopolitical fault line between "oceanist" (and often liberal) countries and "continentalist" (and often illiberal) systems. The oceanists have access to the sea and benefit directly from free trade (though less and less from the free circulation of people); they tend to be more open to progressive ideas incubated on one of the two American coasts. The continentalists, on the other hand, have a tendency to look inward; they see their country as far from the traditional roads of commerce and see China's Belt and Road Initiative as an opportunity rather than a threat; they also see illiberalism as a model worth pursuing, to follow "continental" examples from the Eurasian landmass. In this regard, it is useful to quote extensively part of Viktor Orbán's speech at Băile Tuşnad in 2014, a genesis of his illiberal trend of thinking, which also informs us about his continentalist vision of the world:

> a trending topic in thinking is understanding systems that are not Western, not liberal, not liberal democracies, maybe not even democracies, and yet are making nations successful. Today, the stars of international analyses are Singapore, China, India, Turkey, Russia. And I believe that our political community rightly anticipated this challenge [...]. We are searching for (and we are doing our best to find, ways of parting with Western European dogmas, making ourselves independent from them) the form of organizing a community, that is capable of making us competitive in this great world-race. In order to be able to do this in 2010 and especially these days, we needed to courageously state a sentence, a sentence that, similar to the ones enumerated here, was considered to be a sacrilege in the liberal world order. We needed to state that a democracy is not necessarily liberal. Just because something is not liberal, it still can be a democracy. Moreover, it could be and needed to be expressed, that probably societies founded upon the principle of the liberal way to organize a state will not be able to sustain their world-competitiveness in the following years, and more likely they will suffer a setback, unless they will be able to substantially reform themselves.[98]

Viktor Orbán is careful to include Singapore and Turkey, two formal allies of the United States, as well as India, which has been moving closer to Washington for several years, in his illiberal models so as not to cut bridges with conservative American circles, but the general message is clear: the liberal West is culturally and politically in advanced decadence, and continental powers, first and foremost China (but also Russia) are the future. The logical conclusion to this presentation is that any sensible mind would recommend alignment to the continental model to be competitive in the twenty-first century – which can be interpreted simply through not only economic success but also political success. By taking the continentalist train before the others, a country would then be able to take a competitive advantage over its neighbors and dictate its conditions over them. What is emerging from this picture is that the overspill of the China–America rivalry is already taking place in Europe. Of course, at present the rivalry is mostly economic, but it is not without ideological foundations, insofar as it opposes a Chinese continental model based on particularism, exclusivism, illimited government intervention, harmony and hierarchy against an oceanic model based on universality (inherited from the Enlightenment), freedom, inclusivity, individualism and freedom.[99]

This description itself shows how incompatible the two value systems are: freedom, which is probably the most important value in Western thinking can only be real if it includes the freedom to challenge the established order and hierarchies. As some European states come dangerously close to adhering to the continentalist world view, their realignment threatens to usher in new ideological (and ultimately territorial) divisions within Europe, with two camps emerging like in the Cold War. Except that, unlike in the Cold War, these divisions would not follow the geographical logic of a continuous Iron Curtain descending from Stettin to Trieste. Indeed, even if public opinion in Central and Eastern Europe seems more sensitive to illiberal discourse than in Western Europe (although similar divisions also exist within countries, for example within France and Germany, where the internal East/West geographic fault line is particularly salient), the dividing lines between the countries operating within Beijing's orbit and those still loyal to the Atlantic Alliance would not be as clear-cut this time, as there is little homogeneity between nation-states and no army advances to clearly delimit borders as in 1945. In this instance, it is difficult to imagine geographically homogeneous blocs forming in the absence of external military intervention. It is indeed perfectly imaginable to see illiberal, continentalist leaders being elected in France, for example, while other countries in the Baltic States, Czechia or Romania remain under liberal oceanist leadership. In case of an irreconcilable divorce between a continentalist and an oceanist Europe, the chances would be that Europe would look more like it did at the beginning of the wars of religion, a patchwork of states that will have embraced a new ideology or stuck to the old one, rather than geographic blocs of countries. Europe would thus become a chessboard, before logically becoming a battlefield between the great powers.

Whether Europeans like it or not, their divisions also matter in a world that is no longer as peaceful and neutral as they once thought. As the jungle grows back, it makes Europe's surroundings more dangerous, but it also threatens to take Europeans into conflicts they would not necessarily have joined by choice. How external issues can threaten the peace of Europe will be the subject of the next chapter.

Notes

1 As early as November 1951 (following the decision of Winston Churchill's cabinet not to join the European construction project), future Prime Minister Harold MacMillan (then Minister of Housing and supporter of the project) had anticipated the possible long-term consequences of a Europe without the United Kingdom and with a weakened France: "There would be a European Community which would dominate Europe and would be roughly equal to Hitler's Europe in 1940. If we stay out, we risk that German domination of Europe which we have fought two world wars to prevent"; Quoted in Andrew Adonis et al., *Half In Half Out: Prime Ministers on Europe*, London: Biteback Publishing, 2019, p.47.
2 See Andrew Adonis et al., *Half in Half out: Prime Ministers on Europe*, London: Biteback Publishing, 2018, pp.195–196 et 226–227.
3 Ashoka Mody, *EuroTragedy: A Drama in Nine Acts,* Oxford: Oxford University Press, 2018, p.303.
4 https://www.euractiv.com/section/energy/news/how-us-sanctions-could-hit-russias-nord-stream-2-gas-project/

5 Hans Kundani, *The Paradox of German Power*, Oxford: Oxford University Press, 2014, p.110.
6 https://www.politico.eu/article/germany-economy-the-end-angela-merkel-economic-miracle/
7 In 2015, only Greek public opinion saw in Germany "the main threat to the security of your country." Source: Europe-wide Gallup poll fielded in 2015, quoted in Pascal Orcier, *Représenter la peur: la carte de la menace ressentie par les Européens*, April 2019, http://geoconfluences.ens-lyon.fr/informations-scientifiques/a-la-une/carte-a-la-une/menace-ressentie-par-les-europeens
8 Source: World Bank, 2018.
9 See David Broder, *First They Took Rome: How the Populist Right Conquered Italy*, London: Verso, 2020.
10 On the Euro-wide rise of Euroscepticism in the 2010s, see for example ECFR's study, and notably https://ecfr.eu/archive/page/-/ECFR79_EUROSCEPTICISM_BRIEF_AW.pdf; *The Instituto di Affari Internazionali*, based in Rome, does regular polling about Italians' attitudes about the European Union; they all show large-scale dissatisfaction with the EU, even during the times of the COVID-19 pandemic: https://www.iai.it/en/pubblicazioni/italian-euroscepticism-and-covid-19-pandemic-survey-insights.
11 https://www.politico.eu/article/european-league-matteo-salvini-switches-to-team-eu/?fbclid=IwAR2ArYIO_8lp7En1sEDvfM-hEIKhNGvbsSya-GWCBOOHmhfX5ALEJSHO1Tw
12 Daniel Gros, *Who Holds Italian Governemnt Debt*, CEPS Policy Insights, no. 2019–11, June 2019, https://www.ceps.eu/wp-content/uploads/2019/06/PI2019_11_Italian-public-debt-holdings.pdf
13 https://www.politico.eu/article/why-europe-china-investment-deal-will-poison-transatlantic-relations-joe-biden/
14 https://www.dw.com/en/german-minister-dont-link-navalny-with-nord-stream-2/a-56483949
15 Germany's pre-1945 anthem, the *Deutschlandlied*, is better known for its first stanza, which begins with the famed *Deutschland über Alles*, dubbed by Nietzsche "the dumbest lyrics of the world" (*die blödsinnigste Parole der Welt*). It has been too often caricatured as proving Germany's domination instincts, although it speaks of Germany above all else, not of Germany above everyone else. See https://www.spiegel.de/kultur/literatur/deutsche-nationalhymne-die-bloedsinnigste-parole-der-welt-a-422419.html
16 Geoffrey Blainey, *The Causes of War* (3rd edition), New York: The Free Press, 1988, p.122.
17 In their recent book published just before the 2019 election, Sylvain Kahn and Jacques Lévy argue that the most important fault line in the European Parliament lies in the opposition between an "enlightenment bloc" and a neo-nationalist "nebula," which can also be described as reactionary. This division not only is expressed geographically but intersects with a historical reality, not unlike the one we experienced in Europe between 1815 and 1848, with a more liberal bloc led by Great Britain and France gaining ground against a conservative and anti-liberal bloc led by Prussia, Austria and Russia at the time – the Holy Alliance. Sylvain Kahn and Jacques Lévy, *Le Pays des Européens*, Paris: Odile Jacob, 2019, pp.198–202.
18 Benedict Anderson, *Imagined Communities: Reflections on the Origin and Spread of Nationalism* (revised edition), London: Verso Books, 2016.
19 https://www.economist.com/graphic-detail/2018/11/21/imperial-borders-still-shape-politics-in-poland-and-romania
20 https://euobserver.com/political/139771
21 https://ecfr.eu/article/commentary_can_slovakia_and_the_czech_republic_overcome_europes_east_west_d/

22 See Dominique Reynié et al., *Démocraties sous tension: une enquête planétaire*, Paris: Fondapol, 2019, also available online: http://www.fondapol.org/etude/enquete-planetaire-democraties-sous-tension-volume-i-les-enjeux/
23 The Magyar Creed, installed by Admiral Horthy's dictatorship in the 1920s and 1930s, was taught as early as elementary school, with children having to recite it before each school day. See Paul A. Hanebrick, *In Defense of Christian Hungary: Religion, Nationalism and Antisemitism, 1890–1944*, Ithaca: Cornell University Press, 2006, p.112, for the origins of the creed
24 https://balkaninsight.com/2020/05/07/orbans-greater-hungary-map-creates-waves-in-neighbourhood/
25 See Article D of Hungary's Constitution, as well as https://visegradinsight.eu/dreams-of-power-hungary-politics-history/
26 https://www.nytimes.com/2018/10/05/world/europe/ukraine-hungary-ethnic-languages.html
27 https://www.euractiv.com/section/defence-and-security/news/hungary-blocks-nato-statement-on-ukraine-over-minority-rights-row/
28 https://foreignpolicy.com/2019/10/22/hungary-ukraine-feud-viktor-orban-trump-russia/
29 For a better understanding on how the definition of power relations between nations and the imposition of one actor's will on the other are the main causes of the transition from a state of peace to a state of war, see Geoffrey Blainey, *The Causes of War* (3rd edition), New York: The Free Press, 1988.
30 https://www.lemonde.fr/idees/article/2017/10/11/la-menace-d-une-balkanisation-de-l-espagne-et-de-l-europe-est-reelle_5199240_3232.html
31 Geoffrey Blainey, *The Causes of War* (3rd edition), New York: The Free Press, 1988, p.30.
32 Patrick Pasture, *Imagining European Unity since 1000 AD*, Basingstoke: Palgrave MacMillan, 2015, p.8.
33 Ernst Nolte, *Der europäische Bürgerkrieg, 1917–1941: Nationalsozialismus und Bolschevismus*, Berlin: Propyläen, 1987.
34 Geoffrey Blainey, *The Causes of War* (3rd edition), New York: The Free Press, 1988, p.70.
35 Peter Pomerantsev, *This Is Not Propaganda: Adventures in the War against Reality*, London: Faber & Faber, 2019, p.208.
36 Francis Fukuyama, *Identity: The Demand for Dignity and the Politics of Resentment*, London: Profile Books, 2018, p.18.
37 Ibid., p.56.
38 https://www.livescience.com/34228-will-humans-eventually-all-look-like-brazilians.html
39 Ivan Krastev, *After Europe*, Philadelphia: University of Pennsylvania Press, 2017, p.59.
40 Patrick Pasture, *Imagining European Unity since 1000 AD*, Basingstoke: Palgrave MacMillan, 2015, p.8.
41 Ernest Gellner, *Nations and Nationalism*, Ithaca: Cornell University Press, 1983.
42 See Stanislav Kirschbaum, *A History of Slovakia: The Struggle for Survival* (2nd edition), New York: Saint Martin's Press, 2006.
43 See Jérôme Fourquet, *L'Archipel Français: naissance d'une nation multiple et divisée*, Paris: Seuil, 2019.
44 See David Goodhart, *Head Hand Heart: The Struggle for Dignity and Status in the 21st Century*, London: Allen Lane, 2020,
45 The question of identity in Muslim populations is particularly sensitive, precisely because of the great diversity of responses to the alienation of life in Europe's inner cities. And if much has been written about the Islamist temptation among some individuals, others have chosen full service to the nation, whether in France, Germany, Sweden or Britain, among others. In France, as Jérôme Fourquet recalls,

"7 of our 77 soldiers who fell in Afghanistan between 2001 and 2015 while fighting the Taliban were immigrants, representing a proportion of nearly 10% of French losses. The soldiers killed by Mohamed Merah (Imad Ibn Ziatnen, Abel Chennouf and Mohamed Legouad) were also all of North African origin, as were Ahmed Merabet, the policeman shot dead in front of Charlie Hebdo's offices by the Kouachi brothers, and Samir Bajja, the French soldier who fell in Mali during an operation against jihadists. Following the example of the United States, enlistment in the armed forces is a path to professional integration for minority groups (Blacks and Hispanics in the United States, people from French overseas territories or immigrants in France), who often suffer from a less developed network of relationships, weaker cultural capital and discriminatory practices on the labor market." See Jérôme Fourquet, *L'Archipel Français: naissance d'une nation multiple et divisée*, Paris: Seuil, 2019, p.150.
46 Ibid., p.68.
47 Ibid., p.71.
48 Ibid., p.130.
49 Ibid., p.164.
50 Justin Gest, *The New Minority: White Working Class Politics in the Age of Immigration and Inequality*, New York: Oxford University Press, 2016.
51 Justin Gest, *Apart: Alienated and Engaged Muslims in the West*, New York: Columbia University Press, 2010.
52 David Thomson, *Les Francais jihadistes*, Paris: Les Arènes, 2014.
53 For an exhaustive analysis of Islamist terrorism in the world, see the Islamist Terorrist Attacks in the World: 1979–2019 published by Fondapol and available online: http://www.fondapol.org/wp-content/uploads/2019/11/ENQUETE-TERRORISME_GB_2019-11-18versionfinale.pdf
54 Michel Houellebecq, *Submission: A Novel*, New York: Picador, 2016.
55 See Eugen Weber, *The Hollow Years: France in the 1930s*, New York: Norton, 1996, notably pp.87–146.
56 See Jérome Fourquet, *L'Archipel Français: naissance d'une nation multiple et divisée*, Paris: Seuil, 2019, pp.140–143.
57 Serge Métais, *Histoire des Albanais: Des Illyriens à l'indépendance du Kosovo*, Paris: Fayard, 2006, pp.323–345.
58 Justin Gest, *The New Minority: White Working Class Politics in an Age of Immigration and Inequality*, New York: Oxford University Press, 2016, pp.14–15.
59 https://www.economist.com/special-report/2013/06/13/the-merkel-plan
60 See David Goodhart, *Head Hand Heart, the Struggle for Dignity and Status in the 21st Century*, London: Allen Lane, 2020.
61 Ibid.
62 Jérôme Fourquet, *L'Archipel Français: naissance d'une nation multiple et divisée*, Paris: Seuil, 2019, p.96.
63 A similar process is at work in the United States, and it has much to do with the political polarization that Americans have experienced since the 2000s. See my article in *Le Figaro* during the US election campaign in 2020 https://www.lefigaro.fr/vox/monde/comment-la-fracture-generationnelle-s-est-invitee-dans-la-campagne-americaine-20201015, and for a deeper dive Thibault Muzergues, *The Great Class Shift: How New Social Class Structures Are Redefining Western Politics*, London: Routledge, 2019.
64 Ibid., pp.333–350.
65 Richard Florida, *The Rise of the Creative Class – Revisited*, New York: Basic Books, 2012.
66 Justin Gest, *The New Minority: White Working Class Politics in an Age of Immigration and Inequality*, New York: Oxford University Press, 2016.
67 See Christophe Guiluy, *La France périphérique: Comment on a sacrifié les classes populaires*, Paris: Flammarion, 2014.

68 Thibault Muzergues, *The Great Class Shift: How New Social Class Structures Are Redefining Western Politics*, London: Routledge, 2019.
69 https://www.opendemocracy.net/en/real-divide-between-plebian-and-patrician-visions-of-democracy/
70 Peter Pulzer, *Political Representation and Elections in Britain* (3rd edition), London: Allen and Unwin, 1975, p.102.
71 https://www.lopinion.fr/edition/politique/thibault-muzergues-ralliement-classe-moyenne-aux-gilets-jaunes-est-169783
72 Max Weber, *Wirtschaft und Gesellschaft: Grundriss der verstehengen soziologie* (5th edition), Tübingen: JCB Mohr, 1922.
73 https://www.politicshome.com/news/uk/political-parties/conservative-party/news/108646/tories-now-more-popular-working-class
74 Edward Luce, *The Retreat of Western Liberalism*, Little, Brown Book Group, New York, 2017, p.13.
75 Larry Diamond, *Liberation Technology: Social Media and the Struggle for Democracy*, Baltimore: John Hopkins Press, 2012, p.71.
76 https://www.nytimes.com/2012/02/19/books/review/how-an-egyptian-revolution-began-on-facebook.html
77 https://www.washingtonpost.com/news/monkey-cage/wp/2013/12/04/strategic-use-of-facebook-and-twitter-in-ukrainian-protests/
78 http://www.fondapol.org/wp-content/uploads/2018/06/Ipsos_Jeunes-familles_et_addictions_ANALYSES_2018_05_30_web.pdf
79 Clint Watts, *Messing with the Enemy: Surviving in a Social Media World of Hackers, Terrorists, Russians, and Fake News*, New York: HarperCollins, 2018, p.226.
80 David Patrikarakos, *War in 140 Characters: How Social Media is Reshaping Conflict in the Twenty-First Century*, New York: Basic Books, 2017, pp.12–13.
81 https://gnet-research.org/2020/11/06/social-media-and-the-murder-of-samuel-paty/
82 https://theconversation.com/christchurchs-legacy-of-fighting-violent-extremism-online-must-go-further-deep-into-the-dark-web-133159
83 See Cyrus Krohn, *Bombarded: How to Fight Back against the Online Assault on Democracy*, Issaquah, Made for Success Publishing, 2020.
84 Ibid., p.9.
85 https://www.bbc.com/news/business-34324772
86 David Patrikarakos, *War in 140 Characters: How Social Media is Reshaping Conflict in the Twenty-First Century*, New York: Basic Books, 2017, p.113.
87 In her latest book, Anne Appelbaum gives a perfect example on how liberals and other groups on the right have split in the past decades, although her account is one-sided and at times unwillingly gives reason to those that have drifted away from liberalism. See Anne Appelbaum, *Twilight of Democracy: The Failure of Politics and the Parting of Friends*, New York: Allen Lane, 2020.
88 For John Mearsheimer, "it is because liberalism fails to provide individuals with a sense of community that it cannot provide the glue to hold a society together. It does not make them feel they are part of a large and vibrant group that is special and worthy of esteem, which is important to people psychologically as well as for keeping a society intact." John Mearsheimer, *The Great Delusion: Liberal Dreams and International Realities*, New Haven: Yale University Press, 2018, p.107.
89 Yascha Mounk, *The People vs. Democracy: Why Our Freedom is in Danger and How to Save it*, Cambridge, MA: Harvard University Press, 2018, p.13.
90 See Viktor Orbán's defining speech in Băile Tuşnad (Romania) on July 26 2014, available in English on the *Budapest Beacon* website: https://budapestbeacon.com/full-text-of-viktor-orbans-speech-at-baile-tusnad-tusnadfurdo-of-26-july-2014/
91 https://www.dw.com/en/hungarys-viktor-orban-calls-for-right-wing-union-in-europe/a-44865138

92 There is confusion within Orbán's alliance between the Christian ultraconservatives who seek to save fundamental values as defined by the Church (and which includes, among Catholics, some influence of the Vatican in political affairs) and a nationalist and secular extreme right that is indifferent to religious values and rejects any interference by the Church in national political life. See Olivier Roy, *L'Europe est-elle chrétienne?*, Paris: Seuil, 2019.
93 John B. Judis, *The Populist Explosion: How the Great Recession Transformed American and European Politics*, New York: Columbia Global Reports, 2016.
94 Giuliano da Empoli, *Gli Ingenieri del Caos: Teoria e tecnica dell'Internazionale populista*, Venice: Marsilio, 2019.
95 https://www.marianne.net/societe/casse-democratie-haine-anti-flics-enquete-au-coeur-de-la-pensee-black-bloc
96 Eugen Weber, *The Hollow Years: France in the 1930s*, New York: Norton, 1994, p.114.
97 Yascha Mounk, *The People vs. Democracy: Why Our Freedom is in Danger and How to Save it*, Cambridge, MA: Harvard University Press, 2018, p.13.
98 See Viktor Orbán's defining speech in Băile Tuşnad (Romania) on July 26 2014, available in English on the *Budapest Beacon* website: https://budapestbeacon.com/full-text-of-viktor-orbans-speech-at-baile-tusnad-tusnadfurdo-of-26-july-2014/
99 Graham Allison, *Destined for War: Can America and China Escape Thucydides's Trap*, New York: Mariner Group, 2017, pp.140–147.

Bibliography

Adonis, Andrew et al., *Half In Half Out: Prime Ministers on Europe*, London: Biteback Publishing, 2018.
Allison, Graham, *Destined for War: Can America and China Escape Thucydides's Trap*, New York: Mariner Group, 2017.
Anderson, Benedict, *Imagined Communities: Reflections on the Origin and Spread of Nationalism* (revised edition), London: Verso Books, 2016.
Appelbaum, Anne, *Twilight of Democracy: The Failure of Politics and the Parting of Friends*, New York: Allen Lane, 2020.
Blainey, Geoffrey, *The Causes of War* (3rd edition), New York: The Free Press, 1988.
Broder, David, *First They Took Rome: How the Populist Right Conquered Italy*, London: Verso, 2020.
da Empoli, Giuliano, *Gli Ingenieri del Caos: Teoria e tecnica dell'Internazionale populista*, Venice: Marsilio, 2019.
Diamond, Larry, *Liberation Technology: Social Media and the Struggle for Democracy*, Baltimore: John Hopkins Press, 2012.
Fourquet, Jérôme, *L'Archipel Français: naissance d'une nation multiple et divisée*, Paris: Seuil, 2019.
Florida, Richard, *The Rise of the Creative Class – Revisited*, New York: Basic Books, 2012.
Fukuyama, Francis, *Identity: The Demand for Dignity and the Politics of Resentment*, London: Profile Books, 2018.
Gellner, Ernest, *Nations and Nationalism*, Ithaca: Cornell University Press, 1983.
Gest, Justin, *The New Minority: White Working Class Politics in an Age of Immigration and Inequality*, New York: Oxford University Press, 2016.
Gest, Justin, *Apart: Alienated and Engaged Muslims in the West*, New York: Columbia University Press, 2010.
Goodhart, David, *Head Hand Heart, the Struggle for Dignity and Status in the 21st Century*, London: Allen Lane, 2020.

Guiluy, Christophe, *La France périphérique: Comment on a sacrifié les classes populaires*, Paris: Flammarion, 2014.
Hanebrick, Paul A., *In Defense of Christian Hungary: Religion, Nationalism and Antisemitism, 1890–1944*, Ithaca: Cornell University Press, 2006.
Judis, John B., *The Populist Explosion: How the Great Recession Transformed American and European Politics*, New York: Columbia Global Reports, 2016.
Kahn, Sylvain, and Lévy, Jacques, *Le Pays des Européens*, Paris: Odile Jacob, 2019.
Kirschbaum, Stanislav, *A History of Slovakia: The Struggle for Survival* (2nd edition), New York: Saint Martin's Press, 2006.
Krastev, Ivan, *After Europe*, Philadelphia: University of Pennsylvania Press, 2017.
Kundani, Hans, *The Paradox of German Power*, Oxford: Oxford University Press, 2014.
Luce, Edward, *The Retreat of Western Liberalism*, Little, Brown Book Group, 2017.
Mearsheimer, John, *The Great Delusion: Liberal Dreams and International Realities*, New Haven: Yale University Press, 2018.
Métais, Serge, *Histoire des Albanais: Des Illyriens à l'indépendance du Kosovo*, Paris: Fayard, 2006.
Mody, Ashoka, *EuroTragedy: A Drama in Nine Acts*, Oxford: Oxford University Press, 2018.
Mounk, Yascha, *The People vs. Democracy: Why Our Freedom is in Danger and How to Save it*, Cambridge, MA: Harvard University Press, 2018.
Muzergues, Thibault, *The Great Class Shift: How New Social Class Structures Are Redefining Western Politics*, London: Routledge, 2019.
Nolte, Ernst, *Der europäische Bürgerkrieg, 1917–1941: Nationalsozialismus und Bolschevismus*, Berlin: Propyläen, 1987.
Pasture, Patrick, *Imagining European Unity since 1000 AD*, Basingstoke: Palgrave MacMillan, 2015.
Patrikarakos, David, *War in 140 Characters: How Social Media is Reshaping Conflict in the Twenty-First Century*, New York: Basic Books, 2017.
Pomerantsev, Peter, *This Is Not Propaganda: Adventures in the War against Reality*, London: Faber & Faber, 2019.
Pulzer, Peter, *Political Representation and Elections in Britain* (3rd edition), London: Allen and Unwin, 1975.
Roy, Olivier, *L'Europe est-elle chrétienne?*, Paris: Seuil, 2019.
Thomson, David, *Les Francais jihadistes*, Paris: Les Arènes, 2014.
Watts, Clint, *Messing with the Enemy: Surviving in a Social Media World of Hackers, Terrorists, Russians, and Fake News*, New York: HarperCollins, 2018.
Weber, Eugen, *The Hollow Years: France in the 1930s*, New York: Norton, 1994.
Weber, Max, *Wirtschaft und Geselschaft: Grundriss der verstehengen soziologie* (5th edition), Tübingen: JCB Mohr, 1922.

5
BABY IT'S A WILD WORLD
Europe's external challenges

If one is to follow Clausewitz, war is merely the continuation of politics by other means. Indeed, much like political debate, war proceeds from a disagreement, which ushers in conflict and ultimately into belligerents taking arms against each other. This means that war is principally born of a conflict that is internal to the protagonists. And for what concerns this book, war in Europe would necessarily have been caused by disagreements between Europeans or conflict between Europeans and external power. This already opens the possibility that outsiders could play a role in the return of war in Europe, but more generally, as Geoffrey Blainey reminded us in his study of the causes of war, outside powers play a role even when they are not stakeholders in the decision to go to war: "every decision to wage war is influenced by predictions of how outside nations will affect the course of war."[1] For example,

> when Japan went to war in 1937 she assumed that no European nation would intervene on China's side. When Poland went to war with Germany in 1939 she believed she would receive crucial aid from Britain and France: Hitler on the contrary suspected that Poland would receive no useful aid. In the Suez War and Hungarian uprising of 1956 expectations of how outsiders would behave were crucial to the beginning and ending of those wars.[2]

Of course, war becomes more probable if a foreign power decides to intervene militarily, directly or via a proxy, in the internal affairs of a European country. When Russia decides to invade part of Ukraine, it attacks and occupies a territory on the European continent, and there is no guarantee other than NATO for a small EU country sitting next to Russia that it will not suffer the same fate. Taken from a different perspective, when the Islamic state decides to conduct

DOI: 10.4324/9781003215790-8

terrorist operations in Paris, Nice, Brussels or Berlin, it exports (even for a brief moment) war to the heart of the European Union. In both cases, an attack is made easier by the fact that Europe, in general, and the European Union, in particular, currently look much more vulnerable than in the late 2000s. Sure, it remains prosperous, but from a geopolitical point of view, it has already become peripheral, while commerce and growth have already moved toward the Pacific and the Indo-Pacific. Europe's 2010s and their slow growth have weakened all its security architecture, to the extent that Europeans now find themselves confronted with multiple challenges, inside and outside the European Union.

This chapter will explore the external factors that could lead to war or aggravate internal European conflicts to the point where they would usher in war. Just like current divisions, these factors should not be considered as threats (sometimes the "threat" is rather that these outside factors would actually retreat from Europe) but rather as challenges that could, in a not-so-distant future, contribute to the further weakening of the continent's security architecture, possibly until breaking point. Unsurprisingly, the biggest of these challenges is the future relationship that Europe will have with the one power that has for more than 75 years guaranteed peace: the United States.

America and Europe

It might seem counterintuitive to begin a chapter on the external challenges to European security with the very power that has been guaranteeing peace in Europe for so many years. During the Cold War, the United States was the leader of the West and the counterbalancing power to the Soviets who encouraged Europeans to come together into a common organization and make war between them impossible. The United States was, therefore, both a guarantor of security against the Soviet threat and a stakeholder in Western European security, seen as a key to the global struggle between capitalism and communism Europe was so key that both the United States and USSR preferred to freeze any conflict there rather than risk causing a war in Europe. Within what was their zone of "control" during the Cold War, the United States managed to create an area of peace and prosperity without encroaching on the sovereignty of the Alliance states, leaving each one free to conduct its own affairs, even when these were contrary to American interests: there were no American tanks rolling over Paris after Charles de Gaulle pulled France out NATO's integrated military structure – Budapest and Prague were not so lucky. After 1991, Europeans and Americans seemed to join forces to enlarge the peace and prosperity guaranteed by Euro-Atlantic structures: America's continued presence in NATO allowed to keep the "German question" under control in the post-reunification period, while a new imperium of peace and liberal democracy expanded Eastward to get close to the "Europe Whole and Free" that President George H. W. Bush had envisaged in his Mainz speech of May 1989. Yugoslavia, which was originally not part of this expansion, should have given Europeans and Americans a lesson of what can happen when the United States is not involved. Georgia, Moldova or Ukraine would also have liked to benefit from this protection after their independence.

Undoubtedly, the United States has been a factor of peace in Europe since 1945. How could it become otherwise? Before asking this question, one must understand the situation in which America finds itself as the United States tries to extricate itself from direct entanglement in the Middle East. In fact, and without there being a need to embark on a discussion over the reasons for the "endless wars," America's interventions in Iraq and Afghanistan have had a catastrophic effect on Americans' self-confidence and on the country's finances.[3] And even if the 2008 crisis was primarily due to domestic causes, the financial abyss represented by the American interventions in the Middle East was clearly an aggravating factor in the Great Recession that followed. America's weaker position, combined with China's then meteoric rise in the world system, has since 2008 prompted the United States to rethink its long-term strategy – something which was both natural and healthy: back in the 1970s, as it extricated itself from the Vietnam War, Richard Nixon's administration started a similar process of US foreign policy realignment that continued after he left the White House and paved the way for Ronald Regan's triumph over Soviet communism.

Truth be told, America had already started this realignment in the late 2000s, during the Obama Administration. The "pivot to Asia" is a symbol of Washington's new priorities, as the United States tries to adapt to a fast-changing world. And while American foreign policy has since seen many variations, the general pattern has remained the same: disentanglement from the Middle East quagmire whenever possible, while freeing up as many resources to respond to the Chinese challenge, notably in the Pacific and Indo-Pacific regions. And while attitudes toward Europe have varied, the general idea has been, whenever possible, to let Europeans deal with their own affairs. This has led the Obama administration to adopt a "lead from behind" strategy in its approach to Europe's neighborhood, before that strategy got caught up by Russian aggression in Ukraine; it has also led the Trump administration to aggressively look for ways to share the burden of Europe's defense with Europeans and the Biden administration to include Europe in its alliance of democracies. In each case, the objectives have remained the same: with Europe more peaceful than it has been in its history, attention has shifted East, and America must now focus as much as possible on containing Chinese power where it threatens its interests most directly, which is in the Asia-Pacific region. Of course, there is no question of a complete US pull-out, even less than in the Middle East – a region much less interesting nowadays as the United States has no global rival in the region, and as it has achieved oil self-sufficiency and become a net exporter of hydrocarbons.[4] Nevertheless, Europe is still a subject for the American long-term strategy of redeployment; in some ways, it is now often thought in Washington through the lens of the threat from Russia or China and not so much as what to do with a continent that has until recently too often been thought as definitely pacified.

Part of the problem here is that Europeans have not got used to the idea that they are no longer the center of attention in Washington, and even less the center of the World. Europe is now a periphery which is losing relevance in terms of geopolitics and economics, and in many ways, the dynamics seem to trend toward a further marginalization of the continent in the next decades, despite economic prosperity[5] that will continue to ensure general relevance. A few telling figures can give us an idea about this relatively peripheral position of Europe: out of the 87 million barrels of oil transported today by maritime traffic (60% of oil trade), 15.2 million are transported through the Strait of Malacca, which connects the Pacific and Indian Oceans (and thus the Arab-Persian production zone and the Chinese, Japanese and West American markets). By comparison, only 3.2 million barrels go through the Suez Canal, the fastest passage from the Persian Gulf to Europe.[6] It is true that some of Europe's energy needs are met through transport from other areas, notably Russia and North Africa, but the statistics are nevertheless very telling. Equally informative are the compared growth figures between Europe and the rest of the world. Between 2010 and 2018, annual economic growth in the European Union never exceeded +2.6% GDP, a maximum figure that the United States surpassed almost half of the years over the same period – and each year, growth in the United States and Canada was superior to those of the European Union. At the same time, China's growth, which has plateaued after 2008, reached its lowest level at +6.5% in 2018, while India returned from its worst score of 2011 at +5.2% – unusually strong figures for most European leaders.[7]

Of course, this does not mean that this is the end of Europe: even with much slower growth over the last twenty years, the EU still accounts for 25% of the world's economy, a figure that is out of all proportion to Europe's weight in the global population (just 7%).[8] But this is precisely the problem for the United States: while Americans have to redeploy their own forces at great expense to new hot spots, they find it difficult to understand why a continent as rich as Europe cannot be left on its own to ensure its own security. The idea that Europeans are free riders, ready to reap the dividends of peace without ever having to pay the price for it, is often heard on both sides of the aisle in Washington, and while Donald Trump expressed this sentiment abruptly, Barack Obama's judgment on Europeans, while more mildly presented, was no less severe.

The problem for any administration, though, is actually paradoxical: Americans would like Europeans to contribute more to their security, but they also want to keep this security architecture to remain centered on NATO. They, therefore, view any European discourse claiming to build strategic autonomy as a move away from NATO and, therefore, as unacceptable. This is, of course, not to say that an EU defense policy cannot necessarily be a complement to NATO, but Washington wants this defense policy to be built inside NATO so as to keep it under control. This is increasingly leading to ambiguity on both sides of the Atlantic, where the United States is asking allies to contribute more to NATO and common security architecture, but only on Washington's terms, and while foreign policy priorities – notably in the Middle East – are not always 100% aligned.

Sooner or later, this ambiguity will have to end, and Europeans and Americans will need to have an honest conversation on this issue. But in the meantime, the United States will continue to rethink its strategy and recalibrate military and geopolitical deployments across the World. As mentioned earlier, the Middle East is clearly the region in which US interest is changing at the fastest pace, as America is pulling out of direct involvement in conflicts and, whenever possible, letting allies like Saudi Arabia, Turkey or Israel counter regional threats. In many ways, this is completely logical: the United States is first and foremost a thalassocracy, a maritime power and any entanglement deep inland, far from the maritime routes, is a nonessential engagement.[9] In this context, the US policy change which left the Kurds on their own in 2019 after having worked with them is very telling of Washington's change in priorities: of course, The United States cares about its allies, but it is above all attentive to its. In landlocked regions without access to the sea, this is often limited – particularly when a much bigger actor, Turkey, who controls the Straits between the Mediterranean and the Black Sea, lets it be known that it opposes support to the Kurds. In areas that have become peripheral to US interests, presence has become a problem for Americans, as they now have to focus on very different and immediate threats. This is not the case in Europe or East Asia, where the strategic vision remains one of involvement: in the words of Robert Kagan,

> the Second World War not only ended the debate over whether the United States was physically secure from attack, but it convinced most Americans that Wilson and the two Roosevelts had been right: Americans and their way of life could not be safe in a world where Europe and Asia were dominated by hostile autocratic powers.[10]

Today, this vision is still widely shared by the American establishment – with the difference that it is indeed an Asia potentially dominated by China that poses the most problems for America, not so much Europe, which has become a secondary theatre.

In this context, what could be the future strategy of the United States toward Europe? One possibility, feared by many Atlanticists, could be departure – which would mean first and foremost a withdrawal from NATO. This scenario was already envisaged by the Norwegian TV crews that filmed the series *Occupied*. This pull-out would probably take some time, as it would mean disentangling America from much more than just a military alliance. It would possibly require negotiations with NATO allies, for example on what to do with the bases in Naples, Aviano, Ramstein and others. It is also not the most probable scenario at this stage, as despite Donald Trump's ambiguity toward the Atlantic Alliance, the US foreign policy establishment (Democrat and Republican) remains committed to NATO. But the Trump presidency has also shown that this possibility is not completely fantasist, as Americans remain wary over the high price they have to pay for the security of a continent that is not theirs – and many consider that not only pacified but also ungrateful. In the context of a long-term isolationist drive,[11] and in the absence of a real and direct threat to their interests in Europe, the United States might be prompted to want to review its alliances, especially if the relationship with Germany continues to deteriorate (it has during the Trump era, and the reasons for it ran much deeper than Trump's personal animosity for Angela Merkel or the 2% defense contribution issue). The choice of withdrawal would certainly be drastic, but it could logically be the result of estrangement with key allies on the continent, notably France and Germany, as visions and interests of continental Europe and the United States can be divergent in places like the Middle East, or even commercial ties with East Asia. In particular, attitudes toward China may well prove to be a thorny issue for the Atlantic Alliance, as Europeans, and especially Germans, are not necessarily willing to side fully with Washington: Germany's export drive has until recently been fed by the emerging Chinese consumer market and its appetite for German quality products and public opinion does not seem that keen to side with any power in the case of a conflict between Washington and Beijing, as a recent ECFR study showed.[12]

Of course, it is elites and not people that decide on war, but the drive for neutrality coming from European people can only lead reluctant European leaders to be careful in their engagement with the United States and China. This overprudent attitude (also justified by the memory of America's adventurous wars in the Middle East during the 2000s) is particularly exasperating for Washington. To the point in which Americans would simply pull out? If that were the case, Europeans would be left to their own device, and it is probable that divisions over geostrategic priorities would then prove unsolvable for the EU – with central Europeans seeking protections from Russia to the East, Southern Europeans prioritizing the security over the South and the Mediterranean, and Germany hesitant to take a position, it would not be long before the deconstruction of the European security system, leaving the door for new actors to jump in – primarily, Russia, China and Turkey.

What is much more probable, in the case of long-term deterioration of US–EU relations, is a change of strategy toward Europe: after all, US interests – geopolitical and economic – will probably ensure continued involvement in the region,[13] but bad blood between the two sides of the Atlantic could lead to strategic rethinking: since the 1989 "Europe Whole and Free" speech of George H. W. Bush, American elites have been convinced that their national interest lies in favoring union and liberty in Europe. But this dominant liberal vision of international relations is not the only one in the United States, and it is increasingly contested by a "realist" school of international relations. For John Mearsheimer, the strategy of liberal hegemony that has been pursued over the past 30 years needs to be reversed and turned into a much more transactional vision of foreign relations in which the (often short-term) interest of the United States must take precedence over anything else.[14] And this interest might dictate that, faced with Chinese influence over key European states, a Europe Whole and Free might not be a strategic objective any longer but rather a problem for US security (Robert Kagan's vision that Americans cannot be safe in a world where Europe and Asia are dominated by hostile autocratic powers[15] finds echoes in realist thinking – the main difference being that the words "hostile" and "autocratic" have become superfluous). In this case, realists would be tempted to play Europeans off against each other to maximize short-term results for the United States.

Although clearly in the ascendant in the past few years, the realist school of thought is clearly not the one favored by the Biden administration. But the fact is that isolationists and realists are increasingly getting their voices heard in the corridors of power in Washington – and they may well continue to gain ground in a new geopolitical environment dominated by US–China rivalry, which will push Americans to be more aggressive, especially on the thorny issue of relations with the commercial giants linked to the Chinese military-industrial complex, of which Huawei is just one example. If Europeans remain divided or worse, tetanized by the brewing conflict between Beijing and Washington, it is not impossible to imagine even the most idealistic of American diplomats abandon their vision of a Europe Whole and Free. In this case, Europe would become once again a chessboard where the rivalry between nation-continents would be played out, with the difference compared to the Cold War that there will be no clear demarcation line between the two camps. Already, the pro-Chinese positions that some European leaders have taken over Hong Kong, human rights or Xinjiang suggest that some of them are toying with the idea of choosing Beijing over Washington. Meanwhile, decisions of other leaders to pull out of Chinese initiatives like the 17+1 format in Central Europe suggest that pawns are already moving on the European chessboard. If divisions were to become more serious and European elites much less committed to the Transatlantic alliance as they have been until recently, Americans could adopt much more cynical strategies over Europe. And without the hard power of *Pax Americana*, it seems unlikely that *Pax Europea* would hold for long.

Of course, we are not there yet: American elites today understand that it is more advantageous for them to continue and even enhance their partnership with a Europe Whole and Free that offers opportunities for their businesses and still contributes to security in areas of strategic interest (as the French and British, among others, do in places like the Baltic States, or in the Sahel). But Americans are also pragmatic, and if they feel that Europeans are not faithful partners in the transatlantic alliance, they could change strategy and look at the continent not as the masterpiece of American statecraft but as a battlefield where it would have to defend its interests against the other great powers: China of course, but also Russia, which has shown since 2014 that it does not intend to stay out of Europe's affairs.

Russia, a low-cost power with a high nuisance potential

If the relationship between the United States and Europe is complex, then that between Europe and Russia is even more complicated, partly due to the fact that no ocean separates them, making the cultural and physical border between the two worlds much more porous, for better and (more often) for worse. Indeed, in many corners of Europe (mostly in the faraway West though), Russia can exert a real fascination – leading in turn to fantasized visions of what Russia really is, whether as a full part of the European larger community or as a new Mongol empire full of bloodthirsty Bolsheviks ready to invade Europe at any time. In these two fantasized visions of Russia, there is a part of truth but also much misunderstanding. It is, therefore, important to figure out what is real and what is not if one wants to understand the Kremlin's vision of Europe. It actually does not take much effort to understand Moscow's point of view if one looks in the right place – in fact, four basic facts help understand Russia's views better than anything else: its extension on both sides of the Eurasian mass, its obsession with geopolitical insecurity, its military potential and its revisionism when it comes to the borders of 1991.

The most common mistake made by continental Western Europeans about Russia is to view it as a European power among others on the continent, hence the idea of "Europe from Lisbon to Vladivostok," as French President Emmanuel Macron put it in 2019.[16] This feeling is generally due to a perception of ethnocultural proximity: Russians are white, Christian and have adopted much of classical European culture, even contributing to it heavily in the nineteenth century through literature, ballet or music. But Russia's sense of "belonging" to Europe is only partial. It is true that, since Peter the Great, Imperial Russia integrated the continental security ecosystem, but it also ejected itself from it in 1917, before successfully crawling back through invasion in 1939–1947. Geographically, if Russia's economic, demographic and political heart is situated on the European continent, West of the Urals, the geographic reality is also that most of its territory is actually in Asia. More precisely, and this is even more true today as global warming releases large parts of Siberia from permafrost and allows the region to become potentially cultivated, Russia (like Turkey) is a Eurasian power that sits in the space between the two civilizational centers of the great Eurasian landmass, Europe and East Asia (to which one can add the Middle East to the South). Thus, Russia is not a European power, it is a steppe power, occupying the steppe highway that had previously belonged to the Sarmatians, Scythians, Huns and Mongols before and providing a link between Europe and East Asia.

This geographical reality is confirmed by historical fact: although parts of the Black Sea littoral was settled by Greek and Italian colonies in ancient and medieval times, what is now Russia was never part of the European empires, and the space's occupation by the Mongols in the late medieval era marked a complete break of much of it with the West. Even after Peter the Great, when Russia embarked on an impressive drive of "modernization" (meaning in actual facts

Westernization[17]), the transition was never complete. The concept of Eurasia means both Asia and Europe, and neither of them at the same time, and Russia has continuously remained in an in-between position, ready to adopt Western customs when it suited its interests but rejecting Western morals and other features as suspicious, foreign, dangerous and decadent. This has translated into what some Westerners call, sometimes too lazily, the "Russian soul," which they have so many difficulties to comprehend, probably because much like the Janus of Roman mythology, it offers two faces at the same time: the first one, familiar to Europeans is the Westernizing school of thought (*Zapadnichestvo* in Russian). The *Zapadniki* see Russia as backward and in need of adopting Western ways to become great; historical figures associated with this school of thought include Peter the Great or Alexander II and nineteenth-century philosopher Piotr Chaadaev. This Westernizing universe is at one extreme opposite of the spectrum, the other one being the Slavophile, or Eurasianist school of thought, which sees Russia as completely separate from the West – rather than trying to copy it, it should protect itself from the corrupting influence of Europe and, in the case of the panslavic Eurasianist, beat the West back as far as possible to create a union of Slavs centered on Moscow.

The conflict between Westerners and Slavophiles is a constant in Russian history, and this ambivalence is also to be found in individual positions: Tolstoy and Dostoevsky (among others) wrote novels that are rightly considered as pretty "western" or "European" because they follow in many ways the cannons of European literature. Yet nobody could deny their specific Russian character (nor would they, as both were professed Slavophiles). Lenin may have been trying to import Marxism, a German ideology, into Russia. But his ways of handling dissent and building socialism in an agrarian (and multicultural) empire meant that the way he built Soviet Russia and the USSR was on a basis totally foreign to what would have been envisaged by socialist Europeans like Jean Jaurès. The list of ambivalences could go on and on and includes tsars, communist leaders, Boris Yeltsin or Vladimir Putin.

In the 1990s and 2000s, Europeans believed that the debate between Slavophiles and Westernizers had been closed, so complete was the victory of Western capitalism over Eastern communism, and the discourses from Moscow were indeed hinting at the full adoption of a Western liberal model of building democracy at home and a political-economic network of interdependence with the West. Russia seemed on its way to becoming part of what Mikhail Gorbachev had called the "common European house." However, what everyone in the West failed to understand was that the slogan was interpreted very differently whether one was sitting in Moscow, Berlin or Washington. In reality, Russia has never abandoned its ambivalence toward the West. Only the hand of the Westernizers was much stronger in the 1990s, because just like in 1856 after the Crimea War and just like in 1905 after the defeat against Japan, Russia's backwardness was now obvious. Moscow needed to adopt the ways of the West to come back stronger, and that is what it tried to do. But as Russia adopted liberal ways between 1990 and 1999, its economy was collapsing and the country was ruined. Russians do not look back keenly on these times, and that made the rejection of the West even more popular. Indeed, as early as 1999, the Russian state services had already announced they were having second thoughts on their belonging to a "common European home" – which at the time meant one clearly dominated by Western Europeans. In its White Paper on its "Medium-term Strategy towards the European Union," Russia already made clear that it did not consider itself as a European country but as "a world power stretching over two continents that should value and uphold its independence."[18] Even before Vladimir Putin's installation in the Kremlin, Moscow was already taking its distance with the West, and despite highs and lows, the dynamics of Russia's positioning since then has continued to be an assertion of its Eurasian-ness – itself encouraged by double-digit growth in China. Russia has in fact gradually closed itself off from the West, seeing its dependence on the outside world not as an opportunity for modernization but as a vulnerability that needs to be corrected.

Today, Russia does not see Europe as a partner but as a rival – not only because of NATO and the alliance with the United States but mainly because Russian leaders have an obsession with security (and control) which is dictated by their history. Covering the steppe highway is as much an opportunity as a strategic misfortune, insofar as there are no major geographical obstacles separating Vladivostok from Moscow, and by extension Vladivostok from Paris. This means that Cossacks can go and camp on Paris's *Champ de Mars* (as they did in 1814) or by the Reichstag in Berlin (as in 1945–1989), but that also means that Russia is equally vulnerable: from the East, as the Mongol invasion of 1244 attests, but most importantly in the modern history of Russia from the West. If St. Petersburg, built by Peter the Great as a window on Europe, was particularly vulnerable, Moscow, the historic inland capital, is also exposed: it was occupied by the Polish-Lithuanian Commonwealth in 1610–1612, burned under Napoleon in 1812 and the Wehrmacht reached its suburbs in 1941. Any Russian who knows his history (and most of them do) has good reason to see the West as a threat, whatever the West's real intentions – in geopolitics, these count less than the internal perception.

The nature of this perception is very well summarized by what Russians say about NATO's enlargement: Russian official discourse (and that of their allies in Europe) often portrays this expansion of NATO as an unbearable provocation for Russia. Apart from the fact that it conveniently forgets to mention that NATO enlargement was indeed eagerly pursued by its new members, it is telling in that it views Russia and the West as two mutually exclusive concepts. There can be either a Russian protectorate to act as a *limes* against the West or a neutralized zone that basically fulfills the same objectives – the other option, a neighbor close to the West, is seen as an existential threat. Without a cultural revolution, which as of now seems unlikely, the Russian elites have condemned themselves to never feel safe in their Eurasian environment. The Russian-born sociologist Pitirim Sorokin actually put this feeling of insecurity into a statistic:

during the last millennium, Russia has lived only one single continuous quarter-century without waging war inside or outside its borders.[19] Indeed, since 1991, Russia has been involved in wars in Transnistria (1992), Chechnya (1994–1996 and 1999–2009), Georgia (2008) and Ukraine (2014–present) – that makes only nine years of peace out of the past thirty.

With such an exhaustive perception of threat and encirclement, what could security mean for Russia? Here again, the pattern is a painfully recurring one in Russian history: to feel safer, Russia has to expand, but the more it expands, the more strategic depth it seeks – and *a contrario*, the more Russia shrinks, the more insecure it feels. The deadly spiral is endless: whatever the extent of its empire, and even when it effectively ends to the West of Leipzig – the Kremlin feels vulnerable in the medium- and long-term, and this, in turn, provokes new tensions with neighbors. The situation today, of course, is one of perceived vulnerabilities, as Russia has effectively been almost entirely pushed out of Europe – the continent that matters for Moscow, and certainly out of the "Club" that counts, the European Union. The question is therefore *how* to enter the European security game and how to rebuild a protective *limes* to the West of Russia. But once it will have built its first line of security, history suggests that this will not be enough: in this sense, Robert Kagan is right when he states that "those who suggest we should recognize a Russian sphere of interest in [Europe] should recall that Russia's historical sphere of interest does not end in Ukraine; it begins in Ukraine. It includes the Baltic States, and it includes Poland,"[20] both of which are incidentally members of NATO and the EU.

As it seeks to regain strategic depth, Russia automatically becomes a revisionist power, questioning not only borders but the whole security architecture of Europe, which is favorable to the West insofar as Russia has practically been expulsed from the European game. Here, Moscow's position is not without its paradox: as French diplomatic expert Dominique d'Herbigny puts it, Russia is "both revisionist of the European order and conservative of its world status, sometimes conciliatory in words but often obstructive in deeds."[21] Russian state officials are, of course, aware of this ambiguity, and their priority has so far been to try and regain ascendancy in the post-Soviet space, which they still call the "near-abroad" – meaning that it is not really abroad. The strategy is not new: already in the early 1990s, the Russian army engineered the secession of Transnistria from Moldova (one of the numerous frozen conflicts which have allowed Moscow to regain some form of control over its former republics). In the mid-2000s, with pockets full, thanks to the commodities bonanza, Russia's approach became more centered of "soft power," which consisted, while continuing to use the sticks of gas diplomacy and ethnic conflict in republics like Moldova or Georgia, in buying up local elites to lure the post-Soviet republic to integrate its Eurasian Economic Union, supposed to become a Eurasian rival to the EU and an indispensable intermediary between the West and China. Failing to do that, it reverted to the stick policy by intervening militarily to weaken states and prevent them from moving West, with Georgia (2008) and Ukraine (2014) the unfortunate victims.

Even though Georgia and Ukraine didn't join Euro-Atlantic structures, Russia is aware of its real problem: the European Union and NATO are the obstacles standing in the way of restoring its status as a European power. And even if the recovery of Ukraine (denied by the 2014 Revolution of Dignity) is a key to Russia's return to Europe, it is only one element among others: the control of the east coast of the Baltic Sea (which includes three members of NATO: Estonia, Latvia and Lithuania) and the search for territorial continuity with the enclave of Kaliningrad also make this region a crucial hot spot for Moscow. There as in Crimea in 2014, the Kremlin intends to use the "protection" of Russian speakers in the Baltic states (a third of the Latvian population and a quarter of the Estonian population speak Russian as a mother tongue) as a pretext to retain influence in these countries, or perhaps even one day bring them back into the bosom of Mother Russia, if Euro-Atlantic structures are weak enough.

From the wars it recently fought in Georgia and Ukraine, the Russian political-military establishment has already drawn a few useful lessons: first, making war is once again possible in Europe, and Moscow can get away with it as long as it is not waged against a NATO member (the question, of course, is what if NATO is no longer considered as protecting its member states?); second, the annexation of Crimea shows that borders in Europe are no longer sacrosanct, and the status of certain territories considered by Moscow as belonging to the "Russian world" (*Russkiy Mir*) can be questioned without the West necessarily going to war. Third, Article 5 of NATO (an attack against one of its members is an attack against all) limits the terrain in which Russia can use the direct military instruments it has at its disposal – but this leaves open the use of non-conventional, hybrid warfare.[22] The equation is therefore simple: a divided West, a weakened NATO and a disoriented Western public would mean that Russia could gain the initiative to recover what it considers to be part of the *Russkiy Mir*, a notion that can vary with Russia's interests and perception of threat: it can end in Kyiv, but it can also end in Riga or even in Helsinki and Warsaw – after all, these two capitals were part of the Russian Empire in the nineteenth century, and they could be again, if Moscow feels it has the capacity to digest them.

The question of capacity is crucial here, for it is often overlooked – or rather badly judged – by European policymakers, notably in Berlin and Paris. In fact, while almost everyone is agreeing that Russia is a revisionist power, there is little consensus over Moscow's capacity to challenge the status quo. France's "realist" and Germany's *Ostpolitischer* circles argue that Russia is no longer a threat and point out that Russia's GDP, the equivalent of Spain's, is too low to give Russia the ambition to recreate its empire, while its limited conventional military potential, much lesser than in the Cold War, makes it impossible for Russia to invade its neighbors. Of course, Georgia and Ukraine have something to say about that latter point, but the conclusion from the so-called "realist" circles in Western Europe is that because of its weak GDP and its limited conventional military capacity, Russia has become a benign actor one can do business with, a country that needs to be seduced if the West is to avoid having it enter China's orbit. This view not only greatly overestimates Europe's soft power capacities but also underestimates Russia's intentions and capabilities. Russia is a revisionist country whose ambitions are blocked by NATO and the EU, and this fact alone should suggest extreme caution when dealing with it, as its whole foreign policy since the early 2000s at least has been to weaken the two poles of Atlanticism, either by promoting a special relationship with Germany and France against the other Europeans or by weakening Europe to the point where it would become inoperative, irrelevant, or even non-existent. As Ivan Krastev and Stephen Holmes remind us,

> unlike the Soviet Union, the Russian Federation cannot hope to defeat the West. What it does hope to do is to bring the West to the point of breaking up into pieces, just as happened to the Soviet bloc and the Soviet Union itself in 1989-1991.[23]

Would Russia be able to gather enough resources to achieve this ambition? Moscow's friends in Europe often quote the figures of Russia's GDP equivalent to Spain for a territory that is 3,283% larger (and a population almost thrice that of Spain), but that argument misses the real point. Russia is what French historian Georges Sokoloff has called a "poor power," which can also translate a low-cost power.[24] It can support a major military effort while depriving its population of goods and services that Westerners would consider as part of the natural law (as Igor Gretskiy recalls, in 1980–1986, Soviet "military spending accounted for more than 30% of the state budget" but the country was not on the verge of revolt, it is only after Gorbachev's *Perestroika* policy that social unrest started to kick in[25]). But even more importantly, Russia knows how to win wars in situations of extreme economic weakness – it convincingly beat richer enemies several times in history, France in 1813, Poland in 1939, Germany in 1945, among others. This is because the Russian General Staff does not necessarily rely on a hyper-sophisticated arsenal and expensive equipment to lead its wars; instead, it is ready to use all types of tactics and hybrid strategies, and its troops are now well-versed in this type of low-cost warfare, as they have been able to test it on many theaters of operation: not only in Georgia, Ukraine, Syria or Chechnya but also in Libya and the Central African Republic through paramilitary structures like Wagner, linked to the Russian state by individuals close to Vladimir Putin.[26]

Russia's current military doctrine, named in the West after its armed forces Chief of the General Staff Valery Gerasimov, thus relies not necessarily on expensive "toys" or an arsenal that allows to strike hard from afar. Instead, it is based on the strengths and weaknesses of the country – and Russians are using this doctrine to move their pawns in Europe, including beyond the enemy line. In doing so, Russian strategists adapt their weapons and tactics to the adversary in a world that has become more fluid: according to Gerasimov, wars are "not declared but simply begin," so that "a completely well-off and stable country" could be transformed into "an arena of the most intense armed conflict in the matter of months or even days." Within this framework, all means "including economic, information, humanitarian and other measures" can be used, and not necessarily to destroy an opposing army but to paralyze and weaken an entire nation until a set of strategic objectives is reached.[27] In other words, while Russia is aware of its relative decline, it considers it strategically desirable to weaken its European neighbors and divide them in order to regain a foothold in Europe.[28] To do this, Moscow seeks to reduce as much as possible its economic dependence on the West (which it considers a weakness) and to maximize dependence on Moscow – preferably a European rather than Western dependence. The idea of a strategic environment pacified by economic interdependence is, therefore, thought of not only as anathema but as Western weakness in the Kremlin,[29] and as long as there will be Europeans to think that such a strategy can work, Moscow will be encouraged to multiply preventive action and provocations.

Until war? Moscow is of course aware that it would probably be difficult to survive a direct confrontation with NATO members. But the Kremlin does not consider NATO as an immortal organization, and while it waits for it to crumble, it tries to maintain a climate of distrust in Europe, using social media and the information flows it controls to sow disruptive messages to target audiences (for example, propaganda TV channel *Russia Today* became the main source of information for Yellow Vests during the crisis of winter 2018–2019). The idea is to encourage further division in Europe – of which we saw there are plenty of potentials, and the expected result is a win on two counts: a divided Europe cannot be a danger in Russia's Near Abroad, and weakening Euro-Atlantic structures can allow the Russians to caress the idea of one day gaining back influence in the geopolitical architecture of a divided, de-Americanized Europe, where it would be a bigger power capable of controlling different actors if taken individually, thanks to the strategic superiority of its low-cost doctrine. As long as Europeans are unable to collectively show a strong hand toward the Russians, the latter will not respect them and will continue to sow discord within and among European nations to gain more influence in European affairs. In this respect, the Russian security challenge is much more direct and immediate than that posed by China.

China's rise, Europe's fall

China's presence in the list of Europe's strategic challenges might sound incongruous to some Europeans. Beijing offers none of the threatening features of other neighbors, and it is not directly present (or at least not yet) on European soil, making the perception of its presence in public opinion, at least until recently, a relatively neutral affair – indeed, Europeans' views on China have been so far very neutral,[30] and while the perception of the People's Republic is changing fast in the aftermath of the COVID-19 crisis,[31] the mainstream discourse often downplays China as a problem for Europe. After all, China has no problem of uncontrolled demographic expansion, no direct borders with the European

Union, no military base in Europe and no territorial ambition on the continent, unlike Russia.

Indeed, from a strictly European point of view, China has actually been perceived as a stabilizer in world politics, as it drove world economic growth (and Northern Europe's export market) in the early 2010s, while the West was stuck in economic, social and political crises. Until recently, China also looked rather keenly on Europe: a stable and affluent Europe was a good end-of-the-line market for Chinese goods, its geopolitical insignificance considered a good thing in Beijing, and it was even often described as a potential ally to break up American hegemony in the long term.[32] While the latter feeling was not shared by the EU's political establishment, who preferred to remain close to the United States and at the same time hang on to the dream of a pacified world environment where trade could be both free and fair, one can say that Europeans (including Britons, notably under the premiership of David Cameron) were themselves fascinated with the rise of China. China's rise was thus perceived, if not positively, at least neutrally in circles of power, with European leaders (and company bosses) queuing up to Beijing to compete for cooperation contracts and technology transfers in exchange for the promise to gain access to a juicy market worth almost 1.4 billion customers.

The offer may have looked attractive, but if Europeans naïvely played by the rules, it is disputable that Beijing fulfilled its part of the bargain: the technology transfers took place (willingly, forcibly, or by stealth), in the process China won new markets, implemented structures and built relationships that now allow the regime to spread its propaganda across the continent,[33] and Europeans got the bits of the markets the authorities in Beijing were willing to leave to them. But in reality, most markets remained closed to Europeans, while China built up its competitivity everywhere. In other words, although it was thought of as a win–win relationship, the Europe–China deals have ended up being primarily to the benefit of China. In some parts of Europe, the relationship actually gradually turned to one of dependence: during the euro crisis, in countries where debt had become a major issue and Northern Europeans were not ready to invest, China was often seen as the only option left to escape the stranglehold of creditors – when the Athenian port of Piraeus was privatized in 2016, it was sold to COSCO, a Chinese state-owned company, for €368.5 million[34]; a few years later, in 2019, another country in financial difficulty, Italy, was the first in Western Europe to sign up to China's Belt and Road Initiative, signing major investment agreements that Chinese authorities are still hoping to translate into some form of acquisition or stakeholder control over the ports of Trieste, Genoa and Taranto,[35] all of them keys to the control of the Mediterranean and, importantly in the case of Trieste and Genoa, access to inland European markets. With Chinese firms now holding large stakes in most of Europe's major ports (including in Northern Europe),[36] a trend is becoming clear: China is trying to progressively take over Europe's port infrastructure, in particular in the Mediterranean where Southern European states need to escape a debt trap – and China has the cash to invest.

The problem here is not so much that the Chinese are actually investing in places like Puglia, Istria or Greece, which all badly need further investments, but the fact that there are far-reaching geo-economic and geopolitical consequences for this Chinese incursion in key European infrastructures. When a Chinese company invests in Europe, it is almost invariably linked to either the Chinese security apparatus or the Chinese Communist Party, and often both. This is the case of not only COSCO, the state company that now owns the port of Piraeus, but also Huawei, a telecom giant whose sector is strategic for intelligence gathering (and potentially for disinformation, as the data the companies gather could in the future be used for mass propaganda purposes[37]). Huawei's founder, Ren Zhengfei, served for many years as an officer in the Chinese army,[38] and many of the company's employees are former secret service agents.[39] In this context, it is difficult for the telecom giant to escape the many suspicions of spying for the People's Liberation Army. And even when the companies or their activities do not directly link them with the Chinese Communist Party or state apparatus, China's big conglomerates are still under the heavy influence of the party, as Alibaba founder Jack Ma experienced at his own expense in late 2020 and early 2021. After having criticized Chinese regulators' attitude toward big business, he disappeared for three months, before reappearing humbled in what was as much a self-criticism show as a warning to other businessmen who would dare not to fall into line.[40]

Chinese business works closely with the People's Republic state apparatus, and this can carry geopolitical consequences, for example in the field of infrastructure or telecommunications. As researchers Robert D. Blackwill and Jennifer M. Harris pointed out,

> as China's economic might has grown, so too has its ability and temptation to use this power to advance geopolitical ends. China is often correctly described as the world's leading practitioner of geoeconomics. […] Nations do not fear China's military might; they fear its ability to give or withhold trade and investments.[41]

Indeed, Chinese companies are never alone when they set up shop anywhere in the world – they bring with them a whole state infrastructure, capital and workers, along with promises of low-cost development, thanks to the Belt and Road Initiative. The offer is often attractive, especially for countries far from traditional financing channels, already indebted and undermined by corruption: the promise of large infrastructure projects at low cost, few conditionalities, with interest rates below market prices, can indeed sound very tempting for politicians whose popularity is often linked to economic growth (something that has not exactly been a definer of Europe's economies over the past few years).

The Chinese government offers a wide range of services, from the construction of a new airport, the development of a new motorway or railway, the prompt delivery of a vaccine, etc. The low conditionalities are often enough to encourage leaders to subscribe to the Belt and Road Initiative and let China invest in their countries. But the experience on the ground is very often far from the promises given by Chinese statesmen and businessmen: in terms of local development, the investments often go from Chinese hands to other Chinese hands, as Chinese infrastructure companies exports their own Chinese workers to do the job, thereby avoiding the complications of having local hires or intermediaries. That is, when money circulates at all, as many projects are late or never happen due to corruption. But state debt, on the other hand, is very real – and added to the previously contracted debt, it turns into a vicious circle that can progressively turn states into protectorates. Some countries in the Indo-Pacific zone have fallen into the debt trap, leading them to make major territorial or military concessions – the most famous case is that of Sri Lanka, a strategic stopover in the Indian Ocean located halfway between the Persian Gulf and the Strait of Malacca: riddled with debt, the country had to cede part of its territory, the strategic port of Hambantota, to China for a period of 99 years to lighten its debt burden.[42] Other countries in the area such as the Maldives or Malaysia are also vulnerable: when the Chinese government controls the country's debt, it can also constrain the government's actions, and it can also control its image toward the local population. It can also organize reprisals against countries or politicians who continue to receive the Dalai Lama, express criticism against the treatment of Tibetans or Uyghurs, or support in any way the Hong Kong demonstrators or the independence of Taiwan.[43] China's rise has political consequences throughout the world, and these often run counter to transparency and freedom of expression,[44] two values that seem to be constitutive not only of the West, in general, but also of one of its political expressions, the European Union.

China's rise, initially seen as a positive factor of development for the world, is now being reassessed by many actors, and its ambitions for leadership is increasingly contested: it now seems clear that China has embarked on a project of *Weltpolitik* not dissimilar to that of Germany at the end of the nineteenth century. The much cruder expression of these ambitions under Xi Jinping has, in turn, led the United States to change its strategy toward China and react to its contestation of America's World leadership. This has translated at the economic level in trade wars between Beijing and Washington, at the technological level, with the policies of technological de-coupling and controversies around 5G and Huawei technologies.[45] But the rivalry has also had concrete military consequences around the South China Sea and beyond as the contest is now going global and turning into a clash between two opposing visions of society: on the one hand, American messianism, with its liberal-democratic ideal and unlimited confidence in progress and the individual and, on the other hand, Chinese exceptionalism, with its model of control on society through surveillance and "reactive authoritarianism," as well as an emphasis on social harmony, collectivism and often long-termism.[46]

The confrontation between the two world-views, with a rising Chinese power that is bound to become more assertive in its challenge to American leadership, does not have to turn into open war: Graham Allison has convincingly made the case that the Thucydides trap is not an inevitable destiny.[47] Nevertheless, Allison's statistics also plead for caution: if war is not inevitable, the number of conflicts between a rising and a sitting power that have degenerated into war is large enough to be a source of worry for future US–China relations. The conflict may not be a general war, or even a direct war – after all, America and the Soviet Union ensured that the contest between them would always remain a Cold War. But that did not mean that war could not be made by proxy, in different theaters of operation, much as was the case in Southeast Asia or in parts of Africa and Latin America. In modern times though, Europe could also become a region where the rivalry between the two superpowers could turn into a hot war. The Europe of tomorrow may not be divided between clearly delimited and militarized camps – indeed, many countries in Europe are tempted to play their own partition when it comes to China, and their presence in a particular strategic environment (the Western Balkans for example) could prove explosive. Moreover, even if it remains rich, Europe is no longer the center of attention today, the piece of the puzzle everyone is afraid to mess with. During the Cold War, the European front line was frozen and all internal conflicts within each camp were dealt with scrupulous respect for each's sovereignty (including during the particularly brutal phases of repression of 1956 in Hungary and Central Europe or in 1968 in Czechoslovakia). The equation was simple: as any realignment risked destabilizing the whole European construct, the great prize of the Cold War, nobody would dare to risk touching it, for fear that it would lead to total nuclear war or total loss (indeed, it is precisely what happened when Gorbachev let go the Soviet satellites in Central Europe). Other parts of the world, and in particular Southeast Asia, were not so fortunate. Is it the turn of a weakened and divided Europe to become a new Southeast Asia where global rivalries would play out? The writing is not on the wall, of course, but this scenario is not unthinkable, even more so as the geographical fault lines will not necessarily follow the hard, military logic that they did in 1947, when the Iron Curtain descended upon Europe.

It is indeed highly unlikely that such a clear division would reappear today. Today, Chinese influence in Europe is everywhere and, at times, extremely effective in Western Europe, as Mareike Ohlberg and Clive Hamilton have shown in their latest book,[48] even though other studies also show that some areas and countries are much more directly vulnerable to Chinese influence – notably in the peripheries of Southern and Eastern Europe, where Beijing has installed a "17+1" cooperation framework that regroups 17 central and southeastern countries with China, a formulation that tells a lot about how the Chinese Communist Party views the region as subject to the one influence of Beijing. The economic, political and cultural penetration (measurable by counting the number of Confucius Institutes per university or inhabitants[49]) varies from country to country, with some showing remarkable signs of resilience, while others are much more permeable. This is the case not only for Greece, for whom a Chinese presence represents a breath of economic oxygen but also for Serbia, where President Alexandar Vučić has clearly bet on China for the future. Proof that things are changing in Europe, in the midst of the first wave of Coronavirus in 2020, Vučić did not hesitate to announce to his fellow citizens that solidarity with China was now much more important than that with the European Union.[50] Even more worryingly for the European Union, one of its own members, Hungary also stands out with reports of high levels of Chinese influence, with more Confucius Institutes per inhabitant than anywhere else in the EU and where the choice of China is also to a certain extent a personal and ideological choice: in his Băile Tuşnad speech of 2014, the genesis of his illiberal doctrine, Viktor Orbán did not hide the fact that at least in certain aspects, the Chinese model represented the future,[51] and the Hungarian leader often defended pro-Chinese positions in the European Council on Tibet[52] or the arbitrary detention of Uyghurs or human rights lawyers.[53] To be fair to him, he was not the only one, as Greece and other countries often proved reluctant to engage in criticism of Beijing.

What we are now witnessing is important, as some European countries are starting to turn their back on the very idea of "the West" and opening their doors to China. This should make Western decision-makers ponder for a while, on both sides of the Atlantic. For sure, money is a powerful incentive for any elite, in particular when it has become a scarce resource (the Western Balkans come to mind here). But is it enough to just understand this move toward China as an economic choice? Should it not also be viewed as the sign of a failure of the European Union to produce a zone of solidarity on the continent it has the ambition to take under its wing? Is there no ideological incompatibility between Western liberal culture and the new illiberal ideologies that are sprouting in the region? The answer is not necessarily self-evident, but there are strong reasons to suspect that all of the above factors play a role in the current trends toward continentalization among some European elites.

As Central European researchers Patrik Szicherle, Grigorij Mesežnikov, Jonáš Syrovátka, Jakub Merc and Péter Krekó pointed out in a recent study, a large number of investments promised by the Chinese in Hungary, may it be the high-speed Belgrade-Budapest line or the takeover of the national airline Malév by Hainan Airlines, have either not seen the light of day or have been greatly slowed down by a number of factors, including corruption.[54] But China considers that at least some money can be wasted, and that time is on its side. It is possible that some political leaders who have consciously made the choice of China take the same approach, as they view the West as decadent. Their thinking is that by being ahead of the curve, they may well gain a considerable advantage over their neighbors, who will be late in taking the continentalization train and will not reap the benefits of an early transition.

If such a development were to happen, could we see those who feel they have taken the train early adopt a different, more assertive attitude toward their neighbors? It looks unlikely in today's Europe, but tomorrow's Europe may not be as peaceful: history shows that when dynamics change, some countries can quickly get an over-inflated sense of what they are able to do, and the resurgence of aggressive nationalisms in and around Europe is certainly something to be worried about if nationalism and power imbalances start to work together in the same direction. The episode of Viktor Orbán's positioning toward Ukraine over Transcarpathia at the very time in which Kyiv had to deal with an invasion in the East shows how quickly long-forgotten territorial ambitions can resurface and then be instrumentalized by elites. Let us also remember that very few French or British leaders in 1929 were considering the possibility that Czechoslovakia, Poland and the Baltic States would have ceased to exist ten years later. The creation of new imbalances in regions as unstable as Central Europe and the Balkans, combined with the destructive potential of a long-term conflict between the United States and China, should make us wary about the rise of China and its destabilizing potential on the balances of the continent.

When Europe imports instability

The expression "Powder keg of Europe" has become a cliché of what the Balkan peninsula had become in the years prior to the First World War. It came back to fashion during the 1990s, when the implosion of Yugoslavia meant entrenched wars on which Europeans had little if any control due to their incapacity to coordinate, let alone act. As they watched helplessly the ongoing bloodbaths in Bosnia-Herzegovina and Kosovo, other powers, sensing a vacuum that needed to be filled, kicked in – Russia, and also Turkey, Saudi Arabia and Iran all tried to gain (or, in some cases, regain) a foothold in the region by pretexting religious solidarity to help clients on the ground.[55] In the end, the United States reluctantly intervened, putting an end to the debates: the Russians had to bow to American power, the Iranian jihadists were for the most part (and under heavy pressure from Washington) evacuated from Bosnia and the Saudis had to keep a low profile in Sarajevo and Pristina after the attacks of September 11.

Nonetheless, it would be too optimistic to claim that the Western Balkans were peaceful. True, the cycle of war had been broken, and a looming conflict in North Macedonia did not happen, thanks to the combined action of the European Union and the United States, then at the pinnacle of their soft power. Indeed, it was thought that the promise of joining one day the European Union would be enough to secure the integration of the region in Euro-Atlantic structures (which did mostly happen for NATO integration). However, attention on the Balkans did not last long – as the 2008 and the following crises kicked in, the region quickly faded away in the list of European and American priorities. In the early 2010s, when the United States started to pivot to Asia and recalibrate its engagements in the World, the Western Balkans was one of the victims of this shift in priorities – in many ways, the Obama administration, following its idea to "lead from behind," was hoping to declare the US mission in the Western Balkans accomplished and leave it to the rich Europeans to take care of this part of Europe.

The idea of letting Europe lead in the Balkans was not necessarily a bad one, but the EU was not ready to put the enormous resources needed to establish itself as a truly uncontested dominant power in the region. Again, as vacuums seldom last long, other powers have moved in to conquer markets, friendships and in some cases souls. As a result, and in the words of Konrad Adenauer Stiftung researchers Lars Hänsel and Florian Feyerabend, today "The West, and here primarily the EU, is no longer unchallenged as the dominant force in the Western Balkans, and Brussels' enlargement policy based on conditionality seems to be reaching its limits as an instrument."[56] The vacuum has allowed the usual suspects to return: as in the rest of Europe, Russia plays a particularly disruptive role, playing on the sensitive chord of orthodoxy and panslavism,[57] but it is not the only actor: the countries of the Persian Gulf (Saudi Arabia, United Arab Emirates and Qatar) have made in-roads, while Turkey, historically linked to this region (courtesy of five centuries of Ottoman presence), has also showed renewed interest. Signs of these soft power inroads may be seen not only on the political and cultural level, for example, by the building of mosques around the region, at the political level with the building of relations with "brother" parties (for example, between Turkey's AK Party and the Bosnian SDA), but also on the economic level, as in the case of urban renovation of the banks of the Sava in Belgrade, thanks to Emirati funds.

With China also showing signs of interest in the region and investing heavily in countries like Serbia, all evidence suggests that we are witnessing a renewed scramble for influence in the Western Balkans. These efforts, of course, all have consequences: investment from the Persian Gulf (including Iran) also translates into cultural investments and those are not necessarily neutral, as the rise in reported cases of radicalization throughout the 2010s suggests. The fact that the Western Balkans became a region disproportionately affected by the departure of young Muslims to Syria during the years 2010[58] is no coincidence, and it should be taken as a sign that behind the welcome investments of perfectly legitimate Gulf conglomerates, some groups with more political objectives have tagged along. Geographically closer, Recep Tayyip Erdoğan's Turkey and its soft power approach are also becoming a factor on the ground. Ankara's efforts to portray itself as the defender of Muslims across the world also concern the Western Balkans, which hold sizeable Muslim communities in almost all countries. Turkey is indeed a historical actor in the region: from the fifteenth to the nineteenth century, the Balkans were part of the Ottoman Empire, and although the ties were never completely severed after the Balkan wars, Turkey became much more active after the demise of Yugoslavia, when identity based on religion became once again an important fault line: Muslim populations (especially in Bosnia and Kosovo but also in the Turkish-speaking minority of Bulgaria) were able to pursue cultural links with Ankara, which also translated in political links. In the meantime, Turkish companies moved in and invested heavily in the region, whether the banking sector, in telecommunications or infrastructures, for example in the airports of Pristina, Skopje, Ohrid and Zagreb (the capital of

Croatia, a member of the European Union). More visibly and in line with the re-Islamization of Turkey's foreign policy under Erdoğan, Ankara also financed the construction of mosques of sometimes pharaonic proportions compared to regional standards. The brand-new Great Mosque of Tirana, the largest in the Balkans, built free of charge by the Turks a few steps from the parliament in a country with a nominal Muslim majority but very little religious practice, is a telling example.[59]

It would be wrong to see Turkey as a kind of Russia of the Southeast, a great disruptor seeking to reconquer territories it ruled a long time ago. Rather, Turkey is seeking more of a soft power foothold in the region, whether by economic means by conquering new markets and offering less demanding alternatives to local entrepreneurs, or by posing as the main defender of Muslims. This explains the construction of new large mosques like Tirana's, or the reconstruction/restoration of places of worship from Ottoman times (such as the Ferhad Pasha mosque in Banja Luka, in Bosnia-Herzegovina's Republika Srpska). In this field, competition is fierce with the Saudis, Qataris and Emiratis as to who will fund what, and it has ideological and doctrinal dimensions, as certain groups such as the Salafists or the Muslim Brotherhood are today sponsored by different countries. In this competition for the hearts and souls of Balkan Muslims, Turkey's ambitions are limited by a relative lack of interest from local Muslim populations (which remain much less religious than in other parts of the Muslim world) and finite resources, unlike the Gulf monarchies. Furthermore distance, with the European Union standing between Turkey and the Western Balkans, complicates Turkey's ambitions in the region. Nevertheless, this influence is real and could lead Turkey to intervene more directly if tensions were to rise again in the Balkans, for example, between Serbia and Kosovo, in Bosnia, where the institutions born of the 1995 Dayton Peace show signs of fatigue, or in North Macedonia, where demographic imbalances between the Albanian-speaking (Muslim) and Macedonian (Slavonic Orthodox) populations could generate tensions in the future. As long as the region is at peace, Turkey's goals and policy remain in line with the interests of the European Union, insofar as Ankara has an interest both in keeping the region stable (unlike Russia) and in promoting its inclusion into Euro-Atlantic structures. It is important here to remember that despite ambivalences, Turkey remains a pillar of the Atlantic Alliance, with the second biggest army behind the United States in terms of personnel.[60] But if the Balkans were to become once again a zone of conflict, it is not impossible that Ankara may opt for more disruptive tactics.

Turkey has in fact shown that it could involve itself directly in disruptive operations where it sees a direct geopolitical gain. This is certainly the case in the South Caucasus, where Turkey's support to Azerbaijan in its short war against Armenia put Ankara directly back not only in the regional game but also in the Eastern Mediterranean, which is of direct concern to the European Union. Turkey is active in all its neighborhood: the South Caucasus, and also Syria and Iraq, where it tries to check the ambitions of Kurdish majorities to build a state, on the island of Cyprus, where it supports a puppet secessionist state, but also in North Africa and more particularly Libya, where its military is involved in the current civil war. This involvement, as well as Turkey's long coastline in the Aegean Sea, make Turkey's ambitions in the Eastern Mediterranean disruptive by nature, and even more so since hydrocarbons have been discovered offshore. Turkey's navy feels that it now needs to control the seas in the Eastern Med to project power in Libya and exploit oil and gas resources in North Africa and off the coast of Cyprus.[61] This has led Turkey to flex its military muscle, not only inland in war-torn Libya or Syria but also at sea, where Ankara's ambitions are hampered by Greek ownership of the Aegean islands and independent Cyprus.

When Ankara flexes its muscles and uses its armies in already unstable Near Eastern zones, often devoid of state structures after a decade of war, one could be forgiven to conclude that this is part of a larger game of influence in the Near East, where Turkey's interests clash with those of several powers, including European ones (principally France). But when this commitment takes a maritime dimension, it pushes Turkey directly into conflict with the sovereign rights of two European Union member states, Cyprus and Greece – the latter being also part of NATO. The conflict, in gestation for years, came out in the open over the summer of 2020, and it involved not only Turkey, Cyprus and Greece but also France, which is also entangled in conflicts around the region and sells weapons to Greece. Fortunately, NATO did play a role in de-escalating the conflict between the different actors, most of which were part of the Atlantic Alliance. However, the tensions and incidents of the summer of 2020 have left traces: France's and Greece's frustration with their NATO and EU allies during the crises have repercussions in other issues such as protecting Europe's Eastern flank, and the Eastern Med issue remains unsolved to this day. With many powers entangled with different actors as well as new (China) and not-so-new (Russia) players appearing in the region, the possibilities for renewed tensions accelerating into war are numerous.

In many ways, the key to the Eastern Mediterranean is currently held by Turkey and its relationship with the West. From the beginnings of the Turkish Republic under Atatürk until Recep Tayyip Erdoğan's illiberal turn, Turkey's strategy has been to look West. This is no longer a given in Turkish politics, and the Islamization of the regime, symbolized by the reverting of the Hagia Sofia into a mosque in the summer of 2020, is a telling sign that Ankara is no longer willing to accept its Western trajectory as a given. The ambivalent rapprochement with Russia in recent years, the renewed tensions around Cyprus and the Greek Islands in the summer of 2020, tensions around migration flows and the increasingly authoritarian nature of the regime in place in Ankara all raise doubts about Turkey's ambitions toward the West and whether Ankara still considers itself as a full-fledged member of the Atlantic Alliance. Ankara likes to cultivate a certain ambiguity, as it sees the European Union weakening in Southeastern Europe and the Mediterranean. Confronted with this situation and understanding very well that a vacuum of powers never lasts long, the Turkish government is looking at ways in which it can exploit others' weaknesses to its advantage.

When it comes to the larger relationship with Europe, Recep Tayyip Erdoğan possesses a massive argument in the heart of North-Western Europe: a close-knit Turkish community that remains poorly integrated, particularly in Germany. This is due not only to the original unwillingness of the authorities to integrate these *Gasterbeiter* but also to factors specific to Turkish-speaking communities, historically very much supervised by Ankara and influenced by the Ottoman historical bias against integration inherited from the millet system, as Jérôme Fourquet has described the Turkish-speaking islet in the French archipelago.[62] The Turkish government has tried in recent years to use this leverage, using inflammatory language[63] and giving voting instructions to "Turks abroad" (even though many of them are born and raised in Europe). Calls to the Turkish community in the Netherlands and Germany to vote against parties defined by the government in Ankara as "anti-Islamic" in 2017 and 2018 have had limited effects so far,[64] but they may become much more potent in the event of a direct and sustained Euro-Turkish confrontation, in which Ankara could use Europe's identity crisis as leverage with the European players, in particular Germany.

Turkey possesses a much more lethal weapon in case of tensions with the European Union: the EU's dependence on Ankara to regulate and stop migratory flows. Indeed, Turkey has become a key player in regulating the migrant flow toward Europe in the 2010s: in addition to the funds that the EU continues to send to Ankara, officially to finance accession prospects that nobody believes in anymore, Brussels also pays what in other times would have been called a tribute to the Turks so that they keep their refugees and migrants in Turkey. The Straits and the Turkish coast of the Aegean Sea, so close to the Greek islands, represent one of the three bottlenecks between the three European peninsulas (Iberian, Italian and Balkan) and the transit zones for migrants. In much the same way as the Roman and Byzantine empires paid tribute to their neighbors to keep their hordes in check in a protective *limes*, Europeans now pay large sums of money not only to the Turks but also to Libya and Morocco to manage the influx of migrants from sub-Saharan Africa and the Middle East, without much concern for the defense of human rights.

This strategy may be the only one possible in the short term, but it is unsustainable in the longer term. The risk is that reliance becomes a permanent state of dependency on third countries and that Turkey could at any time threaten Europeans with floods of refugees similar to that of 2015. The crisis of early 2020, in which Ankara put pressure on Europeans by opening the migration floodgates to obtain a position more in line with its interests in Syria is a strong reminder that dependence has a cost. Many Europeans would be ready to qualify this as blackmail, but they should not ignore the fact that Ankara is playing with the hand it has been given, and Turkey is simply putting a price tag on a service it is genuinely giving to Europeans by keeping its 3.6 million registered refugees on its soil – these represent 4.7% of the Turkish population,[65] a situation that is much more explosive than in Europe due not only to the number of migrants now settled on Turkish territory but also to the clear ethnolinguistic differentiation between Arabs and Turks.

Migration is an incredibly difficult human ordeal for those who undertake it. But once settled, it is also a long-term issue in the host country, with many challenges both for the arriving populations (integration into the labor market and the host nation) and for the local populations, as it became painfully clear during and after the 2015 migrant crisis. As American academic Stephen Smith pointed out,[66] the demographic transition in Sub-Saharan Africa is far from over: while the population across the region "has more than quadrupled from 230 million in 1960 to 1 billion by 2015,"[67] it is expected to continue to grow exponentially over the next 30 years. As a result, Africa's population has already largely surpassed Europe's, and the gap will continue to widen over the next few decades: if the European Union has 447 million inhabitants today for one billion Africans, "in thirty-five years, the ratio will be of around 450 million Europeans for 2.5 billion Africans, that is five times more."[68] When it comes to the Sahel region, the closest to Europe, exponential demographic growth is occurring in an ecosystem that remains Malthusian, with finite resources (including ecological) and weak states that are currently experiencing the greatest difficulty in absorbing new and young populations into their educational, health and socioeconomic systems. Thus, the risk of overexploitation of the Niger and Indus rivers (among others) in an environment already threatened by desertification and climate change continues to destabilize these river basins. Moreover, Smith points out that

> demographic pressure on natural resources, starting with the land but also water, increases the risk of conflicts. In Darfur, the sixfold population increase since independence – the population in western Sudan has risen from 1.3 million in 1956 to nearly 8 million in 2017 – is putting a strain on an ecosystem whose desertification is being accelerated by global warming.[69]

In such a challenging environment, it is not surprising to see many individuals tempted by migration and the promise of pay for their family back home and a more predictable future – if not for them, at least for their children. These individuals, whose personal experience of migration is often no less challenging than that of Homer's Odyssey, are part of a large long-term migration process – not only to Europe but also to other parts of the world, where the arrival of foreigners also causes serious difficulties. This has been the case in post-apartheid South Africa, where anti-migrant violence is making headlines on a regular basis, or in Côte d'Ivoire, where the "Ivorian miracle" of the first decades of independence attracted a very large immigrant population from other French-speaking countries in the region. The debate over "Ivoirité," or Ivorian identity, combined with the toxic slogan of "a quarter of foreigners" living on Ivorian soil is one of the main factors that led the country to violence and civil war between the late 1990s and the early 2010s.[70]

Would such a scenario be conceivable for Europe? The toxicity and spread of "Great Replacement" conspiracy theories seems to hint that demographic anxieties are no longer fringe ideas today. For sure, Europeans need continued migration and young people that they do not produce in large enough numbers, if only to compensate for the ongoing pensioners' bulge[71] (although the example of Japan also shows that robotization can partly compensate for the lack of labor in care positions – however, this also implies having local populations and families taking on themselves difficult and unrewarding jobs). But the advantage of a youth influx from aboard is also partly canceled out by other dynamics – as Smith recalls, adult migrants, when they join the job market (as they often do, in jobs that the local populations often consider below their dignity) contribute to financing the generous welfare state, but the costs of education, training and caring, including for their families, partly (and naturally) compensate for the budget bonus. In other words, as on many other subjects, the cost/benefit analysis of migration is much more complex than presented by either side of the debate and the difficulty for Europeans and others to get a full grasp of the issue, coupled with the rise of incendiary discourses over identity and migration can only make the problem worse.

We have seen the devastating effects of the 2015 migration crisis on Europeans' psyche, in the already unfavorable context of an acute economic and social crisis in the eurozone. The waves of terrorist attacks that followed in Western Europe and the reports of cases of sexual harassment by migrants have only contributed to worsen Europeans' identity crisis by building a perception link between violence and terrorism, on the one hand, and on the other hand, Islam and migration. It is of course easy to condemn far-right parties and populist leaders that make their electoral fortunes on these sentiments but they are also the messengers of real anxiety coming from aboriginal European populations that feel threatened by social and cultural downgrading, in a context where Europe's marginalization compared to the rest of the World is becoming visible for everyone.

Could the identity question, linked to migration or not, degenerate into civil war? The scenario of an armed conflict between Islamists and white nationalists was already envisaged in French writer Michel Houellebecq's fiction *Submission*,[72] and although its prediction of civil war breaking in 2022 now seems far-fetched, it is not totally unrealistic in the longer term: nationalist riots in Chemnitz or the Hanau shooting in Germany have shown that an isolated incident could very quickly degenerate into violence, and if those incidents were to become a common occurrence in Western European societies, they could pave the way to a significant deterioration in European's environment, such that Europeans could envisage taking arms against each other in an "ethnic" civil war.

Britain and Europe: friends or foes?

Britain's status as an external – rather than internal – issue for the EU is something new. Indeed, until January 2020, the United Kingdom was part of the European Union, and more generally Britain's belonging to the European security architecture – or indeed to European civilization, is much less debatable than in the case of Russia or Turkey. Yet, despite this "Europeanness," London's relationship with the continent has always been ambiguous. This ambiguity is primarily the result of geography: Britain's insularity is a fact, and it has fashioned peculiar culture and institutions that have, at times, isolated it from the rest of Europe – in this sense, the United Kingdom is to Europe what Japan is to Asia. This insularity has at times been a curse, as when the fifth-century Roman province of Britannia was left to its own devices in the midst of the barbaric invasions – the result was that within a short period of time, coin-minting and anything but the most rudimentary pottery practically disappeared along with other signs of civilization.[73] At other times, isolation has been a blessing, allowing Britain to cut itself from continental turbulences to avoid maintaining a permanent army (at least after 1603 and the union with Scotland) and to focus on mastery of the oceans – in many ways, it was Britain's peripheral position in Europe that allowed it to conquer the World in the seventeenth and eighteenth centuries. Although Britain surely belonged to the European cultural and diplomatic system, its insularity and position on the verge of Europe and close to the Atlantic Ocean allowed it to answer the call of the open seas. Britain's ascendency over the World in Victorian times is due as much to its connection with Europe (which allowed it to take part in the technological military competition) as to its capability to embrace the oceans and shield itself from Europe.

This fundamental distrust for anything coming from the continent explains why, throughout its glory days, Britain tried to adopt whenever it could a policy of splendid isolation,[74] as it tried to stay away from the affairs of the continent except to ensure that no power was able to achieve hegemony. In all other cases, London's eyes were riven on the oceans – as Lord Canning's biographer pointed out, "Europe's domain extends to the shores of the Atlantic, England's begin there."[75] Of course, this policy was never tenable in the long term: British policymakers understood too late that the unification of Germany was going to fundamentally shift the balance of powers in a way that would threaten *Pax Britannica* in Europe. Indeed, they ended up entangling themselves in alliances and going to war, but the hope to keep a safe distance from the continent didn't disappear after the Great War. Britain still wanted above all else to stay away from the messy politics of Europe and tried in vain through appeasement to avoid war, to no avail. After 1945, the policy was also to stay away: Winston Churchill is certainly one of the inspirers of the European project, but his ambiguity about Britain's status in it is just as remarkable: he may have been a supporter of the concept of the "United States of Europe,"[76] but in his mind, Britain had no place in it – Europe was only one of the three circles of Britain's foreign policy, along with the United States and the Commonwealth. Dates matter here, because Churchill's vision was heavily influenced by his own experience: he knew that Britain could not extricate itself that easily from Europe, but he was also a product of the Empire (over which he still presided in his time as Prime Minister – a large part of Britain's "foreign" trade was with the Commonwealth[77]) and a proponent of the alliance with America, whom he had persuaded to join and win the war against Japan and Germany. Churchill also knew that the European project carried by the likes of Schuman, Adenauer and De Gasperi was an initiative from countries that had been vanquished in the war – as a winner of that war, joining them would have been unthinkable.

Subsequent British Prime Ministers were to prove just as ambivalent about Europe, even after Britain's entry into the European Community in 1975.[78] In many ways, integration was an admission of failure for Britain: between 1945 and 1975, Britain had lost its empire and its industrial power at a time when the continent was rebuilding itself at an impressive pace. It is therefore not necessarily surprising to see that once the United Kingdom had regained a certain status during and after the Thatcher years, a trend reemerged to re-isolate Britain from the continent: now that the United Kingdom was strong, did it really need to be part of a club that was itself losing market shares compared to the rest of the world? The economic dynamism of the City of London, often compared with the stagnation of France's former industrial heartlands (but surprisingly never with Britain's own rust belt), became a powerful argument for those wishing to see Britain walk away from its relationship with the European Union – a relationship that was always seen with ambivalence by the British public and by all British Prime Ministers without exception, as Andrew Adonis, a former adviser to Tony Blair, pointed out.[79]

Whether one likes it or not, Britain is now out of the European Union, and for a very long time. Beyond the rhetoric on both sides of the Channel, which have been more emotional than rational, Britain's departure poses a number of problems for the European Union and, down the line, for Europe's security. First, there is simple mathematics: the EU lost 66 million inhabitants overnight and some of the richest, as with them, no less than $2,500 billion of total GDP also evaporated from the books along with the expected €84 billion of operating budget contribution over the period 2021–2028. Although COVID-19 has for some time eluded this question, with the recovery fund taking most attention, the problem of the long-term financing of the Union remains a thorny issue, as member-states (who still would not consider allowing the EU to directly levy its own taxes) will need to either cut some budget lines or increase other members' contributions.[80] But beyond the simple arithmetic, Brexit has also fundamentally changed the balance of power in Europe: combined with eastward enlargement, it contributes to shifting the center of gravity of the European Union from the North Sea to the interior of the continent, which in turn strengthens Dutch and French fears (among others) of being marginalized in an ensemble centered on the heart of Germany; even more worryingly, it cuts the North Sea, Europe's economic heart since the seventeenth century, in two.

In the long run, Brexit also raises the question of Britain's place in the European security system. And the main question for Europeans today is: should they still consider Britain as an ally, or should they see it as a competitor? Her Majesty's Government has cultivated a certain ambiguity, with not only a rather remarkable alignment of British and European positions on a certain number of fundamental international issues (climate change and the Iran deal for example) but also very different strategies on other issues, such as the stance to take over China or trade relations between Britain and the European Union. This ambiguity is unsurprising: on many issues, Britain and the EU still share a common agenda, but on others, they are indeed in competition – a competition that Britain will sometimes win, thanks to its agility (early COVID-19 vaccination provides an edifying example) and that it will sometimes lose because it will be too small compared to the large EU market.

This ambivalence in the EU–UK relation is also the product of an internal debate currently at play within British elites. On the one hand, the Brexiteer hardcore wants a clear cut with the EU (which necessarily implies rivalry, since Great Britain cannot be satisfied with a quasi-hegemonic position of Germany on the European continent); on the other side, there are still many advocates for a policy of equidistance between the United States and Europe, with the idea that the West should stick together to face the global challenges of tomorrow. The debate is still ongoing today, and in many ways, it is about whether Britain should go back to a sort of splendid isolation (under the disguise of "global Britain") or whether it should stay involved with Europe at all. The risk for Britain was actually already posed by Prime Minister Macmillan in 1960, as he feared "being caught between a hostile (or at least increasingly less benevolent) America and a new, powerful and arrogant 'Carolingian Empire' [understand Franco-German]."[81] In many ways, Britain's geopolitical dilemmas on Europe and the Transatlantic relationship have returned to what they used to be before Britain joined the Union.

Sooner or later, the ambiguity of Britain's position toward Europe will have to end. For a while, an in-between position will be comfortable for both the EU and the United Kingdom, but many things – from Scottish separatism to a rift between MacMillan's "Carolingian" Europe and the United States – could make ambiguity untenable, forcing Whitehall to make a choice. This choice could actually be dictated by internal considerations, as many decisions over Europe in the past: much like Harold Wilson, David Cameron's choice for a referendum on membership of the European Union was primarily dictated by considerations that were not only national but internal to the Conservative Party.

London's position will also be defined by the idea that British elites will have of their position vis-à-vis the rest of the World: Britons may be tempted by a return to splendid isolation even if they disguise it under the slogan of "Global Britain," but the reality is that they will eventually get caught up one way or another by events in Europe, as they did in 1914, 1939 or in a different setting after the 1960s once it became clear that Britain had lost its empire.[82]

What would then be the nature of Britain's renewed interest in Europe? Will it be cooperative, even benevolent? It could be that Brexit has not meant that Britain has reneged on cooperation with the continent, British troops are still stationed in the Baltic states to protect them from the threat of Russian aggression and it has retained extensive defense cooperation agreements, including with France under the Lancaster House treaty, ratified by the British and French parliaments in October 2016, just a few months after the Brexit vote. Britain has left the EU but it can still play a positive role to help strengthen peace in Europe and its neighborhood. Britain can still play its role within NATO and use its presence in the Baltic states and in the Mediterranean (with important bases in Cyprus and Gibraltar) to remain a positive geopolitical actor across and around the continent. In this case, without preempting a capacity to embrace the open sea, Britain would remain a key to European security and Brexit would ultimately have had little influence on the security architecture in Europe. This is the scenario that London, Paris and Berlin (not to mention Brussels) are currently seeking to follow, but it is not guaranteed to succeed.

Indeed, the maintenance of the status quo in British-EU relations presupposes a neutral (or quasi-neutral) impact of Brexit on Britain's economy and politics, and we already know that this will not happen. Brexit allows more flexibility and agility for London (allowing it to take the lead in the vaccine rollout, for example, and to take clear policy stances with regard to China), but it is likely to be a problem for some trade negotiations, and probably for Britain's short-term economic prospects, as trade adapts to the new, post-Brexit customs rules. The balance of power between Britain and the continent is therefore likely to shift over time. If that balance of power tilts in Britain's favor, London will not only consider Brexit a success but will be tempted to consider it legitimate (and in Britain's interest) to encourage other EU countries to follow its example. For many hard Brexiteers, exiting the Union was never an end in itself, and they will continue to push for a fight with the "Brussels monster." Of course, this idea is currently marginal, but so was Euroscepticism back in the 1990s, and if Brexit were to become a success, it is possible that Britain would encourage other countries who might be tempted to follow suit (one could think of the Netherlands or Sweden, where Euroscepticism is strong). By trying to "chip" away other countries from the Union, Britain would, therefore, automatically gain the hostility of Brussels, Paris and Berlin, thus raising tensions over the North Sea. It would not be impossible to see incidents developing over fisheries and leading to direct confrontation, for example, between the French and British navies, while the European Union may (or may not) unravel.

But the EU could not be the only union threatened by Brexit. In fact, another scenario could envisage a net loss for the United Kingdom, which would include marginalization of the city and a secessionist drive in Scotland and Northern Ireland. Such a scenario would threaten not only Britain's flourishing economy but also its security, as the Kingdom would be reduced to a "little England" version of Global Britain. The prospect may look pleasing to some in Brussels who resented the mess that Brexit created on both sides of the channel in 2016–2020, but it would not be a bearer of good news for the continent either. Indeed, a deterioration in living conditions in Britain would necessarily be accompanied by a public debate on what is going wrong, and it is by no means certain that the scapegoats would be found in London, in particular, in case secessionist movements were to turn violent – in that case, the suspicion that violence had been encouraged from outside could also provoke a new rise of anti-European Anglo-nationalism. London could then choose a much more defiant position toward the EU, leading to tensions, and down the road even possibly war, whether on British soil or in the North Sea.

The anti-EU circles in London would be too happy to respond to perceived support for secessionist sentiment in Britain by an assertive policy to try and weaken the European Union, relying on conservative and nationalist American circles that they have very often cultivated for years. In that case (and provided that a sympathetic administration would be in place), US Anglo-nationalists could then provide financial support that London can no longer afford to divide Europeans and promote conflicts between the peripheral nations of the Union (especially in the South) and Brussels or Berlin. Of course, such a scenario looks unlikely today, but if the very survival of the kingdom depended on it, London could revert to an outright anti-continental platform, invoking the memories of 1793–1815 – or 1939–1945, which both remain a point of reference for British nationalism. If such a confrontation were to brew up, it is likely that the Atlantic and the North Sea would become new zones of geopolitical rivalry, and Germany would probably have to rethink its foreign policy. The problem is that Berlin's geopolitical situation would much resemble that of 1914, where a fear of being encircled by hostile powers fueled paranoia at home and agressive behavior abroad. The return of a perception of an oceanic threat for Germany or France would probably lead Berlin to look at other security options, including continentalization and a closer relationship with Russia or China, leading other capitals such as Paris to a choice between the *couple franco-allemand* and the *entente cordiale*. In any case, the security architecture of Western Europe would be profoundly reshaped, and this would certainly not be to pacify relations between nation-states on this part of the continent.

★ ★ ★

Today, Europeans face a very different situation compared to the 1990s, as they discover that history did not actually end in 1991. They are also coming to terms with another reality, that Europe's place in the world is not that of 1914. At the beginning of the twentieth century, Europeans not only were the masters of their own destiny but also controlled that of most people on the Afro-Eurasian landmass. Between 1914 and 1945, Europe lost control of its destiny, but it could still rely on its technological advance and a relatively efficient state structure to count in the world. In the 1990s, the rise of soft power as a major factor in foreign policy even convinced Europeans that they could now ignore the dangers around them: Europe was the first continent to have exited from history, and the incarnation of this European pacification, the European Union, was to extend the reign of prosperity and peace by projecting its model to the rest of the world. If anyone ever believed in this myth, it should have been shattered by the implosion of Yugoslavia – on which Europeans proved incapable to act – and Russia's invasion of Georgia, a country that at the time was begging to enter the Euro-Atlantic club.

Today, after more than a decade of crises in Europe, it has become difficult to ignore that Europe, in general (and the European Union in particular), is no longer an expanding force for peace but, on the contrary, an island of peace under attack. Indeed, many challenges have accumulated on Europe's borders: Russia has clearly positioned itself as a challenger and seeks to weaken the EU to regain the influence and territories it lost in 1989–1991; Europeans are slowly coming to terms with the fact that China's geopolitical ambitions also concern Europe and threaten to tear the continent apart; Turkey's new assertive Muslim identity is now provoking regained tensions with key European countries in the Eastern Mediterranean and possibly soon in the very unstable Western Balkans; finally, the Mediterranean, once imagined as a paradise on earth where tourists would simply flock every summer has become as much a border as a graveyard, with migration flows having the potential to create more internal backlash inside the continent. Finally, over the past decades, many Europeans have grown more distrustful of their American ally: the United States may have guaranteed the integrity of Western Europe since 1945 (and of the entire continent since the 1990s), but following the wars in the Middle East and the Trump presidency, some key foreign policy circles have come to doubt the reliability of the alliance. In some ways, they are right to be skeptical: America is going through a period of self-doubt, and it is likely that Europe will matter less to Washington in the coming years – the question is then whether the US foreign policy establishment will continue to view Europe and the EU as an ally, or whether it sees it as a battlefield where it competes with other powers for influence.

Europeans are very slow in understanding these developments. This leaves the region vulnerable, while war is getting dangerously close to the EU, whether geographically (with the Russian invasion of Crimea and the war in the Donbass since 2014) or temporarily (with the wave of terrorist attacks of 2015–2016, which for very short moments imported war in the heart of the European Union). The term "import" is important here. In fact, from being an exporting power of stability in the 1990s, Europe has now become an importer of instability, and if it is unchecked, that instability could bring war on EU soil. Such an occurrence is even more likely as wars are no longer led in the ways most Europeans are used to thinking it: they have become more complex, less intense and more low-cost, including in their conception. Faced with contradictions they are unwilling to face and the irruption of external actors, Europeans must also face an evolution of military doctrine they are seldom prepared (let alone willing) to face.

Notes

1 Geoffrey Blainey, *The Causes of War* (3rd edition), New York: The Free Press, 1988, p.57.
2 Ibid., p.65.
3 A recent study by Brown University in the United States estimated the total cost of the Endless Wars in Iraq and Afghanistan at $5.9 trillion throughout the 2000s and 2010s. https://watson.brown.edu/costsofwar/files/cow/imce/papers/2018/Crawford_Costs%20of%20War%20Estimates%20Through%20FY2019%20.pdf
4 Crude oil production inside the United States more than doubled between 2010 and 2019, from 5.6 to 12.2 million barrels per day. In 2015, production had already reached 9.4 million barrels per day. Source: Robert D. Blackwill and Jennifer M. Harris, *War by Other Means: Geoeconomics and Statecraft*, Cambridge, MA: Harvard University Press, 2016, p.206.
5 Ian Morris, *Why the West Rules – For Now: The Patterns of History and What They Reveal about the Future*, London: Profile Books, 2010.
6 Source: US Energy Information Administration: https://www.eia.gov/beta/international/regions-topics.php?RegionTopicID=WOTC
7 Source: World Bank – https://data.worldbank.org/indicator/NY.GDP.MKTP.KD.ZG?end=2018&start=2010
8 https://www.economist.com/special-report/2013/06/13/the-merkel-plan
9 Robert D. Blackwill and Jennifer M. Harris, *War by Other Means: Geoeconomics and Statecraft*, Cambridge, MA: Harvard University Press, 2016, p.215.
10 Robert Kagan, *The Jungle Grows Back: America and Our Imperiled World*, New York: Alfred A. Knopf, 2018, p.28.
11 See Charles Kupchan, *Isolationsim: A History of America's Efforts to Shield Itself from the World*, New York: Oxford University Press, 2020, pp.339–350.
12 https://www.ecfr.eu/publications/summary/popular_demand_for_strong_european_foreign_policy_what_people_want
13 For John Mearsheimer, three zones outside the Americas are crucial for American power: "Europe and East Asia, because that is where the other great powers are located; and the Persian Gulf, because it is the main source of an exceptionally important resource: oil." See John Mearsheimer, *The Great Delusion: Liberal Dreams and International Realities*, New Haven: Yale University Press, 2018, p.222.
14 John Mearsheimer, *The Great Delusion: Liberal Dreams and International Realities*, New Haven: Yale University Press, 2018.
15 Robert Kagan, *The Jungle Grows Back: America and Our Imperiled World*, New York: Alfred A. Knopf, 2018, p.28.
16 https://www.elysee.fr/emmanuel-macron/2019/08/20/declaration-de-presse-demmanuel-macron-president-de-la-republique-avec-vladimir-poutine-president-de-la-federation-de-russie
17 Simon Dixon, *The Modernization of Russia: 1676–1825*, Cambridge: Cambridge University Press, 1999.
18 Quoted in Kristi Raik and András Rácz et al., *Post-Crimea Shift in EU-Russia Relations: From Fostering Interdependence to Managing Vulnerabilities*, Tallinn: International Centre for Defence and Security, 2019, p.49.
19 Quoted in Geoffrey Blainey, *The Causes of War* (3rd edition), New York: The Free Press, 1988, p.3.
20 Robert Kagan, *The Jungle Grows Back: America and Our Imperiled World*, New York: Alfred A. Knopf, 2018, p.113.

21 Dominique d'Herbigny, « Partenaires de la Russie ou 'idiots utiles' », in *Annuaire français de relations internationales*, Vol. XII, 2012, p.201.
22 Kristi Raik and András Rácz, *Post-Crimea Shift in EU-Russia Relations: From Fostering Interdependence to Managing Vulnerabilities*, Tallinn: International Centre for Defence and Security, 2019, p.94.
23 Ivan Krastev and Stephen Holmes, *The Light that Failed: A Reckoning*, London: Allen Lane, 2019, p.137.
24 Georges Sokoloff, *La Puissance pauvre: Une Histoire de la Russie de 1815 à nos jours*, Paris: Fayard, 1993.
25 Kristi Raik and András Rácz, *Post-Crimea Shift in EU-Russia Relations: From Fostering Interdependence to Managing Vulnerabilities*, Tallinn: International Centre for Defence and Security, 2019, p.61.
26 https://www.csis.org/blogs/post-soviet-post/band-brothers-wagner-group-and-russian-state
27 Quoted in Lawrence Freedman, *The Future of War: A History*, New York: PublicAffairs, 2017, p.224.
28 Timothy Snyder, *The Road to Unfreedom: Russia, Europe, America*, New York: Tim Duggan Books, 2018, p.249.
29 Kristi Raik and András Rácz, *Post-Crimea Shift in EU-Russia Relations: From Fostering Interdependence to Managing Vulnerabilities*, Tallinn: International Centre for Defence and Security, 2019, p.14.
30 See Dominique Reynié et al., *Democracies under Pressure: A Global Survey*, Paris: Fondapol, 2019, p.132; http://www.fondapol.org/en/etudes-en/new-global-survey-democracies-under-pressure-volume-i-the-issues/
31 https://ecfr.eu/article/commentary_china_europe_and_covid_19_headwinds/
32 See Patrik Szicherle, Grigorij Mesežnikov, Jonáš Syrovátka, Jakub Merc, and Péter Krekó, *Doors Wide Shut: Russian, Chinese and Turkish Authoritarian Influence in the Czech Republic, Hungary and Slovakia*, Budapest: Political Capital, 2019, p.21.
33 See Clive Hamilton and Mareike Ohlberg, *Hidden Hand: Exposing How the Chinese Communist Party is Reshaping the World*, Winnipeg: Optimum Publishing, 2020.
34 https://www.freightwaves.com/news/cosco-to-purchase-majority-stake-in-piraeus-port
35 https://en.difesaonline.it/news-forze-armate/sicurezza/il-dragone-cinese-sul-porto-di-taranto-il-colonialismo-infrastrutturale
36 https://www.npr.org/2018/10/09/642587456/chinese-firms-now-hold-stakes-in-over-a-dozen-european-ports?t=1614617996701
37 See Cyrus Krohn, *Bombarded: How to Fight Back against the Online Assault on Democracy*, Issaquah: Made for Success Publishing, 2020.
38 Laure de Charette and Marion Zipfel, *Chine: Les nouveaux milliardaires rouges*, Paris: L'Archipel, 2012.
39 See Christopher Balding, *Huawei Technologies' Links to Chinese State Security Services*, July 5, 2019, available online: https://ssrn.com/abstract=3415726
40 https://www.theguardian.com/business/2021/jan/23/the-strange-case-of-alibabas-jack-ma-and-his-three-month-vanishing-act
41 Robert D. Blackwill and Jennifer M. Harris, *War by Other Means: Geoeconomics and Statecraft*, Cambridge, MA: Harvard University Press, 2016, p.93.
42 David Shullman et al., *Chinese Malign Influence and the Corrosion of Democracy: An Assessment of Chinese Interference in Thirteen Key Countries*, Washington: International Republican Institute, 2019, p.5.
43 https://www.smh.com.au/world/asia/china-announces-retaliation-for-us-action-on-hong-kong-20191203-p53g7z.html
44 David Shullman et al., *Chinese Malign Influence and the Corrosion of Democracy: An Assessment of Chinese Interference in Thirteen Key Countries*, Washington: International Republican Institute, 2019.

45 Peter Rudolf, *The Sino-American World Conflict*, Berlin: German Institute for International and Security Affairs, SWP Research Paper 3, February 2020.
46 Graham Allison, *Destined for War: Can America and China Escape Thucydides's Trap*, New York: Mariner Group, 2017, p.141.
47 Ibid.
48 Clive Hamilton and Mareike Ohlberg, *Hidden Hand: Exposing How the Chinese Communist Party is Reshaping the World*, Melbourne: Hardie Grant Books, 2020.
49 David Shullman et al., *Chinese Malign Influence and the Corrosion of Democracy: An Assessment of Chinese Interference in Thirteen Key Countries*, Washington: International Republican Institute, 2019.
50 https://www.euractiv.com/section/china/news/serbia-turns-to-china-due-to-lack-of-eu-solidarity-on-coronavirus/
51 See Viktor Orbán's defining speech in Băile Tuşnad (Romania) on July 26 2014, available in English on the *Budapest Beacon* website: https://budapestbeacon.com/full-text-of-viktor-orbans-speech-at-baile-tusnad-tusnadfurdo-of-26-july-2014/
52 Patrik Szicherle, Grigorij Mesežnikov, Jonáš Syrovátka, Jakub Merc, and Péter Krekó, *Doors Wide Shut: Russian, Chinese and Turkish Authoritarian Influence in the Czech Republic, Hungary and Slovakia*, Budapest: Political Capital, 2019, p.22.
53 Benjamin Haddad, *Le paradis perdu: L'Amérique de Trump et la fin des illusions européennes*, Paris: Grasset, 2019, p.250.
54 Patrik Szicherle, Grigorij Mesežnikov, Jonáš Syrovátka, Jakub Merc, and Péter Krekó, *Doors Wide Shut: Russian, Chinese and Turkish Authoritarian Influence in the Czech Republic, Hungary and Slovakia*, Budapest: Political Capital, 2019, p.24.
55 Harun Karčić, "Globalisation and Islam in Bosnia: Foreign Influences and Their Effects," *Totalitarian Movements and Political Religions*, Vol. 11, No. 2, 151–166, 2010.
56 Florian Feyerabend et al., *The Influence of External Actors in the Western Balkans: A Map of Geopolitical Players*, Berlin: Konrad Adenauer Stiftung, 2018, p.4. https://www.kas.de/documents/252038/253252/7_dokument_dok_pdf_53583_2.pdf/194afc48-b3be-e3bc-d1da-02771a223f73?version=1.0&t=1539646959279
57 Ibid., p.5.
58 Ibid., p.7.
59 https://www.csmonitor.com/World/Europe/2018/0912/In-Albania-new-Turkish-mosque-stirs-old-resentments
60 Asli Aydıntaşbaş, *From Myth to Reality: How to Understand Turkey's Role in the Western Balkans*, Policy Brief by the European Council of Foreign Relations, March 2019.
61 This is part of Turkey's "Blue Homeland" strategy https://www.washingtonpost.com/world/middle_east/turkey-greece-blue-homeland/2020/09/26/15cf7afe-fc3b-11ea-830c-a160b331ca62_story.html
62 Jérôme Fourquet, *L'archipel français: naissance d'une nation multiple et divisée*, Paris: Seuil, 2019, pp.171–173.
63 Many French people will obviously remember President Erdoğan's words for Emmanuel Macron when he questioned his mental health in yet another rhetoric war between France and Turkey in October 2020, but this is not the first verbal attack by Turkish officials against Europeans. Tempers ran high in Europe before, for example, when Alparslan Kavaklıoğlu, chairman of the Turkish parliament's security and intelligence committee, declared in March 2018 that "Europe will become Muslim," or when President Erdoğan claimed in an official speech in January 2019 that Turkey's borders "go from Vienna to the shores of the Adriatic Sea, from Turkestan [or Xinjiang for the Chinese] to the Black Sea." https://foreignpolicy.com/2019/05/07/erdogans-long-arm-in-europe-germany-netherlands-milli-gorus-muslim-brotherhood-turkey-akp/
64 https://www.hurriyetdailynews.com/turkey-vows-to-mobilize-islamic-world-against-euro-fascism-110792
65 Source: UNHCR – https://data2.unhcr.org/en/documents/download/70508

66 Stephen Smith, *The Scramble for Europe: Young Africa on its Way to the Old Continent*, Cambridge: Polity, 2019. It is a translation of the original French book, which I am using for the specific quotes (using my own translation).
67 Stephen Smith, *La Ruée vers l'Europe: la jeune Afrique en route pour le Vieux continent*, Paris: Grasset, 2018, p.17.
68 Ibid., p.19.
69 Ibid., p.75.
70 Ibid., p.163.
71 Ibid., p.179.
72 Michel Houellebecq, *Submission: A Novel*, New York: Picador, 2016.
73 Adrian Goldsworthy, *Why Rome Fell*, New Haven: Yale University Press, 2009, pp.345–348.
74 Splendid isolation was only truly theorized and labeled at the end of the nineteenth century under the governments of Benjamin Disraeli and Lord Salisbury. However, it took shape long before and in many ways inspired America's trend of isolationism. See Paul W. Schroeder, *The Transformation of European Politics: 1763–1848*, Oxford: Oxford University Press, 1994.
75 Harold Temperley, *The Foreign Policy of Canning 1822–1827: England, the Neo-Holy Alliance and the New World*, London: Routledge, 2014 (1st edition: 1925), p.342.
76 Winston Churchill's Speech to the University of Zurich, Switzerland, on September 19, 1946 is available online: https://www.churchill-in-zurich.ch/site/assets/files/1807/rede_winston_churchill_englisch.pdf
77 Andrew Adonis et al., *Half In Half Out: Prime Ministers on Europe*, Londres: Basic Books, 2018, p.13.
78 Ibid.
79 Ibid.
80 https://www.theguardian.com/world/2020/feb/16/stressed-heads-to-start-brussels-budget-talks-post-brexit
81 MacMillan's journal, quoted in Andrew Adonis et al., *Half In Half Out: Prime Ministers on Europe*, London: Basic Books, 2018, p.64.
82 Donald Kagan, *On the Origins of War and the Preservation of Peace*, New York: Anchor Books, 1996.

Bibliography

Adonis, Andrew et al., *Half In Half Out: Prime Ministers on Europe*, London: Basic Books, 2018.

Allison, Graham, *Destined for War: Can America and China Escape Thucydides's Trap*, New York: Mariner Group, 2017.

Aydıntaşbaş, Asli, *From Myth to Reality: How to Understand Turkey's Role in the Western Balkans*, Policy Brief by the European Council of Foreign Relations, March 2019.

Blackwill, Robert D., and Harris, Jennifer M., *War by Other Means: Geoeconomics and Statecraft*, Cambridge, MA: Harvard University Press, 2016.

Blainey, Geoffrey, *The Causes of War* (3rd edition), New York: The Free Press, 1988.

d'Herbigny, Dominique, «Partenaires de la Russie ou 'idiots utiles' », in *Annuaire français de relations internationales*, Vol. 12, 2012.

de Charette, Laure, and Zipfel, Marion, *Chine: Les nouveaux milliardaires rouges*, Paris: L'Archipel, 2012.

Dixon, Simon, *The Modernization of Russia: 1676–1825*, Cambridge: Cambridge University Press, 1999.

Feyerabend, Florian et al., *The Influence of External Actors in the Western Balkans: A Map of Geopolitical Players*, Berlin: Konrad Adenauer Stiftung, 2018.

Fourquet, Jérôme, *L'archipel français: naissance d'une nation multiple et divisée*, Paris: Seuil, 2019.
Freedman, Lawrence, *The Future of War: A History*, New York: PublicAffairs, 2017.
Goldsworthy, Adrian, *Why Rome Fell*, New Haven: Yale University Press, 2009.
Haddad, Benjamin, *Le paradis perdu: L'Amérique de Trump et la fin des illusions européennes*, Paris: Grasset, 2019.
Hamilton, Clive, and Ohlberg, Mareike, *Hidden Hand: Exposing How the Chinese Communist Party is Reshaping the World*, Melbourne: Hardie Grant Books, 2020.
Houellebecq, Michel, *Submission: A Novel*, New York: Picador, 2016.
Kagan, Donald, *On the Origins of War and the Preservation of Peace*, New York: Anchor Books, 1996.
Kagan, Robert, *The Jungle Grows Back: America and Our Imperiled World*, New York: Alfred A. Knopf, 2018.
Karčić, Harun, "Globalisation and Islam in Bosnia: Foreign Influences and Their Effects," *Totalitarian Movements and Political Religions*, Vol. 11, No. 2, 151–166, 2010.
Krastev, Ivan, and Holmes, Stephen, *The Light that Failed: A Reckoning*, London: Allen Lane, 2019.
Krohn, Cyrus, *Bombarded: How to Fight Back against the Online Assault on Democracy*, Issaquah: Made for Success Publishing, 2020.
Kupchan, Charles, *Isolationsim: A History of America's Efforts to Shield Itself from the World*, New York: Oxford University Press, 2020.
Mearsheimer, John, *The Great Delusion: Liberal Dreams and International Realities*, New Haven: Yale University Press, 2018.
Morris, Ian, *Why the West Rules – For Now: The Patterns of History and What They Reveal about the Future*, London: Profile Books, 2010.
Raik, Kristi, Rácz, András et al., *Post-Crimea Shift in EU-Russia Relations: From Fostering Interdependence to Managing Vulnerabilities*, Tallinn: International Centre for Defence and Security, 2019.
Reynié, Dominique et al., *Democracies under Pressure: A Global Survey*, Paris: Fondapol, 2019.
Rudolf, Peter, *The Sino-American World Conflict*, Berlin: German Institute for International and Security Affairs, SWP Research Paper 3, February 2020.
Shullman, David et al., *Chinese Malign Influence and the Corrosion of Democracy: An Assessment of Chinese Interference in Thirteen Key Countries*, Washington: International Republican Institute, 2019.
Smith, Stephen, *The Scramble for Europe: Young Africa on its Way to the Old Continent*, Cambridge: Polity, 2019.
Snyder, Timothy, *The Road to Unfreedom: Russia, Europe, America*, New York: Tim Duggan Books, 2018.
Sokoloff, Georges, *La Puissance pauvre: Une Histoire de la Russie de 1815 à nos jours*, Paris: Fayard, 1993.
Szicherle, Patrik, Mesežnikov, Grigorij, Syrovátka, Jonáš, Merc, Jakub, and Krekó, Péter, *Doors Wide Shut: Russian, Chinese and Turkish Authoritarian Influence in the Czech Republic, Hungary and Slovakia*, Budapest: Political Capital, 2019.
Temperley, Harold, *The Foreign Policy of Canning 1822–1827: England, the Neo-Holy Alliance and the New World*, London: Routledge, 2014.

6
WAR AIN'T WHAT IT USED TO BE

Ask military personnel and war scholar experts about war, and disturbing truths about its reality will come to light. One of them is that pretty much like golf, war is an activity where training is everything, and the more it is practiced (preferably in lands far away), the more effective the army becomes. As we saw in Chapter 1, this is indeed the main reason why the ever-fighting Europeans were able, for better and for worse, to dominate the world in the 18th and 19th centuries. But losing in practice, as most Europeans have done for most of the past 75 years, also has its price: it becomes very easy to miss new developments in what ancient Chinese strategist Sun Tzu called 'the art of war,' and then be overwhelmed by these new developments in the first fight – something the French army excelled at between 1870 and 1940.

This is of course not to say that Europeans should start new wars just for the sake of updating their fighting skills. But just as war is too serious a thing to be left to the sole military (to quote French politician Georges Clemenceau), it is also too serious to be ignored as a reality. Unfortunately, this is what most Europeans have done for the past 30 years, and today, as war is coming dangerously close to their shores, they find themselves totally unprepared to face its risks, because they do not know what war looks like. And even though many in the European military are acutely aware of the latest evolution of warfare, very few European politicians and decision-makers are, and this ignorance could turn into a tragic unpreparedness in the future.

For most Europeans, war remains pretty much a Clausewitzian affair: following 19th- and 20th-century European textbooks,[1] they imagine it to be a large confrontation between regular armies, with all the nation's forces mobilized for a final victory that is very often imagined as the total annihilation of the adversary. However, this vision is largely outdated: if Europeans imagine that the threat of nuclear fire alone will moderate the bellicose fervor of the protagonists, they

DOI: 10.4324/9781003215790-9

are pretty much unaware of strategic developments since the 1970s, where the idea of limited nuclear warfare started to emerge. Since then, much more has changed, and while the Cold War did allow for actual war between nuclear powers to happen (via proxies), the fact that it didn't become "hot" in Europe is also the result of its geographic position, ant its central status in the confrontation. And while we may get back to new Cold War-type engagement, military strategy has also much evolved to adapt to new types of situations: the post-1991 wars that took place on European soil, whether in ex-Yugoslavia, Moldova, Georgia or Ukraine, show that war is no longer defined by great battles between states, but often between groups belonging to the same state, or even between a state and another state hiding behind local groups in order to disguise its intervention in a civil war.

The practice of warfare has much evolved since the 1950s, and Russia's successful invasion of Crimea in 2014 provides a particularly convincing example of how far warfare is from what Europeans imagine it to look like. To quote British journalist David Patrikarakos,

> "Putin never officially invaded the Crimea. No war was declared; no Russian soldiers ever officially crossed the border. Instead, several hundred troops marched into Simferopol and seized its regional parliament and Council of Ministers. They were masked and wore green uniforms without any identifying insignia. Of course everyone knew they were Russians, not least when they hoisted Russian flags over the captured buildings."[2]

Were Russia and Ukraine at war? The Ukrainians think so, the Russians deny it, even if they are not fooling anyone in military headquarters.

War, as practiced by the Kremlin in eastern Ukraine today (but also by other powers in other parts of the world), is far removed from the "classical" image developed in the West, with gallant declarations of war, orderly battles, limited battlefields and peace agreements. Actually, war never really adhered to this chivalrous ideal. Today, it is not only the methods of engagement but also the weapons, the terrain and even the rules of the game that have changed. Regular or irregular armies do not (only) fight each other with tanks and infantry regiments, but with drones and small special units that can hit soldiers or individuals, identified or not as "terrorists." Battlefields are no longer the muddy trenches of Verdun or the Ukrainian plain, but small urban areas, cyberspace or the media. As General Valery Gerasimov, Chief of Staff of the Russian military, puts it, "the very rules of war have changed. The role of non-military means of achieving political and strategic goals has grown, and, in many cases, they have exceeded the power of force of weapons in their effectiveness."[3] The new conflicts require not only conventional intervention but also "political, economic, information, humanitarian and other measures."[4]

Hybrid warfare techniques, which the US military staff defines as the simultaneous and adaptive use of "a tailored mix of conventional, irregular, terrorism, and criminal means of activities in the operational battlespace,"[5] push the boundaries of war to the point of blurring the distinction between war and peace. Patrikarakos describes the conflict in the Donbass as "a gray-zone conflict: more than peace, but less than war."[6] In this new world, Europeans often find themselves in denial, because the new realities of modern warfare do not correspond to their clausewitzean "ideal" of what war should look like. This is a problem, as it greatly weakens their capacities to react, and the confusion might actually imperceptibly lead them into war – in some ways, one can even argue that it already has. As Geoffrey Blainey reminds us, "the popular belief that war *should* begin only after an explicit warning is humane. It is also dangerous because it rests on a deep misunderstanding of the nature and causes of both peace and war."[7] Europeans thus need to better understand how modern (and future) wars are fought if they are to avoid them.

Low intensity and low-cost warfare

Anticipating what future wars will look like is a crucial part of the work of military strategists – it is also the source of a genre in literature, which Lawrence Freedman has explored in his book *The Future of War: A History*. Of course, anticipation can be proven wrong, but expertise in the subject is often much more prescient than it may look at the time of publication. As Christopher Andrew recalls in his authorized history of the British counter-intelligence service, the works of William Le Queux and others, which imagined an invasion of Britain where German spies would lead the way for a foreign troop invasion, may have been sensationalist, but they did point to a new threat Britain was ill-prepared for, and it had such an impact that it built pressure to build what was to become MI5, whose professionalism has rendered a service to Britain many times in its open and hidden wars.[8] When they are based on facts, on how present warfare is currently evolving, works of anticipation can thus help us anticipate how the art of war will evolve in the coming years.

Unfortunately, since the end of the Cold War, writers and generals alike have been rather pessimistic about the future nature of warfare. As Lawrence Freedman puts it, "the good news [is] that 'the days of armed conflict between nation-states are ending'. The bad news [is] that this [is] combined with a sudden upsurge of unusually nasty and vicious conflicts."[9] The reason for this is simple: as classical interstate warfare between great powers has become too costly, violence is often shifting to other theaters of war. This often means that conflicts are played inside a given country, whether in a "classical" civil war involving civilians as combatants and targets (this was the case in Yugoslavia in the 1990s) or in the context of a fake civil war, in which a more powerful state hides behind a local belligerent that it more or less controls to hide or justify its intervention in a foreign country (as Russia did in Ukraine's Donbass).

The choice to fight or incite civil war is not inconsequential. Civil wars are by definition low-intensity conflicts as actors often lack (or do not need) the resources to practice Clausewitzian warfare. This in turn leads them to adopt unconventional methods to fight. In the "classic" European vision of warfare, two organized armies are led to a battlefield, and from their confrontation emerges a winner and a loser – with the latter choosing between surrender or retreat to a more favorable place or time. In any case, the conduct of war remains firmly in control of the armies' high command. But in an intra-state conflict, violence is not well organized, and it can easily spin out of control, as armies are not as disciplined. In this non-conventional type of warfare, it is very difficult to distinguish who is the enemy, and what constitutes the target, even for a powerful army. As American sociologist Mark P. Worrell noted,

> "Nazis actually existed and were evil; the Cuban missile crisis was a real event; the Berlin Wall really was where it appeared on a map. By contrast the new war on "Terror" [and many other modern wars] is a virtual reality – a purely political concoction, a "rhetorical device."[10]

Worrel's point is at times far-fetched, but it is nonetheless relevant: during the "War on Terror" Westerners waged war at home, but also in Iraq and Afghanistan. Who was the adversary? Once a Jihadist overground organization is routed by vastly superior military force, what remains of it goes underground. But it is precisely from there that they can launch guerilla operations and terrorist actions, at home and abroad. In this configuration, Western armies have learnt that it is very difficult to recognize an enemy that is everywhere and nowhere at the same time. When dealing with this type of insurrection, is it legitimate to target a whole civilian population in a given area (however small or big), or citizens whose religious practice has become suspicious (which in turn leads to the dilemma of how to define this "suspicious")? The US military was confronted with this problem in Iraq, and in many ways the French are also confronted with it in the Sahel and even at home, as they face an invisible enemy that draws strength from building-up a sentiment of fear, insecurity and mistrust with low-tech, low-intensity attacks that directly target the local populations. These tactics lead to a state of *"unpeace,"* to use Lucas Kello's wording,[11] "somewhere between peace and war, where the action chosen [is] deliberately kept below the threshold that would spark a major war."[12]

Whether analyzed through the lens of Islamist terrorism or that of more "conventional" civil warfare between indigenous groups, it is a fact that war has become cheaper and now requires lower levels of intensity, which conventional armies find very difficult to control and check. As the cases of Iraq, Afghanistan and Mali have shown, the initial military victory on the battlefield may be overwhelming, but the enemy quickly adapts and understands that its survival rests on dissimulation and low-level action. As the enemy withdraws and melts into the civilian population, he works actively to further destabilize an already fragile social compact until the conventional army finds itself sucked into a civil war in which it is a reluctant (and inefficient) actor. Originally a technique used by the weak to check the strong, the guerrilla tactic is now also used by the strong against the weak to impose a low-cost, low-intensity warfare and weaken the adversary. Russia did not hesitate to impose it on Ukraine, with the idea to diffuse war to avoid foreign meddling and to exhaust the enemy and its state structures without having to pay any direct costs.

Whether endogenous or imposed from the outside, low-intensity civil warfare blurs the boundaries between war and peace. And while local civilian populations suffer, they do so in a confined space, which is very often cut off from the rest of the country: today one can walk through the streets of Kyiv without imagining that it is the capital of a country at war: there are few armed soldiers patrolling the streets, and most of the city's citizens are doing their day-to-day business: Kyiv is one of the most dynamic cities on the continent in terms of restaurants and bars. Paris, on the other hand, is the capital of a country that has been at peace for decades, but it is difficult not to notice the heavily armed military that patrols its streets. The city even briefly found itself in a state of siege during the Charlie Hebdo and Bataclan attacks of 2015. It was then easy to say that France was at war, but it was much more difficult to answer against whom. Was it an entity installed in Raqa (which nobody in the West wanted to concede the attributes a state, and therefore a status of belligerent)? A few individuals hidden in the population, impossible to identify because they were wearing no uniforms? Was the whole Muslim population to be considered suspect, since ISIS's ambition was to bring all Muslims together under the protection of one state? The distinction is also difficult to make in the Donbass, since separatists do not necessarily wear uniforms and foreign soldiers certainly do not wear signs that allow them to be identified.

In such a battlefield, confusion is the norm, and it is actually sought by some belligerents to push their advantage. The result is that any sense of rules, so ingrained in our chivalresque idea of war, disappear. While there are conventions to regulate the treatment of prisoners of war, there is none for convicted (or suspected) terrorists, as we came to know after September 11. The non-status of terrorists is actually a very useful tool to ignore rules that would otherwise have applied in a more conventional war. This, of course, does not prohibit such things as an exchange of prisoners between belligerents, even when they do not recognize each other as such: the 2019 prisoners' swap between Russia and Ukraine is a perfect example of this. It was done according to the rules of war, even though Moscow continues to deny any involvement in the Donbass conflict.[13] In this context, the laws of war that we have taken decades, even centuries, to develop are no longer important: the balance of powers dictates the behavior of troops, and it is often to the detriment of basic rights.

Such a state of affairs is not new: as early as the 6th century B.C., Chinese general Sun Tzu reminded his students and readers that "all war is based on deception." But deception also makes war more barbaric, to the point where savagery becomes a military strategy: as Europeans have known long before the colonial wars,[14] the best way found by guerrillas to ensure the support of local populations is to push the adversary into barbarism. In return, the best (may be the only) way for the military to put down a guerrilla-style rebellion is to use extremely brutal methods to force the local population to stop supporting the soldiers, and the soldiers to stop fighting. In modern times, the Russians used this strategy in Chechnya to subdue the recalcitrant populations in the secessionist republic of the North Caucasus – conversely, some strategists today explain that it was because they could not (or refused to) adopt this strategy that the Americans were unable to pacify Iraq or Afghanistan. The temptation of barbarism is especially powerful when the battlefield is geographically limited: when war is limited to a portion of a territory (Donbass, northern Syria or Mali, etc.), and part of the population has already fled the theaters of operation, only the poorest civilians stay, and they pay the full price of war. The press may obviously be present to report possible war crimes, but the remoteness, the fear of a wave of migration or other factors will limit interest by third parties. All of this contributes to build a certain opacity around the concept of modern warfare: without beginning, without end, far from the eyes of even the surrounding populations, war can gradually take hold and turn into a bloodbath (or a boring routine) without anyone really noticing.

Mars's new toys

The slide from *unpeace* to war is now even easier as new types of conventional weapons contribute to blurring the boundaries between war and peace. For the purpose of this book, we mean by "conventional" all lethal instruments generally used by armies in combat with a physical enemy: rifles, cannons, combat aircraft and ships, among others, fall into this category. This definition is of course imperfect, but it will allow us to study the new non-conventional, hybrid tools used by states and armed groups in the following pages. But while conventionality may be a subject for discussion, the concept of "novelty" is more problematic: in reality, few of the weapons we consider as "new" truly are. While chemical arsenals used against civilian populations in Syria by the Assad regime (or by the Russian government against specific individuals in Britain) may be the products of later scientific research, the concept of chemical warfare, individual or collective, is not new. Poisoning was a common weapon in the Italian renaissance (at least according to contemporary protagonists and historians), and Geoffrey Blainey reminds us that

> "sulphur was burned at sieges of cities in Peloponnesian Wars nearly five centuries before Christ, while in the Crimean War the British proposed to burn sulphur on a large scale and allow the wind to carry it among Russian soldiers at Sevastopol."[15]

Less than a century later, the use of mustard gas by the Germans to dislodge the French and English from their trenches followed exactly the same logic – though new levels of destruction were reached through research and scientific innovation. The use of chemical weapons by Bashar al-Assad's forces in Syria in the 2010s may be barbaric, but it is not new, insofar as it combines chemical warfare with terror, a very old strategy: before "carpet bombing" was successfully experimented in the 1930s by the Germans in Guernica and the Japanese in Chongqing to subdue civilian populations in Spain and China, the Mongols destroyed entire cities by fire – not for the fun of it, but to set an example and convince the surrounding cities to submit without having to fight.

The new conventional weapons used today to wage war are based on the same philosophy: far from being revolutionary, they are the result of a permanent evolution of armament, as the defense industry and military headquarters try to adapt to new developments in warfare. Thus, the use of drones (or Unmanned Air Vehicles, UAVs) and their deployment in theaters of operation is an (innovative) adaptation of the principles of using aviation on and off the battlefield. Like V1s, UAVs are unmanned, with the difference that a drone can be piloted from a safe place where the V1s followed a predefined trajectory. The development of the drone is the result of a particular need that arose once military powers possessing a decisive technological advantage (particularly in the air) were confronted with guerilla warfare. In a context where air supremacy is often uncontested, it seems more judicious to use a smaller, more maneuverable, also much less expensive aircraft (an F-35 fighter plane costs $89.2 million[16] – a Predator, the most common American drone at present, costs "only" $4 million apiece[17]). This allows for further, more agile aircrafts, without a pilot risking his or her life in operation. The remote pilot can direct a raid over an often extremely precise target (a vehicle or individual, for example) from a remote control center, which can be located nearby or several hundreds or thousands of kilometers away. The economic advantage of the UAV has made it a weapon of choice for US administrations over the past ten years, as Presidents Obama and Trump have used it widely in different theatres during their presidencies.[18] Indeed, it was a drone attack that spectacularly ended the career of Iranian General Qassem Soleimani in January 2020.[19] Other powers, including Turkey, have also used drones and integrated it in their offensive strategies, as seen in the war of Nagorno-Karabakh in 2020 where UAVs greatly helped Azerbaijan gain superiority over Armenia on the battlefield.[20]

The reason why drones are currently so popular is that it seems to be the ultimate, "risk-free" weapon from the point of view of the assailant: the device is relatively inexpensive, it allows to strike without putting a pilot's life in danger, and real-time image transfer makes it possible to strike precisely, taking into account immediate changes in the environment. The "surgical" strike that put an end to Soleimani's life seems to be a perfect example of this: it was effective, precise, inexpensive. UAVs, however, are not infallible and they can also strike civilian populations, either because the adversary has decided to use them as human shields or by the attacker's fault (error by the pilot, bad intelligence which mistakes a legitimate target for a civilian target, etc.). Although counting civilian casualties is an extremely risky and technically complicated business as reliable sources on the ground seldom exist,[21] the fact is that a drone attack is not without danger, and its massive use since 2008 has not made war "cleaner." On the contrary, it tends to trivialize violence on both sides: we know since the Second World War that strikes on civilian populations (whether intentional or not), far from undermining population's morale, tend to unite and galvanize them against an unreachable common adversary. On the other hand, distance and its psychological effects on the drone pilot can only contribute to dehumanize his action, and death becomes a routine that is performed as if in a video game. As Mark P. Worrell reports us in his sociological study of modern warfare, "innovations in the instruments of warfare mean that combatants are no longer required to possess extraordinary physical or intellectual prowess; pushing buttons and operating unmanned aircraft can be performed by the 'average Joe,' which means that, like the world of employment, an ever-increasing pool of candidates is made available for duty. One does not have to possess culinary training to work at a fast-food restaurant. Likewise, most combatants do not have to possess exotic or precious martial skills to succeed in battle [...]. In a sense technology has made war easier to prosecute."[22]

Somehow ironically, while the West has gradually abandoned the principle of mass conscription by professionalizing its army, war has, on the contrary, become more democratic. Take the example of Ukraine, whose official army, known for its corruption and inefficiency, neared collapse in the aftermath of the 2014 Revolution. It was able to be reconstitute itself in record time, in part as a volunteer force that checked the Kremlin's most ambitious plans to run over the Eastern bank of the Dnieper and the south of the country. The war as it unfolded in the Donbass remains a European model of a "low-cost" conflict where military engagement remains limited, even in a potentially very open battlefield like the Eastern Ukraine steppe. This is true both in terms of heavy weapons and in human resources, as a limited number of soldiers is required to be present on the battlefield, thus compensating for the relative lack of cannon fodder caused by Europe's current demographic crisis. Precisely, it is because interstate warfare between ultra-trained armies and with ultra-sophisticated equipment has become extremely expensive that states (and with them non-state actors) have sought other means to wage war. It has thus become more economical, and therefore more likely, insofar as any decision to wage war is based on an a priori rational calculation of its possible gains and costs: if the price to pay is a potential nuclear Armageddon (since one can expect symmetry in retaliation), then actors will be more inclined to seek compromise to avoid war. If, on the contrary, actors believe that conflict will remain localized, short and without too much collateral damage, with a strategic or technological advantage for some time, they will be more inclined to go to war.

In reality, practically all recent technological or strategic military developments have lowered the expected costs of a military intervention. We may of course deplore it, but we also need to be realistic about it. In some sense, it is good news for soldiers: Lawrence Freedman reminds us that "war has become 'less lethal'. Between 1946 and 2008, there was a 50 per cent decline in known battle deaths," despite "only a 20 per cent decline in estimated battle casualties."[23] But that also makes war easier to make, precisely because the costs associated with it (and the costs of entry) have become much lower.

Modern warfare has thus turned into a paradox: while Westerners are spending huge sums of money on increasingly sophisticated equipment that enables them to face larger armies and overcome potential disadvantages in hostile environments (terrain, demography, etc.), they also have to prepare for much more asymmetric, and cheap ways of waging war. In fact, a low-cost war, resembling that waged in ex-Yugoslavia in the 1990s or in the Donbass today, makes the use of basic weapons such as Mikhail Kalashnikov's famous AK-47 assault rifle (or even a kitchen knife in the case of terrorist warfare) potentially very effective, as the objectives are clear and limited. We are thus witnessing a democratization, even a privatization of war: while in the 20th-century warfare (at least in Europe) was considered to be part of states' monopoly on violence, it is now no longer their sole prerogative, and indeed proto-state entities can easily create their private armies to wage war over their adversary. The example of the self-proclaimed Islamic State and its small army of terrorists in Europe of course comes to mind, but it is not the only one. Following the revolution of 2014, faced with what needs to be called a Russian invasion, the Ukrainian government found itself helpless in the face of the disorganization and corruption that crippled its army, which contrasted with the professionalism of the Russian army. In the initial stages of the war, a collapse of the Ukrainian military was not totally unconceivable, but what is remarkable is that the restructuration, recruitment and rebuilding of the army not only happened in record time but mostly from the bottom up, as the post-Maydan movement pushed for the reorganization of the army. This meant incorporating battalions of volunteers who had taken part in the Maydan revolution. In the meantime, in the face of the state's financial weakness, ordinary Ukrainians mobilized their fellow citizens at home and abroad in impressive crowdfunding operations to equip the new army.[24] The Russian military and their local surrogates had expected feeble resistance in their drive toward the Dnieper, but were surprised by the combativity of these newly formed units, so much so that Russian propaganda quickly had to downplay its rhetoric about the constitution of a new *Novorossiya* which, in its original form, was thought as comprising the entire South and East of Ukraine, and would have allowed Russia to control the entire northern shore of the Black Sea and provide a land link to its Transnistrian protectorate, situated on Moldovan territory.[25]

Ukraine's war offers many lessons to Europeans as to what war may look like under their latitudes. Lessons from that war can be comforting, as it showed the limits of Russian military prowess, but they are also distressing, in the sense that it is not ultimately the state, but society and private actors who have de facto saved the Ukrainian State. This is a sign of the "democratization" of war. But it also shows that war is becoming "counterproductive," to use Ian Morris's terms, as it weakens rather than strengthens the capacities of states whose absence makes wars longer and more vicious.[26] The phenomenon also has a dynamic of its own: as war democratizes, new sub-state actors require more cheap weapons; these weapons circulate easily in alternative markets, and their wider availability in turn makes violence more common – with sub-state groups and individuals armed to the teeth.

The counterexample to the Ukrainian miracle in Eastern Ukraine is of course the Islamic state, which has also used crowdfunding and private fundraising to acquire the critical mass that has enabled it to conquer territories; in its terrorist campaigns in Western Europe in 2015–2016, it was also greatly helped by the presence of an illicit trafficking of light weapons in the Balkans, with branches and relays both outside and inside the European Union.[27] As even these weapons have become more difficult to obtain when EU states clamped down on these illicit traffics, ISIS terrorists have adapted and used even less sophisticated weaponry, such as civilian trucks (in Nice in July 2016), or even knives (in London on several occasions since 2017, or again in Nice in October 2020). As violence spreads, it gains some form of legitimacy while at least some citizens consider *in fine* that the state is no longer able to protect them. In a European environment where the state is defined by its monopoly on legitimate physical violence, the perceived weakness of the state becomes highly problematic: at what point does particularly brutal individual violence (killing, terrorist attack, etc.) become an act of war? Should it lead to an ultra-targeted response by the authorities, and do they have the means to do so? If not, can a sub-national community take it upon itself to make justice, since the necessary weapons are at hand, and the state perceived as too weak to act? The democratization of war and the rise of low-cost warfare only increase the potential for diffuse violence to turn into open warfare if the socio-economic situation continues to deteriorate. And since the borderline between war and peace is no longer as clear as it was in the time of the great national armies, the risk of a slow but certain slide from a state of peace to a state of *unpeace* and then to war becomes real.

The effects of economic warfare

Modern warfare, however, is not limited to the physical battlefield. Indeed, the potential long-term costs of open warfare, even in its low-cost version, have encouraged states and governments to find new, less lethal ways to wage war. Among them, the economic sphere has gained market shares since the late 2000s, to the extent that "trade wars" and "geo-economics" have made a notable comeback in the foreign affairs vocabulary.

As always, definitions are important, and if war and trade seem to get along pretty well these days, the two terms should not be confused, for just like trade is most easily done in periods of peace, wars can be led without trade. More specifically, an important distinction must be made: if economic warfare is part of geo-economics, i.e., "the systematic use of economic instruments to accomplish geopolitical objectives,"[28] the reverse is not necessarily true. Indeed, geo-economics offers a much broader range of actions than economic warfare, which aims at forcing a geopolitical outcome through offensive economic weapons. When a Chinese state-owned company buys the port of Piraeus following a privatization to pay off Greece's debt, China is not waging war, even economically, on Greece or Europe. Similarly, when Russia grants preferential tariffs for the purchase of its gas to client countries to keep them in line, it is using a geo-economic instrument to influence political choices, but it is not waging an economic war. Similarly, when the Kremlin decides to end these preferential tariffs to bring them in line with those of the market (as it did with Ukraine in 2006), the move may certainly be assimilated to an unfriendly economic gesture, but not yet to economic warfare. That being said, when a state imposes excessive customs tariffs or orders economic sanctions against an individual, national companies or a state, the act is clearly offensive, and it is then fair to speak of commercial, or economic warfare.

As we can see, the very definition of economic warfare is not self-evident: at what point will a customs tariff become sufficiently unfriendly to trigger reprisals, and thus a trade war? In this sense, economic wars are blurring even further the boundaries between war and peace, and between the state of peace and the state of *unpeace*. However, it should be noted that, from a liberal point of view, this state of *unpeace* remains preferable to a state of open war. The principle of an economic or commercial war as a substitute for physical armed conflict is not new. Already in 1814, Swiss economist Benjamin Constant wrote that "war and trade are only two different means of achieving the same goal: that of possessing what one desires."[29] At the time, Napoleon had been waging economic warfare with Britain through his Continental Blockade, and the fact that he lost this battle had much of an influence on the end of the Napoleonic wars. Britain used the economic weapon extremely efficiently throughout the 19th century to keep a balance in Europe and protect its interest around the World.

Today, economic warfare has almost become part of our daily lives. The "trade wars" made a massive comeback in journalists' vocabulary during the Trump years, but the truth is that US decision-makers had been using this weapon long before Trump. Trade sanctions were already a weapon of choice for the Obama administration: researchers Robert D. Blackwill and Jennifer M. Harris pointed out already in 2016 that

> "the United States in September 2014 had twenty-six sanctions programs and thousands of designated entities – more than double the number in place during President Clinton's time – covering countries as far-flung as Cuba, Belarus and Syria. The Obama administration [had then] sanctioned more entities than any other administration (perhaps even several administrations combined)."[30]

And while the Trump administration used sanctions and tariffs aggressively and without parsimony (notably, but not only against China), Americans had been using offensive geo-economic instruments long before 2016. Already in 1998, Republican Senator Jesse Helms looked at sanctions as one of the limited options available by governments to resolve international crises:

> "There are three tools in foreign policy: diplomacy, sanctions and war. Take away sanctions and how can the United States deal with terrorists, proliferators, and genocidal dictators? Our options would be empty talks or to sending in the Marines. Without sanctions, the United States would be virtually powerless to influence events absent war. Sanctions may not be perfect and they are not always the answer, but they are often the only weapon."[31]

Sanctions can thus be seen as a substitute for armed conflict: rather than going into an extremely costly and necessarily hazardous armed conflict, a rich country would naturally prefer to use economic weapons to settle a dispute with another party, especially when it is economically weaker. And even if the balance of power is more stable and the opponent retaliates, a trade war is still preferable to military confrontation, as the former remains less costly (including in direct loss of life). But that doesn't mean that there is no real cost, as economic warfare has direct consequences for populations: in July 2013, a few months before the start of the Revolution of Dignity and as tensions mounted over Ukraine's trajectory, Russia closed its markets to Ukrainian chocolate maker Roshen (owned by no other than politician and future president Petro Poroshenko). The pretext was that sanitary authorities (who are anything but independent in Russia) had found cancerogenic products in Roshen's chocolates – although those had been on sale in Russia for years. This was a perfect pretext to pressurize Ukraine, whose food exports to Russia then represented a sizeable portion of the country's economy: as Russian customs intensified border controls to all food products coming from Ukraine, any fresh product was left to rot on the spot, and Ukraine is estimated to have lost no less than $500 million[32] in trade, which in turn translated into income and job losses for ordinary Ukrainians.

For Russia in 2013, economic warfare was a useful substitute to conventional warfare: less costly, less aggressive, less dangerous. But is it a perfect substitute? As economic warfare is used more and more frequently in the modern world, it would be tempting to answer by the affirmative: the Trump administration was certainly keen on using that weapon and used it widely throughout its mandate: in the trade wars against China, to put "maximum pressure" against Iran, or to strengthen economic sanctions against Russia (sanctions that are jointly applied with the EU, proof that the Union is also involved in some form of warfare). None of these three modern examples have led to open war, and so it could be assumed that economic warfare often is an effective substitute to sort tensions, even if the results (or objectives) are not necessarily those stated by the belligerents. In the case of Iran, US sanctions have considerably weakened the mullahs' regime to the point of forcing Tehran to reduce its support for its allies throughout the Middle East – it may not be as good as regime change, but it certainly corresponds to US strategic objectives. Likewise, although economic sanctions did not change Russia's behavior to the point that it gave Crimea back to its rightful owner, it considerably weakened its economy and limited its capacities to project further power in Ukraine and beyond (soldiers, after all, need to be paid, even in Russia, and a weaker economy also means less money to wage war). To say that "sanctions don't work" is therefore missing the point, and economic warfare is often not only a substitute but also a preventer of physical war.

However, sanctions and tariffs are no miracle solution. True, trade sanctions can work, but they do not do so on their own: to be effective, an embargo must be imposed in the long term, as in this type of confrontation the endurance of the sanctioner is as important as the endurance of the sanctioned. Imposition requires force, i.e., military instruments, and the use of those instruments *makes* war. It is precisely because Napoleon was not able to implement and force the continental blockade over the whole of Europe that the strategy didn't work – and it is because the strategy didn't work that he felt compelled to invade both Spain and Russia, two disastrous interventions that cost him his throne. In the Napoleonic context, economic warfare, precisely because it could not be implemented fully enough, led to direct warfare.

Economic warfare can also lead to full-scale war when it becomes too effective. The war of 1812 between America and Britain is a textbook example of geo-economic failure: the US declaration of war was in fact a tacit admission that the 1807 embargo was not working, as it dealt far more damage to the US than the British economy. This led the Americans to change strategy, with a limited set of choices: they could either back down and admit defeat or go to war, which had a cost: even though some battle victories (most famously at New Orleans) gave American historians a reason to call it a draw, the nation's capital was occupied, and both the White House and the Capitol burnt to the ground. There were nonetheless useful lessons to be learnt here. As historian Geoffrey Blainey puts it, "a successful economic blockade, in the final resort, [depends] more on the exercising of military than economic power."[33] If trade wars can replace physical confrontation, the failure of this strategy will likely lead to war.

On the other hand, if sanctions become too effective, they can also lead to war. The start of the Pacific War of 1941–1945 probably provides the best example of this. The trigger was of course the Japanese attack on Pearl Harbor, but the "date which will live in infamy," although not directly provoked, certainly had a background: Tokyo had launched a vast military expansion effort in the 1930s to ensure larger access to raw materials (indispensable to realize Japan's autarky policy). By 1941, this had already led to the occupation of China and the then European colonies in Southeast Asia. The Japanese invasion of French Indochina following the French debacle of June 1940 had convinced the British, Australians and Americans that their turn was next, and the three had reacted in kind, by freezing Japanese assets and imposing an oil embargo that was supposed to hurt the Japanese economy and force the military government to the negotiating table. For sure, the sanctions worked, in particular the embargo on oil, which Japanese forces desperately needed to fuel their military campaigns in China and Southeast Asia. Tokyo needed the sanctions to go away and could not back down. Thus the military government came to think of one single, devastating pre-emptive strike that would dramatically change the balance of power in the Pacific and force the Americans to negotiate (and, ideally for the then Japanese government, leave the Asia and Pacific region to them). As we know, the US response was radically different, but the trade wars had led to Pearl Harbor, and Pearl Harbor had led to full-fledged war in the Pacific.[34]

Nearer to us, we have seen recently a similar process take us on the brink of armed conflict in 2019–2020 as tensions mounted between the United States and Iran. Only this time the stroke was decisive enough for one actor to back down. The Trump administration's "maximum pressure" campaign against Iran may not have forced Tehran back to the negotiating table on the nuclear deal, but it clearly crippled the Iranian economy and the state's budgetary capacities. Much like the Japanese high command though, the answer from Tehran was actually to double down and take a more aggressive behavior, as it pushed the patience of the United States and its allies (especially Saudi Arabia) to the limit, with the objective to force Washington to back down. Of course, a full-fledge attack would have been too risky, and so Iran operated by proxies: for example by multiplying acts of sabotage and piracy against Saudi and British oil tankers in the spring and summer of 2019, or by organizing drone attacks on Saudi oil installations in September 2019.[35] The more time went, the bolder the attacks became. Escalation could have continued if the US administration had not struck a big blow, which came with the drone attack that killed Iranian General Qasem Soleimani in January 2020 on Iraqi soil. Tehran's answer might have been dramatic for the cameras, but its "counter-attack" was clearly an admission of weakness: before launching their air raid against US installations, Iranian authorities had taken great care to inform Washington's Iraqi allies where and when they would strike to avoid any American losses.[36] Donald Trump's gamble had paid off, but the fact is that to "pacify" a trade war, brute force had to be employed – and if this strike hadn't been decisive, a new Gulf War would probably have become unavoidable at some point.

The Iranian incident of 2020 is yet another example of the complementarity nature of the relationship between economic and military warfare: they actually go hand in hand, not as a substitute to each other. True, economic confrontation may initially be a good tool to replace war, but it does not constitute an absolute weapon for "pacifying" international relations. More importantly, there is no clear "rule" as to when open warfare becomes inevitable following a trade war: economic sanctions can be as diverse as the Megaran decree preceding the Peloponnesian War, the Anglo-American oil embargo against Japan before Pearl Harbor, the Eisenhower administration's economic sanctions against Britain during the 1956 Suez Crisis or the Trump administration's policy of maximum pressure against Iran. All these policies, similar in their logic and conception, led to different outcomes, some imposing peace (as in the case of Suez), others leading to war (in 432 BC or again in 1941), and the last one to a bold US strike that could have triggered a regional war but did not because the brute force had tilted the balance of power clearly in one single direction.

In reality, economic warfare is rarely decisive by itself. It therefore contributes to blur the distinction between peace, *unpeace* and war. In a trade war, one can gradually move from one to the other, without realizing that a point of no return has already been crossed. Between the imposition of tariffs on targeted products in the name of distorted competition and an unlimited trade war, where is the borderline between the peaceful defense of national interests and the state of *unpeace*? At what point should a tariff war lead a party to think it is legitimate to use force to put an end to it? Answers to these questions are not straightforward, and in the case of a blockade, its necessary enforcement by an army or navy already brings a military, physical dimension to the conflict. Economic warfare, now a crucial component of modern warfare, thus contributes to blurring the lines between war and peace.

The virtual weapon

When in June 2019 the Iranian army shot down an American surveillance drone over the Strait of Hormuz, US President Donald Trump's reaction was swift and threatening: "Iran made a very big mistake!," he tweeted on June 20, a few hours after the attack.[37] Considering the ongoing tensions in the Gulf between Iran and Saudi Arabia and the unpredictability of America's 45th president, such a statement clearly signaled the risk of a quick military escalation. But the world didn't hold its breath for long: it quickly transpired that President Trump had recalled the retaliation strike. Pundits then commented that the recall was a sign of weakness and that the Iranians had called the president's bluff, until it transpired that instead of an airstrike, the United States had engineered and launched a massive cyber-attack against the Iranian Army's servers, blocking their missile launching systems and erasing the databases of their paramilitary proxies. In a nanosecond, the United States had dealt a serious blow to Iran's sabotage program on Saudi tankers in the Gulf.[38] A few months later, another large-scale cyber-attack targeted the Iranian intelligence and propaganda services.[39] Other attacks and counter-attacks would follow, making this series of incidents a secret war within the Gulf crisis of 2019–2020.

The United States had responded to a physical attack by inflicting considerable damage to the enemy without killing anyone or directly destroying a single piece of equipment. This incident between Tehran and Washington demonstrated how effective the "virtual weapon" can be in today's world: according to Lucas Kello, who coined the term, its

> "payload, which, like all computer codes, consists of just 0's and 1's in the form of electrons, can travel through cyberspace to destroy nuclear

enrichment turbines, paralyze the operations of large firms, incapacitate tens of thousands of workstations at large multinational firms, or disrupt stock-trading platforms."[40]

Kello does well to mention the nuclear enrichment turbines, for the virtual weapon's effectiveness is not limited to the economic or technological sector. Beyond its impact on production and other economic aspects, it can actually totally reshape a physical battlefield. As Lawrence Freedman once remarked,

> "what if one side suddenly found itself in the dark, with screens either blank or full of misleading information, and was unable to send out orders to local commanders or else had these orders substituted by false instructions? In such circumstances even the strongest military machine would be left helpless and hapless"[41]

This is not a fiction: it happened to the Iraqi army twice, during its two wars against the United States in 1991 and 2003: before the start of the physical operations, the US armed forces had cut the Internet and satellite transmissions, depriving the Iraqis of all means of communications – the result was confusion and panic, and neutralizing the enemy became like "shooting fish in a barrel," as some US pilots reported after the operations.[42] The cyber weapon may not have killed directly, but it had completely changed the shape of the battlefield, building a fog of war that incapacitated the enemy.

Let us go back to Freedman's narrative, and let us now imagine that a sophisticated cyber-attack could be launched against a country's IT infrastructure – knowing that

> "if all key functions of a modern society – energy, transport, banking, health and education services – depended on these flows of information, might it be possible to bring a country to its knees without firing a shot? Stopping the flow would be like pulling out a gigantic plug. Everything would go dark, screech to a halt, or clatter and bang, leaving an economy in tatters and a society struggling to meet its most basic needs."[43]

Here again, this scenario happened in real life: in December 2015, the Russian malware "BlackEnergy" hit the power grid of the Ivano-Frankivsk region, cutting off the electricity for 230,000 Ukrainians in the middle of winter.[44] Two years later, on June 27, 2017, another malware called "Petya" – also Russian – neutralized the Ukrainian government's online networks and banking system. The results were devastating: suddenly, the most simple government action (such as the payment of pensions, etc.) was no longer possible. Ordinary Ukrainians were also directly impacted: for several days, people could no longer withdraw money from any bank or even pay in shops, even in cash, as the entire transaction system is now dependent on computers, including the cash registers.[45] The incident was not isolated, nor was it a first: ten years earlier, in 2007, groups informally linked to the Russian state had led a large-scale Denial of Service cyber-attack against Estonia after a Red Army statue was moved from downtown Tallinn to a military hospital. The attack also neutralized all government and financial sites in the country – it took more than three weeks for Estonia to get back to normal, and the government considered for a while the possibility of invoking Article 5 of the NATO treaty for assistance in what it could have reasonably considered to be a direct attack against Estonia.[46]

These three attacks, all attributed directly or indirectly to Russia, show us how much the virtual weapon has changed the practice of warfare in recent years. A cyber-attack is difficult to trace: identifying bots and other malware developers is extremely difficult, as the attackers hide behind their computer screen and can blur or falsify their identity. To get back to the Estonian case, the actors directly responsible for the attack were all private, although it clearly became obvious that they were coordinated by the Russian state – the latter of course denied any involvement. This is possible because the virtual weapon is immaterial: it can be triggered from anywhere, and it can hit months or even years after one's system has been infected. A cyber-attack requires access to the computer or network – that is often done through "phishing," where an unsuspecting individual target (a careless employee for example) downloads a compromised file from a fake "official" email or is brought to a fakepage where he or she is led to give his or her passwords. Once the password is captured, the hacker can get full access to all the victim's data and extend control on a network and then an organization (or a group of linked organizations). Once this is done, the hacker can then drain terabytes of data without being detected, and the malware can remain dormant for years before being activated to neutralize the system or destroy data at the most convenient time.[47] Finally, although this only gets to the front page every once in a while (as in December 2020 when the attack on the US government via SolarWind became public), cyber-warfare is actually a daily business: the British Ministry of Defense estimates that it deals with "hundreds or even thousands" of daily attempts to intrude or disrupt its networks, while the US State Department recently counted more than 50,000 intrusion attempts in a single six-month period. These numbers are especially high, but anglosphere countries are not the only targets: France recorded 24,000 cyber-attacks against its military and defense systems in 2016 alone.[48]

Cyber wars seldom make the headlines: denials of service often occur months, even years, after the networks get compromised, and despite the massive costs these attacks can inflict, they rarely cause spectacular, TV-news-worthy direct damage. This will not last though: already the Israeli–American "Stuxnet" attack against Iran has shown how a cyber weapon could actually destroy thousands of centrifuges at the Natanz power station, and physically neutralize years of efforts by Tehran to acquire atomic weapons.[49] It will not be long before direct casualties will be directly traced back to a computer virus, as *The Economist* reminded its readers in its outlook for 2021.[50] But as of now, cyber-attacks do not incur direct loss of human life – "ethically, legally, politically and theoretically"[51] the highest form of damage in warfare. This can be seen as a plus for decision-makers: it means that using the cyber weapon allows getting the message through while reducing the intensity of the conflict to the point that most citizens are unaware that it is taking place. Of course, this takes us back to the state of *unpeace* described by Kello and in this sense the virtual weapon contributes to blurring the boundaries between war and peace: today, a US president can respond to a military attack with a massive cyber-attack, while Russia can order the neutralization of Ukraine's banking system while the two countries remain officially at peace. In the absence of a smoking gun (rarely found in cyber-warfare) who would consider a failure in the country's computer systems an act of war?

The Estonian government was directly confronted with this dilemma in 2007 during a massive attack on its infrastructures, a reprisal for the transfer of a Soviet monument to the Second World War soldiers from downtown Tallinn to a military hospital. For a while, the Estonian government toyed with the idea of invoking NATO's Article 5 – but in the end it had to change its mind, as it realized it was technically impossible to trace Russia's direct involvement with certainty. All the attackers were private persons and organizations, and nobody could provide a tangible proof that the hackers had been coordinated by the Kremlin. In the absence of a smoking gun, the case bore enough resemblance with Austria's investigations over the 1914 assassination of Archduke Franz Ferdinand in Sarajevo in 1914 to convince Tallinn not to take the risk of triggering a direct confrontation between NATO and Russia.[52] The scenario, of course, could have ended differently, and the fact is, as Kello puts it, that virtual warfare "is enabling new forms of antagonism and expanding the range of possible harm between the binary notions of peace and war. The most damaging cyber-actions are not war – so far – but nor are they peace."[53]

As the virtual weapon blurs the borders between war, peace and *unpeace*, it becomes more dangerous: no escalation or de-escalation protocol exists, and in an ever-more connected world where even our cars are to a certain extent controllable from a virtual cloud,[54] the deadly potential of a cyber-attack increases by the day. The virtual weapon remains largely inexpensive, while its potential impact grows every day. This combination provides a clear advantage to the offensive side, leading in turn to a dangerous military imbalance: decision on war is always made on the basis of a cost–advantage analysis, and whenever a leader is convinced to be equipped with a weapon that can give the attacker an absolute advantage to the opponent, that leader is more likely to take unconsidered risks.

This bonus to the assailant makes a confrontation more likely, as risk-taking often leads to more tensions and more reasons between leaders to make war – even more so if they believe that they hold a temporary advantage that can secure victory at low cost and in a short period of time. Of course, one could consider that this is not such a problem as long as war stays locked into the cyber-sphere, but as the Estonian example reminds us, the borders between the cyber and the physical battle space can be blurred, and offensive behavior can be misinterpreted – especially when the consequences of a cyber-attack take only a few seconds to appear plainly. As Graham Allison notes, "cyber-attacks disrupt communication and intensify the fog of war, creating confusion that multiplies the chances of miscalculation."[55] The virtual weapon is a new technology that we do not master yet completely, and this basic fact actually makes war more likely, not less. This leads David Rothkopf, professor of international relations at Columbia University, to conclude that "while cyber-conflict may avoid 'hot' exchanges, it has to date produced almost constant escalation."[56] The Persian Gulf crisis of 2019–2020 gives us a good example of this: America's cyber-attack of June 2019 against Iran and its allies of course incapacitated them, but it also encouraged them to become more restless, in an attempt to compensate for America's technological advantage in the cyber space. This led to blockades of oil tankers of various nationalities and attacks on the Saudi refineries of Abqaiq and Kurais. The escalation continued online and offline until the strikes that killed Qassem Soleimani – in the end the real trigger to de-escalation. Far from easing tensions, the cyber-attacks instead encouraged the belligerents to search for other means of retaliation until the use of force became the only option to resolve the crisis. This leads to a conclusion that looks incredibly similar to the one we developed for economic warfare. Almost mirroring Blainey's comments on economic blockades, Lucas Kello reminds us that "cyber-attacks can augment but not replace traditional military power. Even in conventional war settings […] it can only achieve partial tactical results."[57] When those results are not decisive enough, the only way forward is military escalation.

Disinfo-wars

Even more than cyber-warfare, information warfare has seen a spectacular expansion over the past ten years. It has blurred even more the distinction between war and peace, while making the differentiation between combatants and non-combatants even more difficult. As Clint Watts reminds us, "the Russians meddling with Americans, Europeans, Ukrainians, Turks and Syrians" are not regular troops but "computer whizzes and journalists, young contractors hired by the hour for a specific purpose, interchangeable widgets in a simple yet effective media machine."[58] Because of the intrusion of the Internet and social networks into mass-media life, disinformation has become an integral part of cyber-warfare, even more dangerous because its effects are even more diffuse in society.

Of course, disinformation is not new. The Trojan Horse is probably the oldest documented example of its use in an armed conflict,[59] and as early as the 5th century B.C.E, Sun Tzu had made it a key to his *Art of War*. He went even one step further, claiming that "all warfare is based on deception." Confusing the enemy has since become an integral part of military strategy. Operation Fortitude was a remarkable Anglo-American success as it made the German High Command believe that the 1944 invasion of Europe would not take place in Normandy, and then that D-Day was merely a diversion – the confusion that followed on June 6 and in the following days delayed enemy troop deployment, allowing the Allies to consolidate their fragile bridgehead in Western Europe.[60] Today, as British researcher Peter Pomerantsev points out, information warfare continues to take a central role in modern military doctrine, but with a twist: "Propaganda has always accompanied war, usually as a handmaiden to the actual fighting. But the information age means that this equation has been flipped: military operations are now handmaidens to the more important information effect."[61]

As a journalist specialized in post-Soviet politics and the son of a Soviet dissident, Pomerantsev has an extensive knowledge of the subject: Russia is probably the country in which informational warfare has been theorized the most, from the very beginning of the revolution in 1917, when the new elites put effective propaganda at the heart of their project of society's radical transformation. They quickly saw that an effective propaganda could indeed control the masses, mobilize allies, help quiet down dissent at home and bring disquiet abroad. As a result, propaganda was integrated into all aspects of the USSR's efforts, including mass murder. Propaganda proved useful at home, as it helped mobilize soldiers and population, notably during the Great Patriotic War of 1941–1945. But it was also used abroad extensively by the Soviet embassies for various purposes, with a tailored approach depending on the target audiences: for the friends of the USSR, the idea was – as on the home front – to mobilize and obtain support, including for the sometimes brutal reversals of Soviet foreign policy (this included the adherence of Western communists to the Molotov–Ribbentrop pact of 1939). For all the others, propaganda was aimed at sowing doubt in the minds to defuse any criticism: during the Ukrainian famine in the 1930, when a few brave reporters managed to document the carnage that collectivization was causing in the Ukrainian countryside, Soviet propagandists invited guests such as former French prime minister Édouard Herriot to visit Ukraine in a well-choreographed organized tour. The guests traveled to locations carefully controlled by the Communist Party, where an illusion of abundance had been created. Visitors were astonished by these Potemkin villages, which had been cleaned up of their inhabitants the day before, had seen their stores miraculously filled up with bread and were now peopled by Komsomol disguised as Ukrainian farmers who explained them how beautiful life was in the Kolkhoz. Of course, they didn't see that just a few miles off-stage, Ukrainians were dying of hunger by the millions. But that didn't matter, for when they came back home, they could and did send out messages that contradicted the accounts of famine and repression. Herriot remarked: "I travelled through Ukraine, and I can tell you that what I saw was a garden in full yield."[62] He was not the only one fooled: many senior politicians and intellectuals (George Bernard Shaw and H.G. Wells among them) fell in the disinformation trap, and the Soviet regime continued to instill doubt about the reality of the Great Famine until Perestroika, and even beyond: today, despite the evidence and recognition by previous governments, the Russian post-Soviet establishment continues to deny forcefully the reality of the *Holodomor*, probably here again to instill doubt in people's minds more than for the sake of denying the obvious.

Of course, this is not the only example of intoxication to deny mass crime – similar techniques were used to deny the massacre of Polish officers at Katyn, for example, and these have inspired similar tactics by other communist governments, some of which are still in activity. This is obviously the case in China, where the Chinese Communist Party has used similar tactics of infiltration, information and disinformation to influence political outcomes, as Maeike Ohlberg and Clive Hamilton have described in a recent book on the workings of China's hidden hand in the West.[63]

The principles of informational warfare may be old, but they are still widely used today, and it is remarkable to see how communist China and post-communist Russia have adopted similar approaches, with one major difference: while the Chinese have many resources at their disposal but little experience (yet), Russia has perfected an already well-trained system of *maskirovka* and propaganda warfare that necessitates few resources, thanks to the power of social media. The Russians and Chinese have of course modernized their techniques, and have been able to make full use of new tools to disseminate "alternative" messages on a much larger audience than during the Cold War, thereby strengthening the information bubbles that are proving so disruptive to Western societies today. Lucas Kello has summed up the core tenet of the Russian strategy, which is increasingly being adopted (and adapted) by the Chinese Communist Party:

> "In sum, Russia's century-old theory of information warfare refutes the idea of a decisive military clash that is so central to Western security thinking. Its core tenet is that the psychological element of conflict is as important as the physical one. On the backdrop of a contest of perceptions of international order, Russian strategists exhort actions that seek to deny adversaries the internal political cohesion necessary to act purposefully abroad.[64]"

The Kremlin demonstrated the remarkable sophistication of its information warfare strategy during the war in Ukraine. When it became clear that Kyiv was not going to join the Eurasian Union that Vladimir Putin had created to provide an institutional framework for the restoration of the Soviet empire, the Russians could have sent uniformed and badged Spetsnaz commandos to occupy Crimea, pretexting the protection of Russian speakers in the peninsula. They could also have sent regular troops and equipment to the Donbass, a move which at another time would have made sense considering that the region's flat terrain would have allowed the Russian army to make use of its superior heavy armament and equipment.

And yet, Moscow chose to hide behind "little green men" wearing no distinctive signs, puppet separatist republics led by local thugs and other irregular troops. Why? The first objective was to disorient the Ukrainians so that they would pose as little resistance as possible – this was done, for example, through the use of Russian-speaking television channels that sent contradictory messages to the public. The more the enemy was confused about what was happening, the weaker local resistance would be on the ground. To quote former Deputy Supreme Allied Commander in Europe Sir Richard Shirreff, the strategy was clear: "undermining the integrity of a target state from within, but keeping such actions under the threshold that might trigger a NATO reaction."[65]

The information battlefield was much larger than just Ukraine or the post-Soviet space; it also included the West, where Moscow instigated doubts about the reality of what was happening. This way, Western publics remained confused and divided over what was really going on and what should be done about it, leaving room for Russia to operate at will in Ukraine. The idea was to paralyze Western decision-making, which remains highly dependent on public opinion. As long as Moscow could shape (or, rather, de-shape) the narrative, the potential for action on the part of the West would remain limited: there would be no (then little) arms delivery to Ukraine, no outside support to the new Ukrainian army, etc. These limitations on the West's power to act gave – and in many ways still give – Russia a considerable strategic advantage in the war it continues to wage against Ukraine.

To understand how Moscow acts to divert the narrative and prevents action from the West, it is worth analyzing one of the many incidents involving the Kremlin's propaganda machine: in July 2014, flight MH17 from Malaysian Airlines, carrying mainly Dutch citizens from Amsterdam to Kuala Lumpur, was shot down by a Buk surface-to-air missile, a modern weapon used widely in the Russian army. This action constituted a proof of direct Russian involvement in Ukraine, and therefore had the potential of ruining all the Kremlin's efforts to keep Westerners away from Ukraine. The Russian informational services immediately responded and disseminated dozens of alternative "facts" and narratives through different medias – official of course, but also social media via dormant Twitter accounts. The messages often contradicted each other, but they were not made to be credible. Instead, they aimed at spreading confusion to slow down and, if possible, to prevent reactions. Indeed, the only common message in these narratives (some of which were particularly fantasist) was that they all denied what should have been obvious to all: that a civilian airplane with Dutch passengers onboard had been shot down by a Russian missile system while flying above Ukraine. In the end, the informational counter-offensive, notably thanks to independent websites such as Bellingcat, allowed the truth to prevail, but enough doubt had been instilled in the minds of the Western public to slow down – and downsize – reactions.[66] This is what many Western pundits fail to comprehend about Russia's information war against the West: as Journalist David Patrikarakos puts it, the truth may in the end (imperfectly) prevail, but even when that is the case, "to describe Russia's information warfare as a complete failure is […] to overstate the case. Its primary goal […] is generally not to convince but rather to confuse, and in the case of Eastern Ukraine even to reinvent reality."[67] Of course, the best way to achieve this is to use social networks, which have greatly disrupted the flow of information in our societies, atomizing broadcasters, narratives and audiences.

Russia is certainly not the only country to have integrated social networks into its information warfare doctrine. As early as 2006, Israel was confronted with the real-life consequences of bottom-up social media campaigns in Palestinian Territories and Lebanon, and it was forced to react by incorporating special social network units into its military personnel. In a same reactive fashion, the United States also woke up to the dangers of information manipulation after the 2016 election, once Russian involvement to destabilize the electoral process had been exposed. On its side, the new Ukrainian army is also tech-savvy and has used the power of social networks creatively to organize its supply lines. The Islamic state and the various terrorist groups that compete with it have also made noticeable use of the tool, with specific online propaganda units in charge of recruiting, conditioning and training fighters.[68] David Patrikarakos may be exaggerating when he writes that "the narrative dimensions of war are arguably becoming more important than its physical dimension,"[69] but the dynamics are clearly pointing in this direction. Just like economic or cyber-warfare, information and social media need actual brute force to win battles, but their integration in military doctrine has the potential to reshape the battlefield entirely. The integration is such that war is now "conducted perpetually, on many fronts, with military action, particularly that of special operation forces, blended with political, economic and, most important, information campaigns."[70] Online propaganda can therefore come to support the move of troops on the ground, facilitate them, or even provoke them: in his book anticipating a military conflict between NATO and Russia, British General Sir Richard Shirreff shows how a pro-Russian demonstration organized by FSB operatives on social media can be transformed into a full-scale military invasion of Latvia, a NATO member.[71]

One of the remarkable features of the short case studies that have been enumerated so far is that whenever Europe and European powers are involved, they often play the role of passive victims. As they very often deny the existence of this type of warfare, Europeans find themselves lagging behind and very lightly equipped to withstand a full informational assault. In doing so, they run the risk of seeing the continent become a battlefield where foreign powers (states and non-state actors) try to take advantage of Europeans' weaknesses: in a world where the Islamic state can recruit and train its future suicide commandos and lone wolves on social networks provided by Western funds,[72] in a world where Russia Today (RT), a news channel clearly affiliated with the Russian state can encourage some Yellow Vests to take down the French government,[73] it might seem timely to wake up to the dangers that these covert foreign wars carry for Europe's stability.

However, it is remarkable how few countermeasures have been designed so far on the continent: beyond individual initiatives by NGOs and on the part of a few countries like France or Estonia, along with NATO's Communications Centre of

Excellence (STRATCOMCOE, based in Riga), and Cooperative Cyber Defence Centre of Excellence (CCDCOE, based in Tallinn), continental strategies to counter disinformation and online radicalization operations remain remarkably modest, and their development is often hampered by national atomization. There may be a few individual victories, such as Emmanuel Macron's campaign team's response to a Russian hacking effort a few days before the 2017 French presidential elections,[74] but Westerners in general and Europeans in particular are still moving forward much more slowly than their opponents, who so far have retained a considerable offensive advantage. As Clint Watts (here focusing on the US case) reminds us, "Russia didn't create the Trump bubble or the Snowden groupies. Those bubbles created themselves and the Kremlin harnessed them."[75] Creating disinformation antibodies to increase the resilience of European societies is a difficult effort that requires a lot of time and always remains under the threat of different actors (including domestic ones), and it is difficult at this stage to assess with certainty whether Europeans are doing enough, or have enough time, to build these informational dams that can make their societies more resilient.

By disorienting publics and pushing them against each other, information warfare continues to blur the boundaries between war and peace. But perhaps even more dangerously, it also contributes to democratizing war: today one no longer needs to carry a weapon to become a combatant – sitting quietly in front of a computer might suffice, and while rhetorical declarations of war are multiplying (including against viruses), it might seem reasonable to ask whether something seemingly as benign as posting messages on social media can be considered an act of war – and what this would mean for the combatant. By making the battlefield accessible to anyone, war thus becomes atomized, and in turn more difficult to control. Paradoxically, this democratization also gives a bonus to organization: today, Internet trolls hunt in wolfpacks, and well-organized "fake news factories" can mobilize or, on the contrary, demobilize populations, thanks to the power of collective messaging. This constitutes a remarkable advantage for the assailant, who gains a tactical advantage in military operations: in the words of David Rothkopf, "new technologies make it easier for the technologically empowered to strike out and dominate adversaries without putting human lives or military assets at risk."[76] Here again, this can only encourage risk-taking, with potentially tragic consequences.

The recent trend to weaponize social networks and new information channels has thus contributed to further blur the distinctions between war and peace. In the words of David Patrikarakos,

> the degree of global financial integration that exists today means that the capacity to wage war through nonmilitary means has never been greater. The boundaries between war and peace are crumbling, and this new status quo threatens international stability; if war has increasingly become the practice of politics (and its attendant economics), it has no clear end because politics never end.[77]

In a world where virtual and rhetorical calls to war are multiplying, where violent discourse spreads like wildfire on social media, are we really still at peace? The question deserves reflection, and the answer is not necessarily straightforward. But if we are already at war, can we say who is our enemy? Are we fighting against an elusive terrorist nebula? A whole religion? A foreign state like Russia or Turkey? Or are we waging this war against ourselves, and in the case of Europeans is it between nations, inside nations, inside the Union, as more and more debates are now unfolding on a continental scale, with heroes and villains designated in different countries?

★ ★ ★

"You may not be interested in war. But war is interested in you." The phrase, attributed to Leon Trotsky,[78] seems well suited to Europe today. Europeans may have thought that war was behind them, but their daydream is over, and the awakening painful: once a model and an exporter of stability, Europe now finds itself confronted with threatening (and evolving) internal contradictions, external threats, and remains ill-prepared to face the challenges of new forms of low-cost warfare. As war has changed in nature, new weapons have blurred the lines between war and peace: to quote Lucas Kello,

> the absence of war no longer means the existence of peace – if peace means not only merely the silence of guns but, more fundamentally, a state of affairs to which statesmen can generally aspire as the maximal conditions of coexistence within the system of international anarchy.[79]

In a way, this is a return to normality: every society is traversed by contradictory dynamics that can degenerate into war, and the idea of "external threats" is enough rooted in our collective memory that we do not hesitate to invent them for ourselves when we do not have them. Our mistake is to have forgotten these fundamental truths as we came to believe a bit too literally that we had reached the end point of history, without necessarily following through on Fukuyama's reasoning – his conclusions about the future after the end of history were actually rather more pessimistic than often acknowledged. Boredom and inaction, as we now know, lead to frustration and passivity, which can in turn lead to anger, violence and, ultimately, war.

Hybrid warfare has also returned war to a form of historic normal. As it continues to depart from its Clausewitzian model to a more ambivalent form, it gets closer to Sun Tzu's ancestral model.[80] Thus, war only follows a more general pattern of Easternization and relative decline of the West, hardly a reason for Europe to rejoice: from the military strategies of the Crusaders and their heavy cavalry charges against the Mamelukes to the early practices of colonial warfare in 18th-century India, Europeans have always been more comfortable with war when it meant orderly and organized battles, much less so when conflicts became multifaceted. Europeans are thus not (or hardly) ready to understand the very concept of "limited world wars,"[81] even though they have been theorized since the 1970s by Russian, American and other military staffs, even less hybrid, low-cost or low-intensity wars. Because of this, they can much more easily get caught up, unwillingly or not, in a war whose mechanisms and causes they no longer comprehend.

Notes

1 Carl von Clausewitz, *On War*, London: Penguin, 1982.
2 David Patrikarakos, *War in 140 Characters: How Social Media Is Reshaping Conflict in the Twenty-First Century*, New York: Basic Books, 2017, p.153.
3 Quoted in Clint Watts, *Messing with the Enemy: Surviving in a Social Media World of Hackers, Terrorists, Russians, and Fake News*, New York: HarperCollins, 2018, p.137.
4 Lawrence Freedman, *The Future of War: A History*, New York: Public Affairs, 2017, p.224.
5 Quoted in David Patrikarakos, *War in 140 Characters: How Social Media Is Reshaping Conflict in the Twenty-First Century*, New York: Basic Books, 2017, p.4.
6 Ibid., p.261.
7 Geoffrey Blainey, *The Causes of War* (3rd edition), New York: The Free Press, 1988, p.173.
8 See Christopher Andrew, *The Defence of the Realm: The Authorized History of MI5*, London: Allen Lane, 2009.
9 Lawrence Freedman, *The Future of War: A History*, New York: Public Affairs, 2017, p.143.
10 Mark P. Worrell, *Why Nations Go to War: A Sociology of Military Conflict*, New York: Routledge, 2011, p.24.
11 Lucas Kello, *The Virtual Weapon and International Order*, New Haven: Yale University Press, 2017, pp.77–78.
12 Lawrence Freedman, *The Future of War: A History*, New York: Public Affairs, 2017, p.285.
13 https://www.bbc.com/news/world-europe-49610107
14 Lawrence Freedman, *The Future of War: A History*, New York: Public Affairs, 2017.
15 Geoffrey Blainey, *The Causes of War* (3rd edition), New York: The Free Press, 1988, p.278.
16 https://www.f35.com/about/cost
17 https://en.wikipedia.org/wiki/General_Atomics_MQ-1_Predator
18 For Obama's use of drones as a favored weapon: https://www.thebureauinvestigates.com/stories/2017-01-17/obamas-covert-drone-war-in-numbers-ten-times-more-strikes-than-bush; for Donald Trump's: https://www.bbc.com/news/world-us-canada-47480207
19 https://www.theguardian.com/world/2020/jan/03/baghdad-airport-iraq-attack-deaths-iran-us-tensions
20 https://www.rferl.org/a/drone-wars-in-nagorno-karabakh-the-future-of-warfare-is-now/30885007.html
21 https://www.law.columbia.edu/sites/default/files/microsites/human-rights-institute/files/COLUMBIACountingDronesFinal.pdf
22 Mark P. Worrell, *Why Nations Go to War: A Sociology of Military Conflict*, New York: Routledge, 2010, p.18.
23 Lawrence Freedman, *The Future of War: A History*, New York: Public Affairs, 2017, p.128.
24 See David Patrikarakos, *War in 140 Characters: How Social Media Is Reshaping Conflict in the Twenty-First Century*, New York: Basic Books, 2017, pp.91–111.

25 https://carnegieendowment.org/2015/05/29/why-kremlin-is-shutting-down-novorossiya-project/i96u
26 For more on the "productive warfare" versus "unproductive warfare" dichotomy, see Ian Morris, *War: What is it Good for? The Role of Conflict in Civilization, from Primates to Robots*, London: Profile Books, 2014.
27 https://www.economist.com/europe/2016/04/16/ask-not-from-whom-the-ak-47s-flow
28 Robert D. Blackwill and Jennifer M. Harris, *War by Other Means: Geoeconomics and Statecraft*, Cambridge, MA: Harvard University Press, 2016, p.1.
29 Benjamin Constant, *De l'esprit de conquête et de l'usurpation*, Paris: Charpentier, 1842, p.132.
30 Robert D. Blackwill and Jennifer M. Harris, *War by Other Means: Geoeconomics and Statecraft*, Cambridge, MA: Harvard University Press, 2016, p.196.
31 Jesse Helms, *Here's Where I Stand: A Memoir*, New York: Random House, 2005, p.239.
32 https://www.nytimes.com/2013/10/30/business/international/ukrainian-chocolates-caught-in-trade-war-between-europe-and-russia.html?pagewanted=all&_r=0
33 Geoffrey Blainey, *The Causes of War* (3rd edition), New York: The Free Press, 1988, p.252.
34 Ibid., p.251.
35 https://www.cnbc.com/2019/09/20/oil-drone-attack-damage-revealed-at-saudi-aramco-facility.html
36 https://www.theguardian.com/us-news/2020/jan/08/irans-assault-on-us-bases-in-iraq-might-satisfy-both-sides
37 https://twitter.com/realdonaldtrump/status/1141711064305983488?lang=en
38 https://www.nytimes.com/2019/08/28/us/politics/us-iran-cyber-attack.html
39 https://www.timesofisrael.com/us-conducted-cyberattack-on-iran-following-strike-on-saudi-oil-report/
40 Lucas Kello, *The Virtual Weapon and International Order*, New Haven: Yale University Press, 2017, p.5.
41 Lawrence Freedman, *The Future of War: A History*, New York: Public Affairs, 2017, p.230.
42 Graham Allison, *Destined for War: Can America and China Escape Thucydides's Trap*, New York: Mariner, 2018, p.163.
43 Lawrence Freedman, *The Future of War: A History*, New York: Public Affairs, 2017, pp.230–231.
44 Clint Watts, *Messing with the Enemy: Surviving in a Social Media World of Hackers, Terrorists, Russians, and Fake News*, New York: HarperCollins, 2018, p.139.
45 https://www.wired.com/story/russian-hackers-attack-ukraine/
46 Lucas Kello, *The Virtual Weapon and International Order*, New Haven: Yale University Press, 2017, p.174.
47 Robert D. Blackwill and Jennifer M. Harris, *War by Other Means: Geoeconomics and Statecraft*, Cambridge, MA: Harvard University Press, 2016, p.62.
48 Lucas Kello, *The Virtual Weapon and International Order*, New Haven: Yale University Press, 2017, pp.39–40.
49 See Kim Zetter, *Countdown to Zero Day: Stuxnet and the Launch of the First Digital Weapon*, New York: Broadway Books, 2015.
50 https://www.economist.com/the-world-ahead/2020/11/17/a-murderous-cyber-attack-is-only-a-matter-of-time
51 Lucas Kello, *The Virtual Weapon and International Order*, New Haven: Yale University Press, 2017, p.60.
52 Ibid., p.187.
53 Ibid., p.249.
54 https://www.economist.com/the-world-ahead/2020/11/17/a-murderous-cyber-attack-is-only-a-matter-of-time

55 Graham Allison, *Destined for War: Can America and China Escape Thucydides's Trap*, New York: Mariner Group, 2017, p.164.
56 David Rothkopf, "The Cool War," *Foreign Affairs*, February 20, 2013, https://foreignpolicy.com/2013/02/20/the-cool-war/
57 Lucas Kello, *The Virtual Weapon and International Order*, New Haven: Yale University Press, 2017, p.120.
58 Clint Watts, *Messing with the Enemy: Surviving in a Social Media World of Hackers, Terrorists, Russians, and Fake News*, New York: HarperCollins, 2018, pp.207–208.
59 Vladimir Volkoff, *Petite histoire de la désinformation: du cheval de Troie à Internet*, Paris: Éditions du Rocher, 1999.
60 Thaddeus Holt, *The Deceivers: Allied Military Deception in the Second World War*, New York: Scribner, 2004.
61 Peter Pomerantsev, *This Is Not Propaganda: Adventures in the War against Reality*, Londres: Faber & Faber, 2019, p.140.
62 Iryna Dmytrychyn, *Le Voyage de Monsieur Herriot: Un épisode de la Grande Famine en Ukraine*, Paris: L'Harmattan, 2018.
63 Clive Hamilton and Mareike Ohlberg, *Hidden Hand: Exposing How the Chinese Communist Party Is Reshaping the World*, Melbourne: Hardie Grant Books, 2020.
64 Lucas Kello, *The Virtual Weapon and International Order*, New Haven: Yale University Press, 2017, p.227.
65 Richard Shirreff, *2017 War with Russia: An Urgent Warning from Senior Military Command*, London: Coronet, 2016, p.19.
66 See David Patrikarakos, *War in 140 Characters: How Social Media is Reshaping Conflict in the Twenty-First Century*, New York: Basic Books, 2017, pp.167–202.
67 Ibid., p.197.
68 See Ibid.
69 Ibid., p.5.
70 Clint Watts, *Messing with the Enemy: Surviving in a Social Media World of Hackers, Terrorists, Russians, and Fake News*, New York: HarperCollins, 2018, p.137.
71 Richard Shirreff, *2017 War with Russia: An Urgent Warning from Senior Military Command*, London: Coronet, 2016.
72 Lawrence Freedman summarizes the advantage that the Islamic State has been able to extract from social networks: "The most obvious advantages of the Internet [are] found in their smartphone apps: the ability to disseminate messages to vast audiences around the world without interference, harass opponents, post videos of their victims and martyrs, while they [take] advantage of encrypted communications. When it [comes] to killing one feature of many terrorist atrocities [is] the simplicity of their methods – knives, bombs and guns, or driving trucks into crowds. These weapons [are] crude but effective, well understood by those using them and with proven capabilities, demanding no special expertise to make them work." Lawrence Freedman, *The Future of War: A History*, New York: Public Affairs, 2017, p.247.
73 https://www.lexpress.fr/actualite/medias/gilets-jaunes-et-rt-france-une-histoire-d-opportunisme_2056512.html
74 https://www.weforum.org/agenda/2017/05/how-macrons-team-thwarted-the-hackers-with-one-simple-trick/
75 Clint Watts, *Messing with the Enemy: Surviving in a Social Media World of Hackers, Terrorists, Russians, and Fake News*, New York: HarperCollins, 2018, p.228.
76 David Rothkopf, "The Cool War," *Foreign Affairs*, February 20, 2013. https://foreignpolicy.com/2013/02/20/the-cool-war/
77 David Patrikarakos, *War in 140 Characters: How Social Media Is Reshaping Conflict in the Twenty-First Century*, New York: Basic Books, 2017, p.8.
78 Trotsky may never have uttered those words, but it was attributed to him following a series of errors and/or paraphrases. See Michael Walzer, *Just and Unjust Wars: A Moral Argument with Historical Justifications* (5th edition), New York: Basic Books, 2015.

79 Lucas Kello, *The Virtual Weapon and International Order*, New Haven: Yale University Press, 2017, p.77.
80 The Chinese High Command has incorporated the idea of the "three techniques of hybrid warfare" (economic, media and legal) in its official military doctrine long before the West, or even the Russians, in the years 2000. See Peter Pomerantsev, *This Is Not Propaganda: Adventures in the War against Reality*, Londres: Faber & Faber, 2019, p.208.
81 Douglas Alan Cohn, *World War 4: Nine Scenarios*, Guilford: Rowman & Littlefield, 2016, p.5.

Bibliography

Allison, Graham, *Destined for War: Can America and China Escape Thucydides's Trap*, New York: Mariner Group, 2017.
Andrew, Christopher, *The Defence of the Realm: The Authorized History of MI5*, London: Allen Lane, 2009.
Blackwill, Robert D., and Harris, Jennifer M., *War by Other Means: Geoeconomics and Statecraft*, Cambridge, MA: Harvard University Press, 2016.
Blainey, Geoffrey, *The Causes of War* (3rd edition), New York: The Free Press, 1988.
Clausewitz, Carl von, *On War*, London: Penguin, 1982.
Cohn, Douglas Alan, *World War 4: Nine Scenarios*, Guilford: Rowman & Littlefield, 2016.
Constant, Benjamin, *De l'esprit de conquête et de l'usurpation*, Paris: Charpentier, 1842.
Freedman, Lawrence, *The Future of War: A History*, New York: Public Affairs, 2017.
Gomart, Thomas, *Guerres Invisibles: Nos prochains défis géopolitiques*, Paris: Tallandier, 2021.
Hamilton, Clive, and Ohlberg, Mareike, *Hidden Hand: Exposing How the Chinese Communist Party is Reshaping the World*, Melbourne: Hardie Grant Books, 2020.
Helms, Jesse, *Here's Where I Stand: A Memoir*, New York: Random House, 2005.
Holt, Thaddeus, *The Deceivers: Allied Military Deception in the Second World War*, New York: Scribner, 2004.
Kello, Lucas, *The Virtual Weapon and International Order*, New Haven: Yale University Press, 2017.
Morris, Ian, *War: What is it Good for? The Role of Conflict in Civilization, from Primates to Robots*, London: Profile Books, 2014.
Patrikarakos, David, *War in 140 Characters: How Social Media is Reshaping Conflict in the Twenty-First Century*, New York: Basic Books, 2017.
Pomerantsev, Peter, *This Is Not Propaganda: Adventures in the War Against Reality*, Londres: Faber & Faber, 2019.
Rothkopf, David, "The Cool War," *Foreign Affairs*, February 20, 2013, https://foreignpolicy.com/2013/02/20/the-cool-war/
Shirreff, Richard, *2017 War with Russia: An Urgent Warning from Senior Military Command*, London: Coronet, 2016.
Volkoff, Vladimir, *Petite histoire de la désinformation: du cheval de Troie à Internet*, Paris: Éditions du Rocher, 1999.
Walzer, Michael, *Just and Unjust Wars: A Moral Argument with Historical Justifications* (5th edition), New York: Basic Books, 2015.
Watts, Clint, *Messing with the Enemy: Surviving in a Social Media World of Hackers, Terrorists, Russians, and Fake News*, New York: HarperCollins, 2018.
Worrell, Mark P., *Why Nations Go to War: A Sociology of Military Conflict*, New York: Routledge, 2010.

PART 3
The future

7
SEVEN SCENARIOS FOR THE FUTURE OF EUROPE

Now that we have understood why war is possible again in Europe, we need to understand how it could reappear, before getting to discuss what can be done to avoid it. Unfortunately, there are no magic solutions to guarantee peace, only options to answer the most urgent needs and reduce *as much as possible* the factors that can most obviously lead to war. This chapter will present seven possible scenarios for the future of Europe. Most should be understood as worst-case scenarios, where the planets badly align and leaders make enough bad decisions to end up in a generalized state of war. Some scenarios will look likely, or at least imaginable by the reader, while others might be brushed away as implausible – this is the nature of this type of exercise. In some cases, the reader will (rightly) castigate the author for not having included other likely scenarios of war, such as a confrontation between Greece and Turkey in the Eastern Mediterranean, or a civil war over Islam and identity in France, for example. All the scenarios presented here have in common that they are all rooted in the factors described in the earlier chapters, and the historical precedents offered by Europe's history, with some elements borrowed from other works of anticipation.[1]

Of course, none of these scenarios is either "perfect" or "perfectly plausible." One could also criticize the invocation of history to predict the future – after all, history never repeats itself in the exact same way. Nevertheless, the study of armed conflicts from the Peloponnesian Wars to the present day shows us that even if events and causes vary, the great mechanisms of the outbreak of war do not; as we saw in previous chapters, there is little to add today to the analysis of Thucydides, who in the 5th century B.C.E. reminded his readers that "honor, fear, and interest" were the main drivers of war.[2]

These seven scenarios should therefore not so much be read as attempts to predict the future – a very perilous art indeed – but rather to consider how current negative developments could take proportions large enough to lead to war.

DOI: 10.4324/9781003215790-11

In this sense, the multiplicity of scenarios, all envisaged within a ten-year framework, gives us an idea of the dangers that await Europe in the coming decade and beyond.

Yet the bad omens should not discourage the reader: if history can lead us to envisage the worst, it has also shown that crises can be overcome peacefully. The return of war in Europe is not yet set in stone, and it is precisely because it is not yet inevitable that this book has been written. Of course, inevitability itself is a relative concept: it is only declared with the benefit of hindsight, and some decisions taken by leaders at a certain moment may decrease the chances of war in the very short term, while increasing them in the longer term – one might think of the Munich conference of 1938, for example. At other times, it is firmness and inflexible thinking that lead more surely to war; in the 1914 crisis, war was declared in a more peaceful environment than in previous years, but there was a catch: as Geoffrey Blainey puts it, "both sides wanted peace, but only on their own terms."[3]

These seven scenarios are very diverse, including in their root causes. Most of them suppose a sudden or gradual weakening of the two institutions that still form the keystone of Europe's continental security: the European Union and NATO. Some Eurosceptic readers might see this as an ideological bias, but they are wrong: whatever one thinks of these two organizations, the reality is that they are institutional guarantors of geopolitical continuity as well as an important forum for relations (including power relations) and conflict resolutions on the European continent. One can, of course, imagine Europe functioning without the EU or NATO – after all, it did so for centuries prior to 1945. One could even imagine that Europe could thrive in the long term without these two institutions. But if history teaches us anything, it is that periods of transition from one regional security architecture to another is a transition from order to chaos, not the other way round – as Italian communist intellectual Antonio Gramsci wrote from his fascist prison cell in the 1930s, "The old world is dying and the new world struggles to be born. It is in this interregnum that various monsters appear."[4] The time of monsters can indeed be very long: Gramsci himself did not live to see that the new order would be a capitalist one, would englobe Italy and make it ever more firmly part of the "West," which eventually triumphed over communism in the late 1980s. But Gramsci's time of monsters is also very short compared to the chaos that followed the disappearance of the Roman Empire, or that of the Holy Roman Empire.

The disappearance of the European Union and NATO would make relations between states much more uncertain, leaving much room for war before a new, stable order could take shape. Of course, this period of uncertainty would not automatically mean the return of war in Europe, but the weakening, or even the disappearance, of these institutions would make it much more likely. As Robert Kagan points out, and the first three chapters of this book confirm, "those who suggest that Europe would be more harmonious without the European Union [or NATO] have history against them."[5]

Having all these factors in mind, the following scenarios will help us understand how war could break out once again in Europe. They will focus on the developments prior to the outbreak (or generalization) of war, and not on how the conflict itself could unfold. After all, war rarely proceeds according to an established plan, and as American military officer Douglas Alan Cohn reminds us, "in war, unforeseen consequences take the conflict in unexpected directions."[6] This chapter will thus remain within the field and uncertainty of political decisions and try to avoid as much as possible to add the subsequent uncertainties of the battlefield.

Paralysis

The first scenario is probably the most frustrating for pro-Europeans, but it is also the least unlikely, as it anticipates a broad sclerosis of European and Euro-Atlantic institutions. As crises continue to accumulate and as the EU-recovery plan fails to produce visible positive effects for European populations, resignation becomes apparent among European peoples and elites – in many ways, the predominant feeling is that everything has been tried, and it hasn't worked. EU leaders continue to hold grand speeches about the future of Europe in symbolic places, but these grand declarations are seldom followed by actions. The leaders of Europe's old nation-states know that the continent must adapt to the changes of a world they no longer control, but the solution they envision are systematically "national" in their outlook, and instead of thinking the EU as a whole and their countries as a nation, they think the EU from their national perspective while hanging to the mirage of a global vision for their country. Thus, the French president continues to envision a French Europe, the German Chancellor a German Europe, etc. Naturally, all these visions remain exclusive of each other, and as everyone stands firm on their position so as not to appear weak in national elections, European Councils become talking shops where much is discussed but nothing gets done. The Commission, once used as a punching-ball by national governments, is now so weak that accusing it of all the ills on earth is no longer a useful game for national leaders – voters have long understood that the real decisions were taken by the national governments in the Council, which has continued to centralize powers around itself, making the EU ensemble even less effective. As the EU has gone back to a purely intergovernmental affair, NATO has also fallen into lethargy: the brewing conflict between France and Turkey over the Eastern Mediterranean has spilled over to guarantee the paralysis of the Alliance's institutions, the United States has lost interest and any move by NATO is blocked by competing requests of regional focus, some wanting the Alliance to focus more on the Mediterranean at the expense of the East (while tensions with Turkey, still a member, have made any action impossible in the region), while others wish that NATO stays focused only on members' defense against Russia.

Political leaders have actually found this sclerosis a rather comfortable situation. At least since Tocqueville wrote down these words, they know that "the most dangerous moment for a bad government is usually when it begins to reform."[7] As Europe faces so many external threats and internal challenges, one might find it logical to avoid disturbing the peace, as doing so might prove fatal to the system as a whole. Why try reforming a system that may well explode if it is even slightly altered?

This situation would look like that of Poland in the 17th and 18th centuries. The *Rzeczpospolita*, or Commonwealth of Two Nations, was the fruit of the Union of Lublin, by which the Kingdom of Poland and the Grand Duchy of Lithuania had chosen to merge, with a common monarch, parliament and currency. In many respects, the Noble Republic was strikingly modern: a very tolerant ensemble for the time, it attracted many ethnic and religious minorities (Muslim Tatars and Jews in particular), and it had adopted several official languages (Latin, Polish, Lithuanian and Ruthenian, the ancestor of modern Ukrainian). It also had constitutional texts, among the first in the history of Europe (among them the treaty establishing of the Union of Lublin, and the Constitution of 1791). The Rzeczpospolita had experienced its golden era in the 16th century, as it extended its civilizational power from the Baltic to the Black Sea and routed enemies as diverse as the Teutonic Knights, the Ottomans (who threatened Vienna at the time), the Swedes and the Russians.

The Commonwealth of Two Nations owed much of its success to a subtle institutional balance between the powers of strong kings under the Jagiellonian dynasty and those of the nobility, represented in a *Sejm*, a parliament of nobles that had to take decisions unanimously. But once the founding dynasty disappeared, the crown lost much of its authority, and the *Sejm*, left to its own devices, did not find the resources to fill the power vacuum. The rule of unanimity guaranteed near-absolute paralysis, and the nobles could not overcome their individual interests to reform Poland and make it adapt to the new realities emerging in Europe. Meanwhile the Commonwealth's neighbors were reforming, centralizing their state and reforming their military. Progressively, the great Polish state weakened, and the neighboring powers took advantage of this to gradually take over the country's politics, imposing their will to paralyze the institutions before carving up the kingdom between themselves. A final, particularly ambitious and innovative attempt at reform failed before the three rising powers of the region – Austria, Prussia and Russia – ended the existence of the Noble Republic. After three divisions – in 1772, 1793 and 1795 – Poland had ceased to exist.

Would such a scenario become conceivable in today's Europe? Although a "physical" disappearance similar to that endured by the Poles is difficult to envisage on the scale of an entire continent, Poland's tragic fate shows how sclerosis can have catastrophic consequences over the destiny of a political construct. Indeed, unanimity rule can lead to a near-complete paralysis of institutions, thereby preventing them to change alongside a geopolitical ecosystem in perpetual evolution. The result is stagnation, and while it can be a comfortable status quo that can allow actors to gain a few years of peace, the final result is invariably catastrophic: Poland is not the only state to have proven unable to adapt to a constantly changing environment. Geographer Jared Diamond has identified a number of cases, from the Mayas to the Greenland Vikings, where the inability of peoples to adapt to new geographical, climatic or political conditions led to collapse for what were once vibrant communities, republics or kingdoms.[8]

Doing nothing thus means condemning Europe to downfall at one point or another, and it can only be accompanied by violence and wars. Societies and states do not die out in either joy or peace, and stagnation is probably the most certain guarantee of a return to war in Europe. The question, of course, is how, and when. History shows that great polities such as the Republic of Venice or the Ottoman Empire can survive a long and slow decadence, and this decadence can sometimes even have notes of comfort for at least some – it is remarkable that many of the attractions we associate with Venice (the Carnival, baroque art or the myths around shady characters like Casanova) all date from the decadent period of the Republic. The European Union and NATO could survive a few years, even decades, in sclerosis and gradual decay before being caught up with reality. But as with Venice and the Ottoman Empire, war would eventually come back, and this would spell doom for the Europeans – the security architecture of the continent would then disappear in a whirlwind of blood and steel, as surely as the Polish *Rzeczpospolita*, the Ottoman Empire or the Republic of Venice before it.

War in the Baltics

At this stage, the most likely and anticipated conflict that could challenge Europe's territorial integrity is an invasion from the East. Not unsurprisingly, it would involve Russia, the loser of the Cold War, whose ambitions to recover at least some of its influence (and, as we know since 2008 and 2014 the territories) it lost in 1989–1991 are a secret to nobody. It is no secret that both NATO and the EU are the main obstacles to this ambition. In many ways, Russia considers at least parts of Central Europe as part of the *Russki Mir*, or "Russian world," the definition of which varies according to time and circumstances. It is therefore perfectly imaginable that the Kremlin could decide, if NATO and the EU were to weaken beyond a certain point, to test the resolve of the West and attack a weaker NATO and more exposed EU member countries. Of course, this perspective remains unlikely now, but suffice it that the United States disengage from Europe, or that its determination to protect its allies is questioned, and the equation could instantly look very much different. A lack of resolve in the West could thus put in jeopardy Central Europe and transform it, once again, into a battlefield. The following scenario, which is inspired from a fiction recently published by Sir Richard Shirreff, NATO's former Deputy Supreme Allied Commander Europe (SACEUR),[9] is one among many others that could be envisaged in a NATO war game. Unfortunately, and like many other war games, it has been chosen as an exercise precisely because it corresponds to a real threat, should the resolve of

Euro-Atlantic institutions (and in particular the United States) to deter Russia's revisionist agenda weaken.

At the start of this story, the EU and NATO are still standing, but both are greatly weakened. The EU has not recovered from the consequences of COVID-19 on national economies, and after a recovery plan that has not changed Europe's long-term trajectory, each state has turned back inward to follow its short-term interests, weakening the cohesion of Europe as a whole. For their part, the United States has become even more weary of the weak reactions of partners across the Atlantic, and in a moment of isolationist push, they have substantially reduced their contribution to NATO, thereby sending the wrong signals to Moscow. Not that the United States has completely pulled out, but the closure of a number of large US bases in Germany and Italy has taken its toll on US continental capacities, and the increase in prices for the purchase of military equipment for Europeans – to push them to get to their promised 2% GDP in military spending – has not been met with much enthusiasm. America's partners in Europe accepted the price increases, but their budgets remaining tight after the COVID-19 crisis, they simply decided to buy less equipment from the United States to stay even.

In this favorable context, Russia has proven very patient, but it seems that now is the time to take the initiative. Still in power, Vladimir Putin may be getting old, and long past the age of high-risk gambling, but he still knows seize an occasion when he sees it. The signs of weakening in Western resolve clearly point to what could be a once-in-a-generation opportunity for Russia's physical return into Europe. Moscow may have abandoned the idea of annexing larger parts of Ukraine, but the quick absorption of Belarus has created opportunities in the Baltic region and the North. Following the passing of the Belarusian president (in suspicious circumstances), the Kremlin took the opportunity to propose a plebiscite on the "reunification" of the two republics, which received the support of 96.7% of the population in a referendum. Of course, the vote was not free, and as in 2014 Crimea, "little green men" popped up in the hours that followed the Belarusian president's death to take control of all official buildings. The unidentified gunmen, armed to the teeth and speaking with a heavy Russian accent, had patrolled the country for two months and marked their territory while the "campaign" (a one-way propaganda exercise, actually) took place. The result of the referendum, 96.7% for annexation (just like in 2014 Crimea) was known even before the day of the vote.

The annexation of Belarus had gone almost unnoticed in the heart of the EU. Of course, the Balts and Poles protested vehemently and reminded their peers that the whole operation was suspiciously similar to Hitler's Anschluss – an argument which the "doves" in Brussels had brushed away, dismissing it as "empty Godwin talk": The Germans and the French were seeing little point in imposing new sanctions against Russia – which they suspected would harm their fledging economies. On their side, the Brits and Americans were too focused on their own problems to really care, and the general feeling in the

West was that the disappearance of Belarus represented the end of a historical anomaly, the country having never been able to truly function as a truly independent state. The Kremlin did not need to put much effort into convincing Western European public opinions that its pretensions over Belarus were legitimate and the process of annexation legal, and much of Europe had moved on. Of course, the Balts, the Poles and the Ukrainians had not, and they considered that once again the West was abandoning them. They feared that annexation, far from satisfying Russia, was actually encouraging Moscow to push its luck further – meaning their security was directly endangered. They had reasons to be concerned: with the annexation of Belarus, Russia now gained a strategic protrusion into Europe that allowed it to strike on practically all Ukrainian territory from the North as well as the East; Russia had also gained a long border with Poland, and was now almost entirely encircling the Baltic States, with just a hundred kilometers of forest separating the Northwestern-most Belarusian town of Grodno and the enclave of Kaliningrad. For its Baltic neighbors, there was no doubt that Russia was going to strike. The only question was where, and when?

Westerners may still be hanging to the idea that NATO's Article 5 will itself be enough to deter any Russian aggression, but Vladimir Putin's reading is different: he considers that the United States, the key to Europe's defense, will not intervene in the event of a conflict with Russia. Just like the French and the British were not ready to die for Danzig in 1939, there is little doubt in his mind that Americans will just have to accept the *fait accompli* of a blitzkrieg invasion in the Baltic States.

Russia has to act swiftly if it wants to get what it wants. The operation begins with a demonstration by members of the Russian-speaking community in Riga on May 9, in commemoration of the "Great Patriotic War" – the name Russians give to the Second World War. Violent clashes have broken out on the fringes of the demonstration between groups of "young activists" mobilized by a virulent Russian-speaking media online campaign against Latvia and its "fascist" government. For its part the Latvian population has also been pushed to the limits by the many Russian provocations in recent months, notably a cyber-attack that paralyzed the national electricity network in the middle of the Baltic winter. It is therefore not a surprise to see violence spread in the Latvian capital, although the level of organization on the Russian-speaking side leaves no doubt as to the involvement of Russia's secret service. This of course has the effect of further provoking Latvian security personnel. While the demonstration continues to degenerate, shots are heard in the city center: unidentified snipers have fired into the crowd, killing four young Russians.

The news of the "Riga massacre" (as it is presented by Russian-controlled media) spreads like wildfire on social networks: the power of social media allows for the original information of four young Russian girls killed by unidentified gunmen to become hundreds of deaths murdered by the Latvian "fascists." The Kremlin officially demands that the culprits be immediately arrested and sent to

Moscow for trial, otherwise Russia will intervene directly to defend the security of Russians in the Baltic States. Riga, Tallinn and Vilnius look for allies in Europe, but beyond Warsaw, nobody seems to understand the seriousness of the situation: without a smoking gun, and with so much discussion on social media, France, Germany and the United Kingdom seem hesitant to offer guarantees to the Baltic States as it would surely mean risking a direct conflict with Moscow. Prepared for this situation, the Baltic States answer Moscow's ultimatum by proposing a joint inquiry to elucidate the causes of this tragedy, but it is already too late: the following night, after ensuring air superiority by raiding region's air bases, airborne troops seize all the hot spots of the three Baltic countries, while the infantry crosses border points, reaching the Baltic shore in a few hours. The next day, all three Baltic capitals are occupied, and within a few days, the three territories are "under control," even though the Russian army faces guerrilla resistance by the Forest Brothers, partisan groups reproducing the armed resistance tactics of their namesakes following Soviet annexation in the 1940s. Nevertheless, partisan warfare does not prevent the Russians from imposing three new plebiscites modeled on the Crimean and Belarusian models. As in 1939, with a pistol pointed at their heads, Estonians, Latvians and Lithuanians have once again "chosen" to "join" the *Russkii Mir*.

The military operation has gone fast. Way too fast for the West, where elites have been stunned by the surgical invasion. The dispersed NATO troops stationed in the Baltic States did not have time to fire a single shot: they were picked-up in the middle of the night while still in bed and made prisoners by Russian Spetsnaz. The individuals who managed to escape have joined the Forest Brothers, where they take part in the guerilla. In the meantime, decision-makers in the West (or what remains of it) are facing a dilemma: they can decide to do nothing and let Russia annex another part of its former empire, which would be tantamount to signing NATO's death warrant since its Article 5 would automatically be considered null and void. They can also decide to counterattack and send a task force to the Baltic, but now that Russia is firmly implanted on the ground, this means running the risk of extending the war to the whole of Europe. As the determination of EU leaders wavers, the United States decides to send a naval force to the Baltic Sea to at least prevent it from becoming a Russian lake – Poland has invited the US Navy to take port in Gydnia, next to Gdansk, which the US president immediately accepted.

Western military leaders know that "the Russians have learned to proceed in stages – virtually a national characteristic. Act, pause, and act again."[10] At this point, Moscow hits the pause button, and lets the seeds of hesitation and division further disorganize the Europeans. For different reasons, Paris, Rome and Berlin are tempted to accept the *fait accompli*. There is, however, much less hesitation on the United States and United Kingdom side, as the geopolitical consequences of an uncontested annexation of the Baltic States are plain for Washington and London to see. As the joint US and British Navy task force crosses the Strait of

Kattegat to enter the Baltic Sea, Europeans are becoming spectators of an escalation on their own continent. In a television interview, Vladimir Putin makes it clear that he considers the three Baltic countries are now an integral part of Russia, and any attack on their soil would automatically provoke "nuclear de-escalation," the politically correct term to indicate a nuclear strike targeted on European territory using the tactical weapons deployed in Kaliningrad. Russia's calculation is that, faced with that risk, the French, the Germans and even the British will lobby the Americans to call it a day, rather than risk exposing their cities for the sake of countries whose capitals they often do not know the names of. Russia's president challenges the West to take the risk of a nuclear confrontation, which is enough for Berlin and other capitals to demand peace – better to let Moscow annex some Baltic provinces than risk being swept into war "because of a quarrel in a faraway country, between people we know nothing about," as Neville Chamberlain had put it in 1938.

Not everyone agrees with Berlin: Poland now has to internalize having Russian troops standing permanently a mere 200 km from Warsaw. The Polish government thus logically asks Washington to make up for the Europeans' shortcomings by immediately deploying new divisions of the US Army on its border, and Warsaw offers Gydnia as a permanent US naval base on the Baltic. The "provocation" is unacceptable for the Kremlin, and it strikes Poland to put an end to "NATO's encirclement of Russia." Nevertheless, the attack was much less meticulously prepared than the Baltic invasion of the previous month, and the Russians are stopped in front of Warsaw by a motivated and well-equipped Polish Army. But while Western Europeans breathe a sigh of relief, seeing in Poland's resistance an opportunity for diplomacy to resume its course, they hear of terrifying news: during an air strike on Gydnia, the Russians have sunk (supposedly "by mistake") a recently arrived American warship. This time, war has become inevitable between the United States and Russia, and EU members, unable to take responsibility when the going got tough, now have to choose their side – together as European Union (or what remains of it) or in scattered order.

Europe is at war again. After abandoning their own member-states, EU leaders now have plenty of time to meditate on Winston Churchill's speech the day after the Munich conference: "the government had to choose between shame and war. They have chosen shame and they will get war."[11] In the meantime, and although the fighting takes place in the East, the whole continent is affected by the war. As Sir Richard Shirreff puts it,

> "it does not need Russian soldiers marching through Berlin and Paris for the world as we know it to cease to exist. A militarily victorious Russia, [even temporarily] able to dictate its conditions to Europe and NATO, will be enough for life as we know it in Western Europe to come to an abrupt end.[12]"

Europe, battlefield of a Sino-American Cold War

Another scenario could envisage Europe being locked into a fight between China and the United States, who would use the continent as a battlefield for their confrontation. This would follow and extend the patterns of Graham Allison's works on the likelihood of a Sino-American conflict,[13] only this time the rivalry would be played out in Europe, which would become the Southeast Asia of the new Cold War between the two superpowers.

At the time in which this scenario unfolds, war between China and the United States is no longer a political science prediction – it has already become reality, with formal warfare having taken place for a year now. War started with Taiwan's formal declaration of independence, itself the result of a long rise in tensions in the South China Sea, and the rallying of the Taiwanese Guomindang party to the cause of independence. Put to a national referendum, and with the support of all major parties, the separation with the mainland turned into a real plebiscite, with a resounding victory for independence (78.6%), despite the many warnings and large propaganda efforts by the People's Republic of China. Beijing had been clear that it would consider the formal secession of Taipei as totally unacceptable and that such a move would have immediate consequences. Not unsurprisingly, China's posturing only emboldened the Taiwanese, who voted *en masse* and showed their determination to avoid Hong Kong's fate in the 2020s. In the new, modern China, there is no room for "one country, two systems," and the Taiwanese have acted in consequence by formally breaking away from the mainland.

China knows that it cannot let this go, otherwise all its East Asia strategy would collapse: allow Taiwan to go without a fight, and the People's Republic will no longer be feared across the South China Sea – worse, it might embolden Japan, the Philippines and Vietnam to take advantage of China's evident weakness, and strengthen their claims on contested islets. Immediately after the referendum, and before a proclamation of independence can take place, the Chinese People's Liberation Army (PLA) has begun vast maneuvers in the South China Sea. Beijing knows that it is playing hard ball, and the objective is to intimidate Taiwan into submission: as a naval embargo is put on the island, Beijing tells the Taiwanese authorities that all they have to do to end this is to renounce to the proclamation of independence and allow Chinese military experts to station on Taiwanese soil, which is utterly unacceptable for Taipei. Taiwan knows that it can count on the support of the United States, and the US Navy has been dispatched to break the embargo. When the US and Chinese fleets meet, intimidation degenerates into collision, exchange of fire and full-scale confrontation, thereby drawing the entire Far East into war. Alliances have crystallized almost automatically, with China enlisting North Korea, Laos and Cambodia, while the United States fight alongside the Japanese, South Koreans, Taiwanese, Filipinos and Vietnamese.

The first battles are not decisive. Naval battles in the South China Sea have been inconclusive, engagement on the Korean peninsula is impossible due to the risks of triggering an all-out nuclear war and operations in the mountains and jungle of Southeast Asia have been limited in scope and results. Both Americans and Chinese are looking for ways to fight elsewhere, so problematic is the fight in East Asia. India and China have decided (and managed) to stay out of the war, for different reasons: the Russians know they are not strong enough in the main theater of war, and India in the end prefers not to risk a direct confrontation in Beijing that could lead it to suffer two ground attacks – from China and from Pakistan. Without further options in the Indo-Pacific region, more peripheral theaters of war start to become credible alternatives, much like Italy, the Dardanelles or the Arab peninsula were in the middle of the First World War. European leaders, sensing their vulnerability and indecisiveness as to the best course of action, have managed to find a consensus to declare full neutrality, an easy escape route that has not gone down well in Washington – even though the move was widely popular in the EU's public opinion.[14]

But if neutrality can be decreed, it is not always respected, particularly if the state that has declared it does so by weakness, despite its obvious strategic location (as Belgians in the two world wars can attest). Europeans' neutrality is hiding the fact that member-states are hopelessly divided in their allegiance: some countries have stayed loyal to the Atlantic Alliance (among them the Baltic States, Portugal and Poland); others have followed a continentalist trajectory, and have progressively moved into Beijing's sphere of influence, like Greece, Hungary or Serbia; Greece had to move closer to Beijing to pay its debts to Northern Europe, while Hungary and Serbia seem to have had more direct political motives. Finally, other countries like France, Germany and Italy are divided from within and have therefore found it most convenient to stay out of the conflict, so as not to stir too much trouble at home. Everywhere, different forces have pushed countries in one direction or another – surely, if conflict between Beijing and Washington were to last long, it would become impossible for the EU to stay neutral, whether as an entity or as the sum of its member-states.

As the war lingers, all that is needed is a small trigger, some would even say an excuse, for war to get back to the heart of Europe. That trigger comes from Italy, as parliamentary maneuvers usher in the fall of the neutralist government, with a new parliamentary majority, supported by Beijing, now taking over the reins of a key country in Southern Europe, with US military bases aplenty. Viewed from China, this is a diplomatic game changer that will put enough pressure on the United States to change the course of the war, and potentially force it to release its bases in the Mediterranean.

Immediately upon taking office, the new Italian prime minister decides to "regain sovereign control" over the American bases on Italian soil, which are surrounded the same day by the Italian army. The Americans are summoned to surrender and leave, which they logically refuse, hoping that a parliamentary reversal or new elections might change the situation. Tensions continue to mount, and China is waiting for the pretext to send reinforcements to support its Mediterranean fleet, recently installed in the Gulf of Salamis, near Piraeus. A naval battle in the Mediterranean is expected to decide the fate of the war, but unexpected complications bring the conflict inland. Serbia has seen the latest developments unfold, and its government sees in the US–Chinese war an opportunity to avenge the defeats of the 1990s and regain control over at least part of the territories it lost during the post-Yugoslav wars. It is obvious that a great game is about to take place, and the opportunity to change the borders is way too tempting, even more so as Serbia's alignment to Beijing is now complete. While US and Chinese fleets are busy gathering in the Mediterranean Sea, Belgrade takes the opportunity that little attention is put on the Western Balkans to engineer the secession (and absorption) of Bosnia's Republika Srbska, while Serbian troops, recently equipped with Chinese armaments, clash with the Kosovar army as they try to push toward the ethnic Serb enclave of Mitrovica. As the security architecture of the Western Balkans unravels, Zagreb also enters in the game and convinces the Bosnian Croats to follow suit – leading to the Croatian annexation of Herzegovina. The Western Balkans have plunged back into war, and it is likely that the United States and China will have to get involved in the conflict, either as appeasers or (more likely) as patrons of their client states.

But while the United States and China are busy placing their troops in the Balkans and their navies in the Mediterranean, tensions continue to spill over, this time in Central Europe. During the past years, Budapest has also become a client-state of China, and there is a feeling among Hungarian elites that, with tensions running high and a Chinese victory possible, there is a unique opportunity to wipe out the consequences of Trianon and literally make Hungary great again. Even more so now as China's record investments in Hungary have given it an edge over its neighbors, including militarily. If Serbia managed to get territorial compensation for playing a part in the Sino-American conflict, why shouldn't Hungary have a go at it, even more so as it is clear that the European Union has practically left the region to its own device and will now focus solely on its core in the Northwest of the continent? Hungary has many minorities around its borders, and many potential claims. The question is where to strike – the first enemy identified is Ukraine, where the conflict over the Hungarian minorities in Transcarpathia has never died down, but Slovakia is also seen as a larger possible objective: the country's economy has not recovered from the changes incurred by the post-COVID-19 economic crisis, and its defenses are weak. In this general context, the Hungarian government decides to strike and sends an ultimatum to Bratislava, to surrender parts of its territory to Hungary. Slovakia knows it is not in a position to resist and is therefore tempted to answer favorably, but Poland, which has remained very close to Washington, gets involved to guarantee the present Slovak borders. Romania, feeling threatened if the Hungarians were to get their way in Slovakia, mobilizes its troops and stations them on the border in Transylvania. Tensions are running high, and in the end a border incident on the Danube serves as a pretext for the start of the hostilities, in which everyone now has a stake: the Hungarians because they think they can get territories "back," the Romanians, Slovaks and Poles because they think that they have a unique opportunity to teach the troublesome Hungarians a lesson and China and America because this proxy war might in the end be the best way to play out their rivalry. Without much thinking of the consequences, the Sino-American war has spilled over a good part of Europe, and turned both the Western Balkans and Central Europe (as well as, potentially, the Italian peninsula) into a battlefield. The European Union has proved completely powerless, and Berlin, Brussels and Paris find little consolation in having been able to preserve peace on their territory. Europe was not interested in war, but war was interested in Europe, leaving most of the EU's internal and external periphery under fire.

Southern disintegration

The last two scenarios supposed that the European Union would be a more or less passive importer of conflicts caused by external powers. This should not let the reader conclude that trouble could only come from outside. Indeed, the factors of discord inside Europe are sufficient in themselves to envisage the return of war in the European Union without external help.

One of these scenarios could envisage the breakup of the European Union as the EU core would let its peripheries go. In many ways, this would follow the pattern of imperial breakup, and would undoubtedly be followed by much uncertainty and strife in the peripheries. As Dominic Lieven reminds us in his analysis of the logic of large multinational empires,[15] one of their characteristic feature is the presence of a center and a periphery, which imply a "cost of empire," namely the burden (financial, but not only) that the imperial center has to bear to keep the poorer peripheral regions in line. Of course, this cost also exists in the context of a nation-state (it is indeed costly for London to administer and support the rest of the United Kingdom), but this cost is legitimized by the sense of belonging to a common body, the nation. In an empire or a multinational entity, this solidarity is much less natural, and in times of crisis, the temptation is for the center to let the costly peripheral territories go. This does not necessarily preclude the return of the metropolitan power at a later point – it may indeed be what the center plans to do after the success of its reform. This thinking is what led Soviet Russia to resolve to lose almost without fighting its empire in Europe and Central Asia between 1989 and 1991.[16] The Russians knew that reform was needed, and that reform would more likely happen by getting rid of at least some parts of the empire. This is what explains Boris Yeltsin's appeals to the peripheral republics of the empire (including within the Russian Federation itself) to "take as much sovereignty as you can swallow" – the message was that Moscow was now focused on rebuilding its capacities. Of course, what Yeltsin did not say was that once the center would have regained strength, it would seek to take back that sovereignty.

Would such a process be imaginable in Europe? The EU is often portrayed by Eurosceptics as a new USSR, which shows how little they know of how the EU functions or how the USSR functioned, but the Union is certainly not an empire. It was not formed by constraint, none of its members was forced to join, and as the United Kingdom showed, these members can actually leave the Union. Nevertheless, it is also true that the logic of center versus periphery is a feature of European politics, with Northern Europe now clearly emerging as a core leaving the peripheral territories in the East and South behind. If the core were to decide to let go some of its peripheries – probably with no willingness of getting it back ever, the shock could very well lead to renewed tensions, and even war.

Taking a worst-case scenario, things could unfold in this manner: by 2030, the European Union is still a formal entity, but the North–South and East–West divides have continued to deepen after the failure of the recovery plan: the countries of the South have not been able to take advantage of EU investments and loans to rethink their model, and parts of Central Europe have definitively renounced the German liberal model to build "illiberal" and nationalistic states. The Northerners, often portrayed as the "bankers of Europe" have grown tired of investing money with little return on investment, and the original coalition of "frugal" countries like Austria, the Netherlands, Denmark, Finland and Sweden have not only hardened their stance (focusing less on reform and more on the size of their rebate), but also expanded, as Germany and the Baltic States have joined the coalition. In this way, an informal alternative European Union has emerged, a sort of modern Hansa that now connects the rich economies of the North while letting those of the South on their own. With austerity now looming after yet another economic crisis, Northern workers are clearly taking precedence over the unreformed economies of the South.

Southern Europe is now left to its own device, as the informal division of the past years becomes official. Following yet another monetary crisis, it has been decided that the Eurozone will now be divided into two monetary unions: the N-Euro will remain a strong currency, while the S-Euro will be allowed to float so as to allow Southern economies to regain their competitiveness through devaluations. But what seemed workable on paper has turned into a nightmare: for a brief period of time, Italy, Spain and Greece have been able to regain short-term financial leeway through devaluation, but manipulative monetary policy is not the alpha and the omega of a good economic policy: the interest rates hikes that have followed the devaluation have cancelled up most of the latter's original effects. The result has been a further monetary breakup, with each country returning to its original currency, and starting a "devaluation war" which has further impoverished the three southern peninsulas (Iberia, Italy and the Balkans).

With disaster looming in Southern Europe, the North has remained very cautious and has tried to stay away from any trouble. It has been a long time since the Mediterranean turned into chaos; with the Arctic now open for navigation, it is no longer an interesting trade route for the new Northern Hansa, and Northern Europeans want to stay away from Southern European economic turmoil as much as possible. In any case, the Baltic Sea and the North Sea are now the new *mare nostrum* for the bankers of the region. They look at the general impoverishment in the South with a hint of *schadenfreunde* coupled with a slight despair at seeing their summer holiday destination becoming more dangerous – some creative solutions, however, have been found as some of the Mediterranean islands have been allowed to stay in the N-Euro, making them practically Mediterranean colonies of Northern Europe.

As economic difficulties continue to grow on the mainland, so does the urgency to act swiftly and stop the decline of once affluent areas in Southern Europe. Not unsurprisingly, one result is the rise of identity particularisms: in Spain, Catalonian separatism has bounced back and reaches record high support, while the Basque elites are also showing some willingness to consider breaking away from Madrid. In both cases, the slogan *"Marid nos roba"* (Madrid is robbing us), very much used in the 2010s, has made a surprising come back, only this time the violence is not limited to words and small groups: physical and armed intimidation against Castillan-speakers in the street has become a common occurrence, symbols of the Spanish state or castellan companies have been targeted by direct action, and the situation is generally getting out of hand. In this context, national legislative elections usher in the victory of a hardened right, and the new Spanish nationalist government gets elected in a particularly deleterious context, with much of Catalonia and the Basque country voting overwhelmingly against it, while Castilla, Andalusia and the North West vote in record high numbers for the nationalists. Local elites in Barcelona and Bilbao take this as a sign that there is no other choice for them but to declare immediate and unilateral independence even before the central government in Madrid takes office. In turn, the central government's first action upon arriving in power is to mobilize its army – and any volunteer ready to defend the motherland to put an end to sedition. A second civil war in Spain has become practically inevitable.

In the meantime, the same causes have the same effects in Italy. The third biggest economy in continental Europe is on the verge of bankruptcy, and its historical regional particularities have become more salient as the crisis has unfolded. Under the appearance of a strong, patriotic nation, the Italian Republic has always been a fragile construct (historian Marc Lazar once wrote that one of its problems is that it "is neither hated, nor badly liked, nor loved; it just exists"[17]), and the economic meltdown is threatening the unity acquired in the 1860s. The Northern question has reappeared as secessionist groups have used the rhetoric of Catalan secessionists and Northern Europeans. This time though, the thieves are in Rome and the lazy crooks in Italy's South. The Lega has reverted to a regionalist party and re-embraced the cause of "Padanian" – read Northern Italian – nationalism. Old slogans, like *"Roma, ladrona, la Lega non perdona"* (Rome, thief, the Lega does not forgive), have come back on social media. In the 1970s and 1980s, when those slogans emerged, almost everyone in Italy took this "Padanian" nationalism as racist folklore, an expression of particularism in a country where unity remained recent and not completely digested, but this time circumstances are making the rise of the new Lega much more potent in the North of Italy – and as Italian institutions start to break down, the separatist coalition turns not into Padanian secession, but multiple independences. There was never any Padania, only a Duchy of Milan, a Kingdom of Piedmont/Sardinia a Venetian and a Genoa Republic, etc. As the Italian peninsula melts down, it does not divide itself into "coherent" socioeconomic ensembles, but into small units, like Lombardia, Tuscany and Venice. In the center and South too, centrifugal forces are at play: while Naples claims the ascendant over the rest of the *Mezzogiorno*, it is Sicily's turn to secede, leaving Rome with confetti of territory that still bear the official name of "Italian Republic."

In the meantime, the absence of order in both the Italian and the Hispanic peninsulas has attracted a number of illegal activities: there is now no force strong enough to stop the migrant flow from South to North, and migrants now cross the Mediterranean in numbers to try and find a way in prosperous Northern Europe. Many get stuck in Italy and Spain as they once did in Morocco, Tunisia and Libya, leading to new problems. While some regions, far away from the migration routes, manage to stay away from chaos, others continue to go down in flames, as groups of locals now hunt migrants, and then come to fight with locals over the migrants, leading to a general breakdown of public order. Civil war has now become reality over the entire Western Euro-Med region.

This story ends here: it does not say whether the massive arrival of migrants at Northern Europe's gate will force the "frugals" to finally pay attention to a problem that was bound to be of direct concern to them in the long term or if they manage to lock themselves out of the crisis. What is likely though it that such a scenario will spell the end of Europe, as the continent will then be divided for a long time between a "Hanseatic" and a Mediterranean world, leaving no room for continental cohesion. At this stage, the whole of Europe may not be at war, but Europe as a whole may well have ceased to exist.

The Yellow Vest wars

All the scenarios examined so far have anticipated an outbreak of war in the European peripheries. It is indeed a more likely possibility, as peripheries are naturally the most vulnerable in any political ensemble. As we saw in the last scenario, it is even possible to envisage that the heart of Europe, whether located on the Baltic or the North Sea, would "secede" in order to stay out of trouble – whereby it would make the peripheries even more vulnerable. Nevertheless, envisaging war solely in the European peripheries would be a grave mistake: while armed conflict in Western and North-Western Europe is less probable, it remains possible, and countries like France and Belgium have a long enough history of unrest, and enough difficulties at present, to allow us to envisage the worse. The following scenario actually anticipates France being the center of trouble in the coming years, as it goes through an uprising similar to that of the

Yellow Vests in late 2018, leading to a cascade of events in many ways reminiscent of those that triggered the revolutionary wars of 1792.

In a not-so-distant future, France is still paralyzed by social tensions, after two electoral cycles that have ensured an uneasy political continuity: in 2022, Emmanuel Macron was re-elected against the far right with 55% of the votes, very far from the 66% he had gathered in 2017. In 2027, his designated successor beat Marine Le Pen's replacement once again, with an even smaller gap this time (51% vs. 49%). Not only has the spread between the status quo candidate and the insurgent candidate shrunk, but the campaign itself has been marked by a tense atmosphere, with one camp presenting itself as the only bulwark of democracy in the face of the "fascist threat," and the other as the last hope for the French to make their voices heard against the "dictatorship of the cosmopolitan elites" – American news media had picked on the events and drawn a parallel with the Biden–Trump context of 2020, many were all too happy to take revenge on the Europeans who had dared to mention the risks of "civil war" in the United States at the time.

The parallels between the US elections of 2020 and the French elections of 2027 were indeed remarkable: the end of the campaign was marked by accusations on the side of the insurgent party that a "massive" electoral fraud was in the making, and more generally the "nationalists" believed that the "system" was going to do whatever was necessary to keep them out of power. As the campaign continued to go down the gutter, uncontrolled violence had erupted in cities where public meetings were being held, with street battles between supporters of both camps. Political leaders on all sides had called for calm, but each was actually quick to put the responsibility on the other side and making their calls for de-escalation conditional on a de-escalation from the adversary. Election night had contributed to making the atmosphere even more nefarious, as the small spread between the two candidates had given the opportunity to a number of activists looking for attention to denounce a "massive fraud" in different publics: white working-class cities had given very large majorities to the nationalist candidate, city centers and inner cities had voted in equally large numbers for the candidate of the system, etc.

In many ways, the fault lines of the campaign followed the same sociological logic as those witnessed in previous contests in Europe and the United States since 2015: the large city elites and their affluent suburbs had continued to barricade themselves, while most millenials and zillenials had joined peripheral and poor areas, as the post-coronavirus crisis worsened their situation. With mass unemployment consistently above 10% of the working population since 2020, very few young people had been co-opted into the system, and the repeated defeats of the radical left candidate in the elections had only reinforced their contempt for the "republic of false hopes." In circles outside the Macron mainstream, the electoral defeat was accepted not as an invitation for rival parties to change their ways and enlarge their appeal, but with the feeling that the system was rigged and that French "democracy" was in reality only a façade.

In this nefarious context, the new French President knows that he needs to act, and fast, to put the country back on the right track. But instead of trying to reach out to the other side, he decides to double down on his victory, and a few months after his election, he introduces once again a carbon tax. The carbon tax is an old project that the French bureaucracy insists on putting in place for France to be able to manage its environmental transition, and to refill the empty state's coffers. The project was presented a first time under Nicolas Sarkozy in 2009 and abandoned a few months later after electoral revolt and a historic defeat for the center-right in the regional election of 2010. A few years later, Sarkozy's successor François Hollande tried again to pass it through parliament, only to give up after a localized but spectacular outburst of violence in Brittany. Fast forward another four years in 2018, and a similar project was met with the much more widespread (and violent) opposition of the Yellow Vests. But ten years have passed by, and the new administrations have forgotten popular sensitivity to the problem; it soon becomes clear, however, that the same causes produce the same effects, and Yellow Vests have reappeared in France's *province*, before converging to Paris on the weekends. With violence quickly flaring up, the security forces are tested – but this time many of them join the protesters: the profession's prestige had continued to deteriorate following years of accusations of police brutality and racism, without this leading to much reform in the police system. As many of the insurgent Yellow Vests stem from the same social backgrounds as policemen, junction has become inevitable. Numerous sights of fraternization between policemen and Yellow Vests in the provinces should have alerted state authorities, and public order breaks down. In a weekend of demonstrations in Paris, the mob becomes master of the French capital: what remains of the police is overwhelmed while most policemen have joined the demonstration. Ministries are run over by angry demonstrators, who also take the Elysée: the president has just enough time to escape in helicopter, and takes refuge in Germany.

It is a known fact that power vacuums never last long, particularly in revolutions. With Parliament completely delegitimized after 50 years of power centralization, the beheading of France's executive means that power is here for the taking, and rebel French elites have taken upon themselves to organize a new Committee of Public Safety, modelled on the French Revolution, to govern the country. The feeling that Paris is living another 1789 is overwhelming Parisian minds, and many have started to wear a *tricolore* corcard and to call each other with a "*Citoyen*" in the streets. The ten personalities chosen to head the Public Salvation all stem from "civil society" although everybody knows that they have been carefully selected by a much smaller group of insiders who are the ones that are trying to control the revolutionary process.

With the National Assembly now abolished, power is exercised either vertically, by committee decrees or by referendums, which are showing their own limits: the new "true" democracy may be carried out online, by groups of citizens, but in reality all these theatricals are more or less controlled by the same "Engineers of Chaos"[18] that have been trying for years to sell "real" democracy in their populist environments. While the Revolutionaries have prevailed in France, they have not in most of Europe, and developments have been followed with much horror in the rest of the continent, especially in Germany, as the rise of French nationalism has started to worry even the most Francophiles in Berlin. Images of the French "putsch" have become a classic scaremongering meme on social media, and so have all sorts of information, some true and others not, about the return of the guillotine in French provinces, or the expansionist ambitions of some members of the Committee of Public Safety.

The European Union has managed to come to terms with semi-authoritarian regimes in Central Europe for some years, but the task of dealing with this revolutionary France is completely different: unlike the other governments, the new powers in Paris are claiming their legitimacy not from elections or a parliament (both have been abolished), but from a fantasized popular will; as a result, elites in Berlin, in Brussels and other capitals are wary of a government that they don't really understand, and that does not want to play by the same rules as them: this is a recipe for impulsiveness and unpredictability, two words dreaded in EU institutions or in Berlin. In many ways, the revolutionary wave of 2028 has sealed the divorce in the Franco-German couple. Could balances in Western Europe be maintained within this context?

It was only a matter of time before things would flare up in Belgium. Polarization between French- and Dutch-speaking populations has reached record-highs after the events in France, with Dutch speakers suspecting the francophones of sympathies for the French Yellow Vests and the Flemish deciding to secede. The French, all in their revolutionary craze, decide that it is important to come to the rescue of their francophone brothers, and provide military assistance to the Walloons as the francophone suburbs of Brussels, parts of Flanders become an urban battlefield. Surprisingly, Paris has decided to use its army on the ground, and instead of intervening for "humanitarian" reasons, it has occupied Wallonia and annexed it to France, pretty much like Russia has in Crimea in the 2010s.

The mood in Berlin, to take the language of diplomatic releases, is one of shock and consternation. Such an act of "piracy" may have been common in Napoleonic times, but it is certainly not acceptable in civilized Europe in the 21st century. The fact is that the French and German governments are no longer talking the same language (or with the same references), and the situation continues to deteriorate. The German Chancellor would like to get the Committee of Public Safety to understand that Germany could accept regime change in Paris if the French "revolution" were to stay within the borders of France, but this is not something that the French are ready to hear at this stage: for them 1789 calls for 1793, and they consider it only a matter of time before "their" revolution enlightens the rest of the world.

There is no more room for talks, and Berlin must therefore act quickly to put the French back in line and force them into civilized discussions. Unsurprisingly, the obvious choice is economic warfare: Berlin puts in place a very broad system of sanctions and an economic blockade to convince Paris to get back to the negotiating table. There is logic in this move: Germany is both the primary export market and a much richer country than France, it is therefore expected that using an economic stick will get the French to see their immediate interest and get back to their senses. At the same time as it imposes a large set of economic sanctions on France, Berlin invites Paris to join a larger discussion on the future of Belgium – the Netherlands have also been invited, but not Britain, which has retained its position of splendid isolation ever since Brexit became effective.

The reaction in Paris is completely different to what Berlin hoped for. Much like the Iranians did not respond to American sanctions by capitulation, the French are outraged by this "blackmail." Old discourses about France's "natural borders" being on the Rhine have resurfaced, and the nationalist craze is actually empowered rather than impeded by the German economic sanctions. Those are followed by cyber-attacks from unknown individuals, all with IPs in France. The cyber-attacks hit their targets in the German industry, and Berlin retaliates with a devastating counterattack on France's power grid, leaving many parts of the country without electricity for several days.

Things have clearly spun out of control, but neither German nor French elites have really understood that. As both populations experience a nationalist surge, nobody can back down, and the French are cornered: the last cyber-attack was damaging enough to be considered an act of war, and Paris knows that it has a military ascendant over Berlin, one of the few areas where it has uncontested superiority. In a heated meeting of the Committee of Public Safety, the decision is therefore made to attack Germany militarily before it has the time to organize – the idea is not necessarily to "invade" Germany, but to force it to the negotiation table on terms more favorable to Paris. As commandos of the French Army, already present in Belgium, cross the border at Aachen, France and Germany are once again at war with each other.

The post-Brexit war

Other scenarios could unfold in the economic heart of Europe. One of them could be the development of ethnic tensions in France that could in turn lead to an identity war, which I describe in the French-language version of this book.[19] But equally disturbing, the United Kingdom could also find itself at war with at least parts of the European Union in a post-Brexit worst-case scenario.

A prerequisite would of course be that neither the United Kingdom nor the EU would have made much of a success of Brexit – a diagnosis that currently still hangs in the balance. Not that the divorce between London and Brussels has led to the catastrophe that many Remainers had feared, but neither has it made Britain thrive. Rather, the years following the recovery after the coronavirus pandemic have turned out not to be as promising as initially though, and Europe's growth path has further lagged behind that of North America and East Asia. This has fueled renewed discourses of decline on both sides of the Channel, and the blame game that ensued has rather widened the gap between the United Kingdom and continental Europe. On the one hand, Brits have blamed the continentals for their lack of flexibility and audacity for the disappointing growth numbers across Europe, while the continentals have blamed Britain for sabotaging pretty much every EU move, with acts of economic "piracy" not going unnoticed in Brussels, Paris or Berlin. With memories of the vaccine row still vivid, mistrust is basically the default position of trade negotiators, and each side of the Channel believes that the other is acting in bad faith.

Not that Britain has fared much better than Europe, or the other way around. Economically, the United Kingdom has not done badly per say, but neither the new funds previously dedicated to the EU nor the new investments put in place by the British government for a stronger economic growth have brought much difference to the economic trajectory of the British Isles. The only exception is Northern Ireland, where troubles over the border have meant economic breakdown and a return of sectional violence between the Protestant and Catholic communities. The latter has felt vindicated by a new census that has confirmed their becoming a majority in the province, making a union with Dublin a concrete possibility.

The British and Irish government had initially agreed that they would not bicker over Northern Ireland. Dublin was fine letting time play in its favor and wasn't in a rush to have to subsidize an Irish Ulster. But as always when identity politics kick in, economic takes a back seat as violence in Belfast leads to polarization on both sides. For Irish nationalists, the situation represents a historic opportunity to end a secular struggle for the unity of the island under one government in Dublin. On the other side, confronted with rising nationalist movements in Scotland and Wales, Britons fear a domino-effect on the other side of the Irish Sea. In the end, after a new rise in violence that puts the province on the verge of all-out civil war, and following US pressure, the UK government gives in, and a referendum takes place, giving a short but decisive majority for Northern Ireland to secede from the United Kingdom and join the Republic of Ireland.

Initially, the government in London feels rather relieved to have let go a massive problem that was costing the central government £ 9.2 billion a year, i.e. more than the cost of the United Kingdom being in the EU.[20] But the effect on the British population's morale has been devastating: the loss of Northern Ireland has encouraged the rise of English nationalism, which is also fueled by the endless bickering between Edinburgh and London over devolution and the idea of a second referendum for Scottish independence. The Scottish nationalists themselves are not necessarily happy with the loss of Belfast, as the result has been a massive influx of unionists from Northern Ireland, which in turn has modified Scotland's electoral map.

The Scottish matter has thus far remained an internal British issue from which all major actors on the continent have tried to stay away from. That is, until the news come out that the Scottish National Party, through its affiliation with the European Greens/European Free Alliance, has managed to get some European funding for a cultural project which has in turn been misused for electoral campaign purposes. The amount involved (a few thousand Euros) and the nature of the funds misused would have been brushed off as a sign of Brussels' incompetence by the British government and transformed into a media coup a few years back, but this time it is different. Considering the wave of Anglo-nationalism that has followed the loss of Belfast, the tabloid press and Conservative newspapers in London are taking up arms against the EU, calling it an act of war from Brussels, and pushing the government to answer this outrageous attack on British democracy. Whitehall has to react, and raises tariffs over a range of European products, adding to it a total ban on fishing in all UK territorial waters, in contravention with the Brexit agreement between London and Brussels.

Fishing is not an economically high-stake issue, as it weighs less than 1% of the British and EU economy. But it is nonetheless highly symbolic. For the British government, it is a spectacular way of affirming sovereignty at a time in which it needs to be asserted. But in Brussels, it is seen as a sign that the Brits can no longer be trusted on anything they have signed. The Brexit deal is thus considered null and void, as it has become clear that London can at any time renege on parts of the deal. Europeans also decide to raise tariffs on imported British agricultural products, another touchy subject on both sides of the Channel. Fueled by their respective presses, tensions escalate: the French and Spanish announce they will not discourage their fishermen to go to British territorial waters if they wish to do so. In the meantime, the Spanish government, feeling vindicated by the ongoing tensions in the North Sea and happy to please its nationalist electorate, renews its claim for a "negotiated return of Gibraltar to Spain and the EU."

Needless to say, none of these moves humbles London, and the answer is more tariffs. As the conflict turns to an all-out commercial war, the Daily Mail runs an article according to which the British government servers have been hacked by German actors – the actors were unidentifiable, and the CIA have told MI5 that the attack was actually more likely to have been carried by Russian agents, but the news itself has devastating effects on British public opinion, which in turn demands swift action. The government is thus cornered to act and chooses to do so, once again, on fisheries: Royal Navy ships will be deployed to protect British territorial waters against foreign fishermen. The idea is to "incite" the French and Spanish governments to tell their fishermen to stay away from British waters, which will then open the way for a negotiated settlement. In normal times, this would have happened, but both French and Spanish populations also have their own pride, and the British fleet's behavior has led to further pressure from the French and Spanish press. As a result, not only have both Spanish and French authorities refrained from giving any specific instructions to their fishermen, they have also doubled down: as happens every time the temperature rises, Madrid has cut Gibraltar off the rest of the continent. On its side, France has actually decided to dispatch its own military vessels to protect its fishing fleet.

British tabloids have quickly reacted: the Daily Mail sent an invitation to the French president and Spanish prime minister to meet off Cape Trafalgar to solve their differences with Britain, and British public opinion now approves an intransigent line, even more so as after a few days of hesitation Germany and the rest of the EU have resolutely sided with Paris and Madrid. But the British government knows that despite the appeals to the past, the French fleet is nothing like a pirate flotilla off the coast of Somalia, and the ministry of defense is rather favorable to some de-escalation. This is also the mood in Paris, as the general sentiment is that the situation is getting out of hand. But as always, unforeseen events disturb the plans of French and British diplomats. They take the shape of an incident between a British and a French fishing vessel: finding a small French fishing boat in British waters, and without any assistance from the Royal Navy, British fishermen decide to take matters in their own hands and forcefully board the French vessel, to "teach the Frogs a lesson." Of course, the French are not willing to let go, and the two crews fight with harpoons and distress rockets, resulting in deaths both sides.

At this stage, neither the French nor the British can back down and everybody knows that one incident can trigger war. French and British military ships come face-to-face on the Channel, while they try to discipline their own fishermen. A series of miscalculations and unfortunate circumstances lead the Royal Navy ship to open fire on a French ship, leading to immediate retaliation from the French Navy and the sinking of a British warship. This time, war has become inevitable.

A difficult reform

The six scenarios explored thus far are worst-case scenarios resulting from a long and almost uninterrupted sequence of unfortunate events and bad decisions. It is possible to imagine them only unfolding partially, or even not at all, as there are still numerous pathways for Europe as a continent (and as a European Union) to become again the beacon of peace and stability it had become only a couple of decades ago. Beyond these depressing scenarios, it is also possible to imagine a much more positive outcome for the European continent in the next ten years.

Such a scenario would take us in a future where the European Union has overcome its paradoxes and reached stability. It is certainly not a superpower (as the United States-China duopoly has consolidated), and it has its weaknesses, but like India, it has managed to assert itself on the international scene as a respectable and respected player – the EU has built its capacities of self-defense while remaining within NATO, and this has actually helped appease the Transatlantic relationship, allowing for Europeans to take matters in their own hands in their neighborhood. Agreement with the United States on common interests in Europe's periphery has allowed Washington to focus more on the Far East without leaving Europe. Of course, Europeans know they remain vulnerable, but Brussels and national elites are carefully monitoring their internal weaknesses, no longer allowing them to weaken their hand in their dealing with outside powers. The North–South, East–West and intra-national divisions are still there, but European leaders have learnt after the EU-recovery plan that reform was possible within a broad (if not fully consensual) framework, with more integration being agreed upon in key regal sectors while others have been more readily devolved to the national area. The times in which Eurosceptics accused Brussels of being anti-democratic are also long gone as, following a series of crises, the European Parliament has managed to impose itself as a true parliament, with much wider powers of control over the Commission – and the Council. Europe's better functioning and relative strength have in turn pacified the relationship with Russia, which now has to face its own problems, and also with Turkey, as the powers that be in Ankara have understood that, like in the 1990s and 2000s, a more co-operative approach is a preferable path to deal with a more cohesive European Union. Growth has also come back on the continent after a few difficult years, and while economic development is not as strong in Europe as in the United States, the recovery fund and subsequent budgetary efforts to support national economies have managed to make the EU popular again in Southern and Eastern Europe. In the North, the EU is no longer being seen as a burden for the hard-working German and Swedish workers: those are seeing the dividends of a much more integrated, prosperous internal market with renewed orders and economic dynamics. Of course, this does not mean that all is well: Europe still faces continuous demographic pressure from the South, and the relationship with Turkey and Russia still goes back and forth between economic co-operation and strategic rivalry, but European leaders have learnt to live with these and other challenges.

There is, however, a shadow in this idyllic picture: reforming the Union was no easy task. Tocqueville's famous quote from *The Old Regime and the Revolution*, "the most dangerous moment for a bad government is usually when it begins to reform,"[21] has not become a classic of political science for nothing. And indeed, the moment of reform, a few years after the end of the coronavirus crisis, was no exception, as some of the contradictions described in this book reached boiling point. In many ways, European unity has followed the same trajectory as that of Switzerland in the 19th century, as it went from "a loose confederation of states to a federation in a threatening geopolitical context."[22] Switzerland's unity, achieved in a context of religious, ethnic and political divisions, was not without its problems. The formation of an alliance between the most conservative confederalist Catholic cantons (gathered in the *Sonderbund*) against the radicals' project of forming a full federal government actually led to a short conflict, the Sonderbund War of October–November 1847. The insurgents' defeat paved the way for a fundamental reform of Swiss institutions and the formation of a true federation with a common currency, a truly common market and a common army. A few years later, it was the turn of the United States to build a true federal state, this time at the cost of a much longer and bloody civil war – between 600,000 and one million people died.

Mathieu Calame, author of a remarkable book on France's ambiguous relationship with the EU, reminds us that "the transition from a confederal structure to a centralized or federal entity is generally violent, in particular because of the resistance that local governments and administrations can be capable of when their prerogatives are threatened by a higher authority which, in the long run, condemns them to a secondary role. Thus, federation is only possible when there is an overriding need to federate.[23]"

Switzerland came together in a difficult context where German and Italian unity were threatening to pull away German- and Italian-speaking cantons toward Rome and Berlin (while Paris had always kept a close watch over the francophone cantons). The question therefore arises whether the menacing context described in Chapter 4 will be enough to federate Europe's old nation-states together – not necessarily in a Swiss-style federalization process but conceivably by agreeing on a constitutional framework strong enough to allow Europe to keep malevolent external actors out, while building a common, logical doctrine toward its neighborhood.

Of course, federalization is not the only scenario for Europe and the European Union. The EU's institutional framework could very much stay as it is now – although as we saw at the beginning of this chapter it would probably mean a sclerosis that will continue to debilitate Europe's cohesion. Down the line this would make disintegration more likely, and more deadly. We can also imagine a deconstruction of the EU that we know today, with each state taking back its individual sovereignty to re-create its own environment while the United States pulls out of Europe completely to let every nation fully express its sovereignty. History tells us that these moments of deconstruction of a European political order or security framework, may it be in the 5th century, in 1793–1815 or in 1931–1945, are hardly moments of peace and prosperity. Reform and questioning may not be easy solutions, but they are certainly the least bad options available to European leaders at this stage, and this book suggests that a "federal" jump needs to be envisaged to move forward. It may not follow a linear path – after all, the Indian and American federations are very different in their history and structure, and yet both became viable political constructions. And indeed, the transition would not be without its own risks: further European integration will be met with resistance and skepticism, some of it legitimate, and it may be that tensions lead Europeans to the brink of war. In any case, and even short of a physical war, there will be winners and losers – but if peace is to be preserved on the continent, winners will have to be magnanimous in their victory, while losers should have a chance to redeem themselves by cultivating a "culture of defeat,"[24] digest past events and move forward, as all peoples and regimes have done before them.

★ ★ ★

Depending the alignment of planets and on factors they do not necessarily control, Europeans and their leaders may well be faced with difficult choices in the future, if they are to preserve peace in the EU and beyond, in the larger European continent. Some of these choices may even be between two evils, and the question will therefore be not only what the lesser evil is in the short term, but what can best ensure peace in the long term. These choices will of course be criticized, and European leaders may even be accused of bringing the continent toward civil war. Nevertheless, they are necessary: we saw earlier in this chapter that when unattended, challenges degenerate into war, and inaction would probably in the long term have as dreadful consequences as badly thought action.

As history has made a comeback in Europe, European leaders are being faced with momentous decisions that can decide whether their citizens will experience one (or another) catastrophic scenario described in this chapter, whether war can be contained or whether Europeans can successfully engage in a path to reform that will strengthen peace not only in the EU but also its neighborhood. Of course, reform has its own logic and dynamics – it is indeed a dangerous path: the seventh scenario, despite its optimistic note, does not entirely rule out the possibility of war, which could be as short as the Sonderbund War for Switzerland, or as long and traumatic as the American civil war.

Having answered why Europe needs reform to preserve peace, it remains to be seen how this reform can be led. This will be the subject of our next chapter.

Notes

1 See Richard Shirreff, *2017 War with Russia: An Urgent Warning from Senior Military Command*, London: Coronet, 2016; Douglas Alan Cohn, *World War 4: Nine Scenarios*, Guilford: Rowman & Littlefield, 2016; Graham Allison, *Destined for War: Can America and China Escape Thucydides's Trap*, New York: Mariner, 2018; and finally Lawrence Freedman, *The Future of War: A History*, New York: Public Affairs, 2017.
2 Quoted in Donald Kagan, *On the Origins of War and the Preservation of Peace*, New York: Anchor Books, 1995, p.8.
3 Geoffrey Blainey, *The Causes of War* (3rd edition), New York: The Free Press, 1988, p.264.
4 Antonio Gramsci, *Quaderni del carcere, Edizione critiza dell'Istituto Gramsci*, Turin: Giulio Einaudi, 1975, p. 311.
5 Robert Kagan, *The Jungle Grows Back: America and Our Imperiled World*, New York: Alfred A. Knopf, 2018, p.129.
6 Douglas Alan Cohn, *World War 4: Nine Scenarios*, Guilford: Rowman & Littlefield, 2016, p.134.
7 Alexis de Tocqueville, *L'Ancien Régime et la Révolution*, Paris: Lévy, 1866, p.259.
8 Jared Diamond, *Collapse: How Societies Choose to Fail or Survive*, London: Penguin Books, 2013.
9 Richard Shirreff, *2017 War with Russia: An Urgent Warning from Senior Military Command*, London: Coronet, 2016.
10 Douglas Alan Cohn, *World War 4: Nine Scenarios*, Guilford: Rowman & Littlefield, 2016, p.54.
11 Quoted in Donald Kagan, *On the Origins of War and the Preservation of Peace*, New York: Anchor Books, 1995, p.411.
12 Richard Shirreff, *2017 War with Russia: An Urgent Warning from Senior Military Command*, London: Coronet, 2016, p.13.
13 Graham Allison, *Destined for War: Can America and China Escape Thucydides's Trap?*, New York: Mariner, 2017.

14 In 2019, the European Council of Foreign Relations (ECFR) had YouGov make a 14-country poll in Europe, asking views of Europeans on Foreign policy. See Susi Dennison, *Give the People What They Want: Popular Demand for a Strong European Foreign Policy*, ECFR Policy Brief, September 2019, p.10. https://www.ecfr.eu/page/-/popular_demand_for_strong_european_foreign_policy_what_people_want.pdf
15 Dominic Lieven, *Empire: The Russian Empire and Its Rivals from the Sixteenth Century to the Present*, London: Pimlico, 2003.
16 There were notable exceptions to this "peaceful" breakup, notably Transnistria in Moldova, South Ossetia and Abkhazia in Georgia, where short wars often waged by Russian soldiers have created secessionist republics, and of course the two wars in Chechnya, which claimed several hundred thousand victims, mostly civilians. See Jim Hughes and Gwendolyn Sasse, *Ethnicity and Territory in the Former Soviet Union: Regions in Conflict*, London: Franck Cass, 2002.
17 Marc Lazar et al., *l'Italie contemporaine de 1945 à nos jours*, Paris: Fayard, 2009, p.41.
18 Giuliano da Empoli, *Gli Ingenieri del Caos: Teoria e tecnica dell'Internazionale populista*, Venice: Marsilio, 2019.
19 Thibault Muzergues, *Europe champ de bataille: de la guerre impossible à une paix improbable*, Lormont: Bord de l'eau, 2021, pp.223–226.
20 https://sluggerotoole.com/2018/08/04/paul-gosling-it-costs-more-for-ni-to-be-within-the-uk-than-for-the-uk-to-be-in-eu-feile18/
21 Alexis de Tocqueville, *L'Ancien Régime et la Révolution*, Paris: Lévy, 1866, p.259.
22 Mathieu Calame, *La France contre l'Europe: Histoire d'un malentendu*, Paris: Les petits matins, 2019, p.19.
23 Ibid., p.21.
24 Wolfgang Schivelbusch, *The Culture of Defeat: On National Trauma, Mourning and Recovery*, New York: Picador, 2003.

Bibliography

Allison, Graham, *Destined for War: Can America and China Escape Thucydides's Trap?*, New York: Mariner, 2017.
Blainey, Geoffrey, *The Causes of War* (3rd edition), New York: The Free Press, 1988.
Calame, Mathieu, *La France contre l'Europe: Histoire d'un malentendu*, Paris: Les petits matins, 2019.
Cohn, Douglas Alan, *World War 4: Nine Scenarios*, Guilford: Rowman & Littlefield, 2016.
da Empoli, Giuliano, *Gli Ingenieri del Caos: Teoria e tecnica dell'Internazionale populista*, Venice: Marsilio, 2019.
de Tocqueville, Alexis, *L'Ancien Régime et l.a Révolution*, Paris: Lévy, 1866.
Diamond, Jared, *Collapse: How Societies Choose to Fail or Survive*, London: Penguin Books, 2013.
Freedman, Lawrence, *The Future of War: A History*, New York: Public Affairs, 2017.
Gramsci, Antonio, *Quaderni del carcere: Edizione critiza dell'Istituto Gramsci*, Turin: Giulio Einaudi, 1975.
Hughes, James, and Sasse, Gwendolyn, *Ethnicity and Territory in the Former Soviet Union: Regions in Conflict*, London: Franck Cass, 2002.
Kagan, Donald, *On the Origins of War and the Preservation of Peace*, New York: Anchor Books, 1995.
Kagan, Robert, *The Jungle Grows Back: America and Our Imperiled World*, New York: Alfred A. Knopf, 2018.
Lazar, Marc et al., *l'Italie contemporaine de 1945 à nos jours*, Paris: Fayard, 2009.
Lieven, Dominic, *Empire: The Russian Empire and its Rivals from the Sixteenth Century to the Present*, London: Pimlico, 2003.

Muzergues, Thibault, *Europe champ de bataille: de la guerre impossible à une paix improbable*, Lormont: Bord de l'eau, 2021.
Schivelbusch, Wolfgang, *The Culture of Defeat: On National Trauma, Mourning and Recovery*, New York: Picador, 2003.
Shirreff, Richard, *2017 War with Russia: An Urgent Warning from Senior Military Command*, London: Coronet, 2016.

8
WHAT TO DO?

In his last two books, geographer Jared Diamond studied how societies react to changes in their environment. These changes can be geographic, demographic, political or environmental, but all have in common that they threaten these societies' way of life. The results of Diamond's comparative study all point in the same direction: when societies deliberately choose not to change, they ultimately and invariably condemn themselves to collapse.[1] The only way out of crisis is to change and adapt to a new environment, but this is not without danger. If reform is necessary, it is also necessarily risky, and that risk needs to be weighed in. Because of the risk carried by reform, societies often avoid facing the tough questions until they face upheaval.[2] That moment of intense crisis convinces enough people that the costs of inertia now outweigh the risks of change, thus leading to reform.

This book's thesis is that the EU has reached a crisis point obvious enough to bring about change, and if one is to follow Jared Diamond's thinking, this change should follow a process not too dissimilar to the one we encounter when we, as individuals, are facing our own personal upheavals: the first step is to admit the existence of a crisis, the second is to accept one's own responsibility for resolving it and the third is to isolate the problems that need to be solved, before taking the necessary action – usually the most difficult part of the process. Within this framework, Diamond defines ingredients that can prove crucial for the success of reform: the assistance of other nations, the presence of external models, a strong national identity based on common values, a capacity for honest self-criticism, the memory of past crises overcome, the acceptation of failure, flexibility or a favorable geopolitical environment.[3] The process is painful, and it often takes years, even decades to complete, with the end result sometimes different from what was initially intended. In many ways, this is normal: people and societies do change as they go through reform, and not all of these changes are easy to

DOI: 10.4324/9781003215790-12

anticipate. Nevertheless, considering the other option, which is extinction, the process of reform seems a better solution.

As should have become painfully clear to the reader by now, Europe as a continent with a security architecture and the European Union as a political construct find themselves in this type of crisis that involves profound questioning, and profound (if not necessarily radical) change. The European crisis of today is actually manifold: it is the sum of many crises that have been allowed to accumulate over time, and they together have formed a more-than-decade-long upheaval that should convince Europeans to change. After years of denial, it seems that most European elites have finally realized that there was indeed a crisis in the European Union and more widely in Europe's security architecture. This hopefully can lead the way to the next step: to adapt European institutions to a more dangerous world, with the aim of preserving peace.

These general considerations, however, still leave open the question of what exactly needs to change. The aim of this chapter is to open the debate, in the full knowledge that there will be less consensus on what needs to be done than on the existence (or even the nature) of the crisis. Indeed, the suggested paths that follow might end up producing different results from the ones intended by the author. This is no reason for refraining to think of solutions: when Japan embarked on a series of reforms in the second half of the 19th century, it hoped that the result of modernization would be to expel all Westerners and their corrupting influence on the country. The end result, with the preservation of a specific Japanese way of life but also the assimilation of many Western elements, was probably not foreseen by the inspirators of the reform – nor would the following developments in the 1930s and 1940s that brought Japan to the brink of collapse before a spectacular rebirth.

Even when it is thought out, debated and planned, the path of reform is no bed of roses. Debates about what exactly needs to change often turn acrimonious, and they can even lead to civil war. Switzerland's debate about federalization led to the short war that sealed its union, but it was by no means an exception. While Meiji Japan is often hailed as an incredibly successful model of modernization, reform also meant a short civil war: we often forget that the Meiji reforms encountered extremely violent resistance, even after Commodore Perry's expedition of 1854 made it clear that Japan needed to change if it wanted to keep its independence. The Boshin War that opened the way to the modernizers was violent. Conflict was not so much about the final objective – to kick the Westerners out – but rather on what needed to change: whether the Shogunate should stay or whether a heavily centralized administration should replace it, for example.[4] Today, European elites are faced with a big dilemma: for peace to be preserved in Europe, the EU – and probably NATO as well – must reform. But reform is risky, and it can also lead to a polarization that can in turn bring direct conflict. This book takes the bet that the time is ripe for Europeans to be bald again and that they should take the necessary risks to change – the alternative is to slowly slide into war through sclerosis. The task is not impossible, and the first step that Europeans need to take, collectively (and regardless of their membership to the EU or not), is to face their old demons.

Facing the toxic ex-

Europe has a complex relationship with war. Mars somehow looks like that toxic ex- one cannot really get rid of completely, and who periodically appears to tempt his former partner back into his lure. Today's Europe may not immediately be associated with war, but the latter nevertheless forged the continent as we know it, and between the 16th and 20th centuries it was the intense relationship between Europe and Mars that allowed Europeans to set out and conquer the world. From the 1910s (and probably before), the nature of the relationship deteriorated, leading to a divorce that had to be imposed from outside – a division of the continent into a free zone dominated by the United States, and an Eastern zone governed by the Soviets. Starting in the 1990s, the spread of *pax americana* on almost the entire continent allowed Europeans to take peace for granted, and to believe that they had finally got rid of that toxic ex-.

The Europeans of the late 1990s could have been forgiven to think that they no longer had to worry about Mars, happy as they were to live their own fantasy of the "End of History." But after a financial crisis that moved many levees of power away from Europe and a decade that has weakened it to the point that it is no longer safe in its own marches, Europeans can no longer hide their own vulnerabilities. Many mistakes were made during the period of post–Cold War euphoria, but from a security perspective, the main one was to take all these peaceful developments for granted and believe that, almost naturally, Europe's "soft power" would allow pacifying relationships not only over the whole continent but also in its immediate neighborhood. This blind belief in the infinite potential of soft power completely eluded the fact that, for it to function, it needs to be backed up by hard power. As Ian Morris points out, "without the American globocop protecting the peace, Europe's dovish strategy would be impossible."[5] That globocop saw signs of fatigue in the 2010s, and some even hinted that it might no longer protect Europe as it had until then. As a result, Europeans were naturally left on their own device to try and think a strategy for the future. Not unsurprisingly, considering the continent's recent (and less recent) history, the answer has been paradoxical, sclerotic and at times worryingly close to divisions, deconstruction and tensions that, down the road, could lead to the return of war.

The surprise that many have expressed at these developments is itself surprising. As Donald Kagan reminded us in the 1990s, "International balances can never be still, and it is a folly of statesmanship to assume that they ever could be."[6] This is of course not to say that Turkey's erratic behavior in the Mediterranean, or Russia's threatening stance in Eastern Europe, could have been foretold (although many Greek, Baltic or Polish political and military circles would have something to say about that), but none of the developments witnessed over the past 10–15 years has really been surprising. War may be knocking back on Europe's door, but the truth is that Mars was never very far; it was in Algeria, the Caucasus and in the Western Balkans in the 1990s; in Georgia and the Middle East in the 2000s; it just came a little bit closer in the 2010s and the 2020s, just close enough so that Europeans could remember that it existed.

If those Europeans are to keep the god of war at the door, they need to be able to look at him in the eye. Europeans have been accustomed to thinking of themselves as successful, thanks to an invisible hand, but they now need to discover the usefulness of the "invisible fist,"[7] hard power. Indeed, to quote again Donald Kagan, History has shown that "Good will, unilateral disarmament, the avoidance of alliances, teaching and preaching of the evils of war by those states who, generally satisfied with the state of the world, seek to persevere peace, are of no avail"[8] when internal or external forces are determined to question the established order. Europeans need to understand these fundamental truths of foreign affairs if they are to survive in an environment that has become much more dangerous over the past decade.

If Europeans care about their sovereignty and the preservation of their way of life, they have no choice but to regain awareness of the usefulness and importance of force, even violence, in international relations. For all the talks of a "geopolitical" Europe, there has so far been very little action in this sense, and Europeans have often made beautiful speeches about their willingness to act differently in a changed world, only to find themselves humiliated by foreign powers when it became clear that they did not have the means (or sometimes even a mandate) to follow-up with real action.[9] If the European Union really wants to be geopolitical, it needs to be aware of its own internal geopolitical challenges and fix them. Just as important, the EU also needs to build for itself the means for action, the only thing that in the end counts in geopolitics. As Prussian king Frederick the Great put it in the 18th century, when Germany was an archipelago of small vulnerable states, "diplomacy without arms is like music without instruments."[10] The problem is that, with the exception of France and Britain, European diplomats are precisely trying to do diplomacy unarmed. Faced with a world that has once again become dangerous, they have no choice but to rebuild a capacity to act, so that they can protect themselves and face any eventuality.

Contrary to the cliché popularized by well-intentioned but ill-advised pacifists, preparing for war is not the same thing as wanting war. The Latin adage *Si vis pacem para bellum* – if you want peace, prepare for war – sums up the necessity of being well-armed to preserve peace in an international environment that has actually always been a jungle – a bit more manicured during the years of US global predominance, but a jungle nonetheless. The Latin adage takes more sense when looking at the realities of the Cold War: in 1970, West Germany's defense budget ran at 3.13% of GDP, at a time when the Social Democrats were in power, and Chancellor Willy Brandt was venturing into the first attempts at Ostpolitik. This is not to say that there was no pressure from below to disarm in a post-1968 environment, but Brandt knew that disarmament, when it is unilateral, is a dangerous chimera. What is more, he also understood that his policy of opening up to the East was possible without danger precisely *because* Germany had rearmed itself, because its security was guaranteed by the United States, allowing Berlin to see into its neighbors and rivals eye-to-eye. US President Theodore Roosevelt had found a simpler way to sum up that strategy: "Speak softly and hold a big stick, you will go far." The French and Israelis have also understood this, which is why they have built their own deterrence, so that their hands could be free in case of mortal danger. It seems an adequate strategy for the European Union to adopt if it is to survive in this century, which will most likely remain violent and dangerous.

Preparing for war is not just about producing weapons and building a security framework; it is also about building capacities to increase options when facing adversity. During the Cuban missile crisis, the United States had enough and sufficiently varied armaments and strategies to allow John F. Kennedy to choose between several options: the most radical, the shoot'em out option was kept only as a last resort, as it would have automatically meant war with the Soviet Union. But because the United States had built a wide range of military capacities, there was an alternative at hand, embargo (the squeeze'em out option).[11] The latter was not without risks, and on several occasions during the 13 days that the crisis lasted, it could also have led to war. Nevertheless, it was more prudent, and it worked. But it could only work because Kennedy had the military means to enforce an embargo on Cuba – which led the Soviets to send their missiles back home. If that had not been the case, and provided that Kennedy would have still refused the shoot'em out option, the USSR would have continued to gradually encroach upon vital American interests until either the United States accepted defeat without a fight or until breaking point, when Washington would have had no other choice but to declare war on the Soviet Union, just like France and Britain in 1939 did after the invasion of Poland. As the Belgians of 1918 and 1939 know, when faced with powerful adversaries and without sufficient resources to defend oneself, neutrality counts for nothing, and there are few other options than unconditional surrender.

As dangers grow again in Europe's neighborhood, it is important for Europe in general, and the European Union in particular, to look at war in the eye again – not to wage it inside or outside, but to build deterrence. To complete the Latin saying, if you want peace, prepare for war – to dissuade your enemy from imposing it on you. The logic of armament is like that of survival in the animal world, where the crudest forms of violence are found: chimpanzees are both social and extremely violent animals who, like humans, fight to control territories. The primates will naturally tend to attack weaker adversary, hence the importance of good intelligence and anticipation. If the balance of power is eight to one, the group will attack without hesitation. If the balance of power is reversed, the group will not fight.[12] In spite of millions of years of evolution, the logic is exactly the same among humans, and it therefore seems logical to follow this natural law, in Europe as elsewhere.

Europeans' strategy should therefore be to reappropriate for themselves the concept of violence – not to inflict it upon others but to be able to protect themselves from it, as the Swiss have done during the 20th century. Above all, this means being realistic about the potential outside threats that face the continent and the European Union. This is a difficult exercise, insofar as the EU's strategic rivals are also in other respects partners on whom it is dependent. Unlike the United States, which has been blessed by geography, Europe has to contend with difficult neighbors (who are not difficult because they are necessarily evil, but because their own geographical and cultural constraints push them to have interests that clashes with those of the EU). Today, the EU is too dependent on the outside world, and any such dependence is increasingly seen as a vulnerability by outsiders: Europe is dependent on Russia for its energy, on China for the purchase of basic equipment – something that became painfully clear during the COVID-19 crisis, but also on Turkey and other actors like Libya, Morocco or even, as we came to discover in 2021, on Belarus to keep the migration floodgates closed. Even Europe's overdependence on the United States for its defense to counter those potential security threats is becoming an issue, for Americans as well as Europeans, and it is time for all to understand that action must be taken now to reduce these dependences, which in the end are vulnerabilities – vulnerabilities that can lead to war, as malevolent actors will not hesitate to take aggressive attitudes toward Europeans to see what they can extract from them – until there will be no other choice than war or unconditional surrender.

It is high time for Europeans to take their own security seriously, to strengthen their internal resilience (which also means internalizing the continent's – and the Union's – own geopolitical challenges), and to build a coherent security policy: not only inside the EU but also in its immediate neighborhood. In short, it is a matter of accepting the fact that power and not law once again governs international relations, and that there is no other choice but to play by those rules if one is to survive. This of course does not prevent Europeans (or Americans, for that matter) to seek to pacify international relations whenever possible, but they will only be able to do so if they are in a position of strength. Estonian researcher Kadri Liik made a comment about the EU's policy toward Russia, which is equally valid in Europe's relation toward the rest of the world:

> the EU should change its rhetoric: giving up the position of a paternalistic norm-setter, acknowledging that, at the moment, the European worldview is losing out in the world market of ideas and admitting that the West had made some mistakes would make Moscow treat Europeans a lot more seriously than eloquent moralizing that lacks policy to back it up. 'Say less but to mean it more' would be a good recommendation for the times ahead.[13]

To mean more, however, Europeans need to invest and equip themselves. One does not face physical, economic, information or cyber threats without instruments, and that is why Europeans need to build their own capacities to answer their own security challenges. But it is also important to be clear about the threats, which may be perceived differently depending on the capitals: just like the immediate environment is viewed differently for an American living in Seattle or in Miami (or, for that matter, for an Italian living in Sicily, close to the North African shores and in Alto-Adige, on the border with Austria), security threats can be seen differently in Paris, where the main threat will seem to come from the South, or in Vilnius where it will seem to come from the East. Building a common doctrine that can address both threats should be a top priority for the European Union. In that sense, it should consider itself lucky to rely on the pillar of continental security that is the North Atlantic Treaty Organization.

No salvation beyond NATO

The question of Europe's ability to acquire some form of defense, or strategic autonomy, obviously brings the question of NATO's continued relevance, and of the United States' status within it. After all, what difference could there be between Europe's dependence on Russian hydrocarbons for its energy needs, on Chinese production for its markets, and on the US military for its security? At first sight there is none: all of them are unhealthy for the global bilateral relationship, and even if it is true that Europe has successfully relied on the United States for 30 years (and even more so for its Western part) for its security, Europeans got to understand that this dependence could become problematic if, for some reason, doubts were to arise on the US resolve to defend a territory so far from its mainland during a crisis.

Of course, dependence on the United States for Europe's security is in and of itself not necessarily a bad thing. In the same way as Gaul and Britannia benefited physically and economically from being included in the *pax romana* while contributing to the empire's budget, the EU clearly benefits today from the *pax americana* and the opportunities it provides in terms of trade and security; in its turn (and that was probably not emphasized enough over the past few years), the United States also derives great benefits from protecting Europe, as the integration between the two systems provides welcome consumer markets for American firms, may these be in the automobile sector (Ford is the third-biggest car seller in Europe[14]), the cultural sector (Europeans continue to consume more and more products made in Hollywood, Netflix movies and US TV series) or even in the defense industry. European states have long integrated that one of the conditions of the solidarity of NATO's article 5 is what French Defense Minister Florence Parly called rather cynically "Article F-35," which is that Europeans buy American material not only to have NATO-compatible equipment but also to keep the United States interested in the security of Europe.[15]

Europe's dilemma vis-à-vis the United States is thus twofold: too strong a dependence on the Americans does not allow it to defend the specific European interests (may these be defined in Brussels or in the national capitals); on the other hand, a weakening of American protection and friendship would not only reveal a lack of cohesion and vulnerability at a dangerous time for Europe, but it would also completely upset the continent's security architecture. In Eastern Europe, political leaders know too well how vulnerable a divided region can be when it is left on its own to face Russia. In the South, loss of control over the Mediterranean would bring the sea back to the chaos it experienced numerous times whenever an existing order collapsed.[16] In the Southeast, the relationship with Turkey, which is bound to remain problematic in the foreseeable future, will be better managed if America is involved, precisely because the United States is not more dependent from Turkey on migrations. Further out, if Europe is to stay united and strong when facing China's aggressive commercial approach abroad and protectionism at home, a coordinated approach with the United States will be necessary. For the maintenance of peace around the continent, Europeans need to count on their American ally, because the Europe that exists today is a Europe that America made, and of which they are ultimately the guarantor.

But that should not mean that Europeans should quietly rely on the American globocop without working on their own security. The United States now faces a stiff and ruthless competitor in Asia and it must re-calibrate its engagements in many parts of the world, including Europe. Contrary to what some fantasists may imagine, America is nowhere near abandoning Europe altogether, as recent increases in US contributions to Transatlantic security show. But logically, US policy makers are seeking to convince their allies to adapt their strategies and take their share of the burden, especially in budgetary terms. This of course does not mean that the European and American interests are necessarily perfectly aligned, but when they are or should be (for example on keeping Russian out of the Europe's strategic ecosystem), Europeans need to be able to contribute more – and even on their own, should an unforeseen event not allow the United States to intervene. Strategic autonomy should thus not mean a move away from NATO, but it should mean that, should Europeans face a deadly, immediate danger at their own border, they should have the capacity to protect their interest without having to wait for allies that may come late (or may never come). France and Israel both learnt the hard way (in 1940 for France and in 1948 for Israel) that God helps those who help themselves, and Europeans will be more respected, including by their allies, if they apply this motto to their own security.

There are many reasons why Europeans are reluctant to invest more in their defense, and some of them are perfectly acceptable, like the fear of jeopardizing the balance of power within the continent, something to which the Germans are very attentive from a military point of view (less so on an economic point of view). French, Polish and British diplomats may well criticize the Germans today for not contributing enough of their GDP to their defense, but would they really be reassured if Germany seriously started to re-arm? As former British diplomat Paul Lever puts it, "Although Germany spends less, in terms of GDP per head, on defense than Britain or France, its contribution to the NATO common defense has always been substantial,"[17] so substantial, in fact, that in 2018 Germany's defense budget was almost equivalent to that of Great Britain in absolute terms (49.5 billion dollars, or 1.2% of its GDP, compared to 50 billion for the United

Kingdom, or 1.8% of its GDP), but still far behind that of France (63.8 billion, or 2.3% of our GDP).[18] With an economic power far superior to that of France or Great Britain, a proportional alignment of Germany at 2% of GDP would be enough to upset some actors, in particular the Poles, who already have a lot to do with a much more urgent threat to the East.

Europe is caught between opposing currents: on the one hand, the rise of external threats (which some in Brussels, Paris or Berlin, unfortunately, continue to deny); on the other, an American desire to spend more strategically to defend Europe – while staying engaged in Europe. Last but not least, Europeans need to contribute more to their defense while balancing their budgets, a dilemma that will be difficult as post-pandemic budgets will necessarily have to be reduced – during the Euro-crisis of the 2010s, defense was too often the first line to be cut under austerity policies. There is no solution to this dilemma other than building a European defense closely integrated within the framework of NATO, balancing the necessary integration of European defense systems with US systems and the need for Europeans to be able to act on their own if America wants to pull the resources it needs to face another threat elsewhere. In this sense, the United States has a direct interest in encouraging Europeans to mutualize their defense capacities under one common system – as former Belgian prime minister Guy Verhofstadt points out, the EU's

> "Member States jointly spend just over 250 billion euros on their defense, compared to nearly 560 billion in the United States," so not even half of the US defense budget. But even "with half of their resources, we are not even able to develop 15% of the American military capacity and to deploy operations in conflict zones outside Europe."[19]

Pooling European military capabilities to form a European pillar of transatlantic defense, as long as it is thought and guaranteed *inside* NATO, strengthens rather than weakens the alliance and further relieves the United States so that it can focus on more direct threats for its security. It is thus in the interest of both actors to pursue it.

Realist circles in Washington will obviously object to this proposal: their all-risk insurance is to ensure that neither Europe nor Asia is dominated by a single power – and for them, the European Union is very much the embodiment of such domination. They are, however, mistaken: first, because a united Europe is too diverse and too energy-dependent to ever be a threat to global US power, but also because the United States will need a strong European Union if it is to keep China, its real rival in the 21st century, out of its main zones of interests in the Western peninsula of Eurasia. As they face the most formidable challenge to their power since at least 1940s Japan, the United States cannot afford to estrange a Union that was directly and profoundly inspired by the American experiment, and which could prove a useful (though not always easy) ally if Washington is to win this confrontation with a rising power much more economically potent than the USSR ever was. The Europe that we know today is pretty much the Europe Whole, Free and at peace that America spent almost a century building after the disaster of 1914–1918. Just as it is about to become most useful to the United States in its new fight against tyranny, now is not the time to throw the project down the gutter.

Of course, re-thinking the alliance so that it can be useful to both Europeans and Americans requires trust, and as we will see in the next chapter, that trust has been somewhat weakened by recent (and not-so-recent) events, with each side blaming the other for erratic past behavior. Trust is slow to rebuild, but less sermons (on both sides) and more action would be most useful, regardless of who sits in the White House – and especially when the president is a Republican, more distrustful of any superstructure, especially a foreign one. Continental Europeans have too often in their visits to Washington carefully avoided dialogue with conservative circles (who were too often all too happy not to confront their own contradictions with them), while in the current global geopolitical situation there must be ways for a constructive dialogue between allies to take place. On the European side, the best ways to be convincing to all circles is to actually build capacities on the ground and showing how these are actually complementary to NATO – the first discussions may well be difficult, but facts on the ground matter more in the long-term than communication operations, as many politicians are now starting to understand on both sides of the Atlantic.

We will go back in the next chapter to why decision-makers in Washington and London should support the continued unification of the continent, but on the European side, there are equally appealing reasons why they should cultivate and even strengthen their relationship with the United States, despite the past years of estrangement between Europe and the Anglosphere. Whether they like it or not, Europeans today owe much of their unity (and much of the peace on the continent) to US involvement: Washington encouraged Western Europeans to come together after the war to rebuild their economy and face the Soviet threat. And again, in 1989–2001, it was Washington that offered the necessary guarantees for the reunification of Europe to take place in a pacified environment. The fact that the only area on the continent where the United States did not initially get involved was Yugoslavia, the very region that descended into war, should tell us much about the importance of keeping America involved in the security of the continent. Washington and London are often difficult partners, and they should be told when they are, but they are globally objective allies of the European Union: both are part of the same Western cultural and civilizational ensemble, which allows a relative proximity of points of view and political systems despite the specificity of the Anglo-Saxon system. From a European perspective, it would do great damage to continental security if the "Anglo-Saxons" (a concept that holds negative connotations in both Germany and France) were led to break away from Europe's security architecture, if only because this would open problematic relationships and security dilemmas in the North Sea, the Mediterranean and the Atlantic Ocean. For the EU, a divorce with the Anglosphere would automatically open up a security threat to the Union's West, which it clearly does not need at the moment. If Europe is to build its strategic autonomy, it can only do so inside the Atlantic Alliance, by building a European pillar of NATO. This means keeping open the dialogue with Washington, but also with London, whose military capacity is still formidable at the European level, and who also have a vested interest in stabilizing Europe's marches – and even its core (business is not good with a neighbor at war).

Of course, this does not mean that there will be no disagreements or even disputes between the European Union, and the United States. Indeed, NATO continues to function despite real problems between members of the alliance, including with Turkey, whose ambiguous relationship with the West will also remain a challenge for the foreseeable future. This is the hallmark of collective security, allies do not necessarily have the same interests everywhere and the Transatlantic relationship will continue to go through periods of tensions. Managing these tensions, on both sides, will be more important than trying to hide inevitable divergences between European, British, Turkish and American visions and interests.

The continental "sovereignists" who ardently desire the "Yankees" departure should not despair: that time may come one day. But when this happens, Europeans should know they will be left to their own devices to stay safe – and the past 15 years do not really plead in favor of their capacities to face adversity on their own. If only for that reason, Europeans need to look for ways to strengthen their relationship with the United States without surrendering their interests. To do this, there is no other way than to build proper internal capacities within the framework of NATO – which actually already provides many of the tools Europeans need to build on. European strategic autonomy and the Atlantic Alliance are not necessarily contradictory concepts; they can actually reinforce one another with smart thinking and frank discussions. But while the United States has a role to play in strengthening that link, Europeans should realize that it is their responsibility to build their own resilience and unity, in the defense as well as in the economic sector.

Building Europe's internal market

The idea of building a common European defense may be attractive and necessary, but it inevitably raises the crucial question for any matter of public policy: who will pay? If major economies of scales can be found by pulling resources together rather than duplicating 27 small armies, reorganization, the purchase of equipment and the restructuration of the defense industries ultimately take time – and most importantly money. If there was any further need of proof for NATO's continued relevance, the organization is of huge help in providing a framework for this convergence of equipment, organization and strategy. But if Europe is to build its own strategic autonomy, a very heavy investment will be required – and Europeans will have to pay for it.

Who will pay? This question is one of the most problematic in today's European Union, and it highlights North–South divide. We saw it in the early days of the coronavirus crisis, when even in a desperate period for the continent's economy, there was a strong reluctance from countries like Austria, Finland or the Netherlands (among others) to pay for keeping the economies of Southern or Central Europe afloat – they certainly had a point that the money could not be given out without any conditions, but the original reluctance to give out *any* money showed how little solidarity existed between the EU member-states. Subsequent events in 2021, which showed that Northern European countries were not necessarily as virtuous as they may have thought they were,[20] may have for now helped to smooth things out, but it does not mean that Europeans have miraculously become more solidary toward each other. If the Euro-crisis of the 2010s is any indication, the real moment of truth for the European Union is not the moment where crisis hits and there is no other solution but to support the economy, but rather the following years, when the economy will still need a stimulus while demand will grow for austerity.

Let's be clear: a repeat of the austerity episode of the 2010s would lead to disaster. One cannot hope that a patient will recover after a heart attack by following a strict diet of bread and water (although neither will he get better with a burger and alcohol diet). Austerity is not only a bad thing for the general coherence of Europe as an economic and political ensemble, it is also a problem of security, as defense spending is too often the first victim of austerity policies (it definitely was in the 2010s). The case of the sale of the Port of Piraeus to a company controlled by the Chinese State is a stark reminder that austerity also has geopolitical implications, and it is clearly in the interest of Europeans to resolve this kind of problem among themselves, so that the ports of Genoa, Trieste, Taranto and others do not end up in foreign hands; as Austrian economist Ludwig Von Mises rightly pointed out, "It may sometimes be expedient for a man to heat the stove with his furniture. But he should not delude himself by believing that he has discovered a wonderful new method of heating his premises."[21]

If forcing a fellow member-state to sell off its most valuable assets to a malign foreign actor is certainly not a good policy, refraining from austerity does not in itself solve the problem of who will pay for Europe's long-term recovery. Solidarity cannot be decreed; it is built by the feeling of sharing a common destiny, as well as rational economic reasoning. As the recovery plan is rolled out in the EU, the conditions for solidarity between members need to be created so that what we call today a Union can effectively become one. As many have discovered during the crisis, one's financial difficulties are not necessarily the result of laziness or fraudulent behavior. And it is becoming increasingly clear that Northern European countries are currently doing well principally because of their surplus trade balance toward countries that will not necessarily be as open in the future. Nokia, BMW or Philips managed to sell many of their products to the rest of the world because they had made an extra effort of competitiveness on the market, but also because they took the benefit of a currency that was *de facto* undervalued for their products. This advantage is losing relevance, and outside economies are closing their markets fast, particularly on high-added-value products like German cars. The Trump cycle was not a mirage: the world is moving away from globalization, international trade and interdependence, and more into self-sufficiency, introspection and, to a certain extent, mercantilism.

Contrary to what many people would expect, the move away from openness and free trade actually does not date from the election of Donald Trump: it started in the late 2000s, with the United States reversing its policy of over-reliance on imported oil to fuel its economy. In just a few years, between the end of the Bush presidency and the start of the Trump mandate, the United States went from being mostly an importer of oil and gas to being a hydrocarbon superpower, now exporting energy ressources aplenty. Donald Trump only accelerated the trend of economic decoupling through trade wars and a voluntaristic policy that, at least when it came to China, was mostly kept intact by the Biden administration. Everything in the COVID-19 crisis, from the scramble for masks and respirators in 2020 to the vaccine nationalism of 2021 (in which Europe's biggest problem was actually that it had not been able to develop its own vaccine), only confirmed and accelerated this trend for a demand of more self-reliance. If current trends continue, calls to autarky may soon become a mainstream economic discourse around the world.

In 2005, Tony Blair had told his Labour Party conference that wanting to discuss globalization was like asking "whether autumn should follow summer."[22] He could just as well make that argument about protectionism and economic nationalism to free traders these days. The current drive toward self-reliance and global compartmentalization is currently irreversible, and it poses a problem for Europe: while autarkic tendencies may (imperfectly) suit sub-continental nations such as China, India or the United States, it is very poorly adapted to the size of small European nation-states, who have historically thrive thanks to globalization. Self-sufficiency only makes sense if one has enough raw materials for energy needs and a large enough market to consume one's products. The European Union currently has neither: its dependence on outside sources of energy makes it more expensive than elsewhere to move people and machineries, and its market is still way too compartmentalized to produce the economies of scale that the US, Chinese or Indian economies can produce.

Europe itself has gone through phases of inward-looking focus on self-reliance in the past, and these do not plead for peace on the continent; the last one happened during the 1930s, and actually exposed all the raw products that Europe did not have at its disposal: the answer at the time could only be reliance on the colonies (as in France and Britain), or territorial expansion and the acquisition of a *lebensraum*, which brought Italy, Germany, but also Japan and to a certain extent Soviet Russia to aggressive behavior. For countries of relatively small size (as all European nation-states are) and without natural energy reserves, the global trend toward self-sufficiency is a deadly poison: once the Chinese markets will be *de facto* closed to most European products, Northern European exporting economies will no longer have outlets for their growth in China, and they will perhaps be also less competitive on the Indian and the US markets. Retreating toward a purely national (or even subregional) economic model will only increase external dependence, and will risk making Europe, especially its peripheries, a battlefield for external economic (and, down the road, political) influence.

The current trend toward self-sufficiency rewards large companies able to supply strong domestic markets: these in turn enable companies to limit their production costs and rely on a strong domestic market that may from time to time be supported by government intervention. The larger the market, the stronger the supporting state, the more efficient the economy will be. There are different ways to envisage having such a large market. One is to think of the United States as the leader of a vast "oceanic" world that would bring together the Pacific and the Atlantic oceans, with two large free trade zones encouraged (and dominated) by the United States. This was the project of the Obama years, with the transatlantic (TAFTA) and trans-pacific (TPP) free trade zones, which went down even before the US presidential elections of 2016.[23] It now looks highly unlikely that the Biden administration will pick the project where it was left – the world has moved on, and other solutions need to be found.

The other option, probably more viable because it has already been sketched out by the common market, is the deepening of the EU's common market to make it a true internal market, by supporting the emergence of a number of European "champions" in strategic areas, able to compete on the world market, while European internal consumption would be encouraged. This would allow Northern Europe to rebuild outlets closer to home, and Southern Europe to return to a path of growth – provided that financial aid is also thought of as assistance to structural reforms capable of allowing Southern economies to find a complementary model of growth (and not to align or comply with Northern standards in areas where they will never be able to compete).

More than a simple recovery fund, the European Union needs a 15-year-long European Marshall Plan to modernize Europe's peripheries, with concrete projects that will allow the population to see real results in their lives. Of course, this would mean that the prime beneficiaries of this long-term investment effort would be the Southern (and potentially also Eastern) economies, who would be able to finance modernization by stimulating their domestic demand and increasing their tax revenues (which would necessarily involve reforms, although much has already been done in places like Greece). But Northern countries would also benefit as a growing economy in these regions would also mean customers ready to buy quality products from Northern Europe. The Marshall Plan of 1947 was not a purely disinterested operation: if its primary goal was to keep Western Europe afloat to make sure it would not fall prey to communist subversion, the other idea was that at least parts of the investments would come back to America as Europeans would buy US products. This is exactly what happened, and how both US and European growth fueled each other until the 1960s.

As the world turns away from globalization and moves toward self-reliance, it would be folly to go against the current. This inward tendency may not be the best for the long-term wealth of nations, but for the foreseeable future it will be seen by many (including in Europe) as a necessary corrective to the abuses of globalization. With a general trend toward it and at least some popular support for it, the only thing Europeans can hope to do is to control the movement, by formulating intelligent policies that would allow Europeans to regain some autonomy while limiting long-term costs. This cannot be done at the minuscule scale of the 19th- or 20th-century European nation-state, as European companies now have to compete with the industrial mastodons of the United States, China and soon India. The examples of pubic-owned Airbus, but also the private-sector Ericsson or Stellantis show just how competitive European firms can be when they are allowed to concentrate in specific markets where only the major players can survive. The construction of these European champions will only be possible thanks to the transformation of the common market into a true internal market, where demand will be strong enough for supply, so as to reduce European dependencies and vulnerabilities. This would represent the completion of the single market and would require long-term investments, which will need to be paid for. Here again, reminding those who will ultimately have to support these budgets that they are not only doing it for others, but also for themselves, will be a first step toward the construction of a true European market capable of competing in the global economy.

Eurosceptics will answer that the creation of this internal market is a chimera, practically impossible and economically insane. In the current trend of self-sufficiency, the move toward concentration actually follows economic logic. As for the chimera, those who plead against concentration are the same who, back in the 19th century, would have pleaded that neither Switzerland nor Italy nor Germany could form a common or internal market, let alone a nation. None of these entities had fully constituted by the mid-19th century, and in the case of the latter two, they did not even exist on Europe's map until the second half of the century. German unity, which we now take for granted, was achieved mostly thanks to the slow construction of a single market between the German principalities that were not part of the Austrian crown – the *Zollverein*. This was by no means an easy process. Guy Verhofstadt is right to point out that opponents of German economic integration advanced very similar arguments against the *Zollverein* to those heard in Eurosceptic circles today – they foretold insoluble problems for the German regions and city states and advocated "the primacy of the regional interests over the general interest, warming against the laziness of factory owners in Southern Germany, beer-full all day long and taking advantage of the good folk's hard work in the Ruhr area."[24] Verhofstadt is admittedly a passionate advocate of European integration, but his claims have echoes in the discourses of the time, including with the father of German unity, Bismarck, who for a long time actually opposed it. In 1848, he told Hermann Wagener that "We are Prussian and we intend to remain Prussians [...] We do not want to see the kingdom of Prussia contaminated by the frivolous and vitiated carelessness of the South Germans."[25] At least until the war of 1870, Germans were above all Bavarian, Saxon, Hessian or Prussian citizens. The sense of belonging to a common German nation was forged not only through the construction of common cultural referents, but also through the creation of common economic solidarity, commenced with the Zollverein and consolidated after 1870 by the construction of an internal market and a system of social protection. Only by creating these solidarities was Germany able to then withstand the disasters of 1918 and 1945 as a nation. Without it, it would probably not have survived, and Europe would look much different today. If the European Union were to fail to build solidarity between Europeans, it may not survive the next shock, and this would most surely open the path to war in Europe.

In 1867, as Italy had almost completed the great unification movement that came to be known as the *Risorgimento*, Piedmont's former prime minister Massimo d'Azeglio wrote in his memoirs a famous phrase: "Italy is made. Now we must make the Italians."[26] The fact that Italy as a country was formed before a strong civil society (or a strong state) formed itself is often quoted as one of the original sins of Italian national identity,[27] but it has not impeded Italians from building their nation like every other European. Their Republic is sometimes accused of being "neither hated, nor loved or adulated, it just exists,"[28] to use French historian Marc Lazar's words, but it has so far shown remarkable resilience in the face of adversity – may be because it has been surprisingly effective in making Italians in the way d'Azeglio had wished. After more than a half-century of existence, it is time for Europe to finish making itself, and to make Europeans. Building a real internal market is the first step, and monetary union will necessarily call for a federal jump.

Europe's "F" word

The word "Federalism" is a bad word in European politics. It is taboo everywhere else but in Brussels, where it is often used by Eurosceptics to show that the European project was made to kill the nations that naturally constitute Europe, even though these nations exist only since the 19th century. On the other side of the spectrum, too many pro-Europeans have used the term to justify the acquisition of regulatory powers that Brussels often does not even have the means to enforce. American Conservatives see in this the proof that the European Union project is only a continentalist, centralizing project like the USSR – this of course overlooks the fact that the EU in its current form is now completely controlled by the member-states governments through the EU Council, with a budget at only 1% of nation-states' GDP, and without own resources of its own – history has seen scarier versions of absolutist leviathans.

American politicians and think tankers should know better. The Western federal model from which the EU project derives has little to do with the fake socialist federations of the past, and everything to do with the democratic federations like the United States, Canada, Switzerland or India that have precisely constituted themselves to manage territorial or ethnic diversity – something that Europe has aplenty. A democratic federation implies strong decentralization, and thus a relatively weak central state – in Europe, a common misunderstanding about the US central government is that it is powerful in areas where it has a monopoly (defense, foreign affairs, etc.), but rather weak (or even very weak) on other issues. When it comes to internal affairs (including, as we discovered during the 2020 presidential elections, electoral rules), the federated states are often more powerful than the federal state. This is why a good record as a state governor comes as an asset for US presidential candidates – the presidential office often involves resolving a different set of issues than a governor's, but experience as a state executive comes in handy to approach complex issues and deal with powerful other branches of government. In recent history, four of the last nine US presidents were state governors – Jimmy Carter of Georgia, Ronald Reagan of California, Bill Clinton of Arkansas and George W. Bush of Texas, while many presidential candidates, past and future, are also former governors. Of course, these governors now have to compete with Senators, whose prestige has risen over the past decades, but in the race to the White House, former governors can often put forward their experience in running their states – and voters know they often have more power in their home state to innovate than the central government: with all its flaws and merits, Obamacare was largely inspired by the plan Mitt Romney had implemented to extend social security coverage when he was Governor of Massachusetts.[29] Somehow more anecdotal, as every European who has experienced driving a car in the United States will know, turning right at a red light is actually allowed all over US territory (after a stop and with no traffic incoming from the left). The story of this peculiarity is interesting, because it is a result of America's federal system: the rule originated in California, where some whacky libertarians managed to convince their co-citizens that it was worth being tested. It was thus tried and implemented in California first, and success meant that the policy was then extended to the whole of the United States.[30] Federalism is not only about top-down decision-making, but also a way to provide bottom-up pressure for reform.

Since it started to be thought a viable institutional solution in the late 18th century, federalism has become the norm for managing diversity in territories like those of North America, where three states have adopted it (the United States, Canada and Mexico). But is the model useful for Europe? The question can be politically charged, both for some Anglo-nationalist circles who believe that only Anglo-Saxon models of federalism are viable and for European Jacobins who resent decentralization and the dilution of state authority. Yet multinational Switzerland, Germany and Austria are all examples of fully functional federalist states in the heart of Europe that respect individual and territorial liberties and are uniquely effective – so effective in fact that many European states have moved toward federal or near-federal solutions since the end of the Cold War to deal with geographic, economic and identity diversities.

One could of course answer that in the case of Germany and Austria, federalism was actually imposed by the American occupation in 1945, but this explains neither the move toward federalism in Italy after the 1980s (albeit in a very specific and Italian way) nor Swiss federalism, which actually predates America's move from a confederation to a federation. Even in the case of Austria and Germany, the idea of an import of federalism is only partly true: after the catastrophe of Nazism, the German and Austrian elites felt that America was the natural model to rebuild their institutions, but they also could count on the historical memory of proto-federal precedents, including in the old Holy Roman Empire.[31]

This of course does not mean that federalism is a panacea: like other federations today, the United States has no shortage of problems and moving to (or toward) a more federal model does create new issues to deal with. But much like democracy, it is the least bad of all options thus far tested to manage diversity while promoting freedom. Today, of the ten most populous countries in the world, five of them (India, the United States, Brazil, Nigeria and Mexico) are federations,[32] and one (Russia) at least claims to be one. The match between democracies and federations is no accident: almost by definition, federations provide the checks and balances that are necessary for a functioning modern democracy. All democracies may not be federations, and not all federations are perfect democracies, but it seems that federalism is indeed the best way to reconcile democracy with size and diversity. In the case of the European Union, it would be a way to keep in check the Brussels bureaucracy (always an obsession of the Eurosceptics, and not necessarily for wrong reasons) without having to surrender all powers to the nation-states as is currently the case. Some may of course argue that a federation, which presupposes the presence of a federal state far more powerful than the confederal structure we have in Europe today, is not suitable for an area as diverse as Europe, where languages and traditions vary from country to country. But it is precisely a federal state that allows Switzerland to govern relations between cantons that a priori have nothing in common except a history that has been reinvented to form a coherent national novel.

The confederal model that the European Union is currently following has no future. Since the rise of centralized states after the Renaissance, confederations have never lasted long, mostly because they end up producing much lesser capacity against more centralized models of governance. Indeed, the only modern example of a confederation in Europe is Bosnia-Herzegovina, whose ungovernability is increasingly becoming a problem for the Western Balkans. Contrary to what many Europeans had wished in the 1990s, all evidence points toward the idea that the coming quarter century will be once again dominated by states, not multilateral organizations, as their necessity (but also that of constraining their power) has become evident after the past financial and health crises. The problem of a confederal structure is precisely that it has no federal state – and it is precisely what Europe lacks today. The coronavirus crisis that we have just experienced has just given more proof of this: the only European institution that really and quickly took the necessary emergency measures was the European Central Bank (ECB), the only truly federal structure in the current European Union. Its swift and decisive action to avoid a new speculative attack on the Euro contrasts with the general debacle that marked the original member-states response – indeed, it is probable that without the firm response of the ECB in 2020, EU member-states would not have been able to agree on a recovery fund, and the European Union as we know it would have probably ceased to exist.

The European Union has often been the target of criticism and outrage over the past decades – often for being cosmopolitan and not being a "Europe of nations." And yet, it is the confederal model, with national governments dominating the European Council, that renders the EU powerless: the current hypertrophy of the Council makes any rapid decision-making at 27 almost impossible, with difficult compromises that too often in recent years have actually satisfied nobody. With a parliament without the power to constitute the Union's own resources and a Commission that is now mostly doing the Council's bidding, the Union is dysfunctional and reflects only one will: that of the governments of the member-states. The result is that the countries at the economic "heart" of Europe (which are generally the richest) can enjoy unparalleled authority within a mostly powerless institutional framework. This setup is doubly negative, because it hinders the EU's capacity to act, while the formal dominance of the "big" states only provides frustration to the peripheral states – the resulting resentment has grown everywhere in Europe, in the margins but also at the center.

The confederal model is ill-suited to Europe's current situation, in part because it does not deliver on efficiency, but also because it seems to worsen rather than solve the German question, and the center versus periphery dilemma. A federal (or at least more federal) solution actually solves the problem by introducing institutional checks and balances that, if measured well, can actually both preserve efficiency (that's the role of the federal government) and accountability (which should be the role of a parliament with real powers). More generally, a federal solution has the merit of caging the bigger states in an institutional framework that may consolidate their dominance, but also checks it through other institutions. In a construction that has sought to define itself as an "emporium of law," it is surprising how little thinking has been put into the institutionalization of checks and balances as a way to make Brussels, and the EU work.

France and Germany may find themselves hesitant to accept (let alone promote) this institutional framework. But in reality, such a framework would actually preserve their power more than it would constrain it: in federal frameworks like that of India, Switzerland or the United States, there is no doubt that the most populous and the richest states have more power –it is checked only by the federal government (who thinks for the good of the whole ensemble, not a few rich units) and the federal parliament. The United States would probably not have been able to function in periods of high polarization like today without this federal system that assures that the political debate will not always be decided in the states of New York, Texas and California (although it often is), but that other states like Ohio, Iowa or North Carolina may have a say. Of course, the system is not perfect, but it seems preferable to the opaque processes of bargaining between member-states that we saw in 2019 for the appointment of the President of the Commission: the bigger countries helped themselves, left a few consolation prizes for a few and nothing to the others. In a federal system based on the separation and balance (or rather an institutionalized conflict) of powers, Germany (and to a lesser extent France) would remain dominant, but it would be imprisoned in institutions that would force the center to listen to more peripheral voices, however unpleasant those might be for the Brussels bubble. All in all, it is perhaps better for everyone that a real federal government be installed in Brussels and controlled by the member-states (Council) and importantly by the emanation of the people (European Parliament), rather than giving the illusion of intergovernmental governance where Germany is systematically made responsible for any decision – or lack of decision that the EU makes.

If the European Union is to take a federal step forward, the question of its own resources cannot be avoided. Today, the EU budget is paid by the member-states at the level of 1% of their GNP, far from the 21% GNP of the American and Canadian federal budgets, and very far from that of member-states: at €148 billion, the EU's budget for 2019 did not even reach the size of the national budget of Belgium or Austria.

Not only are resources insufficient, but they also largely escape the democratic control of the European Parliament, since the latter can vote on expenditures, but not on revenues. Can one actually qualify it as a parliament when it has been given none of the prerogative of sovereign legislative chambers? Currently, the European Parliament does not levy taxes, it cannot propose laws (these are co-created by the Commission and the Council) and its control over the other institutions is minimal, even though France and Germany have recently seen that under certain circumstances, they could derail some of their plans, such as the Comprehensive Agreement on Investments with China. If the European Union really wants to be effective, the powers of the Commission must be enhanced. If it wants to be more democratic, the parliament will need to take more powers and grow teeth to do so, because no other institution will willingly devolve power to it, except under pressure.

The European Union today needs a federal leap, and the good news is that other confederations have made that jump in history, not least the United States and Switzerland, even though the price to pay in both cases was war, something that Europe wants to avoid. The constitution of a federation is in itself the institutionalization of a confrontation, that between the rights of the member-states, and those of a central government, in other words, between the particular and the general interest. If the initial step of federalization in Switzerland and the United States were resolved through war, all the other developments in this long-term conflict between center and peripheries were resolved peacefully. Europe's situation currently resembles much more than that of 18th-century America, when opaque deals were made in "the room where it happens" to decide about the mutualization of debts of federated states – in that case, murky politics and their following institutionalization into rule of law decided of the federal jump of the then not-so-united states. The tension between state "rights" and federal power never really disappeared in American politics, for better or for worse: if the civil war was fought in part over state rights to preserve slavery or not, the New Deal, with massive federal budgetary intervention, included a conflict between Washington and the states – and between the different branches of government. As economist Ashoka Mody recalls, in 1933, President Roosevelt had to fight hard with Congress to

> "establish a substantial central budget, about four per cent of Gross National Product, to support states on the brink of bankruptcy following the carnage of the Great Depression. The states received these federal funds as grants – not loans – and then distributed them to the most affected populations, creating purchasing power and prolonging the economic stimulus. These transfers from the richest to the poorest states were a mechanism for sharing the suffering; they were crucial to economic recovery."[33]

Today, the New Deal represents a model of good management of federal tensions between states and federal government – and it rings surprisingly contemporary to current European debates.

Institutions are a key to making Europe function better and to resolving the current internal geopolitical problems that the European Union faces. This will not be without tensions, because all politics is about the management of conflict. Those can sometimes overspill into war, and modern democratic norms have been developed precisely to avoid this. The idea of federalism is not to build an absolutist Leviathan that would "force" redistribution between member-states, but rather to imprison that would-be Leviathan in an institutional framework that allows it to balance rather than promote the specific interests of its members. This is what US federalism is all about, but closer to Europeans, this is also the key to the success of Swiss federalism: in the end, the vanquished cantons of the *Sonderbund* accommodated rather well of "Bern's diktat," which from a Swiss perspective was always preferable from that of Berlin, Paris or Rome.[34] That principle actually already exists in EU law – it is called subsidiarity, an import from German federalism, and it is because it has been only seldom applied over the past 20 years that it has been ineffective. There are many reasons for this: the word is often (rightly) considered as too technocratic, but the weakness of European society, as a nation-maker, is also an issue. This may not be that much of an issue in itself – after all, most of Europe's nation-states, may they be Italy, France or Germany, actually built their institutions before they built their nation. But no contemporary system can survive without a sense of common belonging – which can be acquired either through solidarity and state redistribution or through war. If Europe wants to avoid the latter, it will have to build the former.

Federalism and nationalisms

The big problem with the European Union today is that its (con-)federalism has been built upside down: in Switzerland, the United States or India, the federated states have pooled much of their regal activities (diplomacy, army, homeland security) at federal level, and just enough economic power to create an internal market. Europe has done exactly the opposite: as Matthieu Calame puts it,

> "Because of the history of its build-up, today's European Union is an inverted pyramid of subsidiarity: the Union has decision-making power for the composition of chocolate throughout the continent, but has very little power in terms of defense, social policy or even banking regulation. [...] A butcher feels more closely supervised for his sausage production than a bank for the elaboration of its financial derivatives."[35]

This upside-down federalism is naturally a source of countless arguments by Eurosceptics, as they take frustrating regulatory issues at micro-level as proof that the EU is not working (in the process, they often forget to remind their constituents that these rules have often been adopted as the result of negotiations between members-states, which their own government signed up to). To a certain extent, Eurosceptics are right: there are sectors in which the European Union should do less to constrain European citizens. But that doesn't mean that Europe shouldn't do more to protect its citizens, and develop the attributes of a true federal state.

In many ways, the problem of today's EU is that it claims and wants to be involved in pretty much everything, while it is often too weak to really make a difference anywhere. This puts member-states in an ideal situation where they get to decide (in the Council) what they want from the European Union and, whenever that decision is unpopular, they can always get away with it by blaming the European Union. Although this kind of politics is inevitable in any federal or confederal system, it is much more difficult to escape the blame when there is a clearer distribution of competence. This is of course not to say that Brussels is powerless, but in many respects, the "capital" of Europe looks much more like a built-up version of the 1850s Washington than the "omnipotent" American capital of 1940. Would a clearer division of powers go necessarily in the way of further centralization toward Brussels? It would be desirable in some areas, less in others, but it would most importantly make the irresponsible blame game of some member-states much more difficult, which in itself would do a lot to appease current debates about Europe.

The tragedy of the post-1991 European Union is that it has built itself on the premises of an extremely ambivalent relationship with its constitutive nations and nation-states. The idea that a soulless and neutral superstructure would naturally complete with and sometimes outgrow outdated national infrastructures is one of the major mistakes that was made with regard to the Brussels build-up over the past 30 years. This has led to a divorce between the European ideas of liberalism and civic nationalism, which Ivan Krastev and Stephen Holmes have described in their *Light That Failed*[36] – this in turn has meant that liberalism could not tame nationalism when needed and vice versa. For Conservatives like John J. Mearsheimer, the problem goes even deeper: the absolute neutrality of a liberal state is absolutely incompatible with the sense of belonging that populations require for collective action – in other words, there can be no state today without a nation, and no state without nationalism either.[37]

How can Europe reconcile itself with nationalism today, when the European Union was built in many ways in reaction to the disasters that an unleashed nationalist craze had caused on the continent between 1914 and 1945? One solution, proposed by the populist right, is to deconstruct Europe and give back sovereignty to each European state. The proposal is not absurd, and it would have the merit of clarity – at the price, however, of a compartmentalization of economies that is doing more harm than good to the common wealth – we have seen it during the pandemic. A return to the nation-state, while possible in theory, would not only be difficult to achieve practically. It would also lead to a full balkanization of Europe: in an epoch in which ensembles are closing in on each other, the result would surely be further barriers to trade, and a general impoverishment that would actually raise social tensions and make war in Europe more likely.

Another suggestion would be to stop confronting the concept of a European Union with the nation by recognizing the obvious: the EU represents a civilizational ensemble that should have its own government, but which at the same time can only be built and constituted with nation-states as its base. A federal European identity (which needs to be built) does not have to be set against a national identity, it can actually complete it, and both can mutually reinforce each other. The problem with nationalism at the beginning of the 20th century (and the one that is developing right now under the disguise of sovereignty) is its exclusivity: nationalism is based on the myth that one can only be French, German, Italian and Polish, and nothing else. This was always a myth: even while remaining completely loyal to Germany, one can also perfectly feel Bavarian, a citizen of Munich, or someone belonging to a smaller community (neighborhood, interest group, etc.). The important thing is that all these identities complement each other, and as far as the common identity between Bavarians and Germans is concerned, complementarity was not being obvious until the end of the 19th century, and even beyond: Bismarck's words on the "frivolous and vitiated carelessness of the South Germans" date from 1848 and were principally directed at Bavarians, who until 1918 remained a separated kingdom inside Germany, with its separate king, diplomacy and even up to three autonomous army corps.[38] The Great War completed rather abruptly the slow integration of Bavaria into Germany, but this did not prevent Bavaria from keeping its own identity, whether from a cultural, political or administrative point of view: even today, Bavarian tourists visiting other German towns are often greeted by a humorous *Wilkommen in der Bundesrpublik Deutschland*.

One of the constitutive elements of Europe – its definition even – is its diversity. This does not make governance easier, but Switzerland is an example that shows to Europeans that a common good can be achieved in a diverse environment. Today, no one would dare to deny the Alpine republic its status as a nation (nor to invade it, as the Swiss are armed to the teeth and finance an extremely efficient army[39]). Yet the particular identities of each language community and each canton is fiercely defended by the Swiss themselves. Although Switzerland is a multilingual and, in many respects, a multinational country, nobody would deny its coherence or its common identity. And if German speakers, French speakers, Italian speakers and Romansch speakers fiercely oppose each other in Bern, they are just as united when it comes to dealing with the Germans, the French and the Italians (among others).

Can Europe build its civilizational consciousness, its own "national" identity in the way the Swiss did? This would require time and a strong institutional arrangement, but this should not be enough. Europeans are united by a common civilization, but that is not the same as a nation. To function effectively, a federal model needs to build intellectual and emotional solidarities between Europeans. When it comes to the institutions, at the end of the 1980s, Jacques Delors proposed to synthesize the concepts of nationalism(s) with federal institutions, by proposing a "European federation of nation-states."[40] To do this, Delors took inspiration from the American institutional framework and proposed that the European Parliament becomes a low chamber like the House of Representatives (representing Europeans in all their diversity), the intergovernmental council to be reformed into a powerful Senate and the Commission to become an executive with its own powers, checked by the two others. The proposal was immediately refused by Margaret Thatcher, who opposed Delors' threefold proposal her famous "no, no, no."[41] Now that Britain is out of the European Union, the timing seems right to revisit the concept, which is in many ways aligned with the principle of the founding fathers, including that of looking West for inspiration.

The Federation of Nation-States suggested here should not be seen as an absolute, exclusive endorsement of the nation-state. Western federalism is based on a quasi-permanent conflict between the federal state and the federated entities, and its remarkable feature is that these conflicts are settled in courts, in political joust and in elections, not on the battlefield. Just as war is too serious a business to be left to generals, the nation is too serious a thing to be left to Europe's old nation-states. This is why the EU must get to the task of building a common European identity – an identity of civilization, of a shared history that would start in ancient Greece and not in 1945 and a common destiny. This requires the creation of a European grand narrative that gives coherence to the history of the continent and allows everyone, beyond national experience, to answer the question "where are we going" by seeing meaning in the trajectory of the continent, beyond the founding act of March 25, 1957, which is far too modern and technocratic to incite a real sense of belonging. Of course, skeptics will reply that this narrative can only be artificial, but it will be no more artificial than William Tell, an entirely fictional character who became the symbol of the Swiss nation,[42] or the famous myth of the Gallic origin of France, the country that actually took the name of its Germanic invaders in the 5th century. Of course, this does not mean that European nations are purely artificial products, but they draw their sense of belonging from a re-interpreted, a "re-invented" past, as Anthony Smith suggests in his theory of nationalism.[43] In its history, Europe has the elements of glory, victory, but also defeat and division that can make for an epic common narrative, from Charlemagne to Robert Schuman, from King George of Poděbrady to Richard Coudenhove Kalergi, from the cathedral builders to the nation-makers of the 19th century. Agreeing on such a narrative and defusing it through society is a long effort that must be sustained over time, but the history of post-*Sonderbund* Switzerland shows that it can be done on European soil. The project is certainly ambitious, and it will be a long-term project that will take generations to complete (if nation-building ever stops). In many ways, Europe must seek to turn (to some extent) individuals belonging to the same civilization into European citizens, in much the same way as France (or Italy) had to turn peasants into Frenchmen (or Italians) in the late 19th century.[44]

A good starting point would be to get the EU to work out of the Brussels bubble so as to prove its usefulness not only to the elites, who now seem to derive most of the benefits of EU integration but to the population at large. Too often, solutions thought in Brussels make sense and facilitate the life of internationally oriented professionals, but leave ordinary folks without much tangible evidence of the benefits of EU integration. When the EU decides to abolish the exorbitant charges for mobile Internet access within its territory, this is of course a good thing, and another step toward a single market. But the measure mainly benefits the elites who regularly move from one country to another, not the large majority of European citizens for whom travel abroad, even within the Union, remains the exception rather than the norm. The European Recovery Fund is showing just how impactful a well-thought, concrete policy like this can turn the political tables: in Italy, the simple announcement of the availability of this money has been enough to turn the most Eurosceptic political leaders like Matteo Salvini into stakeholders of the project. The populist leader was in this case pushed to embrace support for a pro-European government because his base, made of small and medium entrepreneurs in Northern Italy, knew perfectly well that EU money was a lifeline for their own business and their own livelihood.

The European project must extend from its current elite-status project to become more palpable for the ordinary European. While the Erasmus program is often held up as a model of European integration, it is mainly aimed at wealthier sections of the population: French sociologist Jérôme Fourquet has pointed out that

> "according to the Erasmus + Observatory, out of the cohort of students leaving the school system in 2010, 45% of the children of executives went

abroad during their studies. This was the case for only 25% of the children of employees and 21% of the children of workers."[45]

These numbers are very telling of the parallel lives that communities in Europe are living. They lead those living a comfortable lifestyle and connected to the wider world to embrace the European Union, while those who stay behind have no concrete link to Europe, and therefore believe more easily the fairy tales vehiculated by Eurosceptics about the evil of the EU. As long as systems like Erasmus do little to include children of employees and workers in their programs, as long as those with a manual work background will have no concrete evidence that the European Union works for them and not only elites far away in Brussels, adhesion to the European Union will remain a fragile construct.

The problem, as always in EU politics, is that to reach these marginalized communities, the European Union needs to rely on the nation-states, who are always happy to blame the same European institutions when things go wrong, but take for themselves all the credit when things go right. But reliance on the nation-states can be a blessing rather than a curse, because these nation-states currently hold the infrastructure to reach out to these communities and better their lives. Paradoxically, the nation-state is an indispensable element for European integration to take concrete shape in the communities that are least exposed to it, and the EU should use this power to reach out. Federal action at the macro-level and implementation at the micro-level does not need to be conflictual: in the 1930s, FDR's New Deal was conceived in Washington, but implementation was largely shaped by the states for the direct benefit of their citizens.[46]

Dealing with Europe's borders

European sovereignty has now become a mainstream talking point on the continent, but it is often used as a catch-all term without much thought put into how to reconcile national and European sovereignty in practice. After all, the general feeling is that the former has eroded over time, but the latter never really existed, except in a few key areas such as trade policy, one of the few where the EU can actually exist and get its way in the international arena.

This is a false dilemma: national and European sovereignty are often intrinsically linked. In the case of social security and the investments to re-connect marginalized groups with the economy, the recovery fund is showing how much action at a federal level can be used to empower nation-states that would otherwise have no room to maneuver. The fund is only answering an emergency, but its application has already changed the conundrum of spending and support in many Southern European states. In other areas such as energy, co-ordination is necessary to achieve sovereignty: if Germany wants to achieve energy sovereignty after having unilaterally renounced nuclear energy production, it cannot do it on the back of its European neighbors – the project Nord Stream II, unilateral in nature, is the kind of national, unilateral behavior that should be prohibited so that the general long-term interest of the Union is not jeopardized by the short-term calculus for one country's electorate.

If energy needs mutualization, the protection of Europe's borders is probably the most important issue that needs to be tackled at the federal level in Europe. All sovereignty is based on respect for borders, both by neighboring states like Russia and Turkey and by individuals. Border guarantee is probably the make-or-break area where the European Union needs to prove its efficacy. As became clear during the migrant crisis of 2015, a continent open to any large movement of the population can only lead to internal chaos for the EU but also for each member-state. The European Union cannot function without controlling its borders, and this control raises a number of questions. The first one is to define which borders need to be controlled: sovereigntists often attack the Schengen agreement for doing away with borders, but they are only right if the disappearance of internal borders is not accompanied by the construction of strong external problems. With Schengen, pretty much like with the Euro, the problem is not so much that the EU has decided to move in the direction of mutualization, but that it did not get to the end of the logic and stopped the process in the middle of the road, the most dangerous spot of all.

Experiences in the breakdown of common economic areas, with the imposition of closed, hermetic borders, show how bad the closing into hermetic borders can be for individual nations' economy. But the other extreme, a completely uncontrollable border system, is just as bad, as it totally breaks down any idea of state authority in a given territory – leading to war as surely as winter follows autumn. As Europeans learnt over the past ten years, without functioning borders it is not possible to regulate and control who enters and leaves the territory, an issue that is important from a quantitative point of view as migratory pressure continues to stress European capacities, but also from a qualitative point of view: when Russian jets encroach upon sovereign Baltic air space, it is a direct challenge to European sovereignty and should be met accordingly. In the same way, when Russians set up a bank in Budapest that gives diplomatic immunity to FSB agents and enables to organize their covert operations throughout the European Union[47] and the national government is unable or unwilling to act accordingly, European authorities should be able to step in.

Of course, sovereignty is not an easily mutualized competence, even more so as the pressure is not equally shared across Europe, with the continent's (and the EU's) peripheries more directly exposed. The EU is faced with a choice: it can move backward, unbundle Schengen and return to national border controls, with the knowledge that in the medium and long term the result will necessarily be a negative differential in growth. The other solution is to move forward and give real resources to Frontex, which was set up to help member-states secure their external borders. To give an idea of the size of the challenge ahead, Frontex currently has a budget of 420 million euros[48] to secure a land border of more than 14,000 kilometers and a 66,000-kilometer-long coastline. By way of comparison, to secure 7,500 km of land borders and 20,000 km of coastline (two to three times less than the European Union), the US Customs and Border Protection Agency (CBP) has a 17 billion dollars budget (approximately 15 billion euros[49]), and even this is deemed not enough for half of the American electorate. If the borders of the EU have to be secured, there is no other choice but to invest heavily in border protection. Euroskeptics are actually not necessarily against that idea, "even if it means seeing agents in German uniforms patrolling to defend the Polish borders" as a Polish MP from the Law and Justice Party once told me in private "It would necessarily be controversial, but in the end most of us could live with it, as long as our borders are secure."

How can the European Union secure its 14,000 km long land border, and its 66,000 km long coastline? One solution would be to "build a wall" to protect Fortress Europe. Except in some key areas, this would be a waste of resources: the security of the Eastern land border is mostly about keeping a well-equipped state army out of the European Union, while the maritime borders in the South and Southeast are currently more about keeping individuals out. In the case of the Mediterranean Sea, the challenge is to keep an open access for commerce, while controlling the migration flows, which first of all means control over the three main bottlenecks that are the Gibraltar and Sicily Straits, as well as the Bosporus and the Aegean islands. Ceuta and Melilla show that these bottlenecks can at best be secured, although that security is also dependent on the amount of pressure exercised by neighboring Morocco. Securing the strait of Sicily and access to the South of Italy is a more arduous task, for the area to cover is larger, and Italy clearly needs assistance from the EU to control the straits. The Aegean and Bosporus (or rather, Thracian) bottleneck is, however, the most arduous of all to control, considering that it includes the hundreds of Greek Dodecanese and North Aegean islands. To guarantee control of the migration flow and, in the longer term, of these islands themselves, the EU needs to build a naval superiority that allows it to keep potential adversaries away from the islands and lead the rescue operations when they are needed, while impeding dangerous illegal crossings in the first place. This requires large investments, and the build-up of a naval capacity to free the Eastern Mediterranean from external incursion and migrant weaponization can only be made within the context of NATO, without any delusions about Turkey's intentions or position. Here as always, the continuation of the North Atlantic Alliance is a key to maintaining European security, even though the ultimate objective is that Europeans can take more of the burden in the Mediterranean and the East, not less.

The securing of the borders opens up another question, which is that of the stability of the borders. And over the past 30 years, answers to it have not been clear: this is first because Europe is actually opening up rather than just finishing at the great steppe highway, leaving a vast open space that often works as a no-man's-land and is difficult to control. But this is also because of the great drive East of the Euro-Atlantic world during the post–Cold War years. Today, there is still much debate about the enlargement process and whether it should continue its East-bound course – to include Ukraine, Moldova and even Georgia. There is also a question about the inclusion of much of the Western Balkans in the EU, as every country is a candidate, although the fulfilment of EU integration criteria have stalled recently (some countries like Serbia are actually moving away from the Union to get closer to China). Finally, there is also the question of Turkey, still a candidate for European integration, while everyone, including in Ankara, doubts that it will ever be a full member. This has not prevented Turkey from receiving 9 billion euros in pre-accession aid within the framework of the European multiannual budget for 2007–2020.[50]

Since 1991, the race for an almost never-ending enlargement has become such an orthodoxy that despite the issue becoming much less relevant, it has kept its own Commissioner, while any questioning of the candidate-country status to Albania or Northern Macedonia leads to major nervous breakdowns in Brussels. The problem of course is that it does not serve much to secure a border if that border has to be moved again within a few years. The question of the integration of countries in the Eastern Partnership area and the Western Balkans must therefore be tackled. This may well mean that not everyone will enter – or that there will be longer paths than those taken by Poland, Slovakia or Romania.

Some countries have no vocation to integrate the European Union. This is clearly the case for Russia or Turkey: these are two fundamentally Eurasian powers, too different and too big to digest, they should be kept away from internal European politics as much as possible, which doesn't preclude trade with them. The two powers were virtually expelled from European politics in the 20th century, Turkey in 1919, Russia in 1991, and they should therefore be kept out. This is of course not to say that Turkey or Russia cannot be trading partners, but their status as "other" must be recognized beyond doubt, so that Europeans do not sleepwalk into dangerous relations with powers that have never and will never be fully European. This also means that the EU must also check the influence of these actors within European territory, within its markets (Russia currently controls around 40% of the gas supply to the EU[51]), but also in the EU's immediate neighborhood: that includes the Aegean and Eastern Mediterranean Sea as a whole, where a rivalry with Turkey is building-up and must be managed, but also on-land in the Western Balkans and Ukraine, which has made a clear choice in 2014 to be part of the West and must be offered practical solutions to fulfil its aspirations. This does not necessarily mean that these countries should become full EU members now, but a first step could be to support these countries' ability to sustain their territorial integrity: both Belarus and Ukraine are security guarantees against a return of Russian power to the heart of the continent.

For years, the prospect of full membership to the European Union has been brandished as a magic key to push countries to reform their economies and institutions and become more "European." Today, it is necessary to recognize that these efforts are not working as they used to: while some countries in the Western Balkans are actually giving up hopes of membership and moving away from the West (most notably Serbia), other countries that have not even been given a candidate status are actually moving further to adopt EU-type rules and laws – often pushed more by their own civil society on the government and because of the more immediate Russian threat on these countries' survival.[52] Faced with such deadlock and ambiguities, the integration process needs to be revised. This does not preclude the possibility of integration of countries like North Macedonia, Albania or Ukraine into the Union, but the process should be more progressive, with intermediate statutes in integration, rather than chapters to be closed before integration happens fully. The example of the formation of the United States can be useful here: it is often forgotten in Europe that the Union is composed of 50 states only since 1959, when Alaska and Hawaii joined in. Before, these two entities (and many others in the West) were "territories" of the United States, a status that greatly differed from that of a full-fledged state. Today, the United States still includes a number of these territories, very often islands in the Pacific and the Caribbean, at least one of which, Puerto Rico, may one day join the Union as a federal state, along with the District of Columbia. Although membership can and should remain an objective, other intermediary statuses could be used to smoothen the transition and ensure the essential things Europe can give to these countries while giving time and opportunity for the EU collective system to adapt. If Europe wants to have secure borders, it cannot allow malevolent actors to build their own sphere of influence in territories that are a stone-throw away from the heart of Europe. If it really wants to be geopolitical, the European Union must think about its neighborhood as well as its internal geography in a geopolitical way and act so that rivals do not settle permanently in its peripheries.

Today, however, the question is not only an extension of the EU's borders, but also one of possible narrowing. Of course, Brexit has raised the possibility that one member could leave the Union in the future – in this particular case, it should be noted that EU fundamental law has given member-states a right to secede, and Britain's case shows that, unlike in the USSR, that right was upheld. As this book has argued, it is not impossible to imagine that a country or a group of countries may also leave the EU, either by their own will (although this currently seems much less realistic than some hardcore Brexiteers imagined a few years ago) or against their will (with the Baltic States particularly exposed to the risk of becoming once again part of a kidnapped West). Such scenarios are not unthinkable today, but they would lead to tensions, chaos and down the line even war. Thinking of these possibilities and preparing for emergencies should be part of the EU's geostrategic agenda – it should give as little incentives for member-states to want to leave the Union, and even less incentives to outside powers to encroach on its sovereignty. This means above all facing up to *any* provocation and foul play whenever it occurs, and being ready to face the inevitable tensions that will arise with the outside world. Internally, it means that a clear line has to be drawn as to what are the fundamental principles of European democracy, which means equal treatment to all and measurement in judgments: too often, the political groups in the European Parliament have tried to politicize procedures on the infringement of fundamental freedoms in countries like

Hungary by mixing fundamental issues like the rule of law and media freedom with less central ones like the environment or migrations. Much like in the United States, the over-politicization of this type of procedure undermines the credibility of the case against member-states and gives ammunition to those who seek to take advantage of European funds to consolidate their personal power.

Much like in medicine, prevention is always preferable to amputation, and it must be applied wisely if the EU wants to avoid shrinking further in the coming years and decades, even though there will be advocates inside the EU for select amputation. Of course, these advocates will not necessarily agree on the members that need to go: some Northern Eurosceptics will probably prefer to get rid of the expensive countries of the South, while countries like France would gladly opt for an Eastern amputation, as the enlargement to the East has meant a loss of influence for Paris. Amputation of a territory is a messy business and is often a prelude to war – it should therefore be avoided as much as possible.

Et Tu felix Austria nube

In his book *Upheaval*, US geographer Jared Diamond has identified a number of factors that can help a society to resolve an existential crisis like the one Europe is going through today. Adaptation of outside models features highly in this list.[53] Of course, the model may vary in time and place: it was the West in general for Meiji-era Japan (the country actually cherry-picked different solutions from different countries like the United States, the United Kingdom, France and Germany for sectoral reforms), more specifically North-Western Europe in Peter the Great's Russia,[54] the United States in post-war Germany,[55] etc. Over the past two centuries, countries have often looked at the "Western" model for modernization, although this is less systematically the case today. Whatever the source of inspiration, and even though the model can also be a fantasized version of an indigenous past (for Ronald Reagan, it was the individualist spirit of the pioneers of the American West[56]), societies in times of crisis need to find inspiration from outside after a crisis. In the case of countries that have suffered the trauma of defeat, the adoption of some features of the "other" is part of what Wolfgang Schivelbusch has called the "culture of defeat,"[57] a step in the process that makes societies transition out of the initial trauma of defeat to a new normality.

The European Union, whose developments over the past 12 years could easily be assimilated to a defeat, is in this position today, in need of inspiration to thrive again. And there are quite a number of possible models for the EU – the most obvious being the United States, which provided the original aspiration for European integration. America's success, power, but also its relative cultural proximity (at least compared to other countries such as China or India), the separation of powers and the federal model it proposes to manage its diverse society is an obvious pick for inspiration. From an institutional point of view, and despite the dysfunctional politics of the past decade (or rather, because the dysfunctional politics of the past decade have shown how resilient US institutions were), America and the history of its federalization remain a model for Europe to follow – particularly as the EU goes through the process of mutualizing some debt in a post-COVID-19 environment.

But the United States cannot be the unique reference for the reconstruction of Europe's credibility. In many areas, American and European cultures are drifting away from each other today, and if Bruno Maçães is to be believed, this may well be a permanent parting.[58] The structural challenges on each side of the Atlantic are also different: North America has natural resources that Europe does not have, and importantly Europeans do not have the same societal model as Americans: despite some convergence in the past decades, the gulf separating what Michel Albert called the Rhenian capitalist model focused on safety and a culture of mutualized social security, and the "New American" capitalism based on risk-taking and shareholder mentality[59] is still large – and it may well widen again in the next few years. American and European approaches to diversity are also completely different, by the nature of that diversity: America's identity was created on a terrain in which indigenous populations had been mostly wiped out by viruses and war, and in many ways diversity was imported to the United States, with movements to assimilate it into the American (often Anglo-Saxon) *creed* happening at regular intervals in US history.[60] European diversity, on the other hand, is mostly homegrown and dates back centuries. It does not impede unification (otherwise Germany and Italy would not exist today), but it means specific issues for an ensemble whose sense of common belonging is much newer and for the moment much more fragile.

There are other sources of inspiration the European Union could look at in the future. The United States is not the only federation in the world, and the experience of India could be interesting to study. Like Europe, India's unity under a single state was made only recently. If one makes abstraction of the shared civilization, one could well argue that few things bring together the inhabitants of the state of Tamil Nadu, in the far south of the Indian peninsula, and those of Uttar Pradesh in the north. Yet nobody would seriously deny the reality of Indian unity, which in many ways (and like the first unity of Greece in antiquity) was imposed from the outside: the subcontinent was not completely united until the British came in (the Mughal Empire never included today's Southern India). Although the nature and extent of the foreign domination were different, *pax americana* made a united European Union from Estonia to Portugal just as the (albeit much less peaceful much more extractive) *pax Britannica* made modern India. Despite the obvious limitations of the Indian model, the size of the federation, its centuries-old diversity, the civilizational nature of the country's union and its federal dimension should certainly be studied more carefully by European elites. The current debates about India's national identity and its evolution should also inform Europeans on their options, and also the costs of directly clamping down on diversity.

There are also more familiar examples at hand for the European Union. As described earlier in this chapter, Switzerland is clearly a successful indigenous example of federalization, albeit in a smaller geographical area. The motto of the Swiss state, *Unus pro omnibus, omnes pro uno* (One for all and all for one), provides a great description of the Swiss system, with a highly decentralized and democratic model, and strong cantonal and linguistic identities that do not conflict with a strong unified national identity. The constraints of Swiss nation-building in the 19th century look strangely similar to those of the modern European Union, with

> "few natural resources; cultural diversity, both religious and linguistic, certainly relative to today's standards of cosmopolitanism, but acute in a period when nationalism was spreading in Europe and religious passions were still alive; and finally, a military and strategic weakness that did not allow it to control its political environment".[61]

Although the description is that of 19th-century Switzerland, it is difficult not to think of the EU's situation today.

European leaders should also study Swiss later history, and how internal dynamics dictated the relationship with turbulent neighbors in the 20th century, to think of their options. In 1919, the Austrian province of Voralberg voted by referendum with 80% support to request entry into the federation, as Switzerland's 27th canton. The request was rejected by the Swiss Parliament, for fears that it would upset the fragile balance between the different parts of the country: Italian-speaking and French-speaking people in particular were hostile to the project, since it would have strengthened the weight of German speakers in Bern. In a different way than the European Union, Switzerland has to deal with its own "German question," and federalism has proven to be a good solution to manage it. As founding father Jean Monnet put it in an interview for French newspaper *Le Monde*,

> "we have in Western Europe a long-standing example of a federal community. It is Switzerland. [...] The German-speaking Swiss make up the largest part of the population and hold the largest share of Switzerland's industrial potential. Because Switzerland is federally organized, there is no domination of the German-speaking elements."[62]

Even though the Swiss parallel has its own limitations (notably in terms of size), its own experience of federalism tells us, now as in Monnet's days, about the advantages of building a federal model able to balance the de facto incomplete domination of the ensemble by one of its constituent parts.

Finally, an unlikely source of inspiration could come from a defunct European model: that of Habsburg Austria, or rather how it could have evolved after 1918 if circumstances and a more pragmatic approach had allowed it to survive the onslaught of the Great War. Could the future of Europe be Austria-Hungary?[63] The proposal may seem counter-intuitive: the Emperors are long gone, and post-1918 historiography has traditionally portrayed their demise as the inevitable defeat of imperialism by nationalism.[64] There is of course some truth to this, and the Viennese elites of the early 20th century had actually understood that the old model of a large sovereignty whose legitimacy rested almost solely on the person of the Habsburg monarch had become untenable in the long term. However, seeing Austria-Hungary's demise as the inevitable result of the superiority of the nation is an over-simplification that does not withhold the much more complex reality of the empire. In 1904, American President Theodore Roosevelt had actually praised the Habsburg monarch for having "understood how to treat different nations and religions with justice and to make his country a model"[65] that the United States could follow to better manage its newly acquired possessions in the Pacific. This description is obviously very different from the image of the "people's prison" that the nationalist historiography is still trying to convey in today's history books.

That the empire didn't deserve to die does not mean that one should, like Franco-Hungarian historian François Fejtö, explain the events of 1918–1919 as an assassination perpetrated by Wilson, Clemenceau and the Czech nationalists.[66] The empire died after a long illness called the Great War, but its demise was not inevitable. It is probable that without the war, the empire would probably have lived for many more years, and it could even have survived the war, hadn't it been for a combination of exceptional circumstances, some of which were under the control of the elites in Vienna and Budapest, some not (among others, Franz Joseph's passing before the end of the war, the subsequent political errors of Emperor Charles and Count von Czernin before their legitimacy could have been consolidated, the Hungarian Red Revolution of 1918, Germany's intransigence in 1917–1918, Wilson's Twelve Points and their reading by Czech nationalists in the United States, etc.). A tour of Vienna today tells any visitor how much the Habsburg empire was in full bloom in 1914, with construction continuing as the city expanded while scientists, intellectuals and artists like Sigmund Freund, Gustav Klimt, Egon Schiele and Otto Wagner were enlightening the city with their talent. As French historian Jean-Paul Bled argued, the agony of the empire started in the fateful days following the assassination of Archduke Franz Ferdinand, and death only became inevitable after 1917, not before.[67]

This is of course not to say that the empire was immune from negative dynamics before 1914. The rivalry with Russia in the Balkans, dilemmas of modernization, problems linked to the consolidation of the confederation after the compromise of 1867, the nationalities question (partly linked to Hungarian intransigence on its autonomy on its desire to Magyarize Slavic and Latin populations), all pre-date the outbreak of the Great War and all, together, proved fatal to the empire. Austrian elites were perfectly aware of these dangers, and they knew that the empire needed reform if it was to survive in the 20th century. In this period of great Viennese creativity, political circles had also designed creative solutions to reform the empire, rid it of the burdens of the past and have it embrace a future which at the time did not need to be that of the intransigent, ethnic nationalism witnessed afterward in Central Europe in the 1920s and 1930s. Of course, the old Emperor Franz Joseph was a major obstacle to reform – for which he had his reasons. But reformist cycles had gathered around the presumptive heads of the state, notably Crown Prince Franz Ferdinand and Archduke Charles, and thought with them the future reform of the empire. Neither Charles nor Ferdinand was a convinced democrat, but they all had realized the need to open the empire to modernization, notably to better manage the diversity of the empire, whose cohesion was challenged by the rise of Czech, Slovak, South Slavic, but also German and Hungarian nationalisms.

The Austrian informal think tanks of the time had put much thought to the question, and in 1906, a Romanian intellectual and lawyer loyal to the empire, Aurel Popovici, presented a plan for a United States of Greater Austria, which proposed to transform what was a confederation of Austria-Hungary into a more integrated federation of 15 states with a clear ethno-linguistic majority, along with autonomous enclaves for large multicultural cities and some rural areas with specific ethno-linguistic identities (generally but not exclusively German-speaking[68]). The ensemble would be ruled by an institutional setting (already) inspired by the US Constitution, but adapted to the multicultural reality of the empire. The project, radical though it was at the time, obtained the assent of a large part of the elites in Vienna (although not in Budapest), and there is little doubt that, had he acceded to the throne, Franz Ferdinand would have sought to implement this type of federalism as a way to bring more coherence to his estates while at the same time betting on decentralization to manage diversity. Unfortunately, the tragic events of June 28, 1914, in Sarajevo prevented him from carrying the project, and when reformist Charles picked up the torch in 1916, the empire was already consuming itself from within and would have had to survive the war before any serious reform could be envisaged. The United States of Greater Austria may have made sense, but it was not given a chance in the troubled circumstances of 1918.

★ ★ ★

Bella gerant alii, tu felix Austria nube: "Let others wage war, you happy Austria, marry." The expression, attributed to great Hungarian king Matthias Corvinus, fitted well the strategy used by the House of Habsburg to dominate much of Europe during the Renaissance, with a remarkably effective matrimonial policy. But the Austrian Monarchs' preference for Venus, even then, did not impede them from sacrificing to Mars when necessary: to protect their territory, suppress the rebellion and occasionally face Turkish, Prussian and Russian threats, the Habsburgs waged war – if not by choice, then by necessity. Europeans today may take a few lessons from the Austrian experience – if they are wise to want to "marry" and trade, they should not forget another, much older Latin locution: *si vis pacem para bellum*. To stay safe, and to avoid having to import wars and instability from the outside, it is often necessary to be ready for war, and even at times (though as rarely as possible) to wage it.

The parallel between modern Europe and the Habsburg Empire should not stop there. Like Austria-Hungary of the early 20th century, the European Union of the 2020s is in the grip of a major identity and institutional crisis – in each case the limits of the confederal model have been reached, and the two large multinational groups are now being threatened by strong internal tensions. Aurel Popovici had called this general estrangement in the Austrian empire a "savage kind hatred,"[69] and one might find this savage kind hatred often expressed today in the heated discussions of the Council meetings. Popovici's project of a federalist reform for a United States of Greater Austria, directly inspired by the American and Swiss models and adapted to Central Europe, aimed to bring back coherence to the whole. This was to be done under the umbrella of a common identity, but the project relied on the reality of the diversity on the Habsburg estates, which it proposed to institutionalize so that coherence and diversity would not destroy but reinforce each other. As the Romanian historian Iulian Nicușor-Isac noted, Popovici's plan prefigured in many ways the Euro-integration projects that followed two destructive world wars.[70]

Looking at the Austria-Hungary model, it could also give us a vision of what could happen on the European continent if the European Union and Euro-Atlantic institutions were to disintegrate, in the same way as they did in 1918 around the Danube Basin. The history of the demise of large ensembles in Europe is not a happy one, and considering the rise of identity politics currently at work on the continent (much like in Central Europe in the 1900s), the result of the EU's demise would undoubtedly lead to a Balkanized continent vulnerable to outside influences, conflict and war. This is what happened in the inter-war period in the former Danubian monarchy, which quickly turned into a theater of confrontation between rival little-nationalisms, while the newly formed countries often fell prey to the European Civil War between liberalism, communism and fascism. This ferocious struggle led to a multitude of conflicts between 1918 and 1939, and it was followed by six years of total warfare in which violence reached genocidal proportions, before 50 years of communism ended up ruining a region in which some areas were some of the most developed in Europe during the *Belle Époque*.

Central Europe's tragic destiny in the 20th century proved Habsburg statesman František Palacký right. A Czech descendant from a Hussite family (and father of the Czech revival), Palacký was a tireless defender of the empire, although he too wanted to reform it. In the troubled year of 1848, he wrote with a remarkable taste for anticipation why the Habsburg ensemble needed to be preserved:

> "Truly if the Austrian Empire had not existed for ages, it would be necessary, in the interest of Europe, in the interest of mankind itself, to create it with all speed [...]. Imagine if you will Austria divided into a number of

republics and miniature republics. What a welcome basis for a universal Russian monarchy!"[71]

Palacký's words may not have saved the empire, but the Danubian basin's fate in the 20th century should serve as a practical warning to what could await Europe if its current institutions were left to decay and disintegrate. The cost of this would be so high for Europeans, but also for Anglo-Americans, that it is in the interests of both to act now, and preferably together, to preserve what they have built for the past 75 years.

Notes

1 Jared Diamond, *Collapse: How Societies Choose to Fail or Survive*, London: Penguin Books, 2013.
2 Jared Diamond, *Upheaval: How Nations Cope with Crisis and Change*, London: Allen Lane, 2019.
3 Ibid., pp.50–54.
4 Andrew Gordon, *A Modern History of Japan: From Tokugawa Times to the Present*, Oxford: Oxford University Press, 2002.
5 Ian Morris, *War: What is it Good for? The Role of Conflict in Civilization, from Primates to Robots*, London: Profile Books, 2014, p.344.
6 Donald Kagan, *On the Origins of War and the Preservation of Peace*, New York: Anchor Books, 1996, p.568.
7 Ian Morris, *War: What is it Good for? The Role of Conflict in Civilization, from Primates to Robots*, London: Profile Books, 2014.
8 Donald Kagan, *On the Origins of War and the Preservation of Peace*, New York: Anchor Books, 1996, p.570.
9 https://www.washingtonpost.com/world/europe/an-eu-diplomat-went-to-moscow-to-build-bridges-it-didnt-go-well/2021/02/09/68cfefb0-6ae8-11eb-a66e-e27046e9e898_story.html
10 Quoted in Geoffrey Blainey, *The Causes of War* (3rd edition), New York: The Free Press, 1988, p.108.
11 Donald Kagan, *On the Origins of War and the Preservation of Peace*, New York: Anchor Books, 1996, p.514.
12 See Dale Peterson and Richard Wrangham, *Demonic Males: Apes and the Origins of Human Violence*, New York: Mariner Books, 1997.
13 Kristi Raik and András Rácz, *Post-Crimea Shift in EU-Russia Relations: From Fostering Interdependence to Managing Vulnerabilities*, Tallinn: International Centre for Defense and Security, 2019, p.285.
14 https://www.best-selling-cars.com/europe/2019-full-year-europe-best-selling-car-manufacturers-and-brands/
15 https://www.bruxelles2.eu/2019/03/la-clause-de-solidarite-de-lotan-sappelle-article-v-pas-article-f-35-parly/
16 This is David Abulafia's theory of the five Mediterranean, which are actually many more considering that the sea was often divided into different zones and saw different orders rise and collapse at different times. See David Abulafia, *The Great Sea: A Human History of the Mediterranean*, London: Penguin Books, 2014.
17 Paul Lever, *Berlin Rules: Europe and the German Way*, London: IB Tauris, 2017, p.109.
18 See Nan Tian Aude Fleurant, Alexandra Kuimova et Pieter D. Wezeman, and Siemon T. Wezeman, "Trends in World Military Expenditures," April 28, 2019, Stockholm International Peace Research Institute, https://sipri.org/sites/default/files/2019-04/fs_1904_milex_2018_0.pdf

19 Guy Verhofstadt, *Le Mal Européen*, Brussels: Marque Belge, 2016, p.366.
20 https://www.politico.eu/article/netherlands-coronavirus-response-how-the-dutch-lost-their-shine/?utm_medium=Social&utm_source=Facebook&fbclid=IwAR0c9hqYhONcFOekK5v6Hh7DLG60HPIbTSyxxOxSy73CJW86AUN40l4JNNc#Echobox=1615567597
21 https://www.economist.com/leaders/2006/01/12/danger-time-for-america
22 https://www.theguardian.com/uk/2005/sep/27/labourconference.speeches
23 It should be remembered that it was Hillary Clinton, under pressure from the Sanders insurgency during the Democratic Primary, who by voicing opposition to it, probably killed the TPP even before it was debated in the presidential campaign; see https://www.washingtonpost.com/posteverything/wp/2015/10/08/is-hillary-clinton-right-about-the-trans-pacific-partnership/
24 Guy Verhofstadt, *Le Mal Européen*, Brussels: Marque Belge, 2016, p.328.
25 Quoted in Lothar Gall, *Bismarck: le révolutionnaire blanc*, Paris: Fayard, 1984, p.95.
26 Litterally, "*l'Italia è fatta. Restano a fare gli Italiani.*" See Claudio Gigante, *Fatta l'Italia, facciamo gli Italiani.Appunti su una massima da restituire a d'Azeglio*, in *Incontri. Rivista europea di studi italiani*, anno 26, fasc. 2/2011, pp.5–15.
27 Antoine Vauchez, "Entre État et Société civile: justice, administration et politique," in Marc Lazar et al., *L'Italie contemporaine de 1945 à nos jours*, Paris: Fayard, p.81.
28 Marc Lazar, "Une République incertaine, de 1945 à la fin des années 1980," in Marc Lazar et al., *L'Italie contemporaine de 1945 à nos jours*, Paris: Fayard, p.41.
29 https://www.npr.org/sections/itsallpolitics/2015/10/23/451200436/mitt-romney-finally-takes-credit-for-obamacare?t=1587041536655
30 Jared Diamond, *Upheaval: How Nations Cope with Crisis and Change*, London: Allen Lane, 2019, pp.336–337.
31 On the conditions for a successful transition to a federation, Alexandre Vulic considers that the entity must be able to draw a useful precedent from historical experience, that this federalism must be democratic, and finally that it must not be zero-sum. We can see the difference between the failure of federations such as Yugoslavia, the USSR or Czechoslovakia, and others such as Germany, Austria or Canada. See Alexandre Vulic, *L'échec des fédéralismes multinationaux en Europe du Centre-Est: Tchécoslovaquie, Yougoslavie*, Mém. DEA: Etudes soviétiques et est-européennes; Paris: IEP, 1995.
32 The four unitary countries being China, Indonesia, Pakistan and Bangladesh.
33 Ashoka Mody, *EuroTragedy: A Drama in Nine Acts,* Oxford: Oxford University Press, 2018, p.265.
34 Ibid., p.33.
35 Ibid., p.85.
36 Ivan Krastev and Stephen Holmes, *The Light that Failed: A Reckoning*, London: Allen Lane, 2019, pp.57–59.
37 John J. Mearsheimer, *The Great Delusion: Liberal Dreams and International Realities*, New Haven: Yale University Press, 2018.
38 Benno Hubensteiner, *Bayerische Geschichte*, Munich: Süddeutscher Verlag, 1989.
39 https://www.wsj.com/articles/SB928442648233995197
40 Gaëtane Ricard-Nihoul, *Pour une fédération européenne d'États-nations : la vision de Jacques Delors revisitée*, Brussels: Larcier, 2012.
41 Paul Lever, *Berlin Rules: Europe and the German Way*, London: Tauris, 2017, p.62.
42 The William Tell character was invented by association with an old Danish saga. See Mathieu Calame, *La France contre l'Europe: Histoire d'un malentendu*, Paris: Les petits matins, 2019, p.30.
43 Anthony Smith, *The Nation in History: Historiographical Debates about Ethnicity and Nationalism*, Cambridge: Polity, 2000.
44 See Eugen Weber, *Peasants into Frenchmen: The Modernization of Rural France 1870–1914*, Stanford: Stanford University Press, 1976.

45 Jérôme Fourquet, *L'archipel français: naissance d'une nation multiple et divisée*, Paris: Seuil, 2019, p.117.
46 See James T. Patterson, *New Deal and States: Federalism in Transition*, Princeton: Princeton University Press, 2016.
47 https://www.nytimes.com/2019/03/18/world/europe/hungary-russian-bank-spy-orban-putin.html
48 The numbers are from 2020. See the EU's budget: https://ec.europa.eu/commission/presscorner/detail/en/IP_19_2809
49 https://www.americanimmigrationcouncil.org/research/the-cost-of-immigration-enforcement-and-border-security
50 https://op.europa.eu/webpub/eca/special-reports/turkey-7-2018/fr/
51 https://www.e-ir.info/2020/02/24/the-energy-relationship-between-russia-and-the-european-union/
52 See https://www.ceps.eu/ceps-publications/balkan-and-eastern-european-comparisons/
53 Jared Diamond, *Upheaval: How Nations Cope with Crisis and Change*, London: Allen Lane, 2019, p.50.
54 Simon Dixon, *The Modernisation of Russia: 1676–1825*, Cambridge: Cambridge University Press, 1999.
55 Jared Diamond, *Upheaval: How Nations Cope with Crisis and Change*, London: Allen Lane, 2019, pp.217–253.
56 This individualist Western spirit was always a myth, as the pioneers did rely heavily on the US government to settle and thrive in the West. See Richard White, *It's Your Misfortune and None of My Own: A History of the American West*, Norman: Oklahoma University Press, 1991.
57 Wolfgang Schivelbusch, *The Culture of Defeat: On National Trauma, Mourning and Recovery*, New York: Picador, 2003.
58 Bruno Maçães, *History has Begun: The Birth of a New America*, London: Hurst, 2020.
59 Michel Albert, *Capitalisme contre capitalisme*, Paris: Seuil, 1991.
60 Samuel Huntington, *Who Are We? The Challenges to America's National Identity*, New York: Simon & Schuster, 2005, p.129.
61 Mathieu Calame, *La France contre l'Europe: Histoire d'un malentendu*, Paris: Les petits matins, 2019.
62 Quoted in Éric Roussel, *Jean Monnet*, Paris: Fayard, 1996.
63 The expression is a free translation and adaptation of a 1991 book by French author Pierre Béhar. See Pierre Béhar, *Autriche-Hongrie, idée d'avenir: permanences géopolitiques de l'Europe centrale et balkanique*, Paris: Desjonquères, 1991.
64 See Dominic Lieven, *Empire: The Russian Empire and its Rivals from the Sixteenth Century to the Present*, London: Pimlico, 2003.
65 Christopher Clark, *The Sleepwalkers: How Europe Went to War in 1914*, London: Penguin, 2013, p.76.
66 François Fejtö, *Requiem pour un empire défunt: Histoire de la destruction de l'Autriche-Hongrie*, Paris: Perrin, 1988.
67 Jean-Paul Bled, *L'Agonie d'une monarchie: Autriche-Hongrie, 1914–1920*, Paris: Tallandier, 2014.
68 Aurel Popovici, *Die Vereinigten Staaten von Groß-Österreich. Politische Studien zur Lösung der nationalen Fragen und staatrechtlichen Krisen in Österreich-Ungarn*, Leipzig: B. Elischer Nachfolger, 1906.
69 Ibid.
70 Iulian-Nicușor Isac, *The United States of Greater Austria – A Step toward European Union?*, Târgoviste: Centrul de Cercetare a Istoriei Relatiilor Internationale si Studii Culturale Grigore Gafencu, 2011; available online: https://web.archive.org/web/20110912025311/http://www.centrulgafencu.ro/user/image/12isac.pdf
71 Quoted in Samuel R. Williamson Jr., *Austria-Hungary and the Origins of the First World War*, London: Palgrave, 1991, p.4.

Bibliography

Abulafia, David, *The Great Sea: A Human History of the Mediterranean*, London: Penguin Books, 2014.
Albert, Michel, *Capitalisme contre capitalisme*, Paris: Seuil, 1991.
Béhar, Pierre, *Autriche-Hongrie, idée d'avenir: permanences géopolitiques de l'Europe centrale et balkanique*, Paris: Desjonquères, 1991.
Blainey, Geoffrey, *The Causes of War* (3rd edition), New York: The Free Press, 1988.
Bled, Jean-Paul, *L'Agonie d'une monarchie: Autriche-Hongrie, 1914–1920*, Paris: Tallandier, 2014.
Calame, Mathieu, *La France contre l'Europe: Histoire d'un malentendu*, Paris: Les petits matins, 2019.
Clark, Christopher, *The Sleepwalkers: How Europe Went to War in 1914*, London: Penguin, 2013.
Diamond, Jared, *Collapse: How Societies Choose to Fail or Survive*, London: Penguin Books, 2013.
Diamond, Jared, *Upheaval: How Nations Cope with Crisis and Change*, London: Allen Lane, 2019.
Fejtö, François, *Requiem pour un empire défunt: Histoire de la destruction de l'Autriche-Hongrie*, Paris: Perrin, 1988.
Fourquet, Jérôme, *L'archipel français: naissance d'une nation multiple et divisée*, Paris: Seuil, 2019.
Gall, Lothar, *Bismarck: le révolutionnaire blanc*, Paris: Fayard, 1984.
Gigante, Claudio, "Fatta l'Italia, facciamo gli Italiani. Appunti su una massima da restituire a d'Azeglio," in *Incontri. Rivista europea di studi italiani*, anno 26, fasc. 2, 2011.
Gordon, Andrew, *A Modern History of Japan: From Tokugawa Times to the Present*, Oxford: Oxford University Press, 2002.
Hubensteiner, Benno, *Bayerische Geschichte*, Munich: Süddeutscher Verlag, 1989.
Huntington, Samuel, *Who Are We?: The Challenges to America's National Identity*, New York: Simon & Schuster, 2005.
Isac, Iulian-Nicuşor, *The United States of Greater Austria – A Step toward European Union?*, Târgoviste: Centrul de Cercetare a Istoriei Relatiilor Internationale si Studii Culturale Grigore Gafencu, 2011.
Kagan, Donald, *On the Origins of War and the Preservation of Peace*, New York: Anchor Books, 1996.
Krastev, Ivan, and Holmes, Stephen, *The Light that Failed: A Reckoning*, London: Allen Lane, 2019.
Lazar, Marc et al., *L'Italie contemporaine de 1945 à nos jours*, Paris: Fayard.
Lever, Paul, *Berlin Rules: Europe and the German Way*, London: Tauris, 2017.
Lieven, Dominic, *Empire: The Russian Empire and its Rivals from the Sixteenth Century to the Present*, London: Pimlico, 2003.
Maçães, Bruno, *History has Begun: The Birth of a New America*, London: Hurst, 2020.
Mearsheimer, John J., *The Great Delusion: Liberal Dreams and International Realities*, New Haven: Yale University Press, 2018.
Mody, Ashoka, *EuroTragedy: A Drama in Nine Acts*, Oxford: Oxford University Press, 2018.
Morris, Ian, *War: What is it Good for? The Role of Conflict in Civilization, from Primates to Robots*, London: Profile Books, 2014.
Patterson, James T., *New Deal and States: Federalism in Transition*, Princeton: Princeton University Press, 2016.

Peterson, Dale, and Wrangham, Richard, *Demonic Males: Apes and the Origins of Human Violence*, New York: Mariner Books, 1997.
Popovici, Aurel, *Die Vereinigten Staaten von Groß-Österreich. Politische Studien zur Lösung der nationalen Fragen und staatrechtlichen Krisen in Österreich-Ungarn*, Leipzig: B. Elischer Nachfolger, 1906.
Raik, Kristi, and Rácz, András, *Post-Crimea Shift in EU-Russia Relations: From Fostering Interdependence to Managing Vulnerabilities*, Tallinn: International Centre for Defense and Security, 2019.
Ricard-Nihoul, Gaëtane, *Pour une fédération européenne d'États-nations: la vision de Jacques Delors revisitée*, Brussels: Larcier, 2012.
Roussel, Éric, *Jean Monnet*, Paris: Fayard, 1996.
Schivelbusch, Wolfgang, *The Culture of Defeat: On National Trauma, Mourning and Recovery*, New York: Picador, 2003.
Smith, Anthony, *The Nation in History: Historiographical Debates about Ethnicity and Nationalism*, Cambridge: Polity, 2000.
Verhofstadt, Guy, *Le Mal Européen*, Brussels: Marque Belge, 2016.
Vulic, Alexandre, *L'échec des fédéralismes multinationaux en Europe du Centre-Est: Tchécoslovaquie, Yougoslavie*, Mém. DEA: Etudes soviétiques et est-européennes; Paris: IEP, 1995.
Weber, Eugen, *Peasants into Frenchmen: The Modernization of Rural France 1870–1914*, Stanford: Stanford University Press, 1976.
White, Richard, *It's Your Misfortune and None of My Own: A History of the American West*, Norman: Oklahoma University Press, 1991.
Williamson Jr., Samuel R., *Austria-Hungary and the Origins of the First World War*, London: Palgrave, 1991.

9
WHAT'S IN IT FOR THE ANGLOSPHERE?

In its original French-language version, this book's last chapter looked at what role France could and should play in a post-Brexit Europe, both to consolidate its rank as a regional power and reform itself after 30 years of stagnation.[1] Considering that this type of reflections would be of much lesser interest for a non-French public, this final chapter will take a different angle at the future of Europe and the preservation of peace, but this time from the perspective of the Anglosphere, as the relationship between the two English-speaking nations of the Transatlantic World and continental Europe are probably one of the victims of the series of events that have shaped the 2010s.

There are currently speculations on whether the relationship between continental Europe and the "Anglo-Saxons" in Britain and the United States has reached a low point from which it can ever recover. For sure, things have been worse in the past (the early 1940s come to mind[2]), but things have also been much better, and unfortunately too little attention is currently put on the real causes of the current estrangement between the Anglos and the Euros, why they still matter to each other and why the United States should invest more in strengthening a Europe Whole and Free. These topics are obviously very large, and a single chapter in one book is too short to either analyze it in depth or define in detail long-term solutions. Nevertheless, it is worth opening paths of exploration for future research and reflection to discern what exactly went wrong in the relationship over the past 20 years; and most importantly what can be done to fix it.

Indeed, there are voices in the Anglosphere who seem perfectly happy to let the relationship go from bad to worse. For some, the events of the past decade have only been the confirmation that the freedom-loving English-speaking people were always different and at odds with the bureaucratic and "authoritarian" continentals. While events over the past few years seem to have given them some (though not all) reason to claim victory, this chapter will argue that, while

Anglos and Euros may have different attitudes to certain issues and should now accept that their cultural paths are not always convergent, their alliance into the "West" is such a strong factor of certainty, predictability and security in a world that has become more dangerous that it is worth investing in. The Europe that Britain and America have shaped for the past two centuries is worth saving, not only in Europeans' but also in Britain's and the United States' interest. Both America and Britain will thus need to build a new partnership with Europe to push back against continentalist and authoritarian narratives coming from China and Russia, and this should be done not by retreating to a small, Anglo-centered vision of the world, but by reclaiming and enlarging the idea of the "West."

2016: a turning point

First, we need to be clear about the diagnosis: the Transatlantic relationship is currently not doing well. There are many dimensions in this crisis of the "West" as we've traditionally come to understand it since the Cold War, i.e. as the Transatlantic World, or NATO allies. These include, among others, Turkey's drifting away from the West as it tries to assume a more specific, Islamic and Eurasian position in the world, but the main challenge has to be the ongoing rift between Anglosphere countries (namely Britain and the United States) and continental Europe. In many ways, the trigger to the crisis was the year 2016 with three distinct events that marked a break between Anglos and Euros: Donald Trump's election as the president of the United States; Brexit; and, more anecdotal but no less important, the Transatlantic row over France's ban on burkinis in the summer of 2016.

Brexit was probably the most spectacular sign of the divorce. First, it was a hard separation, and the vacuum that it leaves will not be easily filled in: culturally but also institutionally and strategically, Britain provided a cultural bridge between Europe and America. Not that the United States needed British universities to study Kant and Rousseau, but Britain's in-between position provided useful links between both sides of the Atlantic: it is often through British universities that ideas travelled, whether from Europe to America in the 19th century or more recently from America to Europe. Culturally, Britain had that capacity to translate into a European cultural world ideas and concepts that had been developed in the United States: the English language was an asset to take from America, and Britain's European cultural tradition was a filter that reshaped American ideas in a way that would often give them sense for continentals. A large number of Europeans going to British universities from the late 1990s to the late 2010s allowed them to be in constant contact with Anglo-Saxon ideas – many of which they adopted.

Because Britain is English-speaking, it is culturally close to the United States. Because it was in the European Union, it could provide this Anglo-Saxon vision of commercial and political liberalism that for a long time Europeans tried to copy. More importantly, because Britain was both in the European Union and part of the Anglosphere, it could provide the key cultural link between two universes that sometimes have radically different approaches to economics and politics: while the Anglos embrace risk-taking and flexibility, and consider radicalism when it comes to policy making (what I will call the "Thatcher" option), continentals are much more averse to risk, often more bureaucratic, and because of Europe's 20th century, they often tend to favor consensus over radical political choices – the "de Gasperi" option, taking from the experience of the Italian Christian Democrat politician who, in the crucial post-war years, preferred to open up his majority to the left and center to preserve peace rather than rule alone with the Catholic right.

While Britain was a member of the Union, it kept one foot in continental Europe and one foot in the Anglosphere. For continentals, this often meant that Britain was "inside the tent pissing out rather than outside the tent pissing in." But there were other advantages: inside the European Union, Britain had the possibility to shape policy, and in some ways "anglicize" it. London was probably not as influential as it could or should have been – the result of coming late into the EU-integration process (which de facto kept Britain out of the building of a core centered on the Franco-German partnership[3]) but also of bad decision-making. When David Cameron decided that his Conservative Party should leave the European People's Party and form a rival group in the late 2000s, he pushed the Tories toward the fringes of the EU parliamentary political system, which rewards consensus rather than disruption.[4]

Britain was always half-in, half-out of the EU, but at least with one foot in, it could influence the debates, make Europe a little bit more Anglo-Saxon, and this also suited the interests of the United States, as there would always be a very strong voice in the EU Council for a more Atlanticist, free-market, freedom-oriented approach to the World. Now that the continent's second economy is gone, that voice is no longer, and Britain's departure represents a clear break whose real impact will be uncovered in the years, even decades to follow: Britain's power and influence guaranteed that Europe's center of gravity would remain in the North Sea – it has now moved fundamentally inland, and this can accentuate continentalist tendencies among European elites, especially in Germany. In the longer term, this may well lead to further cultural estrangement: as less European students will apply for British universities, they will be less exposed to ideas incubated in Britain or the United States, due to the rise in tuition fees and more red tape for students wishing to settle down in the United Kingdom during or after their studies.[5]

More immediately, the Brexit divorce has created a policy rift which is as political as it is philosophical, and much effort will be required to keep up the relationship. After four excruciating years of internal bickering and difficulties in getting Brexit done, Britons have discovered in early 2021 that Brexit also had its good sides: it allowed the United Kingdom to gain agility and audacity on the world stage. London took a stronger stance against China and Russia, on Hong Kong and Ukraine, for example (much to Washington's agreement), and it scored a remarkable success in vaccinating its population much faster than anyone except Israel. But being on one's own also has its disadvantages, in particular when it comes to trading with a much bigger market that can impose regulations, but also taxes, levies, paperwork on the smaller actor. The spats between Britain and the EU over fisheries or vaccines, with both sides claiming the moral high ground, may well be a sign of how UK–EU negotiations will look like in the future.

The second major earthquake of 2016 was the election of Donald Trump as president of the United States. In the end, it didn't lead, as many feared, to anything like a US withdrawal from NATO, but the Trump presidency did see a deterioration of the relationship between the core of the European continent and the United States: President Trump's style didn't suit the more consensual Europeans (although it did force them to step up their spending on NATO); his hostility toward Germany and the European Union as an institution made most European leaders uneasy about a partner that he at times labeled as a foe.[6] More generally, the Trump presidency raised question marks among allies about America's strategy for Europe: until then, Europeans had not questioned America's willingness to step in and protect Europe should it be needed. Now, many Europeans question whether America can be relied on *at all* in the long term. This has led to very different reactions: in places like Warsaw or Bucharest, the strategy has been to double-down on offers of partnership, with increases in the contribution to NATO, the offer of a Fort Trump in Poland, etc. But in other places, the mood has rather been to prepare for a post-American Europe – whether the United States would be leaving on its own or whether competition with China would open the way to a new geopolitical configuration. Approaches may have been different in Berlin, Paris, and Rome, but the trend has been to continue to commit to the Transatlantic relationship with a much more realist, cynical view of America and its ultimate goals in Europe. That Europe should not be an unconditional junior partner in a post-Trump America was made very clear by the EU's attempt to fast-forward negotiations on a Comprehensive Agreement over Investment (CAI) with China on December 30, 2020, just a few weeks before Joe Biden's inauguration. True, the European Parliament (the only institution that is both federal and democratic in the EU) managed to force the suspension of the ratification process, but the signals sent by the EU officials who supported the project all pointed in the same direction: the EU has learnt its lesson from the Trump years. It knows that America could one day become hostile to the Union and it wishes to find its own way in a world that is much less American than it was a few decades ago.[7]

On the other side of the Channel and the Atlantic Ocean, Brexit and the Trump movement represented the victory of an Anglo-nationalist view of the world, and an Anglo-nationalist view of the West: it was difficult to argue in 2016 that this West was not in decline – or at least that it was not challenged from all sides. For the Anglo-Conservatives who followed the Pat Buchanan school of thought, the problem was that the Anglo-Saxon system of government had been perverted by outside influence, most prominent of which from continental Europe and the European Union. In his book *The Death of the West*, Pat Buchanan had set the tone for much of the Trump agenda, with a fundamental distrust, even disgust for the European Union, portrayed as a "socialist superstate."[8] For Buchanan, Europe already committed suicide through the construction of a nondemocratic, cosmopolitan, and un-Christian superstate, but there was still time for the United States and Britain to avert decline and fall. Buchanan was one among many who portrayed the formation of the European Union as a monstrosity, a new "evil Empire" that needed to be unconstructed because it was unnatural and corrupting the Anglo-Saxon tradition. Buchanan (and with him many Eurosceptics in think tanks like the Bruges Group) influenced a whole generation of Conservative thinkers into viewing not only the European Union but also continentals as decadent, and above all socialists: exactly the countermodel Americans and Britons should avoid. Even though there was much rationale for Britain to leave the European Union at the time of the referendum, as described in previous chapters, the fact is that much of the intellectual reasoning for Brexit was developed in Anglo-nationalist circles in the late 1990s and early 2000s.

Although this was not completely true, the feeling in Brussels, Berlin, Paris and other capitals was that with Brexit and Donald Trump, this brand of Anglo-nationalist conservatism that had portrayed them as a deviance was now in charge. Unsurprisingly, the result was a rejection among Europe's center-left and center-right elites, even though there were many on the fringes who adopted much of the techniques and discourse of the Anglo-Nationalists. This has resulted in a divorce between much of the European center and center-right (which essentially holds power in Brussels) and the Anglo-American right. The fact that some adventurous American entrepreneurs came to the help of fringe anti-EU parties in continental Europe actually made matters worse: for EU politicians, Brexit was not only about cutting Britain and the United States from "degenerative" continental influence, it was also about putting an end to the EU experiment altogether.

In the words of Ralph Waldo Emerson, "The only way to have a friend is to be one,"[9] and on both sides of the Atlantic Ocean, Conservatives felt that their counterparts were not behaving like one. Where ideas were flowing freely between West and East before, it seemed that they now stopped at the North Sea and were systematically met with hostility on either side of it. In the final years of Donald Trump's presidency, the relationship turned from mutual distrust to practical divorce, with Republicans often seen as too toxically rightist to many European mainstream Conservatives, while Europeans were often portrayed as hopelessly soulless, even socialistic by many American Conservative intellectuals. In the meantime, while sovereigntist continental Conservatives may have found some favors in Washington, their power remains limited in Europe as they often remain on the fringes of European (and often their countries') politics, and their foreign policy outlook is not always compatible with that of the United

States: many embrace Vladimir Putin's politics and have relations (including financial) with the Kremlin, and some are even betting on China rather than the United States for the future.

If the divorce between the European and Anglo-American right had been in the making for some time and did not come necessarily as a surprise, the divorce between the American and the European center-left came much more brutally, and in many ways the debate over France's ban on the burkini in 2016 served as a catalyst for that divorce. Prior to that, the European left had looked at the souring of relations between Conservatives with a hint of *schadenfreunde*, as the election of Barack Obama had inspired many center-left parties, notably in Scandinavia, Italy, and France to stage an electoral comeback after years in the wilderness. If the Transatlantic right was no more because of nationalism, parties on the center-left were to make up for the deficit, as European Social Democrats adopted many of the postures and policies of the Obama Democrats. The honeymoon, however, was short, and as the left was confronted to a rejection of multiculturalism by much of the European electorate, declining polling numbers and a wave of Islamic State-sponsored terrorism in the mid-2010s, much of Europe's Social-Democratic establishments reverted to a more classical European social-liberal program, which in many places like France included a focus back on integrationist policies and a partial rejection of multiculturalism.

In the summer of 2016, right in between the victories of Brexit and Donald Trump, and while France was still going through a wave of Islamist terrorist attacks (the last of which had killed 87 people in Nice during the Bastille Day celebrations), a polemic grew in France over the use of burkinis on public beaches, with several mayors, some Socialist, banning it altogether. As the center-left government of Manuel Valls supported the mayors, the public debate quickly became international, and foreign news outlets like CNN and Al-Jazeera covered the controversy. Perhaps naively, the French socialists, and with them much of Europe's social left, hoped that the *New York Times* and other mainstream news outlets which they considered beacons of reason and enlightenment would side with them or at least stay neutral. After all, to them the burkini (and with it the burqa) was an expression of women's submission to religion rather than emancipation through reason, pretty much like the religious scarf for women had been in the days where governments had to enforce secularism on religious authorities, at least in Catholic Europe. They had not calculated that American secularism had been built to protect religions against persecution, while theirs had been constructed against religious persecution.

The fact that the *New York Times* not only sided with the burkini wearers, but also explicitly condemned what they considered French racism and bigotry[10] opened another intellectual rift between the politics of both sides of the Atlantic, with the center-left in the United States embracing part of the identity politics agenda, while the French, German, or Italian lefts remained either indifferent or much less permeable to the identity politics promoted in the United States. Nowhere has this divorce been more profound as in France, where many on the center-left have viewed the accusations of racism from the *New York Times* as a treason against the ideals of the Enlightenment, at a time in which they had to contend with the rise of home-grown Islamist terrorism and far-right politics. Many prominent French intellectuals broke with the American left, as the oppositions on the burkini crystallized over two views of universalism and liberalism: the one defended by Europeans (and, in its most extreme version, by the French) was more anticlerical and integrationist in nature, while the one defended by the Americans was more multicultural and, in many ways, moral and religious in its undertones.[11] The conflict has only intensified in the following years, with Emmanuel Macron's efforts to bring France back toward a more integrationist model condemned by the *New York Times*[12] and the *Washington Post*[13] as an authoritarian turn. The French government, on its side, did not hesitate to point out that some journalists of the venerable newspapers had not hesitated to willfully falsify information to persuade their readers that France was a racist and Islamophobic country.[14]

With European rights and lefts now skeptical about their American counterparts (and vice versa), there is now little space left in Europe for a healthy debate and exchange of ideas between the two sides of the Atlantic. Even the center has started to become less pro-American, as the extremes against whom centrists are fighting are often perceived (rightly or wrongly) as imports from the Anglo-Saxon political and intellectual system. As Europeans and Anglo-Americans realize that they are not as similar as they thought they were, this opens the way for further tensions and the fact that these tensions are now present on both left and right means that crisis looms at every corner: when the United States or Britain fared more poorly than Germany in the first wave of coronavirus in 2020, condescendence was pretty much on the menu in the German press. It even turned into a sort of *schadenfreunde* as many German liberals (and French intellectuals, among others) retreated into a told-you-so position after the storming of the US capitol on January 6. A few months after, it was the turn of the Anglos to have a go at the Euros' sluggish vaccination process with accusations of "vaccine nationalism" – those were even more unacceptable to Europeans, because they were actually exporting vaccines produced in Europe to Britain and America (following contracts better drafted by British and American authorities with the pharmaceutical companies), while no British- or American-made vaccines initially made their way back to Europe. Finger pointing continued throughout 2021, with the disastrous exit of Afghanistan and frictions over AUKUS providing more fuel to the partisans of a "strategic autonomy" designed to be an autonomy "from" rather than an autonomy "to do". Even after Brexit and the Trump presidency, European and Anglo-American paths continue to show signs of divergence, and although divorce is not for tomorrow, it is now contemplated by some, and not only on the fringes. The question is not whether this estrangement is an exception due to the passions created by Brexit and Donald Trump (we now know that it is not the case), but how deep the spat is, and whether the Transatlantic relationship can or even should be saved.

Are we all Americans?

"*Nous sommes tous Américains.*" On September 12, 2001, Jean-Marie Colombani, the director of France's main newspaper of record *Le Monde*, dared a headline for his editorial that many young Europeans may find strange today.[15] Yet it looked completely natural at the time, and it was thought as much of an expression of solidarity after the horror of the 9/11 terrorist attacks as an homage to the long-term relationship that Europeans and Americans had built over the past decades. Colombani's "We are all Americans" was a direct reference to John F. Kennedy's *ich bin ein Berliner* speech of 1963. Just like Kennedy had expressed his solidarity with the besieged Berliners of the time, Europeans could only express theirs to New Yorkers after 9/11. If such terrible events were to happen today, would the reaction be as generous? It is of course difficult to imagine the consequences of a life-changing shock like this, but considering the reactions in the 2010s by the American press on Europe's tragedies and by the European press on recent events in America, it is likely that solidarity would be expressed in a much more austere, even muted manner.

The contrast between the hyperbole of Colombani's editorial and the much more low-key reactions to the attacks on the Capitol of January 6, 2021, give a good idea of how Transatlantic relations have evolved in 20 years: 2001 represented a remarkable high point for the unity of a Transatlantic West, as NATO allies reacted to 9/11 by invoking Article 5 of the treaty (for the first and thus far only time) and sending troops to Afghanistan, in a war which was then seen as a fight not between the West and Islam, but for an ideal of freedom, democracy, and good government. Under America's uncontested and decisive leadership, the West had won the Cold War, defeated communism, and it seemed that the global drive for democracy and a Western way of life was irresistible. For sure, the nature of this Western way of life was hotly debated as some saw Europe as a worthier model than the United States (and vice versa), but the dominant idea of the time was one of a never-ending extension of the West and one of ever-closer relations between the two sides of the Atlantic. Ten years after 9/11, American thinker Francis Fukuyama actually quoted Denmark as the model toward which everyone, including the United States, would and should aspire to,[16] a proposition that certainly did not sound that attractive to British or American voters in 2016.

Europeans had also started drifting away from the United States prior to 2016. In Western Europe, they had actually done so long before: the invasion of Iraq of 2003 had already pitted many Europeans against the United States, and even though the continent was divided between an "old Europe" that opposed the war and a "new Europe" that supported it, the realities of public opinion pointed to a much larger rejection of American Middle Eastern policy. Intellectuals too had also started to part ways with the United States. In 2004, German liberal philosopher Jürgen Habermas published a vitriolic indictment of US foreign policy. Habermas pointed to American unilateralism and "aggressive" behavior as a betrayal of Western values – the values of the German enlightenment (notably the Kantian notion of peace through deliberation), but also American Wilsonian principles.[17] Whether willfully or not, his book represented an answer to Robert Kagan's *Of Paradise and Power*, in which the American pointed out the differences between the Venus-loving Europeans and the Mars-leaning Americans.[18]

Relations briefly warmed up during George W. Bush's second term, as a genuine effort of reaching out to estranged allies in Europe helped to repair some of the relationship with Berlin and Paris, among others. As the wars in Afghanistan and Iraq failed to produce the hoped-for results and as the number of casualties (including for Europeans) soared, relationships tightened. The arrival of two friends of America, Angela Merkel and Nicolas Sarkozy, at the head of Germany and France in 2005 and 2007, presented an opportunity for tightening the Transatlantic relationship: both leaders had refrained from criticizing the United States prior to and during the operations in Iraq, and they had actually proven much more supportive of repairing the relationship than the rest of their political establishment. But hopes for rapprochement were dashed as the United States entered a financial meltdown in 2008. All of a sudden, America did not seem all-powerful anymore, and it became easy for groups in Germany, France, and other countries to convince political leaders to take their distance – after all, the crisis had originated in the United States and its leadership was not to be taken for granted any longer. For many in the German and the French establishment, the crisis had been caused by greed, Anglo-Saxon greed. And Europeans had a more prudent model to propose. During the crisis, the writings of French economist Michel Albert, who in the 1990s had opposed the "Rhenian" and the "neo-American" capitalist models, suddenly became once again fashionable,[19] as the economic center of the world moved once again away from the Atlantic. In the meantime, American Conservatives who were rallying into the Tea Party movement were rejecting Barack Obama's promises of a more interventionist politics as unacceptable "socialism," a sign that America was taking the European way of decline and fall, symbolized by the US president's preference for Dijon mustard over the American kind.

Politically, the financial crisis of 2008 was devastating for the political image of America in Europe: prior to that, modernization meant in many ways Anglo-Saxon style reforms, a sort of adaptation of the Reagan–Thatcher recipes to European realities. But 2008 had exposed the fragility of the American financial systems, and although French and German banks (among others) had also sinned during the years of financial exuberance, the mood in Paris and Berlin was that this was fundamentally a crisis of the Anglo-American system, and that a new way needed to be trailed for Europe. In many ways, the rise of China – which had already become Germany's main economic partner back then – and the rising power of Russia in the East provided counter-models that fascinated European elites, although differently: the French and Italian center-right proved particularly sensitive to the narrative of Vladimir Putin's interventionism, which contrasted with the more passive image of Barack Obama's verbal type of leadership. On the other hand, German (and British) elites were fascinated by China's economic growth, which promised great returns on investment if only European firms could gain access to Chinese markets first. Even though the short "Obamania" of the late 2000s had revived a fascination for America among the general public (in particular its youth), the general direction taken by European elites toward America was one of skepticism.

Skepticism was in no way limited to Western Europe, as even allies in Poland showed signs of estrangement: in 2014, an illegal recording of a private conversation between the then-foreign minister Radosław Sikorski and his former colleague Jacek Rostowski revealed how bad the relationship between Poland and the United States had become, after the failed "reset" with Russia and the abandonment of the missile defense project in Poland. In the conversation, Sikorski had called the relationship "worthless" and even harmful, "because it creates a false sense of security …. We'll get in conflict with the Germans, Russians and we'll think that everything is super, because we gave the Americans a blow job."[20] The Obama administration had given many reasons for many different leaders in Europe to be dissatisfied: the Poles and Czechs were still furious at the United States for giving up on missile defense, the Germans were not happy because they had learnt that the NSA had been spying on their top officials, including Chancellor Angela Merkel, and French President François Hollande was still fuming over Barack Obama's decision not to intervene in Syria after Al-Assad's crossing his red line and using chemical against his own population – to his defense, Obama was not particularly keen on intervening after the fiasco of the Franco-British intervention in Libya, where the United States had "led from behind."

The events of the year 2016 thus provided a focal point rather than a break for the relationship between Europe and the United States. While they did represent a series of shocks for European elites on a number of issues, they did not completely come as a surprise, as distrust had been mounting over the previous 15 years, despite periods of rapprochement. The Trump presidency may have had the merit of patching up the relationship with a few countries like Poland and Hungary, but it was also at the cost of other relationships in other capitals like Berlin, Brussels, and Rome, which had also made the Transatlantic relationship the cornerstone of their foreign policy. The present difficulties do not come out of nowhere, and it was folly to think that with President Trump out of the way, things would get back to "normal," with goodwill immediately and automatically taking over. The Trump presidency only added another layer of mistrust on top of a series of events and miscomprehensions that could in the long run put the Transatlantic relationship in danger.

Euros versus Anglos: a long story

The question is whether the current dynamic of estrangement is unique in its scope, and whether it can be patched up. The answer to the first question is itself not necessarily straightforward. True, the experience of the past 20 years points toward a long-term degradation of the relations between the Anglos and the Euros, with the high points of the relationship becoming rarer, shorter, and less intense, while the low points seem to get longer and stronger. But this evolution must also be seen in the longer perspective of the history of Transatlantic (and, to some extent, trans-Channel) relations. That long-term perspective may tell us that our starting and ending points might not be the right references to pass judgment on the health of the Transatlantic relationships. There were in fact much lower points, not least of which in the 1920s and 1930s, when Europeans were already resenting America's rise. As Bruno Maçães puts it, "A century ago Europeans were already learning to resent America because it stood for the most dreadful of nightmares: the end of history and the American salesman."[21]

Nor was there much love lost on the American side in earlier days. In fact, the early history of the United States was all about insulating the country (and, if possible, the American continent) from European influence, as Charles Kupchan demonstrated in his history of American isolationism: "The Founders sought to ease Europe out of the Western Hemisphere so as to enable the United States to enjoy strategic isolation and the natural geographic advantage of flanking oceans and territorial girth."[22] Although American culture took all of its references in Europe, the admiration that Americans had for European cultural and scientific achievements, even when it led to copying and adaptation,[23] was often double-edged. As Kupchan puts it, for American elites "the Old World was beset by aristocratic privilege, social hierarchy, class conflict, and economic inequality. The United States, in contrast, would be free of class hierarchy and social impediments to economic opportunity."[24] Even new arrivals from Europe were not particularly keen about life back in the Old World: "immigrants to the New world sought not only economic opportunity and religious freedom, but also escape from the interstate violence that regularly plagued Europe."[25]

The relationship between America and Europe has varied depending on the times and the circumstances: the French cheered for the Anglo-Americans when they liberated them from Nazi Germany in 1945, but were less welcoming when the Americans, locked up in their NATO bases, turned out not to buy their products and seduced their daughters. Likewise, West Germans adored Uncle Sam during the Berlin Blockade or when John F. Kennedy uttered *Ich bin ein Berliner*, but proved much less enthusiastic when the Reagan administration installed Pershing missiles in Germany in the 1980s (it actually took a French Socialist, François Mitterrand, to remind German lawmakers that "the pacifisits may well be in the West, but the missiles are in the East"[26]). Americans' views on Europe have also varied greatly in time: think about the "Freedom Fries" incident of the early 2000s versus the short "bromance" between Emmanuel Macron and Donald Trump in 2017–2018. Much also depended on the people in place: to stay on the French example, while most Democrats were highly resentful of Charles de Gaulle and his willingness to distance himself from American power, Richard Nixon confessed his admiration for him. The other Republican president of the era, Dwight Eisenhower, was a much more convinced Europhile, having served both as supreme commander of the invasion force that liberated Western Europe in 1944–1945 and as Supreme Allied Commander Europe in 1951–1952.[27]

That the relationship has varied in time should come as no surprise to the reader. In many ways, since the end of the Second World War and the beginning of permanent presence on European soil, the ups and downs have gone through a series of short- and long-term cycles in which the good has alternated with the bad: America's image in 1946–1947 was very high among non-communists in the West because the United States was a shield against communism and because the American way of life fascinated Europeans. This image consolidated in the 1950s as West Europeans tried to copy the American dream and adapt it to their realities, while the vast communities of Central and Eastern Europeans who had developed in the United States and Canada renewed and maintained interest toward the other side of the Atlantic. But after 1965, the relationship deteriorated: as Americans lost self-confidence in Vietnam and proved not as virtuous as they thought they were, European intellectuals questioned US culture and policy: it was the time of anti-American demonstrations on European campuses, of the spaghetti Western (that originally mimicked but ended up critiquing John-Wayne epics), of De Gaulle's withdrawal from NATO's military command, and of Willy Brandt's *Ostpolitik*. But as Détente gave space for Europeans to take their distance from Washington, America remained a magnet for Europeans: while critical of the Western genre, Sergio Leone's and Sergio's Corbucci's films (among others) were as much a critique as an homage to American cinema, and despite their critiques for US foreign policy (notably in Vietnam), neither De Gaulle nor Brandt seriously considered leaving NATO itself.

The period of estrangement was followed in the early 1980s by a new rapprochement, which was triggered by the cooling of relations between the United States and the Soviet Union and accelerated with the new wave of optimism and confidence radiating from the United States under Ronald Reagan. The tightening of the relationship coincided with the end of the Cold War and the triumph of the West in the 1990s, triggering a wave of consumption of American goods and cultural products similar to the 1950s. However, the path toward triumph was no bed of roses. The early 1980s were not exactly defined by much trust between Europeans and Americans: the Germans gave Reagan a difficult time over the deployment of Pershing missiles on their soil in the early 1980s, the Spanish transition to democracy was proving chaotic and at times dangerous for US interests, and Ronald Reagan initially didn't trust the French Socialists of François Mitterrand, who had let Communists in the government. The relationship warmed up when Mitterrand proved to be much more reliable than Reagan expected, defending the Euromissiles in Bonn and sharing extremely sensitive information from a double agent turned by the French DST, which allowed in turn the CIA to get a much better grasp of the extent of GRU and KGB infiltration in their own ranks.[28]

Beyond conjunctural highs and lows, the relationship between the United States and continental Europe seems to have followed a 20-year cycle in which the general trajectory seems to be either ascendant (1945–1965, 1982–2001) or descendent (1965–1982, 2001–2022). The question, of course, is whether this means that Europeans and Americans are going to continue this regular cycle, or whether things will continue to deteriorate. Today, many signs point toward a warming up of relationships between Europeans and Americans under the Biden administration. The latter seems keen on renewing the relationship, but the signals coming from Brussels, Paris, and Berlin are not always positive. In diplomacy, it needs two to tango, and it looks like the automatisms are taking time to settle in. Could this absence be the sign that the rift is much more profound than just diplomatic relations?

In the early 1980s, when Europe progressively warmed up to the Reagan administration, two major factors brought the two sides of the Atlantic together: first the immediate threat of the Soviet Union, which was palpable enough to bring a critical mass of Europeans to rally behind America. This is what had led Mitterrand to declare that the Pacifists were in the West but the missiles in the East. The second thing was that for all the differences in approach and the occasional tension in the bilateral relationships, Europeans and Americans in the post-war period tended to see themselves as two parts of a civilizational whole, the "West" that ended up winning the Cold War. This is not necessarily the case any longer: as Bruno Maçães has recently argued, we may well be witnessing "the development of a new, indigenous American society, separate from modern Western civilization, rooted in new feelings and thoughts."[29] In the 1950s and 1960s, even though American culture started to form its own canon with the likes of Jack Kerouac, Elvis Presley, Bob Dylan, and Jason Pollock, its culture and politics remained deeply rooted in a "Western" cultural mold that made it easy for Europeans to identify with America – even when it was to criticize it – and vice versa. Today, the link is still there, but it has become more tenuous: American artists now produce works that are not only distinctly American but also non-European. In the meantime, and for different reasons, the American left and right have distanced themselves from the idea of the West, which is seen by the former as racist and the latter as decadent. On their side, Europeans have questioned with Jürgen Habermas the unity of the West following America's setbacks in Iraq, in Syria or in the financial and public health spheres.[30] Formerly understood as a given, the idea of an overwhelming cultural and political community (if not identity) on both sides of the Atlantic represented by "the West" is now giving way to that of a much more distant relation between Europe and America. The latter no longer considers itself necessarily as part of the West, which the former often understands as a rejection of Europe: during the Trump years (but also before), Europeans often came to question America's commitment to the ideals of liberty and self-government, which in their understanding is a feature of the West's identity.[31]

The fact is, however, that Americans and Europeans have always been different, ever since the Pilgrims landed on Plymouth Rock. Not that they do not share the same roots – more than any other blocs or civilizations, they do share a common culture and have thus found many times points of convergence, but the fact is that both Habermas and Kagan are right. They may not come from different planets, but Europeans and Americans think very differently on many things: social security, gun control, the understanding of the ordering of society and how to separate church and state, what needs to be done in the Middle East, the necessity of war in international relations, etc. Americans also have less sentimental attachment toward Europe: there are much less Eisenhowers today on Capitol Hill, as American demographics are changing and as Europe becomes a more peripheral area in the world. As this relative estrangement continues, the relationship between Europe and the United States (and also to a certain extent with Britain) becomes one of interest more than values, and the question arises: what are the American and the British interests in Europe? Should it be to continue to promote the vision dear to George H.W. Bush of a Europe Whole, Free and at Peace? Or should the Anglos on the contrary look at Europe as a chessboard where they will have to cynically jockey for influence with Russia and China?

Saving the Europe America made

There has been much quoting of Robert Kagan's work in his book, mainly from *Of Paradise and Power*, which came out in 2003, and *The Jungle Grows Back*, published in 2018. The two books are very different in their tone and message but to understand Kagan's thinking it is also worth diving into another book he published in between, *The World America Made*. In 2012, Kagan argued that despite challenges and the havoc called by the 2008 financial crisis, despite the rise of China, maintaining the American-led order was a goal worth pursuing. Indeed, it was a world aligned with American values and, down the line, favorable to US interests:

> "perhaps if Americans had a clearer picture of what might come after the American world order, they would be more inclined to continue struggling to preserve the world they have made, or at least to ensure that changes in the system do not undermine the order from which they, and others, have so greatly benefited."[32]

He also warned against the idea that this system, beneficial as a whole to America, could maintain itself by mere inertia.

> "The assumption […] is that the present world order will more or less persist without American power (or at least with much less of it), that others can pick up the slack, or simply that the benefits of the world order are permanent and require no special exertion by anyone. Unfortunately, however, the present world order is as fragile as it is unique."[33]

In many ways, Europe is a condensed version of *The World America Made*: for more than a hundred years now, it has been shaped by US involvement and intervention more than any other continent outside of North America. For good and for worse, from Versailles to Yalta to Dayton (and even to Maastricht and Lisbon, even though the United States were not a signatory), the Europe that we know today, with its present borders, its prosperity and its democratic governance, is the product of American production or co-production with Europeans. It was the United States that supported the dismantlement of empires in Europe, it was the United States that designed and helped the reconstruction of Europe, and it was the United States that inspired the new project of federating the peoples of the continent in democratic, United States of Europe or, as George H.W. Bush puts it, a "Europe Whole and Free," and at peace with itself.[34] Today, Europeans are still influenced by American culture and ideas more than any continent on earth. Kagan talked about "The World America Made," but in fact it is Europe that was shaped, more than anywhere else in the world, by America. This Europe that America Made, "for all its flaws and miseries [...] has been a remarkable anomaly in the history of humanity."[35] America may have failed to export freedom and democracy in some other parts of the world, but in many ways, Europe is the showroom of what it has been able to achieve, and all the positive impact it has had on people and institutions. If the United States were to leave Europe on its own device, it is likely that the idea of a Europe Whole, free and at peace would soon become a thing of the past.

This is not to say that Europe could not survive without the United States. The continent has lived for hundreds of years as a civilizational entity, and at times thrived without America. But without the United States, Europe would gradually become a very different place. It is likely that without the "oceanist" influence of American liberalism, many countries further inland would become more continentalist, more inward-looking, probably more illiberal, and certainly less democratic. Without an American "globocop," relations between European nations would not be of the same nature[36]: brute force would prevail more often – whether inside Europe or with the outside world. Trade would probably be not as free as it is right now, and in a balkanized system, some nations would be more tempted to dream about rebuilding the great empires they once were – this is what Europeans have always done, and it may well be what they will always do. True, for the first time in their history, Europeans have come together in a great ensemble that almost englobes the whole continent, and that ensemble wants to keep the peace inside Europe. The European Union has been designed to keep the peace among its members, but the problem is that it is currently too fragile, too weak to maintain it alone.

In many ways, pushing Europeans to build up the institutions and instruments they need to keep the peace by themselves would be the ultimate gift America could make to Europe: after extending the emporium of peace and democracy to almost the whole continent, consolidating this "acquis" by encouraging Europeans to strengthen their union and defend themselves on their own against any threats would be the ultimate achievement of more than a hundred years of American presence and influence in Europe. It would also allow Americans to put less focus on what is going on in a zone that is now less important to its interests, allowing it to deploy more attention to the Indo-Pacific zone, where the future will be played. In a world set to be defined for the next half-century by a rivalry between China and the United States, America has a vested interest in keeping Europe on its side.

Sure, interests between both sides of the Atlantic can and do vary, but values and long-term goals do not. Furthermore, it will be much easier for America to deal with one single entity that may at times behave independently but will ultimately be there in times of crisis, rather than having to deal with a patchwork of nation-states, some of whom will inevitably fall into the influence of China. The EU may not always be an easy ally, but neither has France or Germany been in the past – that did not diminish the fact that they were ultimately allies, and were present in real times of need for the United States (the Cuban crisis, the Euromissiles, or 9/11 and Afghanistan come to mind).

Some American Conservatives may argue that the United States does not need Europe and that the European Union is an unnatural ensemble of states that should never have been put together in the first place. Yet they could have argued the same about Germany, Italy or Switzerland, none of which existed as state entities in the early 19th century and are now considered as natural as water and air. As Americans are well aware, identities do evolve, and the fact that the European Union has survived in one form or another for more than 70 years already is a sign that this European identity is taking roots in Europe itself. Indeed, as Ivan Krastev puts it, the crises that have happened over the past 15 years have brought together Europeans as much as they have torn them apart:

> "in reality, the Union's various crises, much more so than any of Brussels's "cohesion policies," have contributed to the sense that we Europeans are all part of the same political community. In responding to the euro crisis, the refugee question and the growing threat of terrorism, Europe has ended up more integrated than ever before, at least when it comes to economics and security."[37]

Indeed, the result of the 2008 economic crisis has ultimately been a more powerful European Central Bank; the migrant crisis of 2015 has led to the creation of the Frontex agency to provide a common solution to protect Europe's borders. And even though the EU has not exactly covered itself with glory with the order of vaccines in 2020–2021, it got it right in the end and also moved forward with the mutualization of debt and a recovery plan that may still remain small in comparison to the US plan but is nonetheless remarkable considering the starting point.

Today, the United States is dealing with a European Union that was mostly inspired from the American experience, with whom the US trades and invests more than any other bloc on the planet, and that is way too diverse (and unwilling) to contest its global leadership. True, Europeans and Americans are different in many ways, when it comes to guns, the role of the state in society, or even about what is best for the Middle East. But while American and European interests are not aligned completely, they are currently the closest that could be in a changing world: apart from the values of democracy and liberty shared among a wide spectrum in Europe and America, both sides of the Atlantic have a common interest in upholding maritime freedom alive in a world where this current reality may be challenged by the rise of other powers. They also have a common interest in making sure that China's dumping practices cease, because workers on both sides of the Atlantic are suffering from Chinese unfair competition. And to fight unfair competition, European and American businesses are actually often complementary to each other: so far the Swedish Ericsson and the Finnish Nokia are the best 5G alternatives to Huawei around the world, while maritime transport has been left for Europeans to ensure on behalf of the West, as the profits were often seen too small for Anglo-American companies.

America has an interest in upholding the Europe that it shaped for more than a hundred years. Not only because keeping the peace in a continent prone to make war is in itself a remarkable achievement, but also because it is in America's interest to do so: billions of dollars in trade and foreign investment are at stake, and return on investment will be more secure if America and Europe talk to each other as two blocs rather than as one entity versus a myriad of others. True, negotiations will be tougher and the United States will not get their way as often as they could in dealing with small nation-states, but the long-term relationship will be much more solid and will keep China out of European markets. There are of course costs to dealing with a united Europe. As Bruno Maçães points out, "the European Union will not create a common defense and security policy without in the process diminishing the inordinate weight of the American defense industry in Europe."[38] But that does not mean that Europeans will no longer buy American weapons – they might actually buy more costly, high-added-value products under one budget, and most importantly they will be able to provide more easily for themselves, allowing Americans to project their power where it needs to be projected: not in West Germany, at peace for the past 75 years, but in the areas where its interest (and more largely those of the West) are most directly threatened.

The idea brandished by some Conservatives that a united Europe would become the main geopolitical threat to the United States has been proven wrong by the test of reality: a more united Europe has not grown to threaten the United States, because it is too diverse and too tired of the world to really want to lead. In many ways, the EU is to the United States what Austria was to Germany in the early 20th century: a useful, even though at times pesky ally, clearly a junior partner but one that needs to be respected. Indeed, Germany's treatment of the Austrian monarchy as a mere sidekick is one of the reasons why the relationship between the two empires worsened after 1915, and in a sense why both led to each other's doom in the last months of the war.[39] In a world that is no longer unilateral, America needs friends, and it will not find any other large actor in the Eurasian (and African) landmass more similar than the European Union. Indeed, it is often integrated, supranational institutions like the European Parliament that align European policy closer to US interests: in 2020–2021, when nation-states like Germany pushed for an investment deal with China detrimental to Europe as a whole (and to US interests), it was the European Parliament, the most supranational of institutions, that proved the most resistant institution against the deal. This should serve as a lesson to the United States: the institutions that most closely correspond to their model of democracy are also those that side the most often with their values and, down the line, their interests.

Britain and Europe – avoiding catastrophe

If America has an interest in preserving the Europe that it has shaped for over a century, Britain's post-Brexit conundrum with the continent is much different. First, because unlike America the United Kingdom has not shaped Europe since the beginning of the Cold War. Rather, whether inside or outside the Union, it has felt that events on the continent were mostly outside its control. Second, even though the United Kingdom has cut formal links with the EU, it is still inextricably linked with it, as only 50 km and one of the busiest straits in the world separate Britain from the continent. For all the talks about Global Britain, the United Kingdom remains fundamentally a European country, even though it is also different from the rest of Europe.

Anglosphere scholars Michael Kenny and Nick Pearce are right when they point out that "when it comes to trade, it seems that 'geography trumps history' decisively"[40]; indeed the EU is Britain's biggest trading partner and will very likely remain so for a long time, even more so as the trend toward localism and a certain extent of de-globalization will probably accelerate in the coming years. But trade is not the only area where geography is a stronger marker than "kith and kin." True, Britain is culturally (and to a large extent institutionally) closer to other Anglosphere countries like Canada, Australia and New Zealand. But politically (and indeed, geopolitically), Britain has always and will always be tied to the European security system, whether it likes it or not. And even though cultural solidarity is a particularly strong form of solidarity, it also has limits, especially when other countries on the other side of the world have other priorities to attend to, as the British discovered at the beginning of the Second World War: it took a direct attack on the United States for it to intervene decisively in favor of Britain – and even then it did not enter the war in Europe before Adolf Hitler declared war on America. As former French diplomat Gérard Araud once said it in the context of the Francophonie, but it also holds for the English-speaking nations,

> "there is a strange notion according to which countries sharing a same language would share the same vision of the world, the same values and

the same interests. A few months working in the United Nations free you from this illusion."[41]

This is of course not to say that the bonds of the Anglosphere are not real. But as everything else, they have limits, as even think-alike countries can have different interests. This is why an overreliance on the concept of "Anglo-Saxon solidarity" would be detrimental to the United Kingdom – not because Canada, Australia, New Zealand or the United States would not care about Britain, but because their capacity to help will always be limited by geography – and their own national interest. Whether it likes it or not, and even though it has cut institutional ties with the EU, Britain remains tied with Europe geographically, and ignoring what goes on inland is a perilous business. Indeed, each time it has been tried, British elites have come to regret it: whether in the 1860s, in the 1890s, in the 1930s, or indeed the 1950s, the drive for "splendid isolation" proved to be an unmitigated disaster for British interests on a continent to which it geographically and geopolitically belongs, if only reluctantly. The more it has tried to ignore events shaping or reshaping the continent, the more violently it has been brought back into the orbit of European politics. Whether it likes it or not, Britain remains in Europe, and it will therefore have to find a new role to play in greater European politics.

In many ways, Britain's conundrum toward a now much more unified continent today is very similar to that of 1950s and 1960s Britain, even though London's hand is much stronger today, thanks to a long streak of higher economic growth. Now that it is out of the European Union, it cannot rein in on the federalist dynamic going on in at least parts of Europe, nor can it directly influence policies and outcomes in the Union. The EU, of course, has lost much with Brexit (notably a major economy of the continent and a source of growth and innovation), but so has Britain. In a relatively peaceful environment, Brexit has also left the United Kingdom isolated between the North Sea and the Atlantic, a situation that the then prime minister MacMillan had already identified as a dangerous walk between a "less [...] friendly America and a boastful, powerful 'Empire of Charlemagne' – [then] under French but later bound to come under German control."[42] Of course, neither the "unfriendliness" (relative of absolute) of the United States nor the imperial nature of Carolingian Europe are given facts. But the reality is that the United States now is culturally much less attached to the United Kingdom than it was 50 years ago, and a Carolingian Europe dominated by France and Germany is a direct result of Brexit, which left France and Germany accounting more than 40% of an EU-27 GDP (a figure that jumps to 55% if Italy is added).

While full of opportunities if it manages to position itself as a tech and financial hub (much to the benefit of Europe, actually), the geopolitical position of post-Brexit Britain is much more fragile and potentially full of dangers. Of course, the Channel has not overnight become the Messina straits, and navigating between the North Sea and the Atlantic is certainly not the same as sailing between Scylla and Charybdis (or inside the South China Sea for that matter). But Britain's position of relative isolation between two blocs carries as many risks as opportunities, even more so when one bloc is geographically much closer than the other. As Paul Lever puts it, "living alongside an economic superpower will present its own challenges." But this may not be all: if the EU gets really serious about building its own military capacity (as this book suggests), this will bring new challenges:

> "living next to a political and military [major power], in the way that Canada lives next to the United States, would mean a fundamental change to Britain's position in the world. It is unlikely that when Boris Johnson mentioned Canada as an illustration of how Britain might negotiate a trade agreement with the EU he had this sort of relationship in mind."[43]

If Britain has quickly grown accustomed to a powerful United States on the other side of the Atlantic, it is reasonably much more uncomfortable with the idea of having a strong, potentially united Europe just a few miles away from its seashore. After all, Britain's security has for centuries been defined by the idea that a balance of powers on a divided continent would give it a free hand on the oceans, where its place really lies. But the problem is that this balance of power, if ever it existed after 1989, no longer exists, and this leaves Britain with a security dilemma vis-à-vis this huge but not very agile vessel that is the European Union: it might benefit by getting close to it and adopting many of its norms, but this will also reduce its competitive advantage toward the rest of the world. On the other hand, if it navigates too far away from it, it risks becoming irrelevant and dependent on events going on inside the continent, for better or for worse. Finally, if the EU were to go down in flames, as some Brexiters still dream it will, this will not only pose new security dilemmas for the United Kingdom, it will also impoverish it: after all, many of the economic opportunities brought by the rise of the City of London are intrinsically linked to access and proximity to the EU market. Take that out, and the City is much less attractive globally (much like Singapore would not be much attractive to the world without its proximity to the fast-growing Asian markets).

Nor does Britain have a vested interest in seeing the European Union doing too well. As *The Economist* mentioned in March 2021, being the neighbor of a huge bloc like the EU supposes that one either accepts and play along that big bloc's superiority in numbers ("being Switzerland") or that it contests this superiority at any occasion (the "Turkey" option[44]). The excruciating scenario of Brexit has led both Britain and the EU to this latter option, and it is not without danger. Indeed, both actors currently have a vested interest in the other doing badly: for the EU, problems in the United Kingdom would confirm that European members are stronger together and that leaving the Union is a risky business. During the Brexit negotiations, the number of candidates, although very thin from the beginning, has actually decreased. On the other hand, if

Britain fares much better without the EU, not only will London feel vindicated in its choice to leave, but it will see it as a sign that it can and should encourage other countries to engineer their own "exit" to further weaken the EU: after all, it remains fundamentally in Britain's interest to deal with a divided continent. The problem is that this can lead both actors to act (or to be perceived as acting) with the purpose of destroying the other's union: hardcore Brexiters are making no secret that for them Brexit was never only about Britain, it was also about freeing Europe from the Brussels monster. Considering the challenges of keeping the kingdom united in the long term, many on the continent would also be tempted to play the Scottish or Irish card should Britain get involved in too much anti-European activity. As described in Chapter 7, this could lead to an escalation that could in turn bring war in a region that has not seen it for so many years.

Of course, things do not need to turn out that way. Smart politics and restraints on both sides of the North Sea can turn a messy divorce into a civil, if at times awkward, neighborly relationship. This does not mean that there will not be tensions between the United Kingdom and the EU, and the immediate post-Brexit period has been full of them. For even if they may have a short-and-medium-term interest in poking at each other, Britain and the EU have a long-term interest in keeping the peace, for their own security and economic interests. At the end of the day, economic relations will be the key as they will define the mood in London and Brussels – and as MacMillan once warned Adenauer, "no British government could continue to take part in the military defense of a continent which had declared economic war upon her."[45] To a certain extent, the reverse is also true, as European countries will have an interest in upholding the peace with Britain over the seas or, indeed, on the Irish border, if their economic relationship does not lead to decent life conditions for everyone. Navigating between the short-term interests of disruption and the long-term interests of good trade and co-operation to ensure the larger security of Europe (and to a larger extent the Atlantic world) will require skill, co-ordination and patience on both sides. Much will depend on diplomats, as well as goodwill on behalf of the United States, who should be able to provide reasons for all to agree on upholding freedom and peace on the continent. For that, Americans, Brits, and Europeans will have to reappropriate the concept of the West to find goals to achieve together in the future.

Reclaiming the West to uphold the peace

The past 20 years have coincided with a long estrangement between continental Europe and the Anglo-Americans, and even though there is no inevitability to this disaffection, there are grounds to fear for the long-term future of the Transatlantic Alliance. Without a common, well-defined foe (which China does not seem to be everywhere in Europe, at least in absolute terms), Transatlantic discipline may prove difficult to maintain in the future. Add to this demographic and cultural trends moving America (and to a certain extent Britain) further away from continental Europe, the risk of divorce is real. Today, too many young Americans are looking at Europe as inherently white (which it mostly is) and racist (which it mostly is not, even though it sometimes is); on the other side of the Atlantic, too many young Europeans see the Americans as irresponsible warmongers or spoiled children, and in between too many Brits have contempt for either or both. The risk is real to see what used to be called "the West" disappear into a number of different, smaller worlds, one American, one European, and in between a British (or English) entity separate from both. Of course, this is exactly what China is hoping for: a divided West will grant Beijing an indisputable moral victory, because it has for years been arguing that China's rise meant a revenge on the West and that the West was in a state of terminal decline. To be fair with the Chinese, it is true that neither the Americans nor the Europeans or Brits have necessarily covered themselves with glory over the past 20 years.

That "the West" is coming out bruised and less united from the past political and economic cycles is beyond doubt: over the past 15 years, while Europe and America underperformed economically and got stuck in endless conflicts, the world moved on, and in the competition between "the West and the Rest," the Rest has caught up spectacularly. But "the Rest," just like the BRICS, seems to be a much less relevant concept nowadays: one of the "Rest," China, has become a global leader, India is rising as an important global (and, importantly, regional) actor but looks at China with much anxiety, Russia is now an impoverished disruptor, while Brazil and South Africa are struggling with internal problems. In the meantime, new regional actors (among them Turkey, Indonesia, Qatar and the Emirates) have emerged, in different ways. In any case, the tendency has been toward a rise of non-Western actors in what Richard Baldwin has called the "Great Convergence."[46] Today, the World looks much less Western than it has ever been for at least the past 200 years, and it is unlikely that the trend will be reversed any time soon. Indeed, as non-Western countries catch up with the West, they increasingly seek to differentiate themselves from it, to assert and promote their own way of development, whether they brand it as Chinese, Muslim, African, etc.[47]

This new World may not be "West-less" but it is certainly less Western. This has caught Americans and Europeans by surprise. After all, the 1990s were the triumph of the West, which had beaten communism. And as the West enlarged in the 2000s to include most of Central and Eastern Europe, there were reasons to believe that the triumphal march toward a more Western world would follow. In the words of Michael Kimmage, one of the trademarks of the West, its messianism, had led "to overreach, excess, hubris,"[48] for which Westerners ultimately paid the price between 2008 and 2020. As the West subsequently retreated, it became clear that serious questioning needed to happen, something which the mainstream managed rather poorly on both sides of the aisle, leaving room to radicals to bring solutions to the decline of the West, either by ditching what it had become or condemning the concept altogether. But as Kimmage points out, these two critics are not fundamentally new: in many ways, they echo arguments that had already been made in the 1960s and 1970s.[49] These critiques in turn echoed in some ways the 1920s and 1930s, where other critiques of the Western way of life emerged from the far-left and far-right. Both pointed out real failings in the West, and it took major reform as well as the charismatic and inspirational leadership of two leaders, Franklin D. Roosevelt in the 1930s and Ronald Reagan in the 1980s, to reinvent the model and revive the West.

It would be easy to take refuge in the idea that such a miracle will inevitably happen once again to save the West, to make America (and Europe) rise once again as the shining city on the hill. But just like peace, power does not preserve itself, and as China now publicizes its ambitions to replace the United States and more generally the West as the new norm-setter, Western reactions have thus far been little inspiring for the rest of the planet, let alone the Transatlantic World. How could it be when Western elites have stopped believing in it altogether? The left of Noam Chomsky and the right of Pat Buchanan had, for different reasons, given up on the West a long time ago, but since 2000, the center also seems to have abandoned the concept: as Michael Kimmage points out, American elites stopped using it totally after 2001,[50] leaving it only for critiques. This *Abandonment of the West*, to use the title chosen by Kimmage for his book, has itself meant that countries (and people) that had been attracted to the West in the past now had second thoughts. After all, if Americans themselves were no longer proud of being Westerners, why should Hungarians or French Conservatives, for example, still root for it? The rise of what I have called "continentalism" in this book, so visible today in many parts of Europe, has been a short-term gift to countries like China who want to relegate the West to the dustbins of history. It is also deadly for the cohesion of the Transatlantic World, and for a Europe whole, free and at peace – the Europe America made. This is why such temptations of deconstructions or rejections of the West need to be fought against, and this is why the West must be revived.

The question, of course, is how to reclaim a concept that is so intensely criticized, and clearly in need of revamping. One option, advanced by some Conservatives, is to use the West in a more restrictive manner to get back to its roots, and those roots are invariably Christian, Conservative and very often Anglo-Saxon. Such a view would amount to close the wagon circle around a defined core, centering it on the Anglosphere, and therefore excluding continental Europe (and much of the rest of the world) from it. As discussed earlier in this chapter, the proposition is not wise: not only does it create a temptation for countries in what Milan Kundera had called "kidnapped West" to re-think themselves as Eastern and continentalist, but it also restricts the idea of the West to an image of the past – an image that may have corresponded to a reality in the past century (although that is debatable) but that fits neither the needs nor the realities of the present times.

The restrictive vision of the West, however, is not without merits, as it focuses on a truth that we have tended to forget – that the West is first and foremost a cultural object. As Kimmage points out, "the Euro-American world, the transatlantic West, was at its heart a textual community, truly more Magna Carta than Magna Mac,"[51] and this cultural dimension cannot be occulted. The question is whether to limit this cultural dimension to religious or ethnic factors, or whether there can exist a much larger, universalist aspiration that can inspire not only people in Europe and North America but throughout the world.

We have tended to forget it, but the appeal of the West is actually neither fully geographical nor limited to a religion or color of skin. In fact, from Roman cosmopolitanism to Christianity's global message to the Enlightenment and democracy, the West has always had a universal ambition. True, that ambition has led at times to unhealthy messianism, but it has also provided genuine and positive inspiration for the whole world: the West can be found in the sermons of Reverend Martin Luther King, in the compassionate homilies of Pope Francis as well as in the contagious optimism of Ronald Reagan or the writings of Montesquieu on the separation of powers and Kant on how to achieve universal peace. It is also present in the conservatism of Edmund Burke, in the feminist writings of Simone de Beauvoir, and in the egalitarianism of the woke movement, whose Christian rules have been brilliantly demonstrated by Tom Holland.[52] This messianism can lead to abuse, but it is also an inspiration of liberation: when Kyiv demonstrators waved Orange and then European flags, when Burmese, Belarusian or Lebanese demonstrators took the streets to defend their rights, they often did so with the intent of building their own West in their country. They are a living example that even when it is at its lowest, the West continues to inspire people in a way that no other system – and certainly not Chinese communism – can.

The idea of the West is not dead yet, and it should not be left to die. But to be successful again, the West needs to focus on itself and reinvent its model. Of course, this new Western renaissance cannot be decreed, and it must come with some political will as well as an intellectual flourishing (which comes with debate, another trademark of the West). But it also needs to be fed with the optimism that a Ronald Regan, a John F. Kennedy, or a Franklin Roosevelt could inspire. To do that, much work needs to be done at home, to regain that sense of cohesion that will then help Western countries move forward. Much has been written (including in this book) about the need to rebuild a sense of belonging to a larger community that can transcend, even for a moment, our ordinary lives. This cohesion is never easy to be found, and it often involves tensions that need to be pro-actively and reactively managed, which is why politics needs to re-take its place in public policy: too many times over the past decades have we given in to the ideology of the market, imagining that they would self-regulate, that the rule of law would sustain itself, that democracy was a given. The past ten years have humbled us, in Europe as in North America, and we must face up to our shortcomings, understand our mistakes, and move forward by accepting disruption and challenges rather than ignoring them because they do not fit our own ideological prejudices.

But while we fix our polities, we cannot cage ourselves into an inward-looking-only version of the West. This would truly be an abandonment of the concept. We need to think bigger. The West is not a fixed concept, which is what makes it so powerful. It can be described as triumphant and declining at the same time, it has cultural as well as geographical or political undertones, and most importantly it is not fixed in one country: the West won the Great War, the Second World War and the Cold War, but in each case it was a different West. In fact, as Michael Kimmage points out, "The West lives most fully in the never-ending battles over what it is, what it means, what is has been."[53] Now indeed is not the time to shut the West down but on the contrary to open it, by example as well as by diplomacy.

Italian diplomats and defense officials have over the years operated their country's foreign policy around three equally important concepts: the Transatlantic relationship, European integration, and a concept they call the *Mediterraneo allargato*, or enlarged Mediterranean.[54] Originally born out of an ambition to make the Mediterranean a *Mare Nostrum* once again, it has since evolved as a concept to advance Italy's interests around the Mediterranean (including in the Muslim world), but its outreach actually goes much further, to include what were important ways of commerce for the Roman Empire: the Red Sea, the Black Sea, the Strait of Ormuz (among others), all of which remain hugely important for the Mediterranean, which is connected to them all (and indeed, connects them all). Today the West needs to imagine its own "enlarged West," one that may not be as strictly Euro-American, but in which countries outside of it have built their own version of a free and open society. This enlarged West could include Taiwan, Japan, South Korea, India,[55] and many others in Africa and Latin America, brought together by a common willingness to preserve their democratic institution and a commitment to freedom and democracy. This enlarged West would certainly be more difficult to co-ordinate as it would include many different countries with different objectives, and actors like India that will remain unwilling, for historical reasons, to entangle themselves in alliances. But the enlarged West currently has two strong raisons d'être: first, a powerful common long-term foe in China, and second an equally powerful commitment to free and democratic institutions. That does not exclude of course a tightening of the Transatlantic Alliance within that enlarged West. But this broad and informal grouping across the oceans would make America – and the more restrictive West it currently leads – much more powerful as it faces the threat of a communist, autocratic China. A humbled, renovated and enlarged West would thus be the most promising way to keep America's world leadership safe – and to ensure the continuation of *Pax Americana* on the European continent.

Notes

1 See Thibault Muzergues, *Europe champ de bataille: de la guerre impossible à une paix improbable*, Lormont: le Bord de l'Eau, 2021.

2 As Michael Kimmage puts it in his history of the West as an idea in US foreign policy, "Never did the fortunes of European or Euro-American or Western liberty seem darker than in the 1930s. Never were Europe and the United States more violently at odds than during the Second World War." Michael Kimmage, *The Abandonment of the West: The History of an Idea in American Foreign Policy*, New York: Basic Books, 2020, p.20.
3 See Paul Lever, *Berlin Rules: Europe and the Germany Way*, London: IB Tauris, 2017, pp.129–164.
4 See Andrew Adonis et al., *Half In Half Out: Prime Ministers on Europe*, London: Basic Books, 2018.
5 https://www.forbes.com/sites/nickmorrison/2021/02/09/uk-universities-face-financial-loss-as-brexit-hits-eu-student-numbers/#:~:text=Universities%20are%20forecast%20to%20lose,slump%20by%20more%20than%20half
6 https://www.politico.eu/article/donald-trump-putin-russia-europe-one-of-united-states-biggest-foes/
7 https://www.economist.com/europe/2020/06/11/europes-sinatra-doctrine-on-china
8 Patrick Buchanan, *The Death of the West: How Dying Populations and Immigrant Invasions Imperil Our Country and Civilization*, New York: Griffin, 2002.
9 Quoted by Franklin Roosevelt in his Fourth Inaugural Address on January 20, 1945, quoted in Gideon Rose, "The Fourth Founding: The United States and the Liberal Order," *Foreign Affairs*, Vol. 98, No. 1, January–February 2019, p.21.
10 https://www.nytimes.com/2016/08/19/opinion/frances-burkini-bigotry.html
11 Tom Holland has demonstrated with remarkable foresight how much of the woke Credo actually derives from Christian thinking. See Tom Holland, *Dominion: The Making of the Western Mind*, London: Little, Brown, 2019, pp.499–525.
12 https://www.nytimes.com/2020/11/25/world/europe/france-macron-muslims-police-laws.html
13 https://www.washingtonpost.com/opinions/2020/12/03/macrons-centrist-tolerant-facade-is-crumbling/
14 https://www.washingtonexaminer.com/opinion/washington-post-staffer-fabricates-story-about-france-targeting-muslim-schoolchildren
15 https://www.lemonde.fr/idees/article/2011/09/09/nous-sommes-tous-americains_1569503_3232.html
16 Francis Fukuyama, *The Origins of Political Order, from Prehuman Times to the French Revolution*, London: Profile Books, 2012.
17 Jürgen Habermas, *The Divided West*, Cambridge: Polity, 2006 (the original version, in German, was published in 2004).
18 Robert Kagan, *Of Paradise and Power: America and Europe in the New World Order*, New York: Vintage Books, 2004.
19 Michel Albert, *Capitalisme contre capitalisme*, Paris: Seuil, 1991.
20 https://www.theguardian.com/world/2014/jun/22/poland-foreign-minister-alliance-us-worthless
21 Bruno Maçães, *History has Begun: The Birth of a New America*, London: Hurst, 2020, p.51.
22 Charles Kupchan, *Isolationism: A History of America's Efforts to Shield Itself from the World*, New York: Oxford University Press, 2020, p.6.
23 Bruno Maçães, *History has Begun: The Birth of a New America*, London: Hurst, 2020.
24 Charles Kupchan, *Isolationism: A History of America's Efforts to Shield Itself from the World*, New York: Oxford University Press, 2020.
25 Ibid., p.65.
26 https://fresques.ina.fr/mitterrand/fiche-media/Mitter00062/le-pacifisme-est-a-l-ouest-et-les-euromissiles-sont-a-l-est.html
27 See Michael Kimmage, *The Abandonment of the West: The History of an Idea in American Foreign Policy*, New York: Basic Books, 2020 (notably), pp.138–139.

28 The double agent story, one of the best-known success stories of France's counterintelligence efforts in the late Cold War, is better known to the public by the code name of its agent, "Farewell." For more details on the story itself, see Sergei Kostin and Eric Reynaud, *Farewell: The Greatest Spy Story of the Twentieth Century*, Seattle: Amazon Crossing, 2011. And for how it influenced US–French relations, see Pierre Favier and Michel Martin-Roland, *La Décennie Mitterrand, Volume 1: les ruptures (1981–1984)*, Paris: Seuil, 1990, pp.94–96.
29 Bruno Maçães, *History has Begun: The Birth of a New America*, London: Hurst, 2020, p.19.
30 Jürgen Habermas, *The Divided West*, Cambridge: Polity, 2006.
31 Michael Kimmage, *The Abandonment of the West: The History of an Idea in American Foreign Policy*, New York: Basic Books, 2020, p.299.
32 Robert Kagan, *The World America Made*, New York: Alfred A. Knopf, 2012, p.135.
33 Ibid., p.134.
34 George H. W. Bush's speech in Mainz is available online: https://usa.usembassy.de/etexts/ga6-890531.htm
35 Robert Kagan, *The World America Made*, New York: Alfred A. Knopf, 2012, p.141.
36 See Ian Morris, *War: What is it Good for? The Role of Conflict in Civilization, from Primates to Robots*, London: Profile Books, 2014, p.344.
37 Ivan Krastev, *After Europe*, Philadelphia: University of Pennsylvania Press, 2017, p.110.
38 Bruno Maçães, *History has Begun: The Birth of a New America*, London: Hurst, 2020, p.175.
39 See Jean-Paul Bled, *L'agonie d'une monarchie, Autriche-Hongrie 1914–1920*, Paris: Tallandier, 2014.
40 Michael Kenny and Nick Pearce, *Shadows of Empire: The Anglosphere in British Politics*, Cambridge: Polity, 2018, p.160.
41 https://twitter.com/GerardAraud/status/1253041493390118912
42 MacMillan's diary, quoted in Andrew Adonis et al., *Half In Half Out: Prime Ministers on Europe*, London: Basic Books, 2018, p.65.
43 Paul Lever, *Berlin Rules: Europe and the German Way*, London: IB Tauris, 2017, p.223.
44 https://www.economist.com/europe/2021/03/20/how-the-british-became-the-new-turks
45 Quoted in Andrew Adonis et al., *Half In Half Out: Prime Ministers on Europe*, London: Basic Books, 2018, p.64.
46 See Richard Baldwin, *The Great Convergence: Information Technology and the New Globalization*, Cambridge, MA: Harvard University Press, 2016.
47 See Fareed Zakharia, *The Post-American World and the Rise of the Rest – Release 2.0*, New York: W.W. Norton, 2011.
48 Michael Kimmage, *The Abandonment of the West: The History of an Idea in American Foreign Policy*, New York: Basic Books, 2020, p.316.
49 See Ibid.
50 Ibid., pp.1–25.
51 Ibid., p.309.
52 Tom Holland, *Dominion: The Making of the Western Mind*, London: Little, Brown, 2019.
53 Michael Kimmage, *The Abandonment of the West: The History of an Idea in American Foreign Policy*, New York: Basic Books, 2020, p.14.
54 https://www.ammiragliogiuseppedegiorgi.it/mc/481/il-mediterraneo-allargato
55 While India is part of the non-aligned movement and has great reservations about the West *stricto sensu*, it also shares many features with it, for better and for worse. As Michael Kenny and Nick Pearce point out: "In a speech to the Oxford Union in July 2005, which caused considerable controversy in his own country and sent a ripple throughout Anglosphere circles, the Indian Prime Minister, Manmohan Singh, observed the imperial sources of many of India's assets and strengths, from its

railroads to its democratic system. 'if there is one phenomenon on which the sun cannot set,' he observed, 'it is the world of the English-speaking peoples, in which the people of Indian origin are the single largest component,'" Michael Kenny and Nick Pearce, *Shadows of Empire: The Anglosphere in British Politics*, Cambridge: Polity, 2018.

Bibliography

Adonis, Andrew et al., *Half In Half Out: Prime Ministers on Europe*, London: Basic Books, 2018.

Albert, Michel, *Capitalisme contre capitalisme*, Paris: Seuil, 1991.

Baldwin, Richard, *The Great Convergence: Information Technology and the New Globalization*, Cambridge, MA: Harvard University Press, 2016.

Bled, Jean-Paul, *L'agonie d'une monarchie, Autriche-Hongrie 1914–1920*, Paris: Tallandier, 2014.

Buchanan, Patrick, *The Death of the West: How Dying Populations and Immigrant Invasions Imperil Our Country and Civilization*, New York: Griffin, 2002.

Fukuyama, Francis, *The Origins of Political Order, From Prehuman Times to the French Revolution*, London: Profile Books, 2012.

Habermas, Jürgen, *The Divided West*, Cambridge: Polity, 2006.

Holland, Tom, *Dominion: The Making of the Western Mind*, London: Little, Brown, 2019.

Kenny, Michael, and Pearce, Nick, *Shadows of Empire: The Anglosphere in British Politics*, Cambridge: Polity, 2018.

Kagan, Robert, *The World America Made*, New York: Alfred A. Knopf, 2012.

Kimmage, Michael, *The Abandonment of the West: The History of an Idea in American Foreign Policy*, New York: Basic Books, 2020.

Kostin, Sergei, and Reynaud, Eric, *Farewell: The Greatest Spy Story of the Twentieth Century*, Seattle: Amazon Crossing, 2011.

Kupchan, Charles, *Isolationism: A History of America's Efforts to Shield Itself from the World*, New York: Oxford University Press, 2020.

Krastev, Ivan, *After Europe*, Philadelphia: University of Pennsylvania Press, 2017.

Lever, Paul, *Berlin Rules: Europe and the German Way*, London: IB Tauris, 2017.

Maçães, Bruno, *History has Begun: The Birth of a New America*, London: Hurst, 2020.

Morris, Ian, *War: What is it Good for? The Role of Conflict in Civilization, from Primates to Robots*, London: Profile Books, 2014.

Muzergues, Thibault, *Europe champ de bataille: de la guerre impossible à une paix improbable*, Lormont: le Bord de l'Eau, 2021.

Rose, Gideon, "The Fourth Founding: The United States and the Liberal Order," *Foreign Affairs*, Vol. 98, No. 1, January–February 2019, pp.10–21.

Zakharia, Fareed, *The Post-American World and the Rise of the Rest – Release 2.0*, New York: W.W. Norton, 2011.

CONCLUSION

It ain't over till it's over

"Peace does not preserve itself." This is one of the great lessons in the history of war and peace, and Donald Kagan taught it to generations of students at Yale University, in what was one of the most popular courses of the venerable institution. For Kagan,

> "a persistent and repeated error through the ages has been the failure to understand that the preservation of peace requires active effort, planning, the expenditure of resources, and sacrifice, just as war does. In the modern world especially the sense that peace is natural and war an aberration has led to a failure in peacetime to consider the possibility of another war, which, in turn, has prevented the efforts needed to preserve the peace."[1]

Too few Europeans seem to have followed this course, which remained a classic of Ivy League teaching for a quarter century. Indeed, the common idea that "Europe means peace" is both a reflection of this misconception and a dangerous aphorism, in the sense that European institutions alone cannot guarantee peace by themselves.

For a very long time, Europe actually meant just the opposite of peace. Until the 20th century, Europe was all about war, and war loved Europe in return. Humans, because of their tribal and territorial nature, are generally tempted by war, but in Europe they found the most favorable terrain in the world to express their martial inhibitions: everything in the geography, the culture and the history of the continent favors war. Between 1492 and 1914, war was even a crucial factor in Europe's rise and its domination over the world. During what Ian Morris called the "Five Hundred Years' War,"[2] Europeans multiplied conflicts between themselves and with the rest of the world; they ended up conquering most of it. Initially, the combination of firearms and viruses allowed a handful of Europeans to conquer vast empires in the Americas, before the multiplication of conflicts in the New World as in the old gave Europeans a decisive military (and productive) advantage over the great Asian empires. By 1900, the countries claiming a European heritage had conquered 84% of the earth's surface,[3] something they could not have done without war. Mars had pushed them into a fierce competition to perfect the art of war and drive the industrial and sanitary revolution. Those in turn gave Europeans the opportunity to conquer the world, for better and for worse.

By its Christian nature, Western civilization often emphasizes the link between the nature of sin and its punishment: hell reserves a special place for those who will be punished by what they have sinned. It is thus rather ironic that the very Europeans who benefited so much from war also fell because of war. Between 1914 and 1945, during the long European Civil War, Europeans destroyed each other and were destroyed through a series of interlinked wars. In the end, it took two extra-European powers to stop the carnage and impose on the continent what was as much a Cold War as a Long Peace. During this period, the construction of a European community under the *pax americana* laid the foundations of a new security architecture, first limited to Western Europe alone, and then extended to almost the entire continent during the 1990s and early 2000s, after the defeat of Soviet communism. It was time for the End of History, as the victor George H.W. Bush proposed to Europeans the vision of a Europe Whole, Free and at Peace.

This triumphant period is probably the one where Europeans should have remembered the teachings of Donald Kagan. Among them is the fact that "international balances can never be still, and it is a folly of statesmanship to assume that they ever could be."[4] The favorable dynamics for Europe and the West could never last in the way they did in the early 2000s, and while Europe celebrated its unification under a single, common political entity (a first in the history of the continent), the first signs of deterioration were already appearing. The first reaction was one of ignorance, followed by disbelief, and Westerners even took the risk of division as the 2008 crisis unfolded, with Europeans quick to condemn the bankruptcy of "Anglo-Saxon greed" before being caught up by their own contradictions. European critiques were forgetting that the world's financial system was primarily Transatlantic and that a crisis on one side of the ocean could also have dire consequences on the other. If the 2000s were a decade of excess and sin, the 2010s were a decade of crisis and punishment, with no redemption in sight as financial, economic, social and identity crises unfolded in Europe while war made a remarkable comeback to the marches of the Union. While Robert Kagan had opposed the peaceful Europeans and the martial Americans in the early 2000s, most commentators had forgotten that "Europeans are from Venus *because* Americans are from Mars. Without the American globocop protecting the peace, Europe's dovish strategy would be impossible."[5] With the *pax americana* now contested or at least promised to change in nature, the European Union found itself with a weak base to convince even its own members that it could provide security to them all. Fifteen years of pure intergovernmentalism, in which the nation-states took over most of the Union's policies, had not solved Europe's sovereignty conundrum. Nor had it consolidated peace and stability inside its borders, let alone in its neighborhood, now almost entirely in flames.

The outside world has indeed become dangerous, and the European Union, once considered a model of peace and recipient of the Nobel Prize in 2012, now seems particularly ill-equipped to operate in a world defined by power. European officials may well proclaim their ambitions to build a "geopolitical Europe," but they seem little (or perhaps too much) aware of the facts of Europe's internal geopolitical weaknesses to be credible: instead of playing geopolitics, the EU (and more generally Europe) has recently been a pawn rather than an actor in the unfolding geopolitical game. It has thus imported instability rather than exported stability. True, the European Recovery Plan decided in 2020 represents a glimmer of hope for the Union, but only if it is considered as a lifeline and a starting point. In fact, Europe is emerging weakened and divided from the series of crises of the 2010s, with evident East–West and North–South fault lines, but also a resurgence of the German question in geo-economic terms and an increasingly harmful opposition between the center and the peripheries. In this respect, the pure intergovernmental model designed after the Treaty of Lisbon has magnified rather than solved these territorial imbalances between nation-states. Beyond these international tensions, Europeans are also divided inside their own nation-states, with new social, political and identity-related tensions threatening to tear them apart. These have been encouraged by the rise of social networks, a new Gutenberg bible that may have democratized access to (and production of) information, but has also had its downsides. In the 2010s, we learnt that Facebook and Twitter could become incredibly potent tools for urban crowds to mobilize against corrupt leaders and topple dictators (as in Ukraine or in Arab countries), but it could also give a voice to radical critiques of democracy, who suddenly could get their message across to disaffected constituents without any filter (and sometimes with the support of foreign powers). The ensuing polarization has not only been about internal issues such as abortion or media freedom but also about the nature of our institutions and international orientations, with "oceanist" and liberal visions of the future of Europe now having to contend with another, continentalist and often illiberal discourse, very often aligned with either Chinese or Russian interests.

This divide in turn opens the way for Europe to become a battleground in the major conflict that looms for the foreseeable future between China and the United States. Even though it has become less central to great power competition, or perhaps precisely because of this peripheral position, Europe runs the risk of becoming the theater of confrontations between the superpowers of the 21st century. Even more so as continentalist versus oceanist realignments may not follow the geographic logic that the advance of the Soviet and US army physically imposed in 1945. America may still be hanging on to a vision of a "Europe Whole and Free" as envisioned by George H.W. Bush in his 1989 Mainz speech, but it is also a pragmatic power that evolves with the times, and if US leaders were to be confronted with a polarized Europe unable to give itself a general sense of direction, it will have no other choice but to look at the continent as a grand chessboard where it will have to jockey for influence with other actors, mainly China and Russia, who are only too keen already to play on Europeans' divisions. For different reasons, both China and Russia have an interest in taking their revenge on "the West" and engineering its atomization would probably be their best way to do it. As they face these challenges, Europeans also have to deal with other powers such as Turkey or the Gulf countries, who have contradictory interests on the continent and its periphery, and it is not impossible to see a geopolitical weakening of the Union spiral out of control, inviting foreign powers in to guarantee a never-ending cycle of violence in at least parts of the continent.

Internally and externally, Europe is vulnerable like it hasn't been in decades, and the construct that has been built for the past 70 years to build peace, the European Union, remains very weak, even though it has proven resilient in resisting the financial, migration and sanitary shocks of 2008–2021. The Union has weakened even further because of Brexit, which amputates Europe from its second-largest economy, and even though this could provide the background for a federal jump in the coming years (as the recovery plan may suggest), the overall picture is one of weakness, in a world where neighbors seem too happy to exploit any weaknesses. One of the problems that the Union faces is of course the current lack of a collective sense of belonging, although this is (slowly) changing. A common, European identity is a new thing politically, even though its roots run much deeper, in actual fact since the Carolingian Empire that moved the center of gravity of "the West" out of the Mediterranean and in the heart of Europe. Transforming this civilizational idea into an identity is one of the major challenges of the Union today – in many ways similar to that of post-colonial India in and after 1947. The EU's geopolitical scenery, however, is much less favorable than India's and there is no time to waste if Europeans want their security architecture to last. In Europe's past, other groups, sometimes decades or centuries-old (Yugoslavia or Austria-Hungary, among others), were found wanting at the moment of truth. If it wants to survive this new, dangerous moment, the EU needs to build resilience and internal solidarity fast.

This is even more important as the methods of war have changed, making warfare less costly and more democratic. Tactics and weapons have become less expensive and more widely available, allowing armies to develop wars of various degrees of intensity, the course of which contrasts with the latest European experiences of Clausewitzian warfare with regular armies, all-out assaults and total war. Sure, today's wars can also be total, but they are more often hybrid and low cost. General Gerasimov, of the Russian military strategic thinkers, rightly points out that today's wars are "not declared but simply begin." In fact, the addition of multiple grey zones between war and peace, these states of "un-peace," as Lucas Kello calls them,[6] have added a new layer of complexity, making it easier to progressively slide from peace to war. Whether it is economic, cyber or informational, war is creeping back into our daily lives, and its combination with conventional warfare is as potent as it is deadly for Europeans. Will they be tomorrow as terrified of AI's remarkable potential of destruction as Chinese soldiers once were when faced with British gunships during the opium wars? This perspective is not so remote today: the West's rivals have understood and internalized Europe's weaknesses, and they are ready to test new strategies in what could quickly become new European battlefields.

Prediction has always been a very hazardous job, at least since Europeans stopped believing in the inevitability of fate. Hannah Arendt once wrote that

> "predictions of the future are never anything but projections of present automatic processes and procedures, that is, of occurrences that are likely to come to pass if men do not act and if nothing unexpected happens; every action, for better or for worse, and every accident necessarily destroys the whole pattern in whose frame the prediction moves, and where it finds its evidence."[7]

While projections rarely become reality, the diversity of the seven scenarios proposed in this book does not hold the ambition of predicting the future, but of showing us how much potential there currently is for war to happen in the mid- to-long term.

We do not necessarily need to have a power representing absolute evil as in 1939 to enter into a war of continental dimensions. As Geoffrey Blainey points out, most of the time when war breaks out, both sides actually "want peace, but only on their own terms."[8] All it takes is uncertainty about the balance of power, or a leader ready at a given moment to take enough risks, to move from peace to war. From a "classic" NATO–Russia confrontation to a much more surprising revolutionary wave engulfing Western Europe, from a Sino-American conflict overspilling in Europe to a post-Brexit war between the United Kingdom and EU members, the multiplicity of scenarios is not intended to predict the future, but rather to sensitize Europeans to the many risks they now face.

Even the decisive, profound reform of Europe that this book proposes may not be enough to save peace on the continent. It even carries its own risks of triggering new conflicts. In the words of Alexis de Tocqueville, "the most dangerous moment for a bad government is usually when it begins to reform."[9] But that doesn't mean that Europeans should shy away from it, as the alternative, stagnation and decay, is even more deadly. That reform of the European security architecture (and with it the European Union) is necessary, and it does incur first of all that Europeans face their old demons, eye to eye. War can be tamed, and Europeans must prepare for it if they want to survive in a dangerous world. Peace will not preserve itself by vain invocations but by concrete actions, and Europeans have no choice but to build their own defense now, using as much as possible the tools offered by NATO to build a strategic autonomy that will enhance rather than weaken the Transatlantic partnership. Strategic autonomy need not be a challenge to America's position in Europe (although it will incur changes in the armaments that Europeans may need). On the contrary, it can allow allies to renew their alliance and ready it for the challenges of the future. This will require a constant dialogue between allies on both sides of the Atlantic, but also with Britain, who will necessarily remain ambivalent about the European project. Europe has enough rivals on its Eastern flank and enough problems to its South, and it does not want to create one to its West as well: the preservation and strengthening of the Transatlantic relationship along with the development of defense capabilities must be an objective for the European Union. In an environment where the United States seeks the support of allies and must rethink its strategic (and geographic) priorities, the timing is actually excellent for Europeans if they manage to convince their British and American partners of their good intentions. They must be warned, however; deeds, not words, will be the main measure of success – and they have thus far been too proficient on the latter, and not enough on the former.

A reform of Europe's defense must also imply a rethink of the EU's larger institutional framework. The intergovernmental method, which has been almost exclusively the one followed by Europe over the last 15 years, has shown its limits over a decade of crisis. It is now time to think about other alternatives, and notably a move toward a more federal model, which will paradoxically only be possible if the Union can rely more fully on its constitutive nation-states to move forward. It is useful here to come back to the spirit of the Founding Fathers and their descendants, notably Jean Monnet and Jacques Delors: each in their own way dreamed not only of a United States of Europe, but of a "Federation of Nation-States," in which a federal state would remain under the control not only of the representatives of the European Demos inside the European Parliament but also of those of the constituent nation-states – though through a legislative, not an executive power. The European Union should neither be a negation of the nation-state nor the ineffective solution of a 27-member executive. It can instead form its own federalism by subliming Europe's small nation-states so that they can exist in a world now dominated by continental economies such as China, India or the United States. This can only be done successfully if the EU builds the solidarity needed for a European national community to emerge – this presupposes building a full internal market and embarking on a serious nation-building project.

To do that, Europeans will need the goodwill and the friendship of Britain and the United States. The problem is that this goodwill must now more than ever be cultivated. Euros and Anglos have drifted away dangerously for the past 20 years, following a pattern that may be only a negative cycle in a fluctuating Transatlantic relationship but may also be more permanent due to the genuine cultural and geographical differences inside the modern "West." The question on both sides of the Atlantic (and both sides of the Channel) must therefore be whether there are still enough common points, enough transcending aspirations to revive the West. This book argues that despite the estrangement of the past years, the United States has a vested interest in saving the Europe America Made, while Britain also needs to be able to befriend a strong business partner if it is to thrive in this world. In the face of a rising authoritarian and communist China, of a disruptive Russia and many other global and regional challenges, Europe, America and Britain cannot afford to divide their forces, and they need to reclaim the West. This does not exclude much questioning, and indeed a humility that has not been present enough in Western minds in the past 30 years. But the best of the West often comes in its moments of need, not its moments of triumph, this is why it is worth working on reviving it.

Will Europeans, and more generally the West, have time to reform before history catches up with Europe? This is a question for future historians to answer, but one thing is clear: the period of comfort Europeans have been accustomed to for the past 30 years is now over. If they are serious about counting in the world, if they are to preserve peace on their soil, Europeans must now act and confront the many threats that they face, may those be internal, external or global.

After this read, it would be tempting to give way to pessimism, particularly in an age where apocalypses are promised – and sometimes delivered. However, this book was not thought as a millenarian prophecy but rather as a wake-up call. It is still up to Europeans to take matters into their own hands and learn how to evolve in an environment that has become much more dangerous – and where they are no longer the center of the universe. The evidence of Europe's decline in the 2010s must push EU leaders to question themselves and embark on reform. It is still time for Europeans to adapt to a brave new world, and they don't have to be the losers – but only if they agree on changing.

Of course, reform will not be easy. It will face strong pushback, and defenders of the status quo will be numerous. Some of them (and some reformers too) might even wish for war to happen. While it is always deadly, war is not always long, and it often provides the trigger to build a stronger new regional or global order. To a certain extent, the Franco-Prussian war of 1870 was necessary to mark the end of a period of European instability that opened in 1848. Its outcome paved the way for 44 years of uninterrupted peace in Europe, a record for the time. Many present-day Europeans have experienced a longer period of peace, itself unimaginable without the *pax americana*, a product of the United States' entry into the Second World War in 1941, and the ensuing Cold War.

In his study of the world history of war, British historian Ian Morris contests American Motown artist Edwin Star's answer to the question: "War! What is it good for?" For Star, *"War, Good God, What is it good for – absolutely nothing,"* but Morris actually answers that war is actually good for something. As Basil Liddell Hart once put it, "War is always a matter of doing evil in the hope that good may come out of it"[10] – and once the guns have fallen silent, it often does. The postwar recovery of Western Europe itself was not only conditioned by the outcome of the Second World War, but it was also a direct product of the Cold War and the necessity for America to build a capitalist showroom on the other side of the Iron Curtain. The conclusion may be depressing, but "despite all the variations, qualifications, and exceptions, over the ten-thousand-year-long run, war made governments, and governments made peace."[11] It is precisely because violence calls for the organization that political order and then states have emerged. And it is because they must mobilize resources more effectively that strong states install peace within their territories.

Of course, "War Is Peace" is also a totalitarian slogan used in George Orwell's *1984*. But it was precisely chosen because it contains a share of truth. To quote Morris once again,

> "War is certainly the worst imaginable way to create larger and more peaceful societies, but it is the only way humans have so far found to make peace. If the conflicts of history could have been resolved through discussion rather than force, humanity could have enjoyed the benefits of functioning in larger societies without paying the heavy price of war. But this was not the case. The idea is depressing in itself, but the evidence is clearly there."[12]

This might be the rationale Europeans will be confronted with in the future, and people who may not want war for the orgy of violence it implies might accept it because it would usher in a new order, replacing the old one that would have become untenable (or, for some, detestable).

Indeed, war may end up being the only way to cut the Gordian knot of Europe's current contradictions. It could prove the Eurosceptics right by showing that such a heterogeneous organization as the European Union (or, indeed NATO) cannot provide the *esprit de corps* needed to survive in a dangerous world. If the EU were to survive the ordeal, it could in the process de facto create the solidarity Europeans have been craving for in the past decades. Contrary to popular myth, the nation-states of Europe are not millenary constructs – they were born rather recently, and more often than not in steel and blood. German unity was achieved in three successive wars against Denmark, Austria, and France, and that of Italy in the military campaigns of the State of Piedmont-Sardinia and the more unorthodox initiatives of Giuseppe Garibaldi. And France's "spiritual" unity was achieved only in 1914–1918, after the French state (and its teachers) successfully turned "peasants into Frenchmen"[13] and made them spend their best years in the trenches of Northern France – many of those peasants, including my great-grandfathers, definitely adopted French as their mother tongue there.

The reality though is that in its current state, the European Union could currently not withstand such a shock. A war on European soil would have the effect the Great War had on Austria-Hungary rather than France. Not only would the Europe that we know disappear, but it would also likely awaken the demons that have haunted it in the past. We tend to see today's Austria as an unmovable, peaceful country, prosperous, with a quality of life unequalled in the world. But during the inter-war period, Austria was anything but peaceful: with the empire gone, Vienna had become an empty megalopolis, too big for a country that had turned insignificant on the international scene. Austria had lost its raison d'être; its national identity was tortured between the previous glue of Catholicism (now in decline) and new pan-Germanic nationalism. And it too got caught up in the European Civil War, as civilian governments tried to keep their regime alive while it was attacked by communists and Nazis. The Viennese know it, just as well as the Romans and many others, the dismantling of large political orders are rarely followed by happiness and prosperity, and that of the Atlantic Alliance or the European Union would be no exception.

This is why the preservation of NATO and the EU, the two structures that have made peace possible in Europe, is so important. Wars that dismantle empires are by no means "productive wars." It was precisely to avoid this kind of cataclysm in Western Europe that the European community, and later the European Union, was created. Ian Morris understood the exceptional character of the endeavor: "a truly astonishing thing is happening. For the first time in history, huge numbers of people – 500 million so far – are coming together to form a bigger, safer, richer society without being forced to do so."[14] This is where the Brussels' elite mantra, "Europe means peace," really takes its meaning. However, the EU will only be able to continue to mean peace if it adapts to a much more dangerous world. That is why it must learn from its recent failures to move forward and build a better future for European citizens.

European elites might have a once-in-a-lifetime opportunity to do so in these post-pandemic times. Europe may currently seem weakened by its decade of trouble, but what is also remarkable is that despite these acute crises, despite the loss of its second economy, despite early announcements of its imminent death, the EU has actually survived. Each crisis has even led to another push toward integration: the euro crisis may have been catastrophic for many Europeans, but its main consequence has been the strengthening of the European Central Bank, which took it upon itself to save the euro. Out of the migration crisis came Frontex, which now presumes that Europeans have understood that if they want to end borders between EU states, they need to strengthen their own borders. Finally, despite an initially slow vaccine rollout, COVID-19 has ushered in the first movement toward the management of a common, European debt – the EU-wide solidarity that it missed in 2010. Europe can be strong when it is united, and although it shouldn't be overstated, its normative power is still remarkable, may that be on data protection or industrial standards.[15] Ivan Krastev may be a pessimist, but he also reminded us at the end of his book *After Europe* that "[i]n reality, the union's various crises, much more so than any of Brussels's 'cohesion policies,' have contributed to the sense that we Europeans are all part of the same political community."[16] It is a fact that European integration has only moved forward through crises, and the ones that it has just gone through may usher in a moment of truth for the EU. The end might be a continent-wide cataclysm or a new leap forward. It is now up to Europeans to decide.

Notes

1 Donald Kagan, *On the Origins of War and the Preservation of Peace*, New York: Anchor Books, 1996, p.567.
2 Ian Morris, *War: What is it Good for? The Role of Conflict in Civilization, from Primates to Robots*, London: Profile Books, 2014, p.165.
3 Ibid., p.223.
4 Donald Kagan, *On the Origins of War and the Preservation of Peace*, New York: Anchor Books, 1996, p.568.
5 Ian Morris, *War: What is it Good for? The Role of Conflict in Civilization, from Primates to Robots*, London: Profile Books, 2014, p.344.
6 Lucas Kello, *The Virtual Weapon and International Order*, New Haven: Yale University Press, 2017, pp.77–78.
7 Hannah Arendt, *On Violence*, New York: Harcourt, 1970, p.6.
8 Geoffrey Blainey, *The Causes of War* (3rd edition), New York: The Free Press, 1988, p.264.
9 Alexis de Tocqueville, *L'Ancien Régime et la Révolution*, Paris: Lévy, 1866, p.259.
10 Basil Liddell Hart, *Strategy* (2nd edition), London: Faber & Faber, 1967, p.368.
11 Ian Morris, *War: What is it Good for? The Role of Conflict in Civilization, from Primates to Robots*, London: Profile Books, 2014, p.8.
12 Ibid., pp.8–9.
13 Eugen Weber, *Peasants into Frenchmen: The Modernization of Rural France 1870–1914*, Stanford: Stanford University Press, 1976.
14 Ian Morris, *War: What is it Good for? The Role of Conflict in Civilization, from Primates to Robots*, London: Profile Books, 2014, p.341.
15 Anu Bradford, *The Brussels Effect: How the European Union Rules the World*, New York: Oxford University Press, 2020.
16 Ivan Krastev, *After Europe*, Philadelphia: University of Pennsylvania Press, 2017, p.110.

Bibliography

Arendt, Hannah, *On Violence*, New York: Harcourt, 1970.
Blainey, Geoffrey, *The Causes of War* (3rd edition), New York: The Free Press, 1988.
de Tocqueville, Alexis, *L'Ancien Régime et l.a Révolution*, Paris: Lévy, 1866.
Kagan, Donald, *On the Origins of War and the Preservation of Peace*, New York: Anchor Books, 1996.
Kello, Lucas, *The Virtual Weapon and International Order*, New Haven: Yale University Press, 2017.
Hart, Basil Liddell, *Strategy* (2nd edition), London: Faber & Faber, 1967.
Morris, Ian, *War: What is it Good for? The Role of Conflict in Civilization, from Primates to Robots*, London: Profile Books, 2014.
Weber, Eugen, *Peasants into Frenchmen: The Modernization of Rural France 1870–1914*, Stanford: Stanford University Press, 1976.

INDEX

Abandonment of the West (Kimmage) 308
Adenauer, Konrad 57–59, 96
Adonis, Andrew 176
After Europe (Krastev) 322
Agadir crisis of 1911 33, 41
Albania 18, 33, 76, 117, 273–274
Albert, Michel 276, 294
Alexander, Tsar II 40, 157
Alexander the Great 24, 29, 109
Alliance of Liberals and Democrats for Europe (ALDE) 73
Allison, Graham 106, 166, 204
Alternativ fur Deutschland (AfD) 98n26, 115
Anderson, Benedict 117
Andrew, Christopher 188
Anglo-Saxons 254, 287–290; greed of 84, 294, 315; modernization 294; political and intellectual system 292; relationship between continental Europe and 286; research on identity 124; solidarity 304; viability of models of federalism 261
Anglosphere 95, 286–310, 312n55; in 2016 287–292; Americans 293–295; condition of Britain and Europe 303–306; countries 303; cultural proximity 94; estrangement between Europe and 254; peace in the West 306–310
antiquity 19–21, 276
Anton, Michael 106
appeasement 3, 175
Arab Spring in 2011 89, 134

Araud, Gérard 303–304
archipelization 126
Arendt, Hannah 318
armed conflict 2; in 2019–2020 199; affect of Syria and Libya on Europeans 2; battles and 23; as concentration of capitalism 105; between constituted political groups 105; economic or commercial war as substitute for 196; internal 32; between Islamists and white nationalists 174; less probable in Western and North-Western Europe 232; sanctions as substitute for 197; Trojan Horse use in 204
armistice: in 1918 2, 39; during the Marxist revolution 48; no end of violence despite peace treaties and 49; in Rethondes 44
Aron, Raymond 6
Atlantic Alliance 54, 310, 322; and bipolarity 56; contradictions of 72, 255; European elites less committed to 155; Europeans faithfulness in 155; Turkey role in 170–171
Austria-Hungary 321; conflict with Serbia 40–41; decline of estates 43, 278; identity and institutional crisis 280; transformation into integrated federation 279

Baker, James 97n5
balance of power 12–13, 197, 199, 249; of Britons/Britain 32, 178, 305;

consciousness of Viktor Orban about the 120; in Europe 33, 67, 112, 116, 176; of Germany 42–43, 61, 95, 175; Hungary's neighbors 121; uncertainty about the 318
Baldwin, Richard 307
Balkan Wars of 1912–1913 33, 41, 169
Baltic States 76, 118, 159; annexation of 224; austerity in 85; British troops stationed to protect the threat of Russian aggression 178; Germany and 230; invasion in 223; Moscow's ultimatum 224; protection of Russian speakers by the Kremlin 160; security of Russians in 224
Belarus: annexation of 222–223; demonstrators 309; migration in 250; plebiscites 224; politics of 196; as security guarantees against return of Russian power 273
Berlin Rules (Lever) 72–73
Berlin Wall 189; fall of 2, 57, 71
Biden, Joe 115, 155
Blackwill, Robert D. 164, 196
Blainey, Geoffrey 106–107, 122, 149, 166, 188, 191, 318
Blair, Tony 78, 176, 257
Bled, Jean-Paul 278
Boer War 43
borders 87, 120, 180, 270–275; closure of during pandemic 3; delimitation of 46, 142; of the European Union 65–66; of France 122, 127, 235; immigration and 91; minorities in Hungary around 228; national 41; natural 14–15, 17, 236; open 79; peace inside 28; political 39; of Turkey 183n63; virtual weapon 203–204
Bossuet, Jacques-Bénigne 20
Brandt, Willy 57, 248; *Ostpolitik* 297
Bretton Woods 59
Brexit 66, 105, 287; on Britain's economy and politics 178; Britain's place in the European security system 177; as Britain's Plan B 94; and coronavirus crisis 66; debacle on the elites in Brussels and Berlin 94; development in Anglo-nationalist circles 290; geopolitics 95; German economy after 74; impact on the balance of power in Europe 176; migration crisis 93; negotiations 3, 305; Polish and Eastern European immigrants becoming easy target for 78; post-Brexit war 236–239, 318; rationale for 93; referendum 93; threat to EU 178
Brezhnev, Leonid 78
Briand, Aristide 4
Brzezinski, Zbigniew 88, 100n68
Buchanan, Pat 289, 308; *The Death of the West* 290
Bucharest Summit 100n64
Budapest Memorandum in 1994 66
Bundestag 60, 98n26
Burke, Edmund: *Reflections on the Revolution in France* 22
Bush, George H. W. 2, 66, 71, 97n4, 150, 154, 299–300, 315
Bush, George W. 294

Caesar, Julius 25
Calame, Mathieu 240–241, 266
Cameron, David 73, 93, 177
Carnot, Sadi 40
Carolingian Empire 27, 177, 317
Catherine the Great 88
Catholicism 21, 322
Catholics 147n92; leading to fratricidal wars 140; and Protestants 22; status as a minority 125
Central Europe 66, 68, 81, 111, 118, 142; borders 65; consolidation of nation-state building in Europe 56; deportations and massive population transfers 53; ethnic composition 55; extermination 51; financial crisis 80; illiberal problem in 113; immigration 78; mass nationalisms 125; North–South confrontation with 5; refugee crisis in 130; *schadenfreude* on social media 93; separation between Western Europe and 21; shift from socialist democracy to market capitalism 76; tensions in 117; "Westernization" fatigue faced by 78; *see also* Eastern Europe; Europe
Chaadaev, Piotr 157
Chagnon, Napoleon 12
challenges, external 149–181; China's rise 162–168; Europe's fall 162–168; instability in Europe 168–174; relationship between America and Europe 150–155; relationship between Britain and Europe 175–181; Russia as low-cost power 156–162
Chamberlain, Neville 46; steps taken against the Czechs and Slovaks 5
Charles V 106

chemical weapons in war 191–192; *see also* war/warfare
Chirac, Jacques 78
Chomsky, Noam 308
Christian/Christianity 4, 18; adopted by the Hungarians 26; anthropology 19; between Catholicism and Orthodoxy 21; Enlightenment 20, 309; as a European religion 19; heritage 22; knights 4; rejecting the polytheism of Greeks 20
Christian Democratic Union (CDU) 72–73, 110, 115
Christianization 26, 35n38
Churchill, Winston 175–176, 225
civil war/warfare: anarchy of 1917 48; atrocities of 48; classical 188; defined 188; ethnic 174; European Civil War 23, 44–49, 122, 132–133, 280, 322; fake 188; in France 127; between indigenous groups 189; internal armed conflicts turning into 32; in Libya 90; of low-intensity 190; risk of 6; social networks 136; in Spain 231; to total war 49–52; violence and 174; *see also* war/warfare
Clark, Christopher: *Sleepwalkers* 39
Clausewitzian 5, 186, 189, 210, 317; *see also* war/warfare
Clemenceau, Georges 45–46, 186
Clovis, Franks 26
Cold War 6, 52, 54, 70, 76, 142, 166; disarmament of Europe after 2; end of 188; post-Cold War period 136, 272; Sino-American Cold War 226–229; tensions in 60; type engagement 187; victors of 65; *see also* war/warfare
collective memory 2, 5, 52, 210
Colombani, Jean-Marie 293
colonization 18, 31–32, 51
Columbus, Christopher 28
Commonwealth of Two Nations 220
communism 50, 55, 122, 150, 157; fascism and 137, 280; between liberal Europe and the Holy Alliance 21; and liberalism 49–50, 122, 137; right-wing nihilism and 23; from Russian Revolution 49; Soviet 76, 151, 315
Comprehensive Agreement over Investment (CAI) 289
conflict 13, 49, 107, 134, 157, 173, 208, 218; between aristocracy and bourgeoisie 133; Austro-Serbian 41; with continental dimensions in Europe 31; between Croats and Serbs 21–22; cyber 204; in Cyprus 55; ethnic 159; between federal state and federated entities 268; between France and Turkey 219; inextricable 21; insecurity and 18; internal 150; internationalization of local 41; leading to colonization and extermination 18; low-cost 193; low-intensity 188; protracted 127; regional 122; Second World War as final 2; Sino-American 226, 228
Constant, Benjamin 196
continentalism 116, 140–142, 308
Corvinus, Matthias 279
COVID-19 pandemic 6, 222, 257, 322; doctors leaving Romania to settle in other countries 79; health crisis 3; mutualize the European Recovery Fund 113; revealing Europe's geopolitical weakness 6
Crimea: annexation of 88, 160; Crimea War 157; illegal annexation of 66; invasion of 120; military operation 89; Russian invasion of 180, 187
cultural identity 19–21, 23; *see also* identity(ies)
Culture of Defeat (Schivelbusch) 58
culture wars 18–23
cyber-attacks 236; consequences of 204; cyber weapon 203; destruction of the national electricity network 223; difficulties in tracing of 202; against Estonia 202; against the IT infrastructure 201; against servers of the Iranian Army 200; *see also* war/warfare
Cyprus War of 1974 54–55
Czechoslovakia 46, 53, 55, 107, 166, 168, 282n31

d'Annunzio, Gabriele 46
Dark Ages for Europe 25–26
Daul, Joseph 73
The Death of the West (Buchanan) 290
de Gasperi, Alcide 57
de Gaulle, Charles 59, 150, 296–297
Delors, Jacques 60, 319
de Maizière, Thomas 92
de Robien, Louis 38
de Saint-Pierre, Abbé 4
d'Estaing, Valéry Giscard 59
de Tocqueville, Alexis 318
d'Herbigny, Dominique 159
Diamond, Jared 221, 245; *Guns, Germs and Steel* 29; *Upheaval* 275

Diamond, Larry 133
disinfo-wars 204–211; see also war/warfare
disintegration, Southern 229–232
Disraeli, Benjamin 42
diversity 14–15; about opinions 134; to the alienation of life in Europe's inner cities 144n45; cultural 277; decentralization to manage 279; European approaches to 276; and flexibility 130; manage territorial/ethnic 261; socioeconomic 126
domination 72; Draghi, Mario 81; foreign 276; of Germany 143n15, 277; over Europe 15, 31, 39, 314; Soviet Union 55; strategies 5; territorial 32; of United Kingdom over Europe 33
drones in war 192; see also war/warfare
Dumas, Roland 61
Dunant, Henri 32
Dylan, Bob 298
Dzurinda, Mikuláš 77

Eastern Europe 81; delimitation of 17; "Eastern" bloc 117; mass nationalisms 125; population transfers 53; public opinion 142; was as matter of survival 51; "Westernization" fatigue faced by 78; see also Central Europe
economic: advantage 75; boom experienced by Germany 42, 44, 60–61, 74–75; crises Western Europe 60; crisis 5, 89, 91, 117, 123, 230; difficulties 231; distribution of 13; expansion 20; and federalism 58; geo-economic 72, 81, 88, 97, 104, 117, 316; geopolitics 152, 154; growth/development 4, 163–164, 237, 240; inferiority 81; integration 59; interdependence 162; liberalism 129; migration grievances against Northern Europe 113; neoliberal consensus 136; obstacles/difficulties 132; opportunity 296, 305; policy of France 60; prosperity 152; protectionism and nationalism 257; recovery 4, 265; of Russia 156, 161; sanctions on France 236; slowdown in Germany 112; socioeconomic 48, 66, 94, 113, 117–118, 123, 126, 139, 173, 195; sovereignty over economic affairs 59; stagnation of 122; transition of 77; warfare 195–200, 235
Eisenhower, Dwight 297
Elizabeth (Empress of Austria) 40

Élysée Treaty 59
Emerson, Ralph Waldo 290
Engell, Norman 7; *Great Illusion, The* 3–4
Engels, Friedrich 71
enlargement/expansion: of Brussels 169; cultural 26; economic 20; of Europe 76; of the European Union 61, 65–66; NATO 158; side effects of 76–81; territorial 257; of USSR 55
Enlightenment 4, 19–22, 117, 133, 291–292, 309
Erasmus, Desiderius 4, 20
Erdoğan, Tayyip 169–172, 183n63
Erzeberg, Matthias 48
Estonia 76–77; attack on infrastructures 203; cyber-attack against 202
Eurasian Union 88, 206
European Commission 59, 74, 85
European Council on Foreign Relations (ECFR) 6, 154, 243n14
European Defense Community (EDC) 53–54, 58
European Deterrence Initiative 71
European Monetary System (EMS) 59–60, 82
European Parliament 73, 78, 143n17, 240, 264, 268, 274, 303, 319
European People's Party (EPP) 73–75, 110, 288
European Recovery Fund 111–114, 269
European Union (EU) 2, 58, 159; Alexander Vučić against the 6; all-out alliance against 112; British decision to leave 95; crisis in 246; defense policy 152; enlargement/expansion of 65–66; geopolitics 248; institutional framework of 241; long-term funding 95; membership of 79; Nobel Peace Prize won by the 6; political entity of 109; political establishment 163; refugee crises in 3; relationship with Britain 177; security guaranteed by NATO 109; semi-authoritarian regimes in Central Europe 235; shortage of manpower 90; Slovenia joining the 76; threat faced by 85; Turkey tensions with 172
Eurosceptics 2, 229, 321; accused Brussels of being anti-democratic 240; in Brussels 260; creation of internal market 259; upside-down federalism 266
Eurozone 230; countries 85; crisis in 94, 105, 113, 174; Greece excluded from

the 86; members 82; monetary stimulus 85
extermination 18, 51
external threats 27, 210, 220, 253

Farage, Nigel 93
fascism 5, 49–50, 122, 137, 280
Fashoda incident of 1898 41
federalism 58–59, 260–270
Fejtő, François 278
Ferdinand, Franz 31, 33, 40, 203, 278–279
Ferdinand, Tsar 42
Fergusson, Niall 18
Feyerabend, Florian 169
financial crisis: of 1929 49; of 2008 68–69, 81, 97, 125, 294, 299; *Fondation pour l'Innovation Politique* (Fondapol) 118; impact on Central Europe 80
Fourquet, Jérôme 126, 129, 144–145n45, 172, 269–270
France: awareness of its economic weakness 60; balance of powers 95; counterintelligence efforts 312n28; economic policy 60; frustration with Germany 114; frustration with NATO and EU allies 57, 171; inability to "reform" its economy 114; monetary policy 60; social tensions in 233; trauma of people in 2; Yellow Vests movement 3, 5
Franco-German 75; initiatives 114; partnership 288; reconciliation 4; relations 114
Frederick the Great 248
Freedman, Lawrence 36n50, 44, 50, 54, 97n9, 201, 213n72; *The Future of War: A History* 188; phraseology of 105
Freikorps (militia of veterans) 48
French Revolution 5, 22, 122, 234
Freud, Sigmund 278
Fukuyama, Francis 12, 65, 123–124, 293
The Future of War: A History (Freedman) 188

Gellner, Ernest 124
Gerasimov, Valery 161, 187, 317
German Democratic Republic (GDR) 56, 74, 118
German question 110–142; center *vs.* peripheries 116–121; continentalism 140–142; identities and secessionisms 122–128; liberalism 136–140; new class struggles 128–132; oceanism 140–142; social media 132–136; *see also* Alternativ fur Deutschland (AfD)

Germany 51; balance of power of 42–43, 61, 95, 175; changing Transatlantic relationship 115; defeated by Allies 57; dominance of 110–111; economic boom affects on other countries 42–43; economic boom experienced by 42, 44, 60–61, 74–75; foreign policy of 115; German Army 47; industrialization 48; long-term economic slowdown 112; loss of control of geo-economic zone 117; military superiority 107; monetary policy of 59; nationalism and continentalism 116; "ordo-liberal" discourse 113; *Ostpolitischer* 160; panic in 60; pre-1945 anthem, the *Deutschlandlied* 143n15; problems of Czechs and Slovaks against 5; Red Army Faction 55; refugee crisis in 130; reunification of 60–61, 81–82; rise as a threat to France 43; semi-hegemony of 96–97; standing in Europe 74; success in Europe 74; suspicion created by François Mitterand in 60; unification of 4, 44; United States frustration with 115
Gest, Justin 126, 128
Goodhart, David 129
Gorbachev, Mikhail 60, 71, 157
Göring, Hermann 47
The Great Class Shift 129
Great Illusion, The (Engell) 3–4
Great Patriotic War of 1941–1945 205
Great Recession 84, 151
Great War 1, 44–49, 125; aftermath the disaster of 4; as bad decision 40; Britain's intervention in 32; *Freikorps* (militia of veterans) 48; general conflagration 5; role of Wilhelm II in the 7; strategic targets during 50; transformation of European warfare 49; *see also* war/warfare
Greece 83–84, 276; anti-austerity demonstrators 75; confrontation with Turkey 217; deficits 83; European civilization 23; excluded from the Eurozone 86; frustration with NATO and EU allies 171; military build-up between Turkey and 3
Grillo, Beppe 93
Guns, Germs and Steel (Diamond) 29
Gutenberg Bible 132–136, 316

Habermas, Jürgen 293
Haddad, Benjamin 68–70
Hamilton, Clive 166
Hänse, Lars 169

Harris, Jennifer M. 164, 196
Hart, Basil Liddell 52, 320
Havel, Václav 77
Hebdo, Charlie 145n45
Helms, Jesse 197
Herriot, Édouard 205
Hitler, Adolf 47, 50–52, 303; decision to declare war on Poland 107
Hobbes, Thomas 12
Holland, Tom 19
Hollande, François 70, 234, 295
Holmes, Stephen 161; *Light That Failed* 267
Holocaust 51
Holy Roman Empire 20, 27–28, 42, 117, 218
Hoover, John Edgar 95
Houellebecq, Michel: *Submission* 126–127, 174
Hoxha, Enver 18
Hungary 14, 16; China's investments 228; ethnic nationalism 119; financial shock 80; illiberal democracy 138; invasions of 55; limited military resources 120; military resources 120; minorities in 228
hybrid warfare 5, 88, 160, 187, 210; *see also* war/warfare

identity(ies): alienation 126; crises 3, 174, 315; cultural 19–21, 23; ethno-linguistic 279; Ivorian 173; linguistic 277; multiplication and diversification of 126; in Muslim populations 144n45; national 268, 276–277, 322; politics 121–123, 125, 127–129, 237, 280, 291; and secessionisms 122–128; tension between uniformity and 124; three legacies of 20
illiberal democracy 138, 140
Imperial Russia 48, 156; *see also* Russia
industrialization of war 32; *see also* war/warfare
internal market 240, 255–260, 266, 319
International Republican Institute (IRI) 6–7, 99n44
Isac, Iulian-Nicușor 280
Islamic State (ISIS) 89, 92–93, 194, 213n72, 291
isolation *see* splendid isolation
Italy 78–79, 321; beneficiary of the European Recovery Fund 113; defeated by Allies 57; federalism in 262; financial leeway through devaluation 230; Germany worried about rise of 114; income gap 86; Red Brigades 55; sign up the China's Belt and Road Initiative 163; as third-largest economy of the EU 113; unification of 4, 32

Janša, Janez 112
Jaurès, Jean 157
Johnson, Boris 3, 131, 177
Joseph, Franz 278–279
The Jungle Grows Back (Kagan) 299

Kaczyński, Jarosław 112
Kagan, Donald 247–248, 314–315
Kagan, Robert 6, 11, 67, 69, 96, 153, 159; *The Jungle Grows Back* 299; *Of Paradise and Power* 61, 294, 299
Kalashnikov, Mikhail 194
Kalergi, Richard Coudenhove 269
Kant, Immanuel: *Towards Perpetual Peace* 4
Kaplan, Robert 13
Keeley, Lawrence H. 13
Kello, Lucas 189, 200–201, 204, 210, 317
Kennedy, John F. 249, 293, 296, 309
Kenny, Michael 303, 312–313n55
Kerouac, Jack 298
Kimmage, Michael 307, 310, 311n2; *Abandonment of the West* 308
Klimt, Gustav 278
Koch, Charles 69
Kohl, Helmut 60–61, 71, 82
Krastev, Ivan 80, 91, 124, 161, 301; *After Europe* 322; on division of the Union by Eurozone crisis 105–106; *Light That Failed* 267
Krekó, Péter 167
Kundani, Hans 111
Kundera, Milan 308
Kundnani, Hans 72, 78; *Paradox of German Power* 43; views on Germany's competitiveness 82–83
Kupchan, Charles 296
Kurz, Sebastian 131
Kwaśniewski, Aleksander 77

Laar, Mart 77
Lagarde, Christine 81
La République en Marche (Macron) 73
Law and Justice Party (PiS) 80, 112, 118
League of Nations 46
Le Pen, Marine 233
Le Queux, William 188
Lever, Paul 82, 305; *Berlin Rules* 72–73; European quota crisis 91
liberal-antidemocrats 140

liberalism 46, 136–140; and communism 49; confrontation between illiberalism and 140; democratic 49; economic 129; and fascism 50; political 137, 287; quasi-monopoly 137; social 137
Lieven, Dominic 26–27, 229
Light That Failed (Holmes and Krastev) 267
Liik, Kadri 250
low-cost warfare 7, 104, 161, 188–191
Luce, Edward 132
Ludendorff, Erich 47, 50
Luxemburg, Rosa 138

Maçães, Bruno 276, 296, 298
Macartney (Lord) 30
MacMillan, Harold 142n1
MacMillan, Margaret 62n11
Macron, Emmanuel 71, 114, 156, 183n63, 233, 296; campaign team's response to Russian hacking 209; *La République en Marche* 73
Manif pour Tous 125
Mann, Thomas 61
Markovits, Claude 29–30
Marshall, Tim 18
Marshall Plan 53, 57, 258
Marx, Karl 71
Marxist revolution 48
massacre 2, 51, 206, 223
May, Theresa 131
Mead, Margaret 12
Mearsheimer, John 146n88, 154
Meloni, Giorgia 113
Members of the European Parliament (MEPs) 72
Merc, Jakub 167
Merkel, Angela 70, 72, 75, 91, 95, 110, 114, 128, 294–295; end of chancellorship 111, 116
Mesežnikov, Grigorij 167
Middle East 16, 19, 24, 28, 68, 151, 153
military capabilities 253
military doctrine 50, 87, 161, 181, 205, 208
Miquel, Pierre 45
Mitterrand, François 57, 60–61, 296
Mody, Ashoka 83
Monnet, Jean 54, 58–59, 96, 277, 319
Morange, Élie 1
More, Thomas 4, 20
Morris, Ian 5, 19, 31, 35n30, 194–195, 247, 314, 320–322
Moscow 56–57, 61; *see also* Russia
Mounk, Yascha 138

Mussolini, Benito 47
Mutually Assured Destruction (MAD) 54

Nagorno-Karabakh 3, 97n2, 192
Napoleonic Wars 4, 31–32, 133, 140
National Security Agency (NSA) 136
Nazi Germany 296; *see also* Germany
Nazism 23, 122, 262
neutrality 227; of Belgian 43; from European people/Europeans 154, 227; institutional 139; of liberal state 267
Nicholas, Tsar II 32–33, 43
Nixon, Richard 151
Nolte, Ernst 23, 49, 122
North Atlantic Treaty Alliance (NATO) 53, 56–57, 63n51, 71, 87, 100n64, 160; alliance and 158; allies 153, 171, 293; Article 5 of 160, 202; confrontation of Russia with 203, 318; Croatia as member of the 76; enlargement 158; European Union 218, 221–222, 322; integrated military structure 150; no salvation beyond 251–255; Slovenia as member of the 76
Northern Europe 18, 86, 91; fiscal policy and financial help offered to South 86; Italians grudge against 113; migrants in 232; *see also* Central Europe; Eastern Europe
Northern France 1, 321; *see also* France
Novorossiya 88–89, 194

Obama, Barack 70
oceanism 140–142
Of Paradise and Power (Kagan) 61, 294, 299
Ohlberg, Mareike 166
Operation Fortitude 204–205
Orange Revolution 67, 88
Orbán, Viktor 77, 80, 92–93, 112, 118–119, 121, 138, 141, 147n92, 167–168
organized violence 12–13; *see also* violence
Orwell, George 321
Ostpolitik (Brandt) 297
Ottoman Empire 41

Pacific War of 1941–1945 103, 198
Palacký, František 280–281
Paradox of German Power (Kundnani) 43
Parly, Florence 251
Patrikarakos, David 134–135, 187, 207–210
Pax Americana 61, 65–72, 76, 96, 155
Pax Britannica 4, 32–34, 42, 175
Pax Europea 61, 65, 72, 155
Pax Romana 24, 32

peace 13, 28, 48, 52–56, 105, 150, 189–191, 195–196, 200, 203–204, 209–210, 300, 314; Peace of Brest-Litovsk 48; Peace of Versailles 46; Pearce, Nick 303, 312–313n55; perpetual 3–4, 6, 32, 65, 87; preservation of 248, 286, 320; prospects for 122; prosperity and 180, 241; stability and 239; transition to war 106; treaties 47, 49; triumph of 56–61
Pearl Harbor 103–104
Peterson, Dale 12
Peter the Great 157–158
Philip II of Macedonia 24, 35n33
Pleven, René 54
Poděbrady, George: *Tractatus* 58
Pollock, Jason 298
Pomerantsev, Peter 123, 205
Popovici, Aurel 279–280
post-Brexit war 236–239, 318; *see also* Brexit
Presley, Elvis 298
Pulzer, Peter 130
Putin, Vladimir 87–88, 100n71, 120, 157–158, 161, 187, 206, 222–223, 225, 291, 294

Radičová, Iveta 85
Reagan, Ronald 71, 297–298, 308
reappearance of war 217–242; post-Brexit war 236–239; reform 239–242; Sino-American Cold War 226–229; Southern disintegration 229–232; war in the Baltics 221–225; Yellow Vest wars 232–236; *see also* war/warfare
Reflections on the Revolution in France (Burke) 22
Reformation 5, 21, 28, 42, 133, 140
refugees 3, 90–93, 105, 113, 117, 130, 172, 234, 301
Regan, Ronald 309
Renaissance 4, 28, 122, 133, 191, 262, 279, 309
"Riga massacre" 223–224; *see also* massacre
Roman Empire 20–21, 27, 33
Roosevelt, Franklin D. 308–309
Roosevelt, Theodore 249, 278
Rostowski, Jacek 295
Rothkopf, David 204, 209
Rousseau, Jean-Jacques 12
Roy, Olivier 19, 22
Russia 17, 51, 88, 158, 187, 291; aggression in the East 121; decision to end the preferential tariffs 196; decision to invade part of Ukraine 149; Denial of Service cyber-attack against Estonia 202; information warfare 207–208; as low-cost power 156–162; propose a plebiscite 222; protection of Russian speakers in the Baltic states 160; resurgence of 67; Russian Army 48; Russian Revolution 49, 122; socialist movement 48; successful invasion of Crimea 187; tensions with neighbors 159; vision of Europe 156; war in Georgia 88
Ryurik dynasty 17
Rzeczpospolita 28, 220–221

Salvini, Matteo 113, 269
same-sex marriage 21, 79, 125
Sarkozy, Nicolas 75, 234, 294; opposite strategy 110
Schiele, Egon 278
Schivelbusch, Wolfgang 58, 275; *Culture of Defeat* 58
Schmidt, Helmut 75–76
Schröder, Gerhard 74–75
Schultz, Martin 73
Schuman, Robert 57–59, 96
secessionisms 122–128, 171, 173, 178, 191, 228, 231, 243n16
Seehofer, Horst 91
self-radicalization 131, 135
Serbia 33, 40–41; bilateral crisis between Austria and 42; color revolutions in 65–66; military and political support of France and Russia 42; nationalists 121; territorial compensation 228
Shirreff, Richard 207–208, 221, 225
Sikorski, Radosław 295
Single European Act in 1986 60
Sino-American Cold War 226–229
Sleepwalkers (Clark) 39
Slovakia 228, 273; fall of coalition government 85; migrant crisis 118
Slovenia 76
Smith, Anthony 269
Smith, Stephen 173–174
Snowden, Edward 136
Snyder, Timothy 38, 49, 51, 100n71
socialism 51, 105, 124, 137, 157, 294
social media 132–136, 235; controlled forums 138; information and 208
social relations 3, 131
social tensions 3, 6, 128, 233, 267
Sokoloff, Georges 161
Soleimani, Qasem 192, 199, 204
solidarity 6, 322; Anglo-Saxon 304; Central Europe 80; cultural 303;

economic 260; EU citizens asked to show solidarity with Greeks 80; between the EU member-states 256; national 91; of NATO's article 5 251; religious 168
Sorokin, Pitirim 158–159
Soros, George 69
South Caucasus 3, 14, 170, 248
Southern Europe 14, 21, 84–86; economic turmoil 230–231; *see also* Central Europe; Eastern Europe; Western Europe
Spaak, Paul-Henri 57, 96
Spanish Civil War 50
splendid isolation 83, 175, 177, 184n74, 236, 304
Stability Pact in 2003 84
Stolypin, Piotr 40
Stresemann, Gustav 4
Stubb, Alexander 74
Submission (Houellebecq) 126–127, 174
Syrovatka, Jonaš 167
Szicherle, Patrik 167

terrorist attacks of 2015–2016 93
Thatcher, Margaret 60
Thomson, David 126
Thucydides 104, 166
Tooze, Adam 80
Towards Perpetual Peace (Kant) 4
Toynbee, Arnold 104, 107
Tractatus (Poděbrady) 58
Treaty of Westphalia 22, 28
trench warfare 2, 44; *see also* war/warfare
Trianon, Treaty of 119
Trotsky, Leon 210
Trump, Donald 70–72, 106, 152–153, 199–200, 296
Tsipras, Alexis 86, 112

Ukraine 2; abandonment of nuclear arsenal in the Budapest Memorandum 66; army 89; color revolutions in 66; crisis in 105; fight of Polish-Lithuanians in 28; internally displaced persons 89; lessons learned by Europeans 194; no membership of the European Union or NATO 120; Russian aggression in 151; Russia neutralizing the banking system of 203; trade loss 197; transition 67
Umberto I (King of Italy) 40
unification 42; European/Europe 27, 60; of Germany 4, 32–33, 42, 44, 60, 77, 81–82; of Italy 4, 32–33

United Kingdom 3, 66; commercial and maritime power of 32; competitive advantage 78; economic power 253; economy and politics 178; liberal bloc led by 143n17; not satisfied with quasi-hegemonic position of Germany 177; Poles as largest foreign minority 79; relationship with Europe 175–181; relationship with European Union 177; United Kingdom Independence Party (UKIP) 93; world trade controlled by 43
United States 5; Constitution of 19; crisis between "old Europe" and 6, 11; defense budget of 67; encouraging Europeans to pool their armed forces 53; Europe's security dependency on 251; Europe's survival dependency on 45; federalization in Switzerland and 264; foreign policy 69; frustration with Germany 115; integrity of Western Europe 180; military capacities 249; relationship with Europe 150–155; relations with the Soviet Union 297; reluctant in rescue of the Allies 45; and Russia 225; weariness of 71
Upheaval (Diamond) 275

Valls, Manuel 291
verbal violence 12; *see also* violence
Verhofstadt, Guy 21, 83, 97n6, 253
Vertov, Vladimir 60
Vīķe-Freiberga, Vaira 77
violence 249; anti-migrant 173; organized 12–13; outbreaks of 131; physical 195; receding in the Western Balkans 36; in the Samoas 34n5; states not mobilizing armies to fight 49; systemic inter-community 127; territorial 12; uncontrolled 233; verbal 12; and war 12
virtual weapon 200–204
"Visegrad Four" (V4) 118
Volodymyr the Great in 988 22
von der Leyen, Ursula 72
von Moltke, Helmuth (the Elder) 44
Vučić, Alexander 6, 121, 167, 282n31

Wagener, Hermann 259
Wagner, Otto 278
Wałęsa, Lech 77
Warsaw Pact 57
Wars of Religion 4, 127, 133
war/warfare 11–34, 186–211; ancient culture 18–23; in the Baltics 221–225; disinfo-wars 204–211; economic warfare 195–200; endless 23–27;

hybrid 5; low-cost 188–191; low intensity 188–191; and peace 13; post-Brexit war 236–239; reasons behind 103–107; and the state of nature 12–13; transition from peace to 106; trench 2; unproductive 5; and violence 12; virtual weapon 200–204
Watts, Clint 134, 204, 209
Weber, Eugen 138
Weber, Manfred 73–74
Weber, Max 131
Western Europe 2, 5, 21, 28, 31, 65–66, 71, 79; *see also* Central Europe; Eastern Europe
Westernization 18, 77–79, 157
West Germany 56; *see also* Germany
Westphalia, Treaty of 22, 28
Wilhelm, Kaiser 44
Wilhelm II (German Emperor) 7, 43
Wilson, Harold 177
Wilson, Woodrow 46
World Revolution 48
Worrell, Mark P. 189, 193
Wrangham, Richard 12

Yellow Vest movement 3, 5, 125, 128, 130–131, 136, 162, 232–236
Yeltsin, Boris 157, 229

For Product Safety Concerns and Information please contact our EU representative GPSR@taylorandfrancis.com
Taylor & Francis Verlag GmbH, Kaufingerstraße 24, 80331 München, Germany

www.ingramcontent.com/pod-product-compliance
Lightning Source LLC
Chambersburg PA
CBHW050527300426
44113CB00012B/1984